Superman on Film, Television,
Radio and Broadway

Superman on Film, Television, Radio and Broadway

Bruce Scivally

McFarland & Company, Inc., Publishers
Jefferson, North Carolina, and London

LIBRARY OF CONGRESS CATALOGUING-IN-PUBLICATION DATA

Scivally, Bruce.
Superman on film, television, radio
and Broadway /Bruce Scivally.

p.   cm.
Includes bibliographical references and index.

ISBN-13: 978-0-7864-3166-3
illustrated case binding : 50# alkaline paper ∞

1. Superman (Fictitious character) in mass media.
I. Title.
P96.S94S37   2008   700'.451— dc22   2007028649

British Library cataloguing data are available

Cover photograph ©2008 Comstock Images

Manufactured in the United States of America

*McFarland & Company, Inc., Publishers
Box 611, Jefferson, North Carolina 28640
www.mcfarlandpub.com*

To my dear wife, Sandra,
and daughter, Amanda,
who, every day,
make this Clark Kent feel like a Superman

Acknowledgments

Undertaking a project of this scope requires a lot of help, and I want to thank everyone who had a part in making this book happen. First and foremost, I must thank John Cork for his support and advice throughout the writing of this book and Steven Smith for his extremely helpful proofreading and suggestions: Steven kept me from making some gaffes that would have been very embarrassing to me had they made it into print. I also want to thank Geoff St. Andrews for his eagle-eyed proofreading, and especially Steven Kirk (George Reeves Memorial), Jim Nolt (The Adventures Continue), Neil A. Cole (Superman Supersite), and Steve Younis (Superman Homepage), four gentlemen whose knowledge of Superman knows no bounds, as can be evidenced from their terrific websites, for their comments and suggestions.

For taking the time to grant me interviews for the book, I want to thank Cynthia Collyer, Caroline Croskery, Sydney Croskery, Jim Hambrick, Casey Kasem, Jack Larson, Peter Lupus, Denny Miller, and Noel Neill. My thanks also to Larry Thomas Ward for helping to contact certain individuals, Howard Mandelbaum of Photofest for the use of his photo archives, and my agent, Robert Lecker, for his continuing support.

I must also thank all of those who have trod this ground before me with their own books about the cinema and TV legacy of Superman—Kirk Alyn, Michael Bifulco, Les Daniels, Gary Grossman, Chuck Harter, Jan Alan Henderson, Sam Kashner & Nancy Schoenberger, David Michael Petrou, Christopher Reeve and Larry Thomas Ward.

I give a very special thanks to the talented filmmakers who brought Superman to the big and little screens, and to the men who have been the living, breathing personifications of Superman for nearly seven decades: Bud Collyer, Michael Fitzmaurice, Kirk Alyn, George Reeves, Johnny Rockwell, Bob Holiday, Danny Dark, David Wilson, Christopher Reeve, Beau Weaver, John Haymes Newton, Gerard Christopher, Dean Cain and the current keepers of the flame, Timothy Daly, George Newbern, Tom Welling and Brandon Routh.

And lastly, a warm thanks to my late father and my Mom, Roy and Aileen Scivally, who indulged my passion for Superman when I was a kid, and my wife, Sandra, who tolerates it with great humor now that I'm an adult, with only an occasional exclamation of "Great Caesar's ghost!"

Table of Contents

Preface

For a superhero who's approaching seventy, Superman is doing remarkably well. As of this writing, he is a movie star (*Superman Returns*), a television star (*Smallville*), and cartoon star (*Justice League Unlimited*). DVD collectors can now own almost every incarnation of the Man of Steel, from Kirk Alyn's 1948 serial (once considered irretrievably lost) to the George Reeves television series of the 1950s to the Christopher Reeve movies and beyond. More arcane items, like television commercials featuring the Man of Steel, can now be downloaded at websites like Google Video and YouTube.com.

As a small boy growing up in rural north Alabama in the 1960s, I was introduced to Superman on television. One of my favorite programs was *Adventures of Superman* with George Reeves. At four years old, I was amazed at how bullets bounced off his chest. When I began learning to read, one of the first things I remember reading was a Superman comic book (one of the early "Death of Superman" stories; I can still picture the image of him peeling a green mask off his face, and the words: "I wore this mask to fool my friends"). As I grew older, I began collecting comic books and watched animated adventures of Superman on Saturday mornings. By the time I was in fifth grade, I had discovered magazines like *Famous Monsters of Filmland* and learned that there was a live-action Superman before George Reeves. I ordered a copy of Kirk Alyn's book, *A Job for Superman*, autographed by the author. By eighth grade, I owned Max Fleischer's first Superman cartoon in Super 8mm, as well as *Stamp Day for Superman*, with George Reeves. When I hit high school, *Superman: The Movie* hit cinema screens, and I devoured Gary Grossman's book *Superman: Serial to Cereal* and David Michael Petrou's *The Making of Superman: The Movie*.

In 1980, I went to Los Angeles to attend the University of Southern California and was fortunate enough to meet Kirk Alyn, albeit briefly, at an award ceremony. Even at 70 years of age, Alyn still had the bearing of a Superman. As the years have passed, I've met others connected with the Man of Steel's cinema and TV legacies, including Noel Neill, Jack Larson, Gary Grossman, Denny Miller and Peter Lupus.

Why did I have such an interest in Superman? Why had this character created in 1938 by two teenagers from Cleveland taken such a hold of my imagination? I believe Superman appealed to me as a small child because children, who feel powerless, like to fantasize that they have the ability to fly and deflect bullets and protect others from harm, that they can be more powerful than their parents and become, in effect, Superparent. I believe Superman has a similar appeal to the powerless, the downtrodden, and the disenfranchised, which is why he became so enormously popular at the end of the Great Depression. He has remained popular because the ideals he stands for—truth, justice, and the American way—are ideals worth aspiring to. Superman has often been called a bland and boring character because he is so good and righteous, without the inner conflicts of Batman, who was driven to become a superhero by revenge. Superman is a hero because he wants to be, because he believes it's the right thing to do. He is indeed, as some have labeled him, the Big Blue Boy Scout.

I decided to write this book to collect in one volume a history of Superman in radio, movies, TV and Broadway, especially given that many of the previous books that cover the subject are now either hard to find or out of print. For readers looking to know more about Superman in comic books, there are no finer references than *Superman: A Complete History* by Les Daniels, which is thankfully still available at most retail outlets, and *Men of Tomorrow: Geeks, Gangsters and the Birth of the Comic Book* by Gerard Jones, which offers a fascinating history of the creators of Superman and other classic comic book heroes.

In writing this book, I went into my Fortress of Solitude and indulged myself in research—watching again the Fleischer cartoons, the Kirk Alyn serials, the various television series with George Reeves, Dean Cain, John Haymes Newton, Gerard Christopher and Tom Welling, and the films of Christopher Reeve. I eagerly awaited the release of *Superman Returns* and the documentary that came out at the same time, *Look! Up in the Sky*, which was a tantalizing encapsulation of Superman in mass media. I dove into newspaper and magazine archives, conducted interviews, and visited numerous Superman-related websites.

I started out thinking that I knew so much about Superman that I could easily write this book off the top of my head. I soon discovered I was wrong. There is such an abundance of information existing on Superman that to explore every aspect would fill several volumes; this book is just the tip of the iceberg. It is my hope that in reading this tome, casual Superman fans will rediscover the rich history of the Caped One in movies and TV, and the most ardent fans will discover a thing or two they hadn't known before.

Enjoy.

Introduction

In the spring of 1938, the fledgling comic book industry was jolted by the publication of *Action Comics*. There had been other comic strip magazines before, but this was something new. The cover depicted a character in a skin-tight blue-and-red costume hoisting an automobile over his head and smashing it against a rock. This was no mere humor or detective strip. This was the birth of the superhero. This was the birth of Superman.

Inside, the introductory Superman story hurtled along at a dizzying, frenetic pace, recounting how the alien arrived on Earth, assumed the identity of newspaper reporter Clark Kent, and vowed to devote his existence to helping those in need. He cleared an innocent woman marked for death in the electric chair, subdued a wife-beater, wooed Lois Lane, collared a crime boss, and began investigating corruption in Washington, D.C.—all in the space of 13 colorful but crudely drawn pages. The story ended with a cliffhanger, and a bit of ballyhoo: "A physical marvel, a mental wonder, SUPERMAN is destined to reshape the destiny of a world."

In the waning years of the Great Depression, on the cusp of events that would soon lead to a second world war, no one could have foreseen how true those words were. Shortly after his introduction, Superman exploded in the media, becoming a star of comic books, newspaper strips, radio, cartoons, movie serials, and eventually television. He became as ubiquitous a figure in American popular culture as Mickey Mouse or Tarzan. He was such an overpowering entity, in fact, that many of those who became associated with him found their own lives overwhelmed and sometimes unmanageable. The first to wrestle with the enormity of Superman were his creators, Jerry Siegel and Joe Shuster.

1

Siegel and Shuster Create a Legend

As the lights dimmed in a movie theater in Cleveland one day in 1934, two teenage boys took their seats. Before the feature, there was a newsreel and then a Popeye cartoon. The teenagers loved the madcap energy of the animated sailor who—after a few gulps of spinach—was able to perform extraordinary superhuman feats. One wallop of Popeye's mighty fist, and villains were sent flying backwards. The cartoons were the very epitome of action. The boys knew that if they could capture that kind of wild excitement in a comic strip, they'd have a success.

Recent graduates of Glenville High School, Jerry Siegel and Joe Shuster had met three years earlier while working on the school newspaper, *The Glenville Torch.*[1] They became fast friends, bonding over their shared love of science fiction. Siegel was the writer, the idea man, with an active imagination and a natural story-telling ability. Shuster was the artist, albeit one with an eye disease that caused him to lean over so that his eyes were just inches away from the paper as he drew. For the previous couple of years, they had tried to come up with something they could sell to a newspaper syndicate. It was the height of the Depression, and the two boys were barely scraping by. A hit newspaper comic strip could put them on the road to fame and fortune.

There were other things weighing on Jerry Siegel's mind. With his love of writing, and his experience on the school newspaper, he had considered becoming a reporter. And, like all teenaged boys, he was interested in girls. However, he was skinny and wore glasses and felt awkward around women.[2] He was also what a later generation would define as a nerd, a social outcast with a great love of science fiction and pulp novels who, like Joe Shuster, had been kept back a year at school.[3] The girls he had crushes on either didn't know he existed, or if they did, didn't care. But what if he could jump over buildings, or had enough strength to throw cars around? How would they feel about him then?[4]

Siegel lived with a very controlling mother in a nice suburb of Cleveland. His father, Mitchell Siegel, had emigrated with his family from Lithuania to America at the turn of the century, before Jerry was born.[5] Mitchell Siegel was a haberdasher with a shop in Cleveland, and Jerry's older brothers either worked in the shop or had other jobs. Jerry, however, was kept at home, encouraged to draw and write and exercise his imagination. He was the one being groomed for college. But all hopes of college and normalcy were stolen from him in October 1929, when his father was murdered in his shop, shot twice through the chest. The assailant, who apparently robbed the cash register, was never caught.[6]

Jerry, just shy of his fifteenth birthday, dealt with the emotionally wrenching violent loss of his father by retreating from the world, escaping more than ever into fantasy.[7] If only his father had been stronger. If only his reflexes had been quicker. If only the bullets had bounced off his chest.

While his mother accepted money from relatives and her working sons so she could keep her home, Jerry Siegel began wondering if he could come up with an idea that would make him suddenly rich, so that he would be able to fill the position of breadwinner and protector of the family that had been his father's.[8] That ambition still consumed him at age seventeen, and one evening, Siegel went home and spent a sleepless night. His brain was exploding with a tangle of ideas. He began reconsidering some of the earlier creative efforts he'd tried with Joe Shuster. Three years earlier, United Features Syndicate had rejected their first collaboration, *Interplanetary Police*. Undeterred, they developed a new character, *Steve Walsh*, a scientific adventurer whose underground laboratory contained a Pentascope, a machine that gave him X-ray vision and super hearing, allowing him to monitor the activities of criminals. This, also, was rejected, but the boys didn't give up. They created their own magazine, *Science Fiction: The Advance Guard of Future Civilization*, which they published using the high school's mimeograph machine. In the third issue, published in January 1933, Siegel—using the pseudonym Herbert S. Fine—wrote a story called "The Reign of the Superman." It was a grim tale in which the superman of the title was a super villain, wreaking havoc and destruction. Shuster provided the illustrations, showing the superman as a bald-headed megalomaniac. Their magazine lasted for only two more issues, and in the meantime Siegel and Shuster kept trying to come up with a commercial comic strip.[9]

In 1933, a new kind of magazine had appeared on the newsstands of Cleveland. *Detective Dan—Secret Operative 48* was published by the Humor Publishing Company of Chicago. Detective Dan was little more than a Dick Tracy clone, but here, for the first time, in a series of black-and-white illustrations, was a comic magazine with an original character appearing in all-new stories. This was a dramatic departure from other comic magazines, which simply reprinted panels from the Sunday newspaper comic strips. When he saw *Detective Dan*, Siegel thought that he and Shuster could come up with an even more exciting comic book character.[10]

They reconsidered their superman idea. If they wanted to make it commercial, they would have to change the main character. Both boys were admirers of Edgar Rice Burroughs, who had created one of the most popular characters in American fiction in 1912 when he wrote the first Tarzan story. Tarzan was a hero, a character admired by the public, and his creation had made Burroughs a very rich man; after his initial appearance in *All-Story Magazine*, Tarzan had spun off into books, movies, a radio program and a popular comic strip. If Siegel and Shuster wanted that kind of success, they would have to change Superman from a power-mad villain into a benevolent hero.[11]

One day, the boys heard that the publisher of *Detective Dan* was coming to Cleveland on a business trip from Chicago. They set to work creating their first Superman comic book. The main character was a man possessed of super powers, but he didn't come from another planet, and he didn't wear a costume. In the cover illustration, Shuster depicted him in a tee shirt and trousers, holding a criminal over his head while being sprayed with machine-gun bullets—which bounced harmlessly off his chest.[12]

When they showed Superman to the *Detective Dan* publisher, he was interested at first, but he later had a change of heart. Shuster was so upset by this latest rejection that he tore up the comic book, except for the cover illustration. It was a very low period for the boys. Fresh out of school, with employment scarce, they were working odd jobs and doing errands to bring in enough money to submit their comic strip ideas to newspaper syndicates, but to no avail. Eventually, money got so tight that Shuster, unable to afford drawing paper, was reduced to doing his illustrations on brown wrapping paper. When he found several discarded rolls of wallpaper, he was ecstatic; the back was white, which gave him enough drawing paper to last a long while.[13]

Now, months after their meeting with the *Detective Dan* publisher, Siegel had a new take on Superman. As the ideas continued coming to him during that restless night, he kept writing them down until, by morning, he had several weeks' worth of stories for a newspaper strip. As the sun rose, he dashed over to his friend's house, twelve blocks away. Siegel's enthusiasm was infectious, and Shuster quickly became caught up in it. As Shuster translated the ideas into drawings, Siegel became ecstatic. The artwork emerging from Shuster's pencil was even more thrilling than he had imagined.[14]

Working together, the pair created a novel character. Unlike the popular science fiction comic strips of the day like *Flash Gordon* which featured ordinary men from the twentieth century in adventures on far-flung planets, their strip centered around a man from another planet who had come to present-day Earth. He was a costumed character, who hid his identity behind ordinary street-clothes—a reverse of heroes who wore costumes to hide their identities when they performed their heroic deeds. In his disguise of business suit and eyeglasses, he was meek and mild, the kind of man a woman wouldn't know existed—or wouldn't care if he did. Combining the names of two popular movie actors of the time—Clark Gable and Kent Taylor—they gave this character a name: Clark Kent.[15] They also gave him an occupation, that of a newspaper reporter, which would allow him to have ready access to news of breaking emergencies. The bespectacled Kent had a crush on a female reporter, Lois Lane, a character inspired by movie actresses Glenda Farrell and Lola Lane (not, as has been often and erroneously reported, Glenville High classmate Lois Amster).[16]

Superman was a distillation of a number of influences. Shuster loved the movies of Douglas Fairbanks, Sr., the swashbuckling star whose most common pose—when he wasn't wielding a sword, leaping from a balcony or swinging on a rope—was standing with legs apart, hands on his hips, his head thrown back in devil-may-care laughter.[17] There was also Hugo Danner, the main character from Phillip Wylie's 1930 novel *Gladiator*, who could lift automobiles, leap 40 feet in the air, and whose skin seemed bulletproof. Siegel had given the book a favorable review in his science fiction magazine. Besides Tarzan, the boys were inspired by another Edgar Rice Burroughs character, John Carter of Mars. Because the planet Mars was smaller than Earth, earthman John Carter had great strength and was able to leap huge distances on the red planet. Siegel wondered if a character that came from a planet larger than Earth would have extra-normal abilities on our planet. And then, of course, there was Popeye. The boys thought that if they could adapt the super strength and action of the animated cartoons to a static comic strip, and play it straight instead of for comedy, the result would be spectacular.[18]

Superman's costume was patterned after the circus strongman outfits of the day, with a couple of exceptions. First, Superman had a cape, to help give the drawings a sense of movement and action as the character performed his amazing deeds. Secondly, there was an "S" symbol on his chest, to make the costume more distinctive. Besides being the first letter in Superman, the boys joked that it was also the first letter in Siegel and Shuster.[19]

By the end of a non-stop day of work fueled by sandwiches, the two boys had created a character that would eventually become a pop-culture phenomenon. But in 1934, no one was interested in Superman. They submitted their strip to newspaper syndicates, who responded that Superman was too crude, too immature and lacking in appeal. *Famous Fun-*

nies—a magazine that reprinted Sunday newspaper strips—returned their package unopened. Once again, the boys' hopes were dashed.[20]

Things began to look up the following year. In February 1935, a former U.S. Army cavalry officer, Major Malcolm Wheeler-Nicholson, launched a new comic magazine called *New Fun*, published by Wheeler-Nicholson's National Allied Publications. Siegel and Shuster submitted two of their comic strips to the major, *Henri Duval* and *Dr. Occult*. One was drawn on brown paper, and the other on the back of wallpaper. When Wheeler-Nicholson bought the strips, he told them to re-draw it. They bought some proper drawing paper, and Shuster readily complied. When the comic strips appeared in the October 1935 issue of *New Fun*, Siegel and Shuster had finally broken in, after four long years of rejections and false starts. This was the beginning of the comic book age, and the young men from Cleveland were in on the ground floor.[21]

After scoring a success with their first two submissions to Wheeler-Nicholson, Siegel and Shuster next submitted *Superman*. The major took one look at the strip and quickly rejected it; he and his small staff found the whole concept ludicrous.[22]

But Siegel and Shuster didn't give up. Other comic books began appearing early in 1936, including *Popular Comics*. Published by Dell Publishing, the magazine was put together by Max Gaines and a teenaged cartoonist named Sheldon Mayer. The comic book was comprised of reprints of Sunday strips like *Dick Tracy* and *Little Orphan Annie* instead of original stories, but Siegel and Shuster submitted *Superman* anyway. Gaines was impressed by this new character, but he declined to publish it.[23]

Wow Comics appeared in July 1936, edited by 19-year-old artist and writer Will Eisner. In what was becoming a frustrating and depressing ritual, Siegel and Shuster submitted *Superman* to the new magazine. Eisner deemed that it was not professional enough for publication (Eisner later gained fame by creating the cult comic character *The Spirit*).[24]

Meanwhile, Major Wheeler-Nicholson had come up with an idea for a new comic magazine—*Detective Comics*. He was looking for action-oriented material, so Jerry Siegel came up with the idea of a man of action with a sense of humor, not unlike Douglas Fairbanks, Sr. He named the character Slam Bradley. The major agreed to include the strip in *Detective Comics*. Illustrated by Joe Shuster, *Slam Bradley* became the first Siegel and Shuster character to appear on a monthly basis. As far as the boys were concerned, this was a dry run for *Superman*—they used it as a testing ground for some of the slam-bang action they wanted to put into their superhero comic, if they ever got it launched.[25]

When Wheeler-Nicholson's comic book company began to founder, he sold it to a pulp magazine publisher and distributor named Harry Donenfeld. Donenfeld changed the name of the comic book company, christening it after the new publication—Detective Comics, Inc. (later reduced to just the initials DC). After he took control of the company, Donenfeld promoted Whitney Ellsworth and Vin Sullivan, two of its artists, to editors. Max Gaines and Sheldon Mayer were also employed by Donenfeld by this time. When Donenfeld asked Sullivan to put together a new magazine to be called *Action Comics*, Gaines and Mayer went to Sullivan and urged him to consider a strip they had seen sometime earlier, which they thought would be ideal to launch the new comic book—Siegel and Shuster's *Superman*. Sullivan agreed to take a look at *Superman*, and—unlike a legion of editors before him—immediately saw its potential. He asked Siegel and Shuster to turn out a 13-page comic book story based on their *Superman* strip, for which they would be paid $10 per page. With a short deadline, Siegel and Shuster cut their already-prepared newspaper comic strips into individual panels and pasted them onto sheets of paper the size of a comic book page.[26] Despite what they would claim later, Siegel and Shuster knew that when they signed their contract, they were signing over the rights to the character to the publisher. It was standard practice in the business, and they had done the same with their earlier creations *Henri Duval* and *Slam Bradley*.[27] The ten-year contract offered them "a percentage of net profits accruing from the exploitation of Superman in channels other than magazines," without specifying how great, or how meager, that percentage would be.[28]

Superman was finally unveiled to the public in *Action Comics* #1, published in the spring of 1938 (though the date on the cover was June 1938).[29] At that early stage, Superman's powers were somewhat limited. He wasn't able to fly, but could leap an eighth of a mile or hurtle over a twenty-story building. He was able to lift tremendous weights, could outrun an express train, and had skin so tough that nothing less than a bursting shell could penetrate it. His back-story was covered in a single page. As an infant, he was sent by rocket ship from a nameless planet just before it exploded. The rocket crash-landed on Earth, where a passing motorist discovered the unharmed baby inside. He took the child to an orphanage, where it grew to manhood. There was no explanation of how Superman adopted the alter ego of Clark Kent, and there was no *Daily Planet*—in the earliest stories, Kent worked for a newspaper called *The Daily Star*, whose editor was George Taylor. Lois Lane, however, was there from the very beginning.

Superman was an almost instantaneous hit, and sales of subsequent issues of *Action Comics* rose quickly. In September, Siegel and Shuster took the train to New York, where Vin Sullivan, *Detective Comics'* business manager Jack Liebowitz and Harry Donenfeld greeted them. They also met with Max Gaines, who was selling items to the McClure Syndicate for newspaper syndication. Gaines made a deal with Donenfeld and, on the strength of the sales of *Action Comics*, finally sold *Superman* as a daily newspaper strip. For agreeing to do the strip themselves, Donenfeld promised Siegel and Shuster fifty percent of the take.[30]

To handle the combined workload of a daily strip and a monthly comic, Siegel and Shuster created their own studio, hiring other artists and writers to help them with the workload. *The Houston Chronicle* was the first newspaper to agree to run the *Superman* strip. *The Milwaukee Journal* and *The San Antonio Express* followed. The strip quickly picked up momentum, and by January of 1939 it was appearing in newspapers throughout America.

Now that he was responsible for four other artists and occasional writers, whose paychecks came out of his and Shuster's percentages, Siegel began to wonder if he'd cut a good enough deal for Superman. When the character was given his own magazine in the summer of 1939, and also became the featured attraction of *World's Fair Comics*, the Siegel and Shuster studio was churning out more than fifty pages of Superman comics every month, at $10 per page. They were also producing the daily newspaper strips and, later, a color Sunday strip, for a sizeable percentage.[31] They were making more money than any other twenty-five year olds they knew, but when Siegel considered that *Action Comics* was selling nearly a million copies per issue, and *Superman* over 500,000 copies per issue,[32] he couldn't help but feel that he'd been robbed. Since his father's death, Siegel always showed a smiling face to the public, while privately feeling betrayed and abandoned and cheated out of what he deserved. Beginning a pattern that would repeat in years to come, he bottled up his anger until he could hold it no longer, and then he over-reacted, spewing out his thoughts in an letter to Jack Liebowitz, demanding that his and Shuster's page rate be increased from $10 to $15. Liebowitz, a canny businessman who rose to the top as an accountant and who knew how to juggle the books, was dismayed.[33] He responded with a letter saying that Siegel's missive took his breath away, adding, "Don't get the idea that everyone in New York is a 'gyp' and a highbinder and because you are treated as a gentleman and an equal not only by ourselves but by Mr. Gaines and the McClure people, that we are seeking to take advantage of you ... so come off your high horse."[34] He did, however, give Siegel and Shuster their raise.

In the spring of 1939, flush with his newfound success, Jerry Siegel began wooing his next-door neighbor, a teenager named Bella. Almost everyone in his family disapproved of the union, so soon after Siegel and Bella were married in June 1939, the couple moved to New York. Joe remained in Cleveland to run the studio, but made trips to the Big Apple to visit Siegel and the DC Comics offices.[35] On one trip in 1940, he attended the New York World's Fair, which declared "Superman Day" on July 3, an event arranged by DC publicist Allen "Duke" Ducovny and sponsored by Macy's department stores. The event helped promote DC's 100-page special edition *New York World's Fair* comic, which was sold exclusively at the fair. A *Superman* radio broadcast was done from the fairgrounds, and a real, live-action Superman appeared for the first time in person, personified by Ray Middleton, a young Broadway actor who would later win acclaim in *South Pacific* and *Annie Get Your Gun*. By the end of the year, Joe Shuster had also moved to New York, bringing his entire family with him.[36]

Hoping to make lightning strike again, Siegel created other comic book characters in the early 1940s. The most successful was *The Spectre*, who was a supernatural crime-fighting ghost. But no other character he would ever create would have the appeal of Superman, and Superman, he felt, was being slowly pulled away from him. Mort Weisinger was placed in charge of editing the comic book stories, and Whitney Ellsworth edited the newspaper strips. Recalling how much fun he and Joe Shuster had had with a Tarzan spoof called *Goober the Mighty* when they were creating comics for *The Glenville Torch*, Siegel came up with a twist on Superman—Superboy. What if, thought Siegel, before he became Superman, the Man of Steel had used his superpowers for practical jokes? Weisinger was not amused; he felt that spoofing the company's number one hero would dilute his value, and that showing the character pulling pranks would set a bad example for their young readers. Siegel was frustrated.[37] He was even more irked when *Superman* became a radio show and Superman merchandise began filling store shelves.

In January 1940, Siegel wrote another letter to Jack Liebowitz, reminding him that he and Shuster had been promised a piece of the licensing. Liebowitz replied, "Get behind your work with zest and ambition to improve and forget about book rights, movie rights and all other dreams. We'll take care of things in the proper manner."

A year later, Siegel was still waiting for his piece of the merchandising pie. Paramount Pictures had guaranteed $100,000 for the animation rights. The sponsors of the radio show put up almost as much for the first full season of programs. At the end of 1941, Siegel wrote again, and Liebowitz responded that the company's figures "show that we lost money and therefore you are entitled to no royalties. However, in line with our usual generous attitude toward you boys, I am enclosing a check for $500, which is in effect a token of feeling."[38] It was also a very, very small token of the $1.5 million that Harry Donenfeld's companies had grossed just off of the Superman toys and spin-off products glutting the market in 1940–41.[39]

Siegel knew that it was ludicrous to assert that Superman had lost money, considering the popularity of the character. By 1941, Superman appeared regularly in over 200 newspapers across the country, reaching 25 million readers. During the war years, every issue of *Superman* sold more than a million copies. A special overseas edition of 35,000 copies was sent to the troops each month. And in 1944, it was reported that in more than 2,500 classrooms in the U.S., children were learning to read from *Superman* workbooks.[40] But despite his wounded feelings, Siegel never pressed for an audit or threatened to take his talents to another publisher.[41] He had created a character who could bend steel in his bare hands, outrace a locomotive and laugh as bullets raked across his chest, but these were little boy fantasies, the dreams of an insecure kid whose father had been ripped from his life in an instant of unpunished violence. Emotionally, Siegel himself was still a child, one who erupted in anger and rage, got reprimanded, and then sheepishly towed the line, until the pent-up anger boiled over again.

When Jerry Siegel was drafted into the Army in the summer of 1943, during the waning years of World War II, he continued writing new comic book stories (Shuster was ineligible for service due to his poor eyesight). Five months after his induction, his son Michael was born. Siegel came home from maneuvers to see his boy, but his marriage to Bella was failing. He would never speak of his first wife or his son in interviews from that point onward.[42]

While Siegel was away, Whitney Ellsworth tried another approach with *Superboy*. Instead of a mischievous prankster, Ellsworth conceived of him as a wholesome do-gooder. Although Fawcett's *Captain Marvel* had juvenile spin-offs with *Mary Marvel* and *Captain Marvel, Jr.*, this was an approach that had never been taken before—the teen adventures of an established comic book hero. The five-page introductory story was the product of the Siegel and Shuster studio; though he would later claim that he was surprised when *Superboy* made his debut in the January/February 1945 issue of DC's *More Fun Comics*, Siegel was, in fact, the writer.[43]

While in the army, Siegel served with a lawyer named Alfred Zugsmith. Finally following the advice he'd been hearing from friends for years, he asked Zugsmith for legal advice. Should he, he asked, sue for greater compensation on *Superboy*? Zugsmith had a better idea—he advised Siegel to fight to get the rights to Superman back. When Siegel was mustered out of the military in 1945, with just three years left to go on his original contract with DC, he began complaining more openly about the tactics of Donenfeld and Liebowitz. He and Joe Shuster had been robbed, Siegel said. But from Donenfeld and Liebowitz's perspective, they'd done the boys a favor. Without a publisher, who would ever have heard of Superman?[44]

Siegel and Shuster came up with a new character, a clown who fought crime with joy buzzers and water-spraying flowers and other clown gags, called *Funnyman*. DC initially showed some interest, but negotiations broke down over Siegel's insistence that he and Shuster would retain all the rights. Siegel next took the idea to Vin Sullivan, who had started a company called Magazine Enterprises and was happy to be in business with the creators of Superman.[45]

When comic book sales dipped following the war, and the revenue from Superman licensing diminished, Siegel and Shuster's profits shrank. Siegel felt there was more to blame for his lessened paychecks than just a downturn in the market. He told Zugsmith that it was time to proceed with a lawsuit. Zugsmith filed the suit in April of 1947, seeking return of the rights to Superman to Siegel and Shuster and $5 million in damages. Outraged, Jack Liebowitz tried to talk Siegel out of the lawsuit, saying he had signed his rights away and his claims had no basis, but Siegel was determined not to back down. Neither was DC; the company immediately fired Superman's creators.[46]

The actual financial situation of Siegel and Shuster during this time is hard to pinpoint. In some newspaper accounts, they are said to be earning $100,000 a year from Superman. Once the suit was filed, Siegel claimed the pair never made more than $30,000 in a year. Whatever the amount, they were living in relative comfort. Siegel maintained homes in Cleveland and New York, while Joe supported his parents and siblings in New York.[47]

That year, as Joe Shuster was preparing to attend the National Cartoonists Society costume ball at the Plaza Hotel in New York City, he learned that Joanne Carter, an acquaintance from Cleveland who had modeled for Lois Lane twelve years earlier, was in town. Joanne was newly divorced, and went to the function as Shuster's date, but it was Jerry Siegel who swept her off her feet. As the lawsuit trudged forward, Siegel asked Carter if she would marry him if he divorced Bella. She said she would.[48]

In 1948, the lawsuit finally went to court. DC had an esteemed copyright lawyer and documents to support their claims. Siegel and Shuster had depositions and righteous indignation. When the verdict came down in May 1948, the court ruled that Siegel and Shuster had surrendered their rights to Superman to DC, and had no claim on the character or any basis for their claim of $5 million in damages. However, the court agreed that *Superboy* had been unfairly exploited and urged the parties to seek a settlement. It was a painful defeat for Siegel. In the end, he and Shuster settled for $100,000, most of which went to Zugsmith's fees. The loss of the court case was made worse by the unremarkable sales of *Funnyman*. The new comic book only lasted six issues, the final one coming out in the summer of 1948. By that time, the Siegel and Shuster byline had disappeared from the *Superman* comics, and when Columbia Pictures released its *Superman* serial, the pair did not profit from it. Siegel wanted to appeal the court's verdict, but Shuster and Zugsmith talked him out of it. Shuster was tired of fighting; Zugsmith saw no point in it. For Siegel, the only bright spot of 1948 came in October, when he was granted a divorce from his first wife and married Joanne Carter a week later.[49]

Siegel sold his house in Cleveland and settled in New York with Joanne. He told Joe he'd try to find something they could do together, but nothing materialized. It had been ten years since they had sold Superman to DC. They had stood up against a corporation made rich and powerful on the strength of their creation, and that corporation had squashed them. The legal defeat effectively spelled the end of the Siegel and Shuster collaboration. Now, at age 35, they were both out of work.[50]

Joe Shuster, with his eyesight getting worse, more or less retired after the lawsuit. After doing some work on a Charlton crime comic in 1954, he disappeared from the comic book scene. His parents died, his sister married, and Shuster and his younger brother moved into a smaller place.[51]

Jerry Siegel went to work for lesser comic book companies, such as Ziff-Davis and Charlton, creating new characters that never caught on. He next tried to find a job in advertising, but to no avail. He sold a few scripts here and there to magazines like *Cracked* and *Panic*, but he wasn't able to bring in enough income to make alimony and child support payments and take care of his new family, which had grown with the birth of a daughter. As he grew more dispirited, his wife Joanne began making appeals to DC. She met with Jack Liebowitz, who told her that DC had done all they could for Siegel and Shuster, only to be repaid with an expensive lawsuit. Joanne threatened to contact newspapers, and asked Liebowitz if he really wanted to see a headline that said "Creator of Superman Starves to Death." Liebowitz gave in. He asked *Superman* editor Mort Weisinger to assign some stories to Siegel, on one condition—Siegel could never claim publicly to be one of the creators of Superman.[52]

After twelve years away from the character he created, Jerry Siegel's stories began appearing in *Action Comics* and *Superman* in late 1959.[53] Before the lawsuits, he had been paid $50 per page. Now he was back to his 1938 rate of $10 per page. In a departure from his previous work, Siegel's new Superman tales were more emotional stories, exploring the pain at the heart of the exile from Krypton, the alien orphan who had been separated from his father as the result of a violent act (the destruction of his home planet). But Siegel was now working for Mort Weisinger, a notoriously ill-tempered editor who wore his writers down and eroded their confidence with a constant barrage of disparaging remarks and insults.[54]

Siegel knew that 1966 would mark the expiration of the first copyright term on Superman, and that when National Comics (formed in 1944 when National Allied Publications merged with Detective Comics, Inc.) went to renew, he could challenge their claim. In 1963, he contacted a lawyer to begin investigating his chances. He also contacted Shuster, but his former partner was unwilling to join in another court case. Siegel also knew that once he challenged the copyright, he would again be fired from DC, so he began looking for other work, using a pseudonym. Stan Lee of Marvel Comics hired him to script some *Human Torch* stories, but Marvel's hip readers found Siegel's work too old-fashioned. In 1964, he began writing for Archie Comics, who were trying a superhero line with *Fly Man* and *Mighty Crusaders*. Then, in 1965, his copyright challenge went to court. As he expected, he was quickly fired from *Superman*.[55]

In a repeat of the events of the previous decade, Siegel's copyright challenge was denied. With pro bono help, he appealed the decision. Archie Comics cancelled its superhero line, and was unwilling to give Siegel any work on its teen humor comics. He went back to Stan Lee, who could only offer him a position as a proofreader. Desperate for work, Siegel took it. When that petered out, he tried his hand at selling magazine stories, but without success. Finally, in 1968, Siegel left New York and headed for the West Coast, hoping for a fresh start.[56]

Siegel and Shuster, who hoped that *Superman* would bring fame and fortune, were living their lives near the poverty line. The lawsuits, instead of enriching them, had bankrupted them. Unable to retain rights to their character, Joe Shuster, now in his mid–50s, was eventually reduced to becoming a messenger boy in Manhattan, but even that did not last. When he became legally blind, he left his job and was supported by his younger brother in Forest Hills, Queens. Siegel took a job as a clerk typist with the California Public Utilities Commission in Los Angeles, earning $7,000 a year. In 1975, he told a reporter, "I can't stand to look at a *Superman* comic book. It makes me physically ill. I love Superman, and yet to me he has become an alien thing."[57]

By this time, a federal court had denied his appeal of the copyright verdict. His only recourse now was to take the fight to the U.S. Supreme Court. Under the strain of the litigation, Siegel suffered a heart attack.[58] He was a defeated man.

But in April 1975, Siegel received a call from his lawyer, who said that with a new Superman movie on the horizon, Warner Communications—who now owned National Periodical Publications, which included DC Comics—wanted to settle Siegel's case. They would offer Siegel and Shuster a yearly stipend if Siegel would drop the lawsuit. Reluctantly, Siegel agreed. When the promised money didn't arrive, he wrote to Warner Bros., and waited. Then he wrote again. And again. By summer, he felt he had made a big mistake. And then he saw an article in *Variety* saying that Warner Bros. had paid $3 million to National Comics for the screen rights to Superman. Indignant, and with Joanne's urging, Siegel sat down and typed out a 10-page, single-spaced press release, detailing his and Shuster's plight:[59] "I, Jerry Siegel, the co-originator of SUPERMAN, put a curse on the SUPERMAN movie! I hope it super-bombs." Superman's publishers, he wrote, "murdered my days, killed my nights, choked my happiness, strangled my career.... WHAT AN INFERNAL, SICKENING SUPERSTENCH EMANATES FROM NATIONAL PERIODICAL PUBLICATIONS ... I consider National's executives economic murderers, money-mad monsters." Jack Liebowitz, said Siegel, "stabbed Joe Shuster and me, Jerry Siegel, in the back. He ruined our lives, deliberately."[60]

Siegel made a thousand copies of the press release and sent it to news outlets all over the country. Then he sat back and waited for reporters to contact him, but the phone was silent ... until Phil Yeh, editor of a free newspaper called *Cobblestone*, called and requested an interview. In late October, another call came, from John Sherwood of *The Washington Star*. Sherwood's paper wouldn't send him to Los Angeles, so he took the train to New York and interviewed Joe Shuster. After that article appeared, Siegel was invited to be a guest on *The Tomorrow Show*, a late night NBC talk show hosted by Tom Snyder. Cartoonist Jerry Robinson, a co-creator of Batman who had become successful in commercial advertising, saw the program and felt empathy for his old friend's plight. He called Siegel and asked what he could do. With the help of esteemed comic book artist Neal Adams, Robinson launched a campaign to get Warner Bros. to live up to its commitment.[61]

In December of 1975, Siegel and Shuster appeared at a news conference at the New York Press Club at which the National Cartoonists Society and the Cartoonists Guild offered their full backing to their attempt to gain more money from Warner Communications for their creation of Superman. Bill Gallo, president of the National Cartoonists Society, said the cartoonists were shocked and outraged that the publishers of Superman refused to share a fair percentage of the millions of dollars the character had spawned with its creators.[62] At the press conference, Irwin Hasen, creator of the comic strip *Dondi*, put up a poster showing the child with a huge tear on his face and the words, "Is it a plane? Is it a bird? No, it's a pity."[63]

The publicity campaign worked. Warner Bros. agreed to give Siegel and Shuster a yearly annuity of $10,000 each.[64] Robinson advised them not to take it, and made a counteroffer on their behalf, asking Warner Bros. to pay Siegel and Shuster's legal fees and provide medical insurance for them. On December 9th, Warner Bros. raised its offer to $15,000 per year, and gave the pair two days to accept. But there was one demand on which they would not budge—restoring the "created by Jerry Siegel and Joe Shuster" credit to Superman. On Monday, December 15, 1975, Siegel flew to New York for a sit-down meeting of all the parties in Warner Bros. Rockefeller Center office. Siegel and Shuster wanted to take the offer before the deal collapsed, but Robinson urged them to hold out for credit. The negotiations dragged through Tuesday and into Wednesday. Finally, Warner Bros. raised their offer to $20,000 with cost-of-living increases, but they still refused to give "created by" credit. Robinson said the offer was unacceptable. On Thursday, Warner Bros. hinted that they were going to withdraw the offer. Siegel was at the breaking point, but Robinson told him to give it one more day. That night, Robinson called Jay Emmett—Jack Liebowitz's nephew—who had been overseeing the negotiations for the studio. By the time he hung up, Robinson had gotten Emmett to agree to restore the "created by" credit on the comic books and also on the upcoming movie. A contract signing was scheduled for the following Wednesday.[65]

On December 25, 1975, at the end of the CBS *Evening News* broadcast, Walter Cronkite told the story of the two boys from Cleveland who created a superhero, lost the rights, fell into poverty and battled for decades for the recognition they deserved. As he spoke of the legal settlement, an image of Superman appeared on the screen, and Cronkite intoned, "Today, at least, truth, justice and the American way have triumphed."[66]

Three years later, after the first *Superman* movie starring Christopher Reeve generated more than $80 million, and after Warner Communications had received more than $250 million of the more than $1 billion earned from Superman movies, television programs and a vast array of commercial products, Siegel and Shuster were given a one-time bonus of $15,000 each. After the release of *Superman II* in 1981, the yearly annuity was raised to $30,000.[67] Jerry Siegel's wife, Joanne, told *New York Times* reporter Aljean Harmetz that compared to the opulent lifestyles of other people connected with Superman, she and her husband lived a very quiet, secluded life. For his part, Jerry Siegel said, "Sometimes I feel like half a corpse rescued from a horrible old age."[68] But having their credit restored meant a lot for their morale, if not their bank accounts. After coming to terms with the Superman creators, Warner Bros. flew the duo across the country to Superman birthday parties and opening days of the movies. At one of the events, Shuster met actor Christopher Reeve, then portraying the Man of Steel on-screen. "He came up and asked me how I liked his portrayal of the part," Shuster told *The Los Angeles Times* reporter John L. Mitchell. "I said he was perfect."[69]

In the final years of his life, Joe Shuster moved to Los Angeles and lived—as he had in his teens—a few blocks away from Jerry Siegel. In an interview with *The Toronto Star* in April 1992, Shuster said, "There aren't many people who can say they're leaving behind something as important as Superman. But Jerry and I can, and that's a good feeling." Joe Shuster died on July 30, 1992, at age 78. Jerry Siegel died at age 81 on January 28, 1996. DC Comics ran an obituary thanking him for helping to create the comic book industry.[70]

However, the legal battles did not die with them. A 1976 copyright law gave authors and their heirs the ability to recapture copyrights of works sold before 1978. After Siegel's death, his widow Joanne and daughter Laura Siegel Larson put Warners on two years' notice that they intended to terminate the 1948 *Superboy* copyright agreement. Two years later, they filed suit against the giant conglomerate, alleging that episodes of the television series *Smallville* produced after they exerted the notice infringed on their copyright. In March 2006, a U.S. District Court judge ruled that the Siegels had, in fact, recaptured the *Superboy* rights in November 2004. Time will tell what effect—if any—the ruling will have on the production of future episodes of *Smallville*.

2

Superman on the Air

When listeners turned on their radios on the evening of Monday, February 12, 1940, they heard this action-packed opening:

"Faster than an airplane!
More powerful than a locomotive!
Impervious to bullets!
Up in the sky, look!
It's a giant bird!
It's a plane!
It's SUPERMAN!

And now, Superman—a being no larger than an ordinary man but possessed of powers and abilities never before realized on Earth: able to leap into the air an eighth of a mile at a single bound, hurtle a 20-story building with ease, race a high-powered bullet to its target, lift tremendous weights and rend solid steel in his bare hands as though it were paper. Superman—a strange visitor from a distant planet: champion of the oppressed, physical marvel extraordinary who has sworn to devote his existence on Earth to helping those in need!"

By 1940, radio was the primary entertainment medium of its time; nearly every home and office had one, and Americans by the millions thrilled to the audio adventures of *The Lone Ranger* and *The Shadow*, or laughed along with *Amos 'n' Andy* and *Fibber McGee and Molly*. It wasn't until after World War I that commercial radio began (the Radio Corporation of America, or RCA, was formed on October 17, 1919), broadcasting to a small audience listening over homemade receivers. But by 1926, there were over 5 million radios in America, and RCA formed the National Broadcasting Company (NBC) to broadcast programs to them. The Columbia Broadcasting System (CBS) was formed the following year. As a cultural force, radio had a profound effect on the nation. For the first time, listeners in New York and Chicago and Los Angeles could hear the same news, laugh at the same jokes, whistle along to the same tunes and hear the same commercial pitches simultaneously. Radio, as a shared experience, united the nation like no medium before it. Catchphrases instantly became a part of the language, and stars were born overnight.[71]

Superman was brought to radio by Allen Ducovny, a press agent with Detective Comics, and Robert Maxwell (the pen name of Robert Joffe),[72] a former pulp fiction author who was in charge of licensing the subsidiary rights of the company's comic book characters. In 1939, the two men prepared sample audition disks of four episodes to take to prospective sponsors, and co-wrote an opening that would make full use of an array of sound effects. At this early stage, a sound similar to that used for flying saucers in 1950s B-films was used to convey Superman's flights through the air; it wasn't nearly as convincing as the whistling wind sound effect that would be used after the series officially premiered.

The four fifteen-minute audition episodes covered Superman's origin, Clark Kent's becoming a reporter, and a two-part adventure that pitted Superman against a villain called The Shark. In the audition disks, Clark Kent's boss was Paris White, editor of *The Daily Star*. White had a secretary named Miss Lane, played by Agnes Moorehead. The episodes did their job; Hecker's HO Oats signed on as the show's first sponsor. Hecker's tried to buy time on the major radio networks but was unsuccessful. Instead, they bought time on ten stations, and syndicated it to others, recording it on sixteen-inch electrical transcription disks.

When the show went on the air, the premiere episode told how Jor-L, a scientist on the distant planet Krypton, and his wife Lara sent their infant son to earth moments before the planet exploded. Playing the roles of Superman's parents were veteran New York radio performers Ned Wever (of the *Bulldog Drummond* radio series) and Agnes Moorehead, who had appeared as Miss Lane in the audition disks. Coincidentally, Moorehead also played the similarly named "Margot Lane" on *The Shadow*. A member of Orson Welles's Mercury Theater, Moorehead achieved lasting fame in the 1960s as the witch Endora on the TV series *Bewitched*.

The real challenge for the producers was finding an actor who could convincingly portray the Man of Steel. At one point, they considered casting two actors in the part, one to play Clark Kent and one to play Superman. Then they met Bud Collyer.

Like Superman, Bud Collyer had lived a life of dual identities. His real name was Clayton Johnson Heermance, Jr. Born into a theatrical family on June 18, 1908 in New York City, he was the grandson of Dan Collyer, who had appeared on stage for fifty years. His mother acted under the name Carrie Collyer. His sister, June Collyer, became a silent film star and married comedian Stu Erwin. His brother, Richard Heermance, became an executive at Monogram Studios. His father, however, was an attorney, and it seemed young Clayton would follow in his footsteps. After graduating from Horace Mann High School, Clayton Heermance Jr. entered Williams College, where he became the leader of a dance band. While the band was performing at a school dance at the St. Regis Hotel, actress and fashion commentator Helen Claire heard him sing. Impressed, she arranged for him to get a part-time job for $85 a week, singing on CBS radio programs. Heermance later attended Fordham University and earned a law degree, intending to become a practicing attorney. He became a clerk in his father's law firm, but tired of it after two years and decided to give acting a chance.[73] Bud Collyer's daughter, Cynthia Collyer, remembers, "Dad was a great storyteller. He worked his way through Law school singing on the radio and found law clerking in his father's office stifling. Hence when some announcing work beckoned, he went that route."[74] On March 28, 1932, using the family theatrical name of Collyer, he made his Broadway debut in *Life Begins* at the Selwyn Theatre, in a cast that included future movie actress Glenda Farrell. The show closed after eight performances, but Collyer kept at it, appearing in other small parts on Broadway and landing more radio jobs. Radio was lucrative for the young actor. He played the part of Abie on *Abie's Irish Rose*, was Pat Ryan on NBC's *Terry and the Pirates* series, and was the announcer on *Ripley's Believe It or Not*.

By the time the Superman producers approached Collyer, he was one of the busiest actors on radio, appearing on two shows, NBC's *Road of Life* and ABC's *Listening Post*. Lucky for him the recording studios were in the same building, on the same floor, one hundred feet down the hall from each other; Monday through Friday at 10:45 A.M., Collyer had thirty seconds to sprint from one studio to the next. But the easy-going actor never complained; he welcomed all the work he could handle. "Those were great days," Collyer later told *The*

New York Times, "because you weren't seen. You could appear on as many as twenty-five to thirty shows a week and grab off $6,000 to $7,000 a year—big dough at that time."[75]

Bud Collyer didn't want to be Superman. Producers Robert Maxwell and Frank Chase found it difficult getting him to take a role on what was widely viewed as a "kiddie program." Appearing on Richard Lamparski's radio program *Whatever Became Of ...* in the 1960s, Bud Collyer recalled that when Robert Maxwell first approached him, he turned the role down; he thought he'd be embarrassed playing a part on a kid's program. Maxwell asked the actor if he would at least do the audition tape, implying that they would hire another actor if the show made it onto the airwaves. Once Collyer did the audition tapes, Maxwell simply told him "You're Superman." Collyer handed the script back to Maxwell and tried to walk off the show, but he couldn't unload it, even though he was still embarrassed by the whole concept.[76]

"He did not want to take the job and it took a lot of persuading," said Cynthia Collyer. "Dad felt it would be limiting." Collyer also had a more practical reason for not taking the job, according to his daughter: he didn't need it. "He was also the announcer on several soaps during the day," she said. In the end, however, he gave in to the producers' pleas.[77]

Collyer's extensive radio experience, plus his singing ability, gave him a tremendous advantage. To help the listening audience differentiate between mild-mannered Clark Kent and powerful Superman, he played the reporter with a tenor voice, and the superhero with a baritone. He was expert at dropping his voice an octave in mid-sentence as he proclaimed, "This looks like a job—FOR SUPERMAN!"

To preserve the illusion that Superman himself, and not an actor, was the star of the radio program, Collyer's casting was not given a great amount of publicity. Some have written that it wasn't until 1946 that he was acknowledged as the actor who voiced the Man of Steel, but on September 13, 1942, *The New York Times* ran a photo of the actor with a caption that identified him as the title role player of Superman.[78] But unlike Brace Beemer, radio's Lone Ranger, who often made public appearances attired as the Western hero, Bud Collyer was one of the few radio performers who was never

Clayton "Bud" Collyer, radio's original Superman. The radio show's producers considered casting two actors, one to play Superman and one to play Clark Kent, until they met Bud Collyer, who was able to suggest the change from one character to the other by simply lowering his voice (Photofest).

photographed attired as the character he played on the air. "He never made personal appearances as Superman," remembered Cynthia Collyer. "I think he liked the mystery surrounding radio and using your imagination."[79]

The instantaneous popularity of the *Superman* radio show had an impact on the character as depicted in the comic books and newspaper strips. In the show's second episode, Superman arrives on earth as a full-grown man, a departure from the comic books where he arrived as an infant and was raised in an orphanage. The episode also introduced Julian Noa as Clark Kent's boss, whose name had evolved from Paris White to Perry White. White's newspaper changed from *The Daily Flash* to *The Daily Planet*. Soon after the radio show appeared, the comic books also changed their *Daily Star* editor George Taylor to *Daily Planet* editor Perry White, giving the character the same blustery persona that Noa brought to the role on radio.

The seventh episode of the series properly introduced spunky reporter Lois Lane. Casting an actress to play the part proved an even greater challenge than finding a Superman. Rollie Bester, wife of Alfred Bester (a science fiction author who wrote *Superman*, *Batman* and *Green Lantern* comics beginning in 1942) was the first actress to play the character, essaying the role a total of three times before the character was sidelined for a couple of weeks. When Lois reappeared on the show, she was played for a short while by Helen Choate before Joan Alexander took over the role. The producers decided Alexander wasn't quite right, either, and fired her after she'd been playing the role for about three months. She was permitted to re-audition for the role only at the insistence of Bud Collyer, and won the part back.[80]

Bud Collyer recalled that Joan Alexander was one of those rare actresses who could go on the radio and read a script cold, without even a rehearsal or a read-through, and her instincts were so good that she could nail the performance. He found her a joy to work with.[81] "Dad got along with everyone," said Cynthia Collyer. "I never heard him say a negative comment about anyone he worked with."[82]

Beginning with the show's twenty-eighth episode, broadcast April 15, 1940, another character was introduced who would come to loom large in all subsequent iterations of Superman—Jimmy Olsen. When he debuted on the radio show, Jimmy was a copyboy who recruited Clark Kent to investigate a protection racket that was preying on his mother's candy store. Jimmy later became a regular character, and was promoted to cub reporter. He began appearing in *Superman* comic books in 1942, and starred in his own comic book series beginning in 1954. During most of the radio show's run, Jimmy was played by Jackie Kelk, who later went on to play "Homer Brown" in the *Henry Aldrich* radio and TV series.

The Superman radio show introduced many other elements that have become firmly associated with the Man of Steel's mythos. It was on radio, in 1943, that kryptonite—a meteorite fragment of Superman's home planet which could weaken and kill him—was introduced (Siegel and Shuster created a comic book in 1939 in which a fragment of Superman's home planet, called "K metal," was discovered and used by villains to overpower him; National Comics refused to publish the story, which Superman's creators considered one of their best works, because it involved Superman revealing his secret identity to Lois Lane). Besides Perry White and Jimmy Olsen, Clark Kent's police liaison Inspector Henderson made his debut on the radio program. And Superman's catchphrases, "Great Scott!," "Up, up and away" and "This looks like a job for Superman!," were radio innovations ("Up, up and away," of course, helped signal to the listening audience that Superman was taking flight).

In the first two years of radio's *The Adventures of Superman*, George Lowther was the narrator as well as its primary writer. In 1942, Lowther authored the first novel about the

Man of Steel, also called *The Adventures of Superman*. Lowther's novel expanded on Superman's origin. Instead of being raised in an orphanage as in the comic books, or arriving on earth as an adult as in the radio series, the novel had him arriving as an infant, where he was found by the farm couple Eben and Sarah Kent and raised as their own son. The novel also marked the first time that Superman's Kryptonian father's name was spelled "Jor-El," instead of "Jor-L," a change that stuck.

Even in syndication, *The Adventures of Superman* radio show became an immediate hit. Within two months of its first airing, it scored a Crossley rating of 5.6, the highest of any thrice-weekly program. Eventually, this captured the attention of the networks, and on August 31, 1942, after a brief hiatus, the program debuted on the Mutual Network, which aired five 15-minute episodes weekly, starting with a new two-part retelling of Superman's origin. Beginning January 4, 1943, Kellogg's became the show's sponsor, using it to promote their new cereal, Pep. Many fans consider this to be the show's golden era, with Superman battling evil around the world, encountering Nazi agents, and having adventures on far-flung planets. "It was a great way to get all your inhibitions out real fast," said Collyer.[83]

In 1943, George Lowther took over the show's directing chores. He was replaced as announcer by Jackson Beck, who had previously played minor roles on the program. The grandson of Joseph Beck, who immigrated to America from Saxony and founded the Joseph Beck & Sons Distillery, Beck entered radio in 1930 and began a long career as an actor and announcer. He was the voice of detective Philo Vance and Western hero The Cisco Kid on radio, and later appeared on the television program *The Edge of Night* as "Willie Saffire" (1968–69 season). He continued doing voice-overs for TV commercials into the 1980s; his last was a 1988 ad for Clairol.

The actors worked hard to keep the fantasy of the program believable. For every show broadcast, they spent an hour doing a quick read-through sitting around a table and then a dress rehearsal before going on the air. During the rehearsals, the cast would horse around and camp it up to get all of the laughs out of their system so the far-out material wouldn't cause them to break-up during a broadcast. Collyer believed that playing the fantasy material with sincerity and honesty added to its charm.[84] "Dad did take the role seriously," said Cynthia Collyer. "It was a gentler time in some ways, but I do think he mirrored Superman's values." She said her father was like Superman "in his fairness, strength and availability. He was strict but fair and respectful of us and other people.

"He did believe in giving back to the community. His church work always included singing in the choir, being superintendent of the Sunday school and teaching the senior class. Talk about feeling intimidated on Sunday morning, having your dad be your teacher. But in fairness to him, he never called on me if I didn't volunteer, never put me on the spot. Whenever I had a test in school and I needed some help, I would leave a note for Dad to ask him the night before and he would wake me up a bit earlier and test me. He was a master in Latin and loved the challenge, along with math. At home he spent lots of time with my sister and me and my brother. Dad took us to school every morning and we sat down to dinner every night at 6:30 sharp all together. He was never too busy, we were always a priority.

"As I grew up I always felt that Dad welcomed every day with joy, because that was what he radiated. Radio and TV were not as public and complicated as they are today with everyone knowing everything about personalities. Of course I was a bit intimidating to my friends because 'my Dad was Superman!' But yes, Dad was totally easy going at home. He didn't like parties *per se*. He loved being at home."[85]

On Richard Lamparski's *Whatever Became Of ...* broadcast, Collyer recalled that when his daughter Pat was three years old, he was taking a walk with her in Manhattan and a little boy about four years of age came up and looked up at him with great admiration. Suddenly, the boy said to Pat, "Gee! Your daddy's Superman, isn't he?" Pat responded, "Bud? No, he's just an actor." "Doesn't that tell you how your own kids cut you off right at the knees?" asked Collyer.[86]

With the show's growing popularity, Bud Collyer came to learn that there was a downside to playing the Man of Steel. In a 1945 *New York Times* article, he told reporter Leonard Buder that once, as he was leaving the WOR-Mutual offices in New York, a kid challenged him, "I bet you can't lift this building." Another time, a little girl rang his doorbell and said, "I came here to decide who I should marry—Superman or The Lone Ranger." Collyer worried that someday a little tot with an overactive imagination would empty a shotgun at him, just to see if the bullets bounced off.[87]

On April 14, 1946, the Superman radio show began to explore a heady topic for what was ostensibly a children's program. For twenty-five episodes, Superman helped an interfaith group take on "The Guardians of America," the misleading name of a gang of hoodlums. In one show, a young Irish boy named Danny O'Neill reported that he had seen some hoodlums set fire to David Hoffman's drug store. Afterwards, the thugs beat up O'Neill. Cub reporter Jimmy Olsen related the events to Clark Kent:

> JIMMY: He knew they'd do something to him for squealing.
> KENT: Don't use that word, Jim. Danny didn't squeal. He reported an act of violence
> against the public. Not only against Dave Hoffman and his drug store but against all of us.
> The fire was only the beginning. There's a lot more to come—unless we nip it in the bud.
> This sort of thing—hating people and trying to destroy them because they don't go to the
> same church you do—is like poison ivy. If you don't kill the roots, it spreads. [88]

The New York Times commended the program, saying that with a simplicity of language the theme was introduced without having Superman preaching from a soapbox, but rather incorporating his views in a way that was "perfectly logical and appropriate to the script. The producers of *Superman* keep their minds on the issue, which is to entertain.... The significance of the new radio *Superman* is not only that he is a reflection of [modern] times but that now he is to be a constructive participant in them." [89]

Newsweek also lauded the program's change of course, saying, "*Superman* is the first children's program to develop a social consciousness." The sponsors were relieved when these programs garnered some of the highest ratings in the show's history, and endorsements from the United Parents Association, the Associated Negro Press, the Boys Clubs of America, and the National Conference on Christians and Jews, among others. The pleas for tolerance were not universally lauded, however; conservative commentator and evangelist Gerald L.K. Smith branded the *Superman* radio show "a disgrace to America."

Later that same year, Superman took on the KKK in a sixteen-part adventure called "Clan of the Fiery Cross." Though the organization wasn't called the KKK, and its leader was a Grand Scorpion instead of a Grand Dragon, listeners knew whom the show was targeting. What most of them didn't know was that the secret passwords used in the show were actual KKK passwords. A Southern writer and journalist, Stetson Kennedy, had infiltrated a Ku Klux Klan klavern and, just for fun, passed the passwords on to the producers of the *Superman* radio show via the Anti-Defamation League. Samuel "Doc" Green, Grand Dragon of Klavern Number One of Atlanta, Georgia, was not amused; every time he heard one of the passwords used on the show, he had to issue a new one. He was reportedly so angered and exasperated by it all that he tried to stop local merchants from selling Kellogg's Pep, to little effect.

As an indication of the show's popularity—and ubiquity—on November 10, 1946, the radio program *Command Performance* broadcast a spoof of Superman with a cast that included Bela Lugosi as the villain Dr. Bikini, Sterling Holloway as his assistant Atoll, Paulette Goddard (an actress who had been Charlie Chaplin's paramour before becoming Mrs. Burgess Meredith) as Lois Lane, the King Sisters as the King Sisters and Bob Hope as Clark Kent/Superman. Dr. Bikini and Atoll were a reference to the Bikini Atoll of the Marshall Islands, where the U.S. tested atom bombs beginning on March 7, 1946. Dr. Bikini makes giant bars of soap out of the King Sisters, and invites Lois Lane to his lair so he can use his soap machine to make soap out of Superman, the only man in the world who contains lanolin. After Superman defeats Dr. Bikini, he has the following exchange with Lois:

> SUPERMAN: "Ah, the forces of justice have once more triumphed over those of evil."
> LOIS LANE: "Oh, Superman, kiss me."
> SUPERMAN: "But I'm Superman, I don't waste time with girls. This is the hardest part I ever played...."

Beginning February 7, 1949, *The Adventures of Superman* began broadcasting three days a week instead of five, but the length of each episode doubled from fifteen minutes to thirty. There was also a cast change, as Jackie Kelk turned over the role of Jimmy Olsen to Jack Grimes (Grimes would later play "Homer Brown" in the 1952–53 season of *The Aldrich Family* TV show, and T.J. Thistle on *Tom Corbett, Space Cadet*). Narrator Jackson Beck also left the program, to be replaced by Sidney Paul and Ross Martin. Martin became famous costarring with Robert Conrad in the 1960s fantasy Western series *The Wild, Wild West*. The last of these shows aired June 24, 1949, and then after a four-month break, *The Adventures of Superman* returned to the airwaves on October 29 on the ABC Network, airing once a week on Saturday evenings.

Clayton "Bud" Collyer made his final radio appearance as Superman on December 10, 1949. The following week, Michael Fitzmaurice took over the role. A radio veteran, Fitzmaurice had been the announcer of Mutual's *Nick Carter, Master Detective* and *Land of the Lost*. Born April 28, 1908 in Chicago, Fitzmaurice appeared in a handful of films in the 1930s before moving to radio. During the time that he was portraying Superman, he also portrayed another DC comics character on radio—*Blackhawk*. In 1951, he had a brief role as a TV announcer in the 20th Century Fox film *Fourteen Hours*, based on the true story of a man who went out on the ledge of New York's Astor Hotel in 1938 and kept the city in thrall.

After the January 21, 1950 broadcast, *The Adventures of Superman* was off the air again for nearly five months, returning June 5, 1950 as a twice-weekly thirty-minute program on Mondays and Wednesdays on ABC. In September, it switched to Tuesdays and Thursdays. The final show was broadcast March 1, 1951.

When it was all over, Bud Collyer's nine years as Superman carried him through over two thousand radio adventures, the longest run of any actor in a radio adventure serial. He had appeared in 325 syndicated Superman broadcasts, 1,610 15-minute shows, and 73 half-hour episodes. Michael Fitzmaurice starred in a total of 78 half-hour programs.

Always busy, Bud Collyer entered the fertile field of a new medium, television, where he quickly became popular as a game show host with programs such as *Beat the Clock, Quick as a Flash* and *To Tell the Truth*. Besides his duties in front of the microphone and camera, Collyer was also active behind the scenes, making sure he and his colleagues were treated fairly through his work with the American Federation of Radio Artists. "Dad and George Heller started the AFRA (it became AFTRA when television began) pension and welfare program, guaranteeing payment in an industry where jobs changed frequently," remembers

Cynthia Collyer. "Dad was president a few times including the blacklisting time."[90] Another founding member of AFTRA was *Superman* announcer Jackson Beck, who carried a union card bearing the number 2. He served as vice-president and president of the New York local branch of AFTRA, and became the first vice-president of the national union.

As more and more people began turning to television for entertainment instead of their radios, the old radio programs either migrated to the new medium or faded into obscurity. However, the generations that came of age during the golden era of radio continued to hold it in special regard. On April 22, 1969, nearly twenty years after *Superman* left the airwaves, Johnny Carson had Bud Collyer as a guest on his late-night television show. They produced a complete 15-minute Superman radio episode that had originally aired on January 5, 1944, about Lois and Jimmy trapped by Nazi spies in an abandoned warehouse, with Superman flying over Metropolis looking for clues. Carson played Jimmy Olsen, Jackson Beck narrated, and Billy Redfield, Frank Buxton and Marian Mercer (as Lois Lane) joined in the fun. Playing Superman again at the age of 61 (and just five months before his untimely death), Collyer's normally gravelly speaking voice became sharp and clear as a whistle when he read his lines as Clark Kent and Superman, as though he had vocally found a way to beat the clock and turn back time. However, unlike radio's *The Adventures of Superman*, TV's *The Tonight Show* had a more adult sponsor. When it came time for the radio show's commercial break, Ed McMahon got a laugh when he announced, "We'll be back to Superman, boys and girls, in just a moment, right after this word from.... Budweiser, the king of beers." When they came to the end of the fifteen-minute recreation, and Jackson Beck announced, "Tune in tomorrow for another thrilling episode of *The Adventures of Superman*," Johnny Carson remarked that he could hear a collective sigh go up from the audience, who didn't want the adventure to end.[91]

3

Superman Paramount

The frantic energy of Max Fleischer's *Popeye* cartoons helped inspire Jerry Siegel and Joe Shuster to create Superman. And in August of 1940, just over two years after Superman's comic book debut, Harry Donenfeld, president of Superman, Inc., made arrangements with Fleischer to begin production on a series of Technicolor *Superman* shorts. The initial release was expected by Christmas, 1940. Due to the complexities of bringing a flying man to life, the actual release was nine months later, on September 26, 1941.

Max Fleischer was born July 19, 1883 in Karkau, Galicia, Austria-Hungary (now Krakow, Poland). When he was four years old, his parents came to America, settling in Brooklyn. As a young boy, he loved to draw cartoons, and in 1909, when he was a teenager, he went to the offices of *The Brooklyn Daily Eagle* and offered to pay them two dollars a week to let him sit in their Art Department and watch the professional cartoonists. Instead, they paid him two dollars a week to go around the city on a horse-drawn wagon and help deliver newspapers. Meanwhile, he studied art at the Art Students League and mechanics at the Mechanics and Tradesmen High School in New York. His persistence and education paid off. Within four years, he was a staff artist on the paper, making him the country's youngest comic strip artist. Another cartoonist working in the department was J.R. Bray who—like Fleischer—was interested in the new art of moviemaking, especially animated cartoons. When Bray decided to venture into the movies, he asked Fleischer to join him, but Fleischer opted to stay at the newspaper. They lost track of each other for about a dozen years, during which time Max began brainstorming with his two brothers, Dave, a photoengraver, and Joe, a mechanic, about speedy ways to produce animated movies. One night, the boys spilled a bottle of ink on the rug. Fearing the wrath of Max's wife, they shifted the rug around so the ink spot was hidden under the piano. Mrs. Fleischer eventually discovered it, but the incident gave the boys a name for their fledgling operation—Out of the Inkwell. After two years, they had completed their first cartoon.

Fleischer got in touch with Bray, who looked at the cartoon and liked it, but thought there might be ways to improve it. With Bray behind them, the Fleischer brothers began working in earnest to develop a way to speed up the process of making animated cartoons. On December 8, 1915, Max Fleischer filed his patent for a "Method of Producing Moving Picture Cartoons." His invention, the rotoscope, was awarded patent number 1,242,674 on October 9, 1917. With this machine, a live-action actor would be photographed, and then that film would be projected and the actor's movements carefully traced to give lifelike, fluid motion to an animated character. By use of the rotoscope, 300 feet of film could be produced in three weeks by the combined work of four or five men.

Using his invention, Fleischer was able to ingeniously combine an animated character with a real person. Thus was born the Out of the Inkwell series, where a live-action Fleischer would be seen at an animation stand, and cartoon characters would climb out of the inkwell and interact with him. The first character they created was Koko the Clown, who became an instant sensation and made Max Fleischer a household name.

In 1921, Fleischer, as an independent producer, entered into an association with Adolph Zukor's Paramount Pictures. As early as 1924, Fleischer was making sound cartoons, called "Song Car-Tunes," that used the "bouncing ball" gimmick. On August 9, 1930, Fleischer released *Dizzy Dishes*, and introduced the world to a floppy-eared dog that sang with a baby voice and said "boop-oop-a-doop." By 1931's *Mask-a-Raid*, the dog had become a human character, Betty Boop, who starred in shorts that highlighted the music of jazz greats like Louis Armstrong and Cab Calloway.[92]

In 1933, Fleischer introduced Elzie Segar's comic-strip character in *Betty Boop Meets Popeye the Sailor*. Later that year, *I Yam What I Yam* kicked off a long series of animated Popeye shorts.[93] Fleischer wanted to be the first to make an animated color cartoon, but Adolph Zukor vetoed the idea and Walt Disney eclipsed him. Fleischer next lobbied to make a feature-length animated cartoon, but Zukor refused. When Disney's *Snow White and the Seven Dwarfs* (1937) became a sensation, it was a bitter pill for Fleischer to swallow (Fleischer had done *Snow White* in 1933 as a Betty Boop short).[94]

But after the phenomenal success of *Snow White and the Seven Dwarfs*, even Adolph Zukor could see the value in producing a feature length cartoon, so he finally gave the green light to the film Fleischer wanted to make, *Gulliver's Travels*. It would be an ambitious undertaking, one that would require a bigger studio than Fleischer's New York offices. When the city fathers of Miami, Florida, offered Fleischer tax incentives to build a studio in their city—where he had a summer home—he leapt at the opportunity. His decision was also influenced, no doubt, by the tough efforts of the Commercial Artists and Designers Union to unionize his animators. Fleischer moved his business from New York to Florida, relocating some two hundred employees and their families.

Fleischer borrowed the money to carry out the entire project from Paramount Pictures, a decision that would eventually prove fatal. Construction of the new studio began in Miami in March 1938. Less than a year later, the new animation studios opened, a single-story concrete structure that covered four city blocks. The building contained everything needed for the production of animated cartoons, including Fleischer's patented rotoscope machines and cutting edge sound recording equipment. It was the first fully air-conditioned building in the state of Florida.

When *Gulliver's Travels* opened on December 22, 1939, it broke house records despite mixed reviews, some of which compared it unfavorably with Disney's *Snow White*. Eight months later, Fleischer began production on the Superman cartoon series. The first one cost $50,000, more than three times what Paramount spent on the production of an average Popeye cartoon. Subsequent entries in the series were budgeted at $30,000 each; the final cost for all seventeen Superman shorts was $530,000. Adjusted for inflation, it was one of the most expensive cartoon series ever produced.

When the first entry, simply titled *Superman* but subsequently known under the alternate title *The Mad Scientist*, was shown in September, 1941, audiences were treated to spectacular full-color animation with the characters shown "in relief" (with shadows), making them seem almost lifelike. The voices were provided by the cast of the radio show, with Clayton "Bud" Collyer, Joan Alexander and Julian Noa as Clark Kent/Superman, Lois Lane and Perry White, respectively (although the newspaper editor wasn't clearly identified as Perry

White until the next-to-last entry). Another of Fleischer's inventions, a stereo optical process that had patent number 2054414, helped give the illusion of characters moving within a three-dimensional environment, as opposed to moving across flat backgrounds. Fleischer had made extensive use of the process with his *Gulliver's Travels* feature.

After a brief summation of Superman's origin, which seems to have been based on Siegel and Shuster's earliest comic book, with Superman arriving on earth as an infant and being taken to an orphanage by a passing motorist, the narrator intones:

> "Faster than a speeding bullet.
> More powerful than a locomotive.
> Able to leap tall buildings in a single bound.
> The infant of Krypton is now the man of steel—SUPERMAN.
> To best be in a position to use his amazing powers in a never-ending battle for truth and justice, Superman has assumed the disguise of Clark Kent, mild-mannered reporter for a great Metropolitan newspaper."

This opening narration was the first time the phrase "Faster than a speeding bullet" was used; it would become an indelible trademark. The Fleischer cartoons were also where Superman was first seen flying, rather than just taking long and mighty leaps.

The initial entry went on to show a dark, shadowy ultra-modern Metropolis being threatened by an unnamed mad scientist. When Lois goes to the scientist's mountaintop lair to investigate, she's taken hostage. The scientist uses his "electrothanasia ray" against the *Daily Planet* newspaper building. Clark Kent runs for the storeroom, saying "This looks like a job for Superman!" After a quick change, Superman emerges, flies out the window, forces the ray back to its source, rescues Lois and captures the mad scientist. As Superman flies over Metropolis with the villain under one arm and Lois under the other, viewers are treated to a Superman's-eye-view of the cityscape passing below. All this action is accompanied by thrilling music courtesy of Sammy Timberg. Timberg had been providing music for Fleischer's Popeye and Betty Boop cartoons since the early 1930s; his "Superman March" would later be used as the theme for the radio broadcasts, where—played on an organ—it lost much of its majesty. *Superman* proved to be a great success, even earning an Academy Award nomination (it lost to *Lend a Paw*—a Disney cartoon).

The first *Superman* cartoon was written by Seymour Kneitel and I. Sparber, animated by Steve Muffati and Frank Endres and directed by Dave Fleischer. Seymour Kneitel began as an animator, working on a slew of Popeye and Betty Boop cartoons before graduating to writer. He would step up to directing with the tenth Superman short, *Japoteurs*. Isidore "Izzy" Sparber was a writer on *Gulliver's Travels* and later on Fleischer's second feature-length animated cartoon, *Mr. Bug Goes to Town* (1941). In the 1940s, he gave up writing to become a producer and director of the Popeye cartoons. Animators Steve Muffati and Frank Endres were also Fleischer veterans who had contributed to *Gulliver's Travels*. Both eventually worked on the 1960s *Felix the Cat* television cartoons. Endres would do more superhero duty as an animator on the *Spider-Man* cartoon series in 1967. Dave Fleischer, Max's younger brother and director of almost all of the Fleischer Studios output, retired from the business in 1948, but returned in 1963 to help animate the avian attackers of Alfred Hitchcock's *The Birds*.

As Philip Skerry and Chris Lambert noted in their essay "From Panel to Panavision," included in the 1987 book *Superman at Fifty! The Persistence of a Legend!*, the second Superman cartoon, *The Mechanical Monsters*, which was released November 28, 1941, was featured within a Superman comic book. In *Superman* #19, Clark Kent accompanies Lois Lane to the movies, where a Fleischer Superman cartoon is showing. As it unspools, Clark realizes he has to keep Lois distracted so she won't see the cartoon Kent changing into Superman, thus revealing to her his secret identity. By feigning a choking incident, and then "accidentally" kicking her purse, he gets her to avert her eyes from the screen at the crucial moments. Returning her attention to the cartoon, Lois stands and cheers when Superman saves her animated counterpart from being crushed under the foot of a giant robot.[95]

The ninth Superman cartoon, *Terror on the Midway*, which opened August 28, 1942, signaled a dramatic change behind the scenes. It was the first of the shorts whose opening title card did not read "A Max Fleischer cartoon," and for good reason—Fleischer had fallen from grace with Paramount. On December 9, 1941—two days after Pearl Harbor—Fleischer's second animated feature, *Mr. Bug Goes to Town*, was released. With the country now at war, the light-hearted children's film was a financial failure. Fleischer still had five years' worth of payments to make on his ten-year loan with Paramount, and the studio became nervous. They called in his loan. In an instant, Max Fleischer lost the animation factory he'd worked so hard to create. Around this time, Dave Fleischer defected to Columbia Pictures after a falling out with his older brother. Picking up the pieces, Isidore Sparber and Seymour Knietel, along with Dan Gordon and Sam Buchwald, formed Famous Studios, legally a separate entity from Paramount Pictures, and continued producing Superman shorts. The Florida operation was closed down, and the animators and their families returned to New York. *Showdown*, the eleventh Superman cartoon, released on October 16, 1942, was the first one released under the banner of "A Famous Studios Production." Max Fleischer's career was effectively over.

Superman as seen in the opening credits of Max Fleischer's *Superman* (1941). The rich colors, Art Deco style and film noir-style shadows of these cartoons would influence the *Batman* and *Superman* animated series of the 1990s (Paramount Pictures/Photofest, © Paramount Pictures).

Without Fleischer, the series shifted tone. Instead of battling mechanical monsters, dinosaurs, giant apes and natural disasters, almost every other episode of the remaining Superman shorts found the Man of Tomorrow after Axis spies. In *Japoteurs* (released September 18, 1942), he stops Japanese agents from sabotaging the maiden flight of the world's largest bombing plane (which is loaded with smaller planes!). In the twelfth entry, *Eleventh Hour* (released November 20, 1942), Clark and Lois are inexplicably in Yokohama, Japan. Each night, as the clock strikes eleven, Clark changes into Superman and sinks a Japanese battleship. *Destruction, Inc.* (released December 25, 1942), had the Man of Steel foiling American traitors at a munitions plant. Interestingly, in this episode, when a driverless truck of explosives is sent barreling down a hill toward the plant, Superman flies up to the truck and gets inside and drives it off a cliff, instead of just picking it up and throwing it off. *Jungle Drums*, released March 26, 1943, had Superman rescuing Lois from Nazis in Africa. The last shot is of Adolf Hitler, hearing a radio broadcast that American dive-bombers destroyed an entire fleet of Axis submarines. Hitler angrily flips off the radio. Over the closing Paramount logo, we hear the song, "Praise the Lord and pass the ammunition, and we'll all be free."

The final Superman short, *Secret Agent* (released July 30, 1943), was the only one of the shorts that did not include Lois Lane. In her place is a beautiful blonde with information about a German spy ring that she must deliver to Washington, D.C. For a cartoon, it's amazingly violent, like a film noir gangster film, with several gun battles. In the end, viewers are treated to a nice animated aerial view of Washington, and a shot of Superman flying past the American flag. With that, Superman would disappear from movie screens for five years.

Like Siegel and Shuster before him, Fleischer's fortunes mushroomed and then quickly collapsed once he took on Superman. After the Superman shorts, he produced and directed cartoons for the Jim Handy Corporation, including *Rudolph the Red-Nosed Reindeer* (1948). Six years later, he left Handy and returned to the Bray Studios, where he had worked nearly four decades earlier. In 1958, he joined with Hal Seeger to produce one hundred *Koko the Clown* cartoons that aired on local TV stations throughout the 1960s. After that, he retired and faded into obscurity and poverty, eventually ending up at the Motion Picture County Home. Fleischer died of congestive heart failure at age 89 on September 11, 1972, just days after signing a deal with King Features for new series of Betty Boop cartoons which, had he lived, would have earned him millions.[96]

4

A Job for Kirk Alyn

Lois Lane and Jimmy Olsen are on a train, speeding away to report on a hot-breaking story. Unbeknown to them, the train track ahead is damaged, sure to cause a derailment. It looks like sudden death for everyone aboard—and it's the end of chapter one of the 1948 serial *Superman*. But the following week, the Man of Steel flies to the rescue just in the nick of time, bending the train rail back into shape and holding it in place until the train passes. Superman has saved the day.

And so it went for 15 exciting chapters of the Columbia Pictures serial, *Superman*. It was an immediate hit with its audience of young children, so much so that another 15-chapter sequel, *Atom Man vs. Superman*, was produced two years later. After two appearances as the Man of Steel, Kirk Alyn made ten more movies, including small, uncredited parts in *When Worlds Collide* (1951), *The Eddie Duchin Story* (1956) and *Beginning of the End* (1957)—a film whose title proved prophetic for Alyn. By the close of the 1950s, Kirk Alyn, the first cinema Superman, was out of work, his career effectively over. "I couldn't get a job in Hollywood," said Alyn. "I was permanently typecast as Superman."

Kirk Alyn was born John Feggo, Jr. on October 8, 1910 at 47 West Central Avenue in Wharton, New Jersey (many sources cite his birthplace as Oxford, 22 miles away). His father was a carpenter, and wanted his son to follow in his footsteps. John Jr. had other ideas; he had fallen in love with the movies, especially the Westerns and mystery thrillers of Eddie Polo, known in the silent era as the "Hercules of the Screen."[97]

At first glance, John Feggo, Jr. didn't seem like the showbiz type. Growing up, he was painfully shy. But he gained a little self-confidence when he asked a school friend who performed in vaudeville shows to teach him some basic steps—tap dance, buck and wing, waltz clog and soft shoe. Once out of school, Alyn tried out as a dancer for a Broadway show, *Heads Up*. This led to a job in the chorus of another production, *Girl Crazy*, with Ethel Merman. The show ran for a year, and led to more stage work. Eventually, he had a long two-year run as part of the company of the George and Ira Gershwin musical *Of Thee I Sing*.[98] By the early 1930s, he had undergone a name change. Billing himself as Kirk Alyn, he appeared as half of the dance act Nadine and Kirk with the Tommy Dorsey orchestra,[99] then paired with Imogene Coca in comedy and song-and-dance routines touring with George Olsen's orchestra.[100] Later in the decade, he joined the cast of Olsen and Johnson's *Hellzapoppin'* revue for another one-year run.[101]

After a decade of appearing in Broadway shows and vaudeville revues, Kirk Alyn came to Hollywood for a short vacation in 1941 and stayed at the home of an old friend, Red

Skelton, who was beginning to make his mark in movies as a comedy performer. Skelton introduced Alyn to one of his co-stars, Virginia O'Brien. O'Brien was a singer who appeared in a number of MGM musicals, among them *Thousands Cheer* (1943), *The Harvey Girls* (1946), and *Till the Clouds Roll By* (1946), and who was known for delivering songs while standing stock-still. Observers attributed this to her performance genius. In actuality, it was due to her crippling stage fright, an affliction with which Alyn sympathized.

By December of 1941, O'Brien had announced to newspaper reporters that she and Alyn were planning to wed. They were married in Yuma, Arizona, on Sunday, October 11, 1942.[102] By that time, Alyn had taken a job in an aircraft plant. He became a father for the first time when O'Brien gave birth to their daughter, Elizabeth.

Alyn eventually found work in films, landing the part of a Portuguese sailor in the film version of the popular radio series *My Sister Eileen* (1942).[103] The following year, Republic Pictures put him under contract; in 1943 and '44, he made nine films for the studio, earning $50 a day. Tall and lean with clean-cut good looks, Alyn played characters on both sides of the law in Republic features. But World War II was now raging, and Alyn's career was interrupted when he was drafted into the Coast Guard. He spent eighteen months as an instructor on Catalina Island, beginning his service after receiving a deferment that allowed him to complete his work in a Hopalong Cassidy Western, *Forty Thieves* (1944).[104]

After entering the Coast Guard, Alyn went one evening to a show for soldiers at Ft. Ord. His wife was one of the performers on the bill. Alyn sat in the audience with the other soldiers, and when O'Brien took the stage, the serviceman next to him said, "Gee, that's the type of girl I'd like to marry, but I hear she's hitched. What a shame. Girls like that always marry the wrong guy. Why couldn't she marry a guy like you or me?"[105]

While he was in the Coast Guard, Alyn's daughter Theresa was born in June 1945.[106] O'Brien had learned she was pregnant while filming *The Harvey Girls* with Judy Garland and Angela Lansbury. Her costars threw her a baby shower.

When the war ended and Alyn's Coast Guard duty was completed, he resumed his film career with a role in Monogram's *The Trap* (1946), a Charlie Chan mystery that turned out to be Sidney Toler's final performance in the role. Alyn then returned to Republic, where he appeared in his first serial, *Daughter of Don Q* (1946). Alyn played intrepid reporter Cliff Roberts, who aids a modern-day descendant of Zorro in her quest to defeat the villainous Carlos Manning. Alyn's success in the serial led to other featured roles in the serials *Federal Agents Versus Underworld, Inc.* (1949) and *Radar Patrol Vs. Sky King* (1950) at Republic, and *Superman, Atom Man Vs. Superman* and *Blackhawk* (1952) at Columbia. After the phenomenal success of his second serial, *Superman*, Alyn was tagged "King of the Serials." "I didn't care what they were," he told a reporter in 1987. "They paid me my salary and I did them and forgot them." But the salary paid by the serials was hardly exorbitant; for *Daughter of Don Q*, Alyn received star billing and $1,800 for about six weeks work.

Quickly produced and shot on shoestring budgets, the serials were frowned upon by actors with loftier aspirations. Intended for juvenile audiences, they were the motion picture equivalent of serialized novels in nineteenth century magazines. They usually began with a half-hour episode that ended with a "cliffhanger," a scene of the hero or heroine in mortal peril. The following week, the next chapter would show how the protagonist escaped from danger, advance the plot a little, and put the hero or heroine in jeopardy again. This went on for twelve and sometimes fifteen chapters, with all of the chapters after the first one running about twenty minutes. The serials would be shown as part of a whole entertainment package that included a newsreel, a cartoon, a serial chapter, and then a feature film. In the days before television, these Saturday afternoon presentations provided fun, thrills and suspense for young moviegoers.

Another medium that catered to young audiences was the comic book. After Superman debuted in *Action Comics* in 1938, it proved an immediate sensation, spinning off into a radio series and starting a merchandizing bonanza. It also spawned a host of imitators; National introduced another crime-fighter, Batman, in *Detective Comics* in 1939. Timely Comics (forerunner of Marvel) had *Captain America*, introduced in 1941. And in 1940, Fawcett Publications unveiled *Captain Marvel*, a character who had enormous strength, flew and wore a cape. National cried fowl over Captain Marvel; they felt his similarities to their Superman character were a copyright infringement. In 1941, they filed suit against Fawcett; the case settled out of court twelve years later, when Fawcett ceased publication of *Captain Marvel* comics and paid National $400,000 in damages (National later bought the rights to Captain Marvel in the 1970s and resumed publication of the hero's exploits).

With their built-in audiences of juvenile readers, heroes from newspaper comic strips and comic books were naturals for adaptation to the serials. Universal brought *Flash Gordon* to the screen, perfectly personified by Olympic swimming champion Larry "Buster" Crabbe, in three serials beginning in 1936; Columbia Pictures had *Mandrake the Magician* (1939) starring Warren Hull. And Republic set their sights on Superman.

After much negotiating with National Comics, Republic Pictures announced on April 26, 1940 that they had purchased the rights to Superman. The following month, on May 30, Republic unveiled their production schedule for 1940-'41 that featured two 15-chapter serials, *Superman* and *Dick Tracy Strikes Again*, and two 12-chapter serials, *Jungle Girl* and *King of the Royal Mounted*. However, by August the Superman deal had fallen apart. *The New York Times* reported on August 17 that it soured when National Comics demanded supervision of the serial.[107]

Making the best of the situation, Republic rewrote the Superman script for a hero of their own creation, a masked avenger with no superpowers called Copperhead (his mask looked like a sack made of fine copper chain mail), who battled *The Mysterious Dr. Satan* (1940). Though the script was changed, the love interest of the hero was still named Lois. A year later, Republic produced what many consider to be the greatest serial ever made, *The Adventures of Captain Marvel*, starring cowboy star Tom Tyler as the Fawcett Comics hero.

After the deal with Republic fell through, National Comics eventually came to an agreement with independent producer Sam Katzman, whose films were released through Columbia Pictures and poverty row studio Monogram. Katzman's films were hardly the hallmark of quality, but he claimed that he never produced a movie that lost money. Then again, his movies didn't cost very much money; Katzman's business model centered on producing movies that would have the widest possible audience appeal made on the lowest possible budgets. Over the years, his output of over two hundred movies included everything from Tim McCoy Westerns in the '30s to East Side Kids films in the '40s to teenage rock-and-roll movies in the '50s to biker flicks and Elvis Presley musicals in the '60s.

Having acquired the screen rights to the character, Katzman contacted Columbia Pictures. A deal was worked out whereby the serial would be independently produced for Columbia through Sam Katzman's cleverly named company—Esskay Pictures (named for his initials).[108] The budget was set at $10,000 per episode, or $150,000 for the entire serial.[109]

To help shepherd Superman to the screen, Katzman hired two experienced action directors, Spencer Bennett and Tommy Carr. Bennett began his career as a stunt performer, when he responded to an ad in a New York newspaper seeking a stuntman who would jump from the Palisades of the Hudson River while dressed in a suit. The stunt paid one dollar per foot of distance fallen. Later, Bennett relocated to California, where he directed his first feature in 1921, *Behold the Man*, shot in a combination of black-and-white and Pathé color. Five years later, he directed the very first Charlie Chan movie, a 1926 silent serial version of Earl Derr Biggers' *The House Without a Key*. In the 1930s, he directed numerous Westerns, but by the '40s he was known as "The King of Serial Directors."

Tommy Carr was the son of actors William and Mary Carr. Born on July 4, 1907, in Philadelphia, Carr began his career as an actor with the 1918 silent film *Virtuous Wives*. He appeared in the two great flying epics of early cinema, *Wings* (1927) and Howard Hughes's *Hell's Angels* (1930). In the 1930s and '40s, Carr acted in a number of serials, including a role as Capt. Rama of the Forest People in *Flash Gordon's Trip to Mars* (1938). The first film he directed was the 1945 Western *Santa Fe Saddlemates* with Sunset Carson, which he also associate produced. A number of other Sunset Carson films followed, but he also directed serials and later TV episodes (including *Dick Tracy*, *Range Rider* and several episodes of the George Reeves *Superman* TV series).

The screenplay for the Superman serial was credited to Arthur Hoerl, Lewis Clay and Royal K. Cole, from an adaptation by George H. Plympton and Joseph F. Poland. Born in Brooklyn in 1889, George Holcombe Plympton wrote scenarios for nearly 300 films in his long career, beginning with *Mrs. Carter's Necklace* in 1912. Prior to *Superman*, his credits included the serials *Tarzan the Fearless* (1933), *Flash Gordon* (1936), and *The Green Hornet* (1940), as well as a slew of Westerns. Joseph Franklin Poland, born in Waterbury, Connecticut in 1892, had over 130 produced writing credits, beginning with 1913's *The Taming of Texas Pete*. Significantly, he was one of the scriptwriters of *The Adventures of Captain Marvel* (1941). Lewis Clay and Royal K. Cole were veteran Republic Pictures scriptwriters; Cole had contributed to the screenplay of Republic's *Captain America* (1944). Hoerl was a newspaper writer with over a hundred film credits to his name, stretching back to the 1920s. His most infamous achievement is the cult favorite *Reefer Madness* (1936), which told of the dangers of marijuana addiction in rather hysterical fashion.

The script for *Superman*—which is really a thin plotline tying together a lot of cliffhanger situations—told the origin story of Superman (based on the George Lowther novel of 1942) in Chapter One before pitting the caped hero against the Queen of the Underworld, the Spider Lady, who plots to steal a weapon called the reducer ray from the U.S. government, and who uses kryptonite to keep Superman at bay. Kryptonite was an innovation of the Superman radio program; the Superman of the comics wouldn't be menaced with kryptonite until 1949, a year after the serial's release.

With a script in hand and directors to help bring it to life, Katzman set about casting the title role. Radio Superman Clayton "Bud" Collyer, who leapt to television in 1948 as the host of the game show *Winner Take All*, was never considered. As Cynthia Collyer recalled, "To my knowledge he was not approached for the movie role. But then I doubt he would have done it because of his identification with the TV host he had become. Also family life was too important to him. He would not have wanted to uproot us to California."[110] For his part, Bud Collyer told Richard Lamparski, "They took one look at me and my physique and said 'Nope!'"[111]

After seeing over one hundred wrestlers and muscle men, none of whom possessed the acting chops required,[112] Katzman remembered an actor who had recently appeared in two films he produced, *Little Miss Broadway* and *Sweet Genevieve* (both 1947). The actor's name was Kirk Alyn. Spencer Bennett was also familiar with the actor—he had directed him in *Daughter of Don Q* (1946).

Katzman called Alyn and asked him to drop by the office to meet the representatives from National Comics, who had casting approval. National wanted to be sure that whoever became the first film Superman met the requirements of their clean-cut, all–American hero. When Alyn arrived, Katzman and the National reps were shocked by his scruffy appearance. Alyn explained that he'd just finished a couple of Westerns, for which he'd let his hair and beard grow. Katzman asked his secretary to bring up some stills from *Sweet Genevieve*, to show the men from National that there really was a handsome face under the shaggy beard. But the comic book men still weren't satisfied; they asked Alyn to take off his shirt, so they could see his build. Alyn complied. He had been working out with barbells, and it showed— at 6 feet 2, he weighed 198 pounds, with a 31-inch waist and 44-inch shoulders. But the men from National still weren't sold. They asked him to take off his pants. Alyn objected, but the men explained that since he would be wearing tights, they needed to see his legs. Off came Alyn's pants, and his muscular dancer's legs satisfied the representatives from the comic book company. Standing in Sam Katzman's office in his underwear, Kirk Alyn was told he was Superman.[113]

Years later, Alyn wrote, "The entire audition took about 15 minutes. Sam told me to go downstairs and sign the contract. When I got downstairs, a girl told me that they had auditioned 125 guys in the last two weeks. 'You mean I'm not the first one Sam called?' I winced.

"I found out later that I got the part because I looked the most like Clark Kent. That must have helped a great deal. That and the fact that a lot of the guys they interviewed could barely speak English; a lot of Greek wrestlers, fighters and big muscle men. They must have gotten so tired of looking at those people that when I walked in they said, 'For cryin' out loud, sign him up, he's all right.'"[114]

In his excitement at landing the role, Alyn had neglected to inquire about the deal terms. He called Katzman, who told him to come in the next day and they would settle it, adding, "You know I always take care of you, kid." Alyn returned to the studio the next afternoon and haggled with Katzman, settling on a fee of $4,500 for eight weeks of work, including overtime. Then Katzman presented Alyn with the conditions for playing the role, which included such provisions as always referring to the Superman costume as "the uniform," never appearing on the lot in the uniform, and never allowing visitors on the set when Alyn was in the uniform—it was to be a closed set.[115] Furthermore, Alyn would only be credited as playing Clark Kent, not Superman, and all of his personal appearances as Superman would be screened and supervised to protect the Superman image. The idea was to give the kiddies the impression that Superman was genuinely a strange visitor from another planet, not a B-actor in a grey-and-cocoa suit (colors that would look like red and blue on black-and-white film).[116]

On January 13, 1948, *The New York Times* announced that Alyn had been hired to play Superman in a new Columbia Pictures serial, which was to begin shooting on January 26. Meanwhile, to sustain the illusion, Katzman put out a press release saying that since no human actor could be found who possessed the requisite qualities to play the strange visitor from the planet Krypton, Superman would be played by—who else?—Superman.[117]

Other comic book and radio-based serials often deviated from their source material; for instance, in *Captain America* (1944), the title character carried a pistol instead of a shield, and The Lone Ranger became more of a Zorro-like character in *The Lone Ranger Rides Again* (1939). But Kirk Alyn's Superman uniform was a near-exact replica of the one from the comic books. And although Alyn looked a little thinner than the muscle-laden comic book Superman then being drawn by artist Wayne Boring—his shoulders weren't as broad, his chest wasn't as deep, his jaw wasn't as square and jutting—he still managed to capture the

Kirk Alyn makes his first appearance as Superman in the 1948 Columbia Pictures serial *Superman*. Alyn joked that he never wore muscle pads as Superman, unlike "the other fellow" (Warner Bros./Photofest, © Warner Bros).

persona of the character, portraying a superhero with confidence and a slight sense of amusement; his Superman *knew* he was a superior being who could kick any puny human's butt, and got a kick out of seeing how the villains would try to kick his.

With Kirk Alyn in place, Sam Katzman set about filling the other roles. To play spunky, inquisitive Lois Lane, he decided to cast a perky young actress who had appeared in the "Teenagers" series of films he had produced at Monogram, Noel Neill.[118] *The Los Angeles*

Times announced her casting on January 10, 1948, and reminded its readers that when Ms. Neill was under contract to Paramount in 1944, she was "the queen of the *Times* Open golf tournament."[119]

Noel Neill was born in Minneapolis on November 25, 1920. Her mother was a former singer and dancer, her father the news editor of *The Minneapolis Star*.[120] With that combination of show business and journalism in her blood, it's as though she was predestined to become an actress noted for portraying one of the most famous reporters in popular fiction. At the tender age of seven, Neill first performed on radio on Minneapolis's WDGY, reciting "The Punishment of Mary Louise" for *The Children's Play Hour* over live radio.[121] By the time she was in her teens, Neill was a seasoned performer, dancing and singing on the Vaudeville circuit.[122] In 1938, she and her mother traveled to California, where Neill sang at the Del Mar Turf Club, which was owned by Bing Crosby.[123]

Agent Jack Pomeroy began representing Neill, and landed her small roles in Monogram's Henry Aldrich film series as well as Shirley Temple's films *Miss Annie Rooney* (1942) and *Salute For Three* (1943).[124] After seeing her in the chorus line of *Lady of Burlesque* (1943), Paramount signed the young ingénue to a seven-year contract; she played a hatcheck girl in the 1946 noir classic *The Blue Dahlia*.[125] She was very active throughout the 1940s, appearing in numerous B-Westerns opposite cowboy stars like Whip Wilson, Johnny Mack Brown and Clayton Moore. From 1945 to 1948, she appeared in nine "Teenagers" films for producer Sam Katzman, who also cast her in the serials *Brick Bradford* (1947) and *The Adventures of Frank and Jesse James* (1948) before offering her the role of Lois Lane.[126]

For Jimmy Olsen, the young photographer of *The Daily Planet* who acted first and thought later, Katzman cast Tommy Bond, already a seasoned performer at age 21. As a child, Bond was seen as "Butch" in Hal Roach's popular *Our Gang* series, bullying Carl "Alfalfa" Switzer and wooing Darla Hood. He retired from the screen after 1951, received a degree in Theatre Arts from Cal State Los Angeles, and became a prop manager on the TV series *You Asked For It* and *The Carol Burnett Show*.

The role of the editor of *The Daily Planet*, Perry White, was filled by prolific character actor Pierre Watkin. Watkin had actually been a real-life newspaper editor, for *The Sioux City Tribune* and *The Sioux Falls Argus*. One of the busiest actors in Hollywood, he appeared in over 300 movies, including such classics as *Mr. Deed Goes to Town* (1936), *Knute Rockne, All American* (1940), and *The Secret Life of Walter Mitty* (1947).[127]

The role of The Spider Lady required an actress who could project menace while being strikingly beautiful and sexy. The part went to Carol Forman (real name Carolyn Sawls), an ambitious raven-haired actress from Epps, Alabama, who had made her first film appearance in the 1946 RKO film *From This Day Forward*. Impressed with their new discovery, RKO had put her under contract, but she bolted after a year and began freelancing. In the 1947 Republic serial *The Black Widow*, Forman played Sombra, also known as the Black Widow, the evil daughter of an Asian king sent to America to steal the secret of a new atomic rocket engine. After *Superman*, Forman continued to work in serials and Westerns for Republic and Columbia, but eventually turned her attention to TV roles, commercials and the theater before retiring from the business in the mid–1960s.

At the end of January 1948, Kirk Alyn made his first appearance before the cameras in "the uniform," at a location outside of Los Angeles. The scene called for the Man of Steel to hold a disabled train rail in place as a locomotive thundered past. Being as this was a low-budget film, the producers had received permission to film alongside a real train track, as a real locomotive came barreling through. The camera was positioned on one side of the track, and Alyn took his place on the other side. The technical advisor from the railroad told the actor that they thought he would be okay, as long as he stood eighteen inches away from the track. As the train approached, the crew retreated to a safe vantage point a good distance away. The camera operators started the camera running, and they, too, moved back to a position of relative safety. Alyn was left alone, with a train approaching at 90 miles per hour, hoping he wouldn't be whipped off his feet by the suction the passing locomotive would create. As the train neared and he could feel the vibration in the rails, his worries increased, but with a "show must go on" determination, he sucked in his fears and thrust out his chest as one train car after another zoomed by, each one whipping him with cyclonic winds.[128]

Finally, the train passed, and Alyn was still standing. The crew came out from their hiding places. Director Spencer Bennett clapped him on the shoulder and said, "Great job, Kirk! That was great! And we got it all in one take!" As shooting progressed, Alyn would find himself in many more hairy situations.[129]

Noel Neill remembers her first reaction upon seeing Kirk Alyn in his Superman outfit— Nice legs, she thought. "You could tell he'd been a dancer," said Neill.[130] Virginia O'Brien, who sometimes visited her husband on the set despite the closed set policy, said, "He was really a fantastic Superman because he could move, because he had been a dancer."[131]

Alyn's strong dancer's legs were a great help in playing the role. He claimed he didn't need a trampoline to get him off the ground, and when he landed, he took care to do it gracefully, since everything was supposed to be easy for Superman. He couldn't land flat on his feet, the way a stuntman would.[132] Alyn, like most actors, liked to claim that he did all his own stunts, but in fact Paul Stader—who doubled for Johnny Weissmuller in the later Tarzan movies—substituted for Alyn in the riskier scenes. Stader also helped fill out the villain's ranks, appearing as "Irwin" in *Superman* and "Killer Lawson" in the first 4 chapters of *Atom Man Vs. Superman* (where he was billed as Paul Strader).

While Alyn had no trouble leaping into the air for his take-offs, shots of him actually flying posed an almost insurmountable challenge. The special effects crew promised the producers that they could fly Alyn on wires, which they would opaque so that they wouldn't show. To rig him for the effect, Alyn, who suffered from a mild form of claustrophobia, had to submit to having a plaster mold made of his chest. Molten steel was then poured into the mold, to fashion a steel breastplate that perfectly conformed to Alyn's build. For the flying scenes, Alyn wore the breastplate under his Superman tunic, with wires attached to hold him aloft. However, there was no provision made for holding up his legs, and after hours spent in a simulated flying posture, with arms forward and legs straight behind, Alyn's stomach muscles were screaming in agony. As if that weren't bad enough, a smoke pot was placed in front of a fan to give the illusion of clouds fluttering past the Man of Steel. But the smoke pot also produced sparks, which blew underneath Alyn's breastplate, setting his chest hairs afire. It took a pitcher of water poured down his tunic to keep Superman from going up in flames.[133]

Later, when Alyn, Katzman, Bennett, and the effects crew gathered to see the results of the flying shots, they were shocked to see the wires plainly visible. The only shots they felt they could safely use were ones of Superman flying beside an airplane, whose metallic fuselage helped hide the glint of the wires. The effects crew was fired on the spot. Luckily— or so they thought—Columbia had an animation department, so the decision was made to animate Superman's flying scenes.[134] This idea probably sounded good on paper, but the execution left much to be desired, though to be fair Howard Swift and his animators weren't given much of a budget to work with; they completed the work for $32 per foot of film. Spencer Bennett felt that if Katzman had paid them $64 per foot, they would have animated Superman "in relief," making him look more 3-dimensional.[135]

With a thick script and a thin shooting schedule, directors Spencer Bennett and Tommy Carr kept things moving at a brisk clip. Interviewed for Gary Grossman's excellent 1976 book *Superman: Serial to Cereal*, Kirk Alyn said, "Some days, we did seventy-six setups and thought nothing of it."[136] He later told Kerry Webster of *The Los Angeles Herald-Examiner*, "The hardest part of the shooting was keeping a straight face. I had to do some pretty silly things, and the bad guys who were supposed to be knocked out would be lying on the ground making faces at me."[137]

After finishing the exterior shooting, the crew moved to the soundstages to film the interior scenes. On that first day in the studio, as Alyn sat in the make-up chair, he noticed that he had a different make-up man than the one who had been with the crew on location. He began chatting with the man, who had seen some of the rushes and praised Alyn's performance. Alyn thanked him for his comments, put out his hand, and said, "My name isn't really Superman as they seem to think around here—it's Kirk Alyn. What's yours?"

"I'm Eddie Polo," said the man.

Alyn almost fell out of his chair. Here he was, face-to-face with the silent serial star whose cinema exploits had thrilled him as a child. For the rest of the production, the morning make-up sessions became a mutual admiration society. Years later, Alyn regretted that in his excitement to share memories with Polo, he neglected to ask for an autograph.[138]

Polo was right—Alyn *was* very convincing in the Superman uniform, so much so that his directors sometimes seemed to mistake him for the genuine article. For instance, in one scene that involved Superman rescuing Jimmy and Lois from a burning room, Alyn—in uniform—rushed in, picked up Noel Neill under one arm and Tommy Bond under the other, and rushed from the room. Unfortunately, there was a problem with one of the cameras. A second take was done, with another technical glitch. After two more tries, everything seemed to go well, but Spencer Bennett wasn't satisfied; he felt the veins in Alyn's neck were bulging too much, showing the strain of his efforts. Alyn reminded him that he was merely an actor, not the REAL Superman, and that with each take, the actors he was carrying seemed to get a little heavier. Bennett apologized profusely, and called for lighter-weight mannequins to substitute for Bond and Neill.[139]

Despite the hardships, Alyn enjoyed the filming. Looking back on the serials thirty years later, he told *Starlog* magazine's Jeff Elliot that playing the role was great fun. He said that as a child, his father never let him play cops and robber. Playing Superman, he was finally able to get that out of his system.[140]

Superman completed production on February 27, 1948.[141] The challenges of the production had more than doubled its budget; the final cost was variously reported as anywhere from $250,000 to $325,000. Upon completion, the serial was vigorously marketed. It was advertised on the *Superman* radio show and in *Superman* comic books. Theaters instituted a "Superman Club Card" promotion—if you could show that you had attended the previous fourteen chapters, you got to see the last one for free.[142] With all the hype, *Superman* quickly became the most profitable serial in film history. In Los Angeles, it premiered in "first run" theaters, the first time a serial had been booked in major theaters both in downtown and in Hollywood at the same time.[143] After fifteen months it had grossed over one million dollars, a remarkable achievement in those days. Some theaters began booking six chapters at a time and running them as a single feature.

But the phenomenal success of the serial had an adverse affect on Kirk Alyn. Before long, he was finding it hard to get other jobs. Consequently, when Katzman and Columbia began making plans to produce a sequel, Alyn was less than enthusiastic about once again donning the uniform. Instead, he planned on returning to New York, and perhaps seeking work in a new medium called television (Alyn had appeared in experimental TV broadcasts while in New York in the late 1930s).[144] But with few other offers on the horizon, he finally decided to star in the sequel, thinking it would help give him some extra dollars to keep him afloat while he hunted for other work. The move to New York would have to wait another few months.

On January 7, 1950, *The New York Times* announced that Sam Katzman's next serial for Columbia would be *Atom Man Vs. Superman*. Alyn, Noel Neill, Pierre Watkin and Tommy Bond returned, and veteran character actor Lyle Talbot was cast as a villain from the comic books—Lex Luthor.

Born Lisle Henderson in Pittsburgh, Pennsylvania, on February 8, 1902, Lyle Talbot was one of the original founders and board members of the Screen Actors Guild (a group of 21 actors which included such diverse talents as Charles Starrett, C. Aubrey Smith and Boris Karloff). Talbot's first film role was in 1931's *The Cline Mystery*, co-starring with Donald Meek and John Hamilton. He quickly established himself as a versatile, dependable actor, and by 1948 was an established character performer whose credits included *42nd Street* (1933), the lead role in *Chick Carter, Detective* (1946), and a turn as Commissioner Gordon in the serial *Batman and Robin* (1949). As Lex Luthor, the actor wore a baldhead cap and glowered menacingly for 15 chapters. "Our approach was never to kid it," said Talbot. "This had to be for real."

Alyn also played it straight. He told a reporter in 1987 that because he didn't want to disappoint the kids, he took the role seriously and patterned his performance on the Superman of the comic books. "We didn't do it tongue-in-cheek," said Alyn.[145]

The plot for the second serial, scripted by George H. Plympton and Joseph F. Poland with an assist by David Mathews (one of the writers of Columbia's 1949 serial *The Adventures of Sir Galahad*, produced by Sam Katzman, directed by Spencer Bennett and starring George Reeves), was even more fantastic than its predecessor. Marking the first on-screen appearance of perennial Superman comic book über-villain Lex Luthor and very loosely based on episodes of the *Superman* radio show, the story has Luthor threatening Metropolis with an array of weapons, including a disintegrating machine that seems like a forerunner of *Star Trek*'s transporter, and a sonic vibrator that can create earthquakes. Luthor also weakens Superman with synthetic kryptonite, and transports the hero into "the empty doom" (similar to the Phantom Zone of the comic books).

In the script, Superman accelerates to a rate greater than the speed of light in order to intercept Luthor's rocket ship. When someone pointed out that according to Einstein's theories Superman would have to pass through a state of infinite mass into a state of mathematical impossibility to reach such speed, producer Sam Katzman commented, "All you fellows need is a little faith."[146]

Scenes of Superman in flight were slightly more convincing in the sequel. Though animation was still used for many of the shots, there were more live-action shots of Alyn soaring through the air, accomplished by having him stand in front of a cyclorama with his head tilted back and arms raised as though he were flying. The camera, mounted on gimbals, was tilted ninety degrees. When projected, Alyn would appear to be horizontal. With the addition of a smoke pot and fan above Alyn to create the illusion of passing clouds, the resultant footage was a passable solution to "the flying problem."[147]

Nonetheless, there was a greater use of animation overall in *Atom Man Vs. Superman*. When the bad guys shot at Superman, animated bullets bounced off his chest (a trick which was later repeated in the 1950s TV series). Shots of Luthor's rocket hurtling into space were also animated.

In early February, the serial was shooting on the streets of Los Angeles, utilizing the Los Angeles Civic Center and the Colorado Street Bridge in Pasadena as locations.[148] Benefiting from the lessons learned on the first serial, the shooting of *Atom Man Vs. Superman* commenced without incident, and completed production on March 10, 1950.[149]

While Kirk Alyn was filming his second Superman serial, plans were in the works to bring the Man of Steel to television. But Sam Katzman was not involved in the TV series; National had chosen Robert Maxwell, producer of the Superman radio series, to bring the character to the small screen. Maxwell chose to "clean house" and start over, with different actors playing the roles of Superman/Clark Kent, Lois Lane, Jimmy Olsen and Perry White, and different writers and directors behind the scene. In interviews, Kirk Alyn claimed that he was initially approached about the TV series, saying it had been discussed when they shot the second serial. However, when the casting director asked him about it, he did it in a manner that discouraged him, saying the money was low and they didn't know if it would catch on. Alyn decided that since he was already having trouble finding work, there was no use in prolonging his agony with an even greater identification with the role. Instead, he went to New York.[150]

Noel Neill remembers it differently. She says the producers of the TV series never approached Alyn initially, and that he was very hurt that he wasn't being asked to continue in the role. In any event, Alyn did not have a very high opinion of the television series. He told interviewers that he only saw one or two episodes of the George Reeves series, and he found that ninety percent of the time, Reeves was Clark Kent in scenes that involved a lot of talking. This, said Alyn, was the opposite of his films, where ninety percent of the time, he was Superman performing amazing feats.[151]

According to Alyn, a few years into the *Superman* TV series, George Reeves asked for an increase in salary. Reluctant to give in to his demands, the producers again approached Alyn. However, he told them that they would have to pay him (Alyn) more money anyway, so they might as well go ahead and give Reeves his raise.[152]

Alyn had a starring role in another serial based on a comic book character, *Blackhawk* (1952), and then roles dried up. Frustrated, he went to see the head of Columbia Pictures, Max Arnow. Arnow explained to him, "Everybody thinks you're Superman, Kirk. They wouldn't believe you in any other part."[153] Virginia O'Brien said that as much as Alyn loved the role of Superman, playing the character led to disappointment. "The thing is," she said, "he felt like he was typed and he couldn't seem to get other types of parts."

In September, 1953, Alyn's son, John Feggo III, was born. But despite the joy of a new son, these were not happy years for the actor. Giving up on Hollywood, he finally returned to New York, home of his earlier successes. But Superman, he found, cast a long shadow. "I couldn't walk ten blocks without people recognizing me," he told *The Los Angeles Times'* William Stephens. "They'd honk their horns and yell, 'Hi ya, Superman.'"[154]

Nonetheless, Alyn did find work. "I did 10–12 Broadway plays," he told a reporter in 1987. "I was in New York only two weeks when I got my first show, *Angel in Paris*, with Ilona Massey. I also did about 125 commercials." After a year and a half in New York, he returned to Los Angeles, taking whatever parts he could find. "I did a lot of television," he said. "I was on *The Donna Reed Show* 12 to 14 times, *Highway Patrol* six times."[155] But with the parts becoming smaller and much less frequent, Kirk Alyn's career seemed to be going the way of Eddie Polo's.

Alyn was also facing difficult times on the home front. As his career disintegrated, so did his marriage to O'Brien. The couple was granted a divorce by Superior Court Judge Lewis Drucker in Hollywood on June 24, 1955.[156] The out-of-court settlement gave O'Brien custody of the couple's three children and the proceeds from the sale of their home at 12155 Morrison Street in North Hollywood. Alyn was obligated to begin paying $75 a month for child support, beginning October 1, 1955. O'Brien remarried twice, in 1958 and 1968, but Alyn remained a bachelor for the rest of his life.

By the 1960s, Alyn was largely forgotten. His Superman serials were never released to television; in fact, for many years they were considered "lost." In any event, children of the TV age had only one image of Superman—George Reeves. So Alyn became a sort of Clark Kent, penning articles for a small newspaper. Since he loved to cook as a hobby, he began writing a food column for *The Canyon Crier*, a local newspaper published for Hollywood's Laurel Canyon area.[157] He also enjoyed fishing, and would sometimes take his camper into the High Sierras on freshwater fishing outings.[158]

Then, in the early 1970s, the nostalgia craze struck America. Kids who had thrilled to serial heroes in the 1950s were now college-age, and wondering what had become of their idols. One morning in 1971, Alyn received his first call to appear at a nostalgia convention in Houston, "and it all just started snowballing from there," he said. He turned down more offers than he accepted. "I don't even have an agent, I'm not listed in the phone book, I never go looking for these things, and yet somehow they manage to find me!" A New York lecture agency guaranteed the actor steady bookings nationwide for fifty-two weeks a year. He turned them down.[159]

"I still can't believe it, but suddenly I'm in big demand as a speaker," he told a reporter. Alyn claimed that suddenly nostalgia groups and colleges all over the country were approaching him. At one convention, a number of prominent men came up to Alyn to tell him what an inspiration Superman had been to them in their formative years. When he first began his speaking engagements, he made jokes about Superman, but found that his audiences didn't like it. "They wanted me to be like the Superman they remembered on the Saturday afternoon matinee." After years of being forgotten, Alyn relished the newfound attention. "Playing Superman ruined my acting career and I've been bitter for many years about the whole thing," he said, "but now it's finally starting to pay off."[160]

In his personal appearances, Alyn usually began by explaining what a serial was, then showed a number of endings from silent film serials. Next, he ran the finale of a chapter from *Blackhawk*, and a ten-minute sequence from *Superman*, while giving comments as he stood beside the screen. Then he would say, "And now, a word from our sponsor ..." and show three of his TV commercials.[161] The *Superman* clips Alyn showed in his appearances came from a 16mm print of the serial that Alyn bought from a collector at a science fiction convention where he was making an appearance. According to Jim Hambrick, curator of the Super Museum in Metropolis, Illinois, this same print was the one used by Warner Bros. when they eventually released the serial on videotape in 1988.[162]

On occasion, Alyn would show up at conventions with his *Superman* co-star, Noel Neill. She noticed that in his public appearances he still wore his hair with a Superman spit curl drooping down in front. "I just thought, 'Oh, Kirk, get over it.'" The actress, who has overwhelmingly fond memories of TV Superman George Reeves, held Alyn in somewhat less regard. "He was very egotistical," she recalled.[163]

In 1971, Alyn penned an autobiography, *A Job for Superman*, which he self-published. It was a curious book offering up anecdotes about his years as the caped wonder, and some additional information about his professional life on stage and in the movies, but divulged precious little about his private life. There's one photograph of him with Virginia O'Brien, Albert Dekker and William "Hopalong Cassidy" Boyd relaxing on a Chicago rooftop, yet there is never any mention in the text that he was married to O'Brien, nor any mention of his children.[164] Alyn claimed that he wrote the book because he was receiving hundreds of letters each week asking questions about his life as Superman. He sold it through mail order and at his convention and lecture appearances.

"That was very lucrative for him, because he already had that turned into a business," said Hambrick. "He was buying his photographs for seventeen cents apiece, and then he would sell them for two dollars a piece with his signature on them. Well, he's making a dollar eighty-three on each one, and he'd always have a line of people waiting, so he'd be pumping out maybe eight hundred or a thousand signatures a day."[165]

Jim Hambrick first met Kirk Alyn in the 1970s, and soon found himself acting as manager for the former serial hero. "I was used to handling a lot of celebrities on the road because I had a mobile museum, and he would tour with it," said Hambrick. "In the process of that, you get to know somebody real well because you're in different locations and it's just like shooting a movie. You're in one location for a couple of weeks, you might be at the Orange County Fair and then a week will go by and then you're up in Santa Barbara at the Renaissance Fair or Sacramento or wherever. Kirk liked to do those things because he could be gone for three or four days and then go home for a couple of days, and back and forth."

Like Jimmy Olsen in the comic books, Hambrick soon became Superman's pal. "He was like my surrogate father. I grew up without a father. He knew that. And he was giving me the do's and dont's, the facts of life. And a lot of times when we'd do those fairs, we'd have to spend the night there. And ultimately, if we were within a hundred mile radius of my house, we'd go back there, and I had a room upstairs in my own house where he stayed. It was a real good relationship. When we were together and doing things, Kirk was my best friend."

"He had girlfriends," recalled Hambrick. "Lots of them. And he always told me that there's one way to forget about a woman, and I said, 'What's that?' And he said, 'A lot of other women.' And I can tell you firsthand, too, that the women did flock around him at these conventions and fair tours. The ladies loved him. He had that personality, you know."

Alyn enjoyed the time he spent with Hambrick and his family, and reveled in the appreciation he received from Hambrick's friends, who were also genuine fans of Alyn's *Superman* serials. "Whenever he would come over to the house, some of my friends would know about it and then of course we'd always pull out the 16mm projector. We wouldn't show any of the George Reeves TV shows when he was around, because he always called George Reeves the impostor."[166]

In 1974, Alyn received national newspaper coverage when he acquired a phone booth from the Burbank Theater in Los Angeles, which was being torn down. He was photographed hauling it (with the help of three workmen) to his home. "I'm going to put it in my living room," he told reporters. "I don't think I'll undress in it, though"[167] (the phone booth is now in Jim Hambrick's collection at the Super Museum).

A few years later, in April 1977, Alyn went to bat for the Man of Steel when he sought $10 million in a libel and invasion of privacy suit in Superior Court in Los Angeles after seeing a plaque produced by the Great American Dream Co. which featured an image of him as Superman with the legend, "Super Schmuck." In his court filing, Alyn claimed the plaque caused him "severe emotional shock and mental anguish."[168]

Alyn told a reporter that he still got acting offers, "but it's only for detective roles. I just turned down two such parts. For one thing, I can't get used to the language they want to use today." His biggest concern was, "I don't want kids saying 'Look at the words Superman is using.'"[169] He did appear, however, on NBC's late-night talk show *Tomorrow*, hosted by Tom Snyder, on September 9, 1978. That evening's program was devoted to movie nostalgia; the guest roster also included old-time B-Western cowboys Roy Rogers, Tim McCoy and Monty Hale.

Noel Neill remembers an unpleasant incident from that same year. After it was reported that she had been asked to appear in *Superman: The Movie*, she received a call from Alyn's manager, who told her in no uncertain terms that Neill had to get Alyn a part in the movie. Neill, who had no control over the film's casting and felt that the manager had been unduly rude, ignored the call. However, when she arrived on the location in Calgary, Canada, there was Alyn, looking at her a little sheepishly. Apparently, even without Neill's help, the manager had prevailed in getting her client a cameo in the new movie.[170]

In interviews, Alyn recalled that in the scene, a very young Lois Lane saw Clark Kent running beside the train. Amazed, the little girl told her mother and father, and the father told her to read her book. When she then said that the boy had jumped over the train, the father asked if she'd like for him to read the book to her.[171]

However, in the original release of the film, their lines were edited out—viewers only got a brief glimpse of Neill and the back of Kirk Alyn's head. Alyn was disappointed, but claimed that he received a beautiful letter from Richard Donner typed on Pinewood Studios' Superman stationery saying that cutting the scene was the hardest thing the director had ever had to do in his life.[172] When the film appeared on television and was released on DVD, Alyn and Neill's scene had been restored.

Nonetheless, his role in the movie and the publicity surrounding it gave him enough exposure to land him a few more film and TV roles. In 1979, he appeared in a two-part episode of the science-fiction series *Battlestar: Galactica*, "War of the Gods," playing "the Old Man." His final film role came in 1983, when he played Prof. Machen in the low-budget horror thriller *Scalps*, directed by Fred Olen Ray.

"He was always trying to continue," said Hambrick. "He knew he was an older guy, so he was going for a lot of these older roles. I think he even was trying out for Jor-El or something at some point. He talked about trying out for Marlon Brando's thing.

"He was doing a lot of television commercials at that time. He would appear in a lot of insurance commercials and things like that; I'd see him all over the place," said Hambrick. "And in the '80s, he was back and forth to Hollywood three times a week, up until the mobile museum kicked in.

"During his heyday, I'll tell you, Kirk was a wild man, I mean, he always had the energy to go that extra mile. And even back then, I mean, he was in his early 80s, but he had the energy to just keep going and tell the stories that people appreciated about him, and taking pictures. He was always a real trouper, you know, very professional.

"He had such a great personality with people," said Hambrick. "It was amazing. He would light up. That kept him alive. In fact, his girlfriend told me that these conventions and the notoriety that he got for doing what he did way back then probably added a lot of years to his life. He was always worried about people not remembering what he did."

Retreating further from Hollywood, Alyn moved away from the Los Angeles area and into the California desert. "He built his own house in Sun City," said Hambrick. "Back at that time, Sun City and Temecula and all those areas around Elsinore were just starting to grow, and now they're huge and everybody's moved out there. But he was one of the first ones that settled out there, and everybody knew about Superman because he built his own house, from the ground up. And that was a big deal for an old man. They even did some newspaper articles out there in Sun City on it back in the early 80s."[173]

As the 1980s progressed, Alyn looked back on his years as Superman with a mixture of pride and regret. Now with grandchildren who called him "Grandpa Superman,"[174] he said, "I couldn't get a job after I did *Superman*.... It took only nine weeks to do something that's going to follow me for the rest of my life. *Now*, I'm very happy I did it. Some of the years in-between it was kind of rough."[175]

On February 29, 1988, Alyn appeared briefly in a CBS-TV special produced by Lorne Michaels called *Superman's 50th Anniversary: A Celebration of the Man of Steel*. In an interview for the special, he said proudly, "I felt like I was a creator. I created it. I made him look like this, I made him strong, and they believed me."[176] He told another reporter that if he had the chance, he'd do it all over again. "The money wasn't much," said Alyn. "It was mostly a labor of love, but today especially, I'd relish the chance to play Superman. The role has taken on a special importance. It's a vital part of Americana. It's an exciting role, a challenging role, a fulfilling role. Sure, I would love to do it again."[177]

In the early 1990s, Jim Hambrick talked Alyn into a joint business venture. "Kirk and I were going to do another book," said Hambrick. "It was more of a coffee table version of that smaller book, *A Job for Superman*, with additional items. We had the photographs. I scoured the countryside for color photographs, colorized photographs, lobby cards that were in good shape. We were going to have a lobby card section, a new cover, everything else. I did all the layout for him, and he said that he had a publisher up in Seattle that was interested in looking at what we had put together." Hambrick stayed behind while Alyn took the materials they had gathered and flew to Seattle to meet with the publisher. When Alyn returned, he had good news, and horrible news. The publisher was very interested, but on the return flight, when Alyn got off the plane, he left all of the materials on board. "He said, 'I got on the plane, we've got the publishing deal going, we're supposed to have another meeting, but how are we going to get all this information back within the next three or four weeks?'" recalled Hambrick. "I said, 'Kirk, what are you talking about? Why didn't you just take copies of everything?' Because we'd always talked about that, you know, being real careful. That was sacred stuff. We're talking photographs that there's no way you're going to replace. I said, 'Kirk, forget it. We're not going to do an addendum to your book without all that research and all that material.' So, that kind of rubbed me the wrong way. And I was really upset with him for that. But it wasn't his fault, you know. It was the Alzheimer's."

This was the first of several incidents that pointed out that Alyn's health was on the decline, and his mental acuity was fading. "I know basically all the stories that he told by heart," said Hambrick. "Even when Alzheimer's really kicked in with Kirk, which is a sad thing, the stories stayed. He could forget faces, he'd forget his own kids, but there's two things that stuck with him—he never forgot me, and I'm not just saying this, but he didn't forget me because he would call me twice a day for five years, every single day. And he never forgot about being Superman."

In 1993, Jim Hambrick completed the eight-year process of moving his Superman collection from his Fountain Valley, California, home to Metropolis, Illinois, and opened a permanent Super Museum to house his vast array of Superman memorabilia. Today, the 8,500 square foot museum, across the square from a bronze statue of the Man of Steel, houses not only the museum exhibits but also a gift shop with a vast array of officially licensed Superman merchandise. "Metropolis had an annual Superman celebration, but I came up with the idea of putting in a celebrity to make it different every year," said Hambrick. "So then you theme parts of the celebration around that celebrity. And so Kirk came in and was the grand marshal for a Christmas parade, and then he came in the following year for the Superman celebration.

"Kirk was always concerned about being the forgotten Superman. That was his own tagline, you know, that he used over and over again. And then the last time that he came into Metropolis, he sat over in his corner of the Super Museum, where the Kirk Alyn section was, and he was sitting there with his girlfriend on a stool and was just staring at the display, and I walked up and said, 'What's up, Kirk?' And they were in the museum for a couple of hours, walking around and looking at things and talking to people, and there was a lot of people and he would go through stories and everything else—with Alzheimer's—and he sat there and he was kind of crying, you know. And he was sitting there in the corner and he says, 'You're gonna make sure, Jim, they don't forget me, aren't you?' And I said, 'Yeah, that's kind of what it was all about. That was our intention from the very beginning, Kirk.'"[178]

Kirk Alyn died at age 88 on March 14, 1999, in Woodland, Texas, 49 years and 4 days after *Atom Man Vs. Superman* wrapped production. At the end of his life, as he looked back upon the unfulfilled promise of his film career, Kirk Alyn may have been disappointed ... but shy, retiring John Feggo, Jr. could be proud.

5

Superman Comes to Television

By 1949, radio and movie serial audiences were in sharp decline. Television had moved beyond the experimental phase of the pre–war years, and was now a practical reality, mushrooming in popularity. In May of 1949, only twelve percent of the people in Baltimore, Maryland, watched TV. Just one year later, Baltimore became the first city where more people watched TV than listened to radio.[179] Over the next year, radio listenership continued to decline dramatically, even for *The Adventures of Superman*. When the radio show's final broadcast occurred March 1, 1951, fans may have wondered if they would thrill to Superman's exploits again. They needn't have worried. The following month, Robert Maxwell, producer of the radio series, was tasked with making the transition to television.

By May 16, *Variety* was announcing Maxwell's arrival in Hollywood. National Comics had signed a thirty-year distribution contract with Flamingo Films, a company formed by Sy Weintraub, Jimmy and Joe Harris, and a fresh-out-of-USC David L. Wolper.[180] Flamingo was formed when insurance brokerage company owner Joe Harris bought a series of travel shorts and decided the best way to get a return on his investment was to sell them to TV stations. His son Jimmy and Jimmy's friend David Wolper began traveling around the country, going from station to station selling the shorts. The company soon added old, obscure movies to their inventory. The TV stations weren't very discerning; as Wolper wrote in his autobiography, *Producer*, written with David Fisher, "It was soon obvious that the real star of television was television. Nobody cared about quality as long as it was on television."[181] That said, Sy Weintraub certainly understood the value of a marquee name. Before the decade was out, he bought the movie rights to Tarzan from legendary producer Sol Lesser, reinvigorating the character in a series of seven globe-hopping films before bringing the Lord of the Jungle to television in 1966. Wolper's ambitions were ultimately too big for Flamingo Films; by the 1960s, he had his own company and was renowned for superior television documentaries. By the 1970s, he was producing feature films such as *Willie Wonka and the Chocolate Factory* (1971) and TV mini-series like *Sandburg's Lincoln* (1975) and the ratings juggernaut *Roots* (1977).

With a distribution deal for the *Superman* television series in place, Maxwell set to work. To help produce the series, he hired someone who had considerably more experience dealing with the intricacies of Hollywood—Bernard Luber, a former Paramount Pictures attorney.[182] According to Gary Grossman's 1977 book *Superman: Serial to Cereal*, Bernard Luber claimed that Maxwell was given a 40 percent interest in the *Adventures of Superman* TV series in 1951. For his part, Luber received 10 percent of Maxwell's share and $500 for each program produced.

The first hurdle the duo faced was finding a new actor to play Superman. Dozens of potential Men of Steel were tested (including, reportedly, bodybuilders from Los Angeles's Muscle Beach), but none seemed to possess the qualities Maxwell and Luber were looking for. The solution came with a chance encounter at a popular Los Angeles eatery. "One evening I was dining in the Cock'n'Bull restaurant," said Luber, "when I saw George [Reeves] looking around rather forlorn." Luber knew Reeves when the actor was under contract at Paramount. "The studios had essentially forgotten about him after the war, but he was just right for us." Luber suggested Reeves to Maxwell, who agreed with the choice.[183] On June 27, 1951, *The Los Angeles Times* reported that Reeves had signed a seven-year contract to play the comic book hero.[184]

George Reeves was born in Woolstock, Iowa, on January 5, 1914, as George Keefer Brewer. His parents, Helen and Don Brewer, divorced soon after his birth, and his mother took him to her sister's home in Galesburg, Illinois. Helen and George later went to stay with family members in Kentucky before settling in Pasadena, California. In Pasadena, Helen met and married a druggist named Frank Bessolo. When George was twelve years old, Frank Bessolo adopted him and gave him his last name. Helen divorced Frank Bessolo in the mid–1930s.

After high school, George Bessolo attended Pasadena Community College, where he showed promise as a boxer, a sport that left him with a broken nose on more than one occasion. In 1932, he was considered a Golden Gloves prospect, but Helen discouraged him from pursuing boxing professionally.[185] George decided to try acting. He trained at Pasadena Playhouse, where his classmates included Victor Mature and Robert Preston. In the late 1930s, Warner Bros. offered the young actor a contract, which he signed as George Brewer, adding that his professional name was Bessolo. The powers-that-be at Warners didn't like either name, and rechristened him George Reeves, feeling Reeves was a name with more box-office appeal. Reeves was put into several of the studio's historical shorts, including *The Monroe Doctrine* (1939) and *Pony Express Days* (1939), in which he played Buffalo Bill Cody.

For his feature film debut, Reeves was loaned out to Selznick Pictures, where he landed a part in *Gone with the Wind* (1939). Reeves and Fred Crane played the Tarleton Twins in the film's opening scenes. After that high-profile assignment, Reeves returned to Warner Bros. for supporting roles in crime thrillers and in three James Cagney films, *The Fighting 69th* (1940), *Torrid Zone* (1940) and *Strawberry Blonde* (1941). By this time, Reeves was a married man, having wed a young Pasadena Playhouse actress named Ellanora Needles on September 22, 1940.

After his Warner Bros. contract expired, Reeves moved to 20th Century Fox, where he appeared in the Charlie Chan film *Dead Men Tell* (1941) and the studio's big-budget, color remake of *Blood and Sand*, starring Tyrone Power (1941). After a year at Fox, Reeves free-lanced, co-starring with William Boyd in several Hopalong Cassidy Westerns. His biggest career break came when he was handpicked by Claudette Colbert to co-star with her in *So Proudly We Hail* (1943), directed by Mark Sandrich. Reeves played the role with the confidence of a seasoned Hollywood veteran, and received glowing reviews. However, before he could capitalize on his success, he was drafted. Assigned to the Army-Air Force's Special Forces Division, Reeves appeared in the New York stage production of Moss Hart's *Winged Victory*, and later toured Army camps with a production of *Yellow Jack*. When the war ended, he returned to Hollywood hoping to reestablish himself. Sadly, Mark Sandrich—the one major studio director who believed in him—had passed away. Reeves's career went on a slow decline, from B-movie programmers (including a turn as the villain in Johnny Weissmuller's initial *Jungle Jim* feature in 1948) to a low-budget Sam Katzman-produced serial, *Sir Galahad* (1949).

With his career on the wane, Reeves and his wife Ellanora divorced; she soon married a prosperous attorney named Edward Rose. Reeves also found a new lover—Toni Mannix, the wife of MGM vice president Eddie Mannix. Eddie, by all accounts, was not only aware of his wife's affair, but approved of it; he was, himself, having affairs on the side. Reeves, like Superman, now found himself living a double life. In private, he was dating Toni Mannix, but in public he projected the image of a wholesome bachelor.

When Reeves and his agent dropped in to see producer Robert Maxwell and director Tommy Carr in 1951, Carr was immediately enthusiastic. "From that moment on," Carr told Gary Grossman, author of *Superman: Serial to Cereal*, "he was my first choice. He looked like Superman with that jaw of his." From Reeves's standpoint, it was just another job, something to tide him over until another chance at his big break came along. "I've played about every type of part you can think of," Reeves was quoted as saying. "Why not Superman?"[186] Little could the 37-year-old actor foresee the impact the role would have on his career.

Unlike Kirk Alyn, George Reeves, though fit and athletic, did not naturally possess Superman's physique. He was slope-shouldered, so he wore shoulder pads as well as muscle pads that covered his upper chest and biceps sewn to a cut-off tee shirt to help bring him up to superhero proportions. Under the hot studio lights, Reeves melted; it was sometimes impossible to hide the perspiration leaking onto his tunic from beneath the padding. But what he lacked in physique, he more than made up for in charisma. The camera loved Reeves; he was handsome in a rugged way, and had a smile that could melt an iceberg.

Finding an actress to play Lois Lane proved as big a challenge as finding an actor for Superman. After screening over 300 applicants, the producers hired Phyllis Coates. Her casting was announced in *The Los Angeles Times* on July 6, 1951.[187] When Coates initially interviewed for the part, she didn't think she would get it. She told Walter Ames of *The Los Angeles Times* that the producer thought she was too short, adding that although she'd lost other movie roles for various reasons in the past, it was "never for being too small. After all I'm 5 feet 4 inches tall and I finally convinced him I could stretch a point with high heels."[188]

Born Gypsy Ann Evarts in Wichita Falls, Texas, the blue-eyed strawberry blonde had experience in USO shows before coming to Hollywood. She had a small role in *So You Want to Be in Pictures* (1947), one of the "So You Want To ..." series of shorts produced at Warner Bros. and starring George O'Hanlon as "Joe McDoakes" (Hanlon was later the voice of George Jetson on the 1960s animated TV series *The Jetsons*). The film, which was nominated for an Academy Award, was directed by Richard Bare, who soon married the young ingénue. The marriage lasted less than eight months, but it was apparently an amicable split, as Coates continued to act in shorts directed by Bare. Coates began winning small screen roles, appearing in numerous Westerns for poverty-row studio Monogram before landing the part of Lois Lane.

The role of Jimmy Olsen went to a relative newcomer, Jack Larson. Born in Los Angeles, Larson's father was a milk truck driver and his mother a Western Union clerk. "I cut classes and didn't do well in school. I hung out in bowling alleys, and went to school when I felt like it at Montebello," said Larson.[189] His time in bowling alleys paid off; he became the junior champion of Southern California, making his first film appearance in an MGM sports short.[190] He was also an avid reader of comic books. "I was a big Superman comics fan," said Larson, "and my dad once said, 'It's about time you got paid from Superman—you're just getting your money back.' I must have kept him broke buying all those comic books when I was a kid!"[191]

After he made the MGM sports short, his father came to him and asked him how he was going to make a living. Larson said he would become a pro bowler. His father said he wanted him to finish school and get a good education. At his father's insistence, Larson entered a program at Pasadena Junior College designed to help ex–GIs to finish high school. "They included youngsters from underprivileged areas to be a part of it with the ex–GIs," said Larson. "You had to have a good IQ, and you were repeatedly tested. I didn't consider myself disadvantaged, I was just bad. I was doing poorly at school." Larson had thought he might want to become a newspaperman, but he got involved in theater and music and writing plays, which were performed at the Pasadena Playhouse. "You were induced to do things you wouldn't think of doing," he said. Larson put on a musical, and three talent scouts showed up, one from MGM, one from Fox, and one from Warners. The Warner Bros. scout asked him to audition for Raoul Walsh, and Jack Larson, at the age of seventeen, landed a role in *Fighter Squadron* (1948).[192]

Larson was put under contract by Warner Bros. (the same week the studio also signed Debbie Reynolds), and more film work followed. But when TV came on the horizon, and a federal anti-trust suit forced the studios to divest themselves of their theaters, Warner Bros. began to cut back, and dropped a lot of their stock contracts. Larson could have gone to another studio, but his dream was to go to New York and become a playwright and theater actor. His agent suggested he might make the money for the trip by auditioning for a role in a TV series that didn't yet have a sponsor and would probably never be broadcast. Larson followed the agent's advice, and won the role of the cub reporter in the *Adventures of Superman* TV series. With a 26-episode commitment, he thought it would be quick money for a show no one would ever see.[193] He also thought it would be the death-knell of his film career. "You were all but blackballed in film if you did TV," he said. "Television was the enemy."[194]

The last two regular roles for the proposed series were filled at the end of July, when Robert Shayne was cast as Inspector Henderson and John Hamilton won the role of Perry White. Both were veteran character actors, and like Reeves, Coates and Larson, both had at one time been under contract to Warner Bros.[195]

To introduce the new Superman to the public, it was decided that a low-budget feature-length movie would be made. The first draft of the script was written by Whitney Ellsworth, who thought it up as he drove his family cross-country from Connecticut to Hollywood beginning May 25, 1951. The drive took them through the oilfields of Oklahoma. The sight of the towering oil derricks planted the seed of an idea in Ellsworth's fertile imagination. When they reached the Grand Canyon, while his wife and daughter enjoyed the scenic wonders, Ellsworth holed up in a hotel room and, over the course of a day and a half, banged out the first draft of a script on his portable typewriter.[196] After he arrived in California, Robert Maxwell helped him refine the screenplay, which was eventually credited to Richard Fielding, the *nom de plume* Ellsworth and Maxwell used on their collaborations.[197] Maxwell had previously worked with Ellsworth on the Superman radio show, on which Ellsworth served as story advisor and script developer, a function he would also fulfill for the first season of Superman's TV run.

According to Ellsworth's daughter Patricia Ellsworth Wilson, the idea was for *Superman and the Mole Men* to be released to theaters to gain publicity and financing for the new TV series. After its theatrical run, the feature would be edited down into a two-part story for TV broadcast.[198]

Superman and the Mole Men was a modest piece of sci-fi noir in which little creatures from inside the earth are met with hatred and prejudice from the fearful earthlings aboveground. The creatures come to the surface when the world's deepest oil well plunges into their domain. Once they appear, glowing with phosphorous, the townspeople unite to destroy them. Superman faces down the belligerent ringleader of the townspeople, and helps the mole men return safely to their domain, which they then seal off with a ray gun. It was a tale of tolerance in a time of Jim Crow laws and Communist witch-hunts, disguised as a comic book science-fiction story.

Superman and the Mole Men began filming on July 30, 1951 at the RKO-Pathé lot in Culver City, California. The mole men were played by a quartet of "little people": Billy Curtis, Jack Banbury, Jerry Maren (who was a Lollypop Guild Munchkin in 1939's *The Wizard of Oz* and played "Buster Brown" in 1960s TV commercials) and Tony Baris.[199] Produced by Maxwell and Barney Sarecky, the 58-minute feature was shot in a quick twelve days by Lee Sholem, a veteran director of B-movies known as "Roll'em" Sholem. According to *Variety*, the feature film and an additional twenty-four half-hour episodes were to come in for $400,000, or roughly $15,000 each.[200]

The feature established how Reeves and Coates would interpret their roles, as tough, hardnosed reporters. "In those days," Coates told *Los Angeles Times* reporter Rip Rense in 1994, "I couldn't even *smile* at Superman. If I even gave a knowing or suggestive look to him ... I was like a horse with a bit in his mouth! But I played her tough and direct ... I had one or two attitudes and that was it."[201]

Jettisoning the comic book image of Clark Kent as a milquetoast, and ignoring the Bud Collyer/Kirk Alyn technique of making The Man of Steel's voice lower than Kent's, Reeves played Kent as a sharp-witted, charming, resourceful newspaperman. As played by Reeves, Clark Kent was already a hero; as Superman, he was a tough-minded avenging angel. As director Tommy Carr once stated, "There was little difference between our Superman and our Clark Kent."[202]

As soon as the feature was in the can, the cast got to work on the remaining twenty-four episodes of the TV series. The shows were split between two directors, Sholem and Tommy Carr. Four shows were filmed every ten days. While one director filmed his shows, the other was prepping the next batch. Interiors were filmed on the stages at RKO-Pathé, while exteriors were filmed on the backlot, which was known as Forty Acres (a decade later, the same Forty Acres buildings that suggested Metropolis would become *The Andy Griffith Show*'s Mayberry).[203] Carr, having put Kirk Alyn through his paces for the 1948 *Superman* serial, relished having another crack at the character. "We had more say with Superman on television for the simple reason that we weren't restricted to animation as we were in the serial," said Carr. "Our TV work looked alive! The writing was better on television, the acting was better, too; it was a more intimate medium."[204] On August 10, 1951, as soon as Sholem finished shooting *Superman and the Mole Men*, Carr began filming his first batch of episodes, starting with "The Runaway Robot."[205] Two of the first season episodes, "The Stolen Costume" and "The Secret of Superman," were adapted from scripts originally used for the Superman radio program.[206]

After Carr filmed his initial five episodes, Lee Sholem began shooting his batch of five on August 24, 1951, including "The Ghost Wolf."[207] During production of this episode, the inevitable happened. While Reeves was executing a take-off, one of the wires of the flying rig broke as he was being hoisted aloft. The actor fell to the hard stage floor. Reeves later said he was hurt as much by producer Robert Maxwell's reaction as he was by the fall. Instead of asking if he was hurt, Maxwell reportedly blurted out, "My god—the star!"

The accident spelled the end for Ray Mercer as Superman's special effects supervisor. He was replaced by Thol "Si" Simonson, who jettisoned the leather harness and wires and substituted a hydraulic counterbalance system. Reeves would lie flat in a steel pan molded in the shape of his torso and thighs. His body, situated between the camera lens and the background screen, hid the hydraulic arm from view. A fan blew his cape, and—voila!—Superman flew.[208] To help facilitate the Man of Steel's lift-offs, director Tommy Carr suggested a springboard.[209]

The rigors of filming in the hot wool costume with the sewn-in muscle pads, not to mention the effects snafus, began to wear on series star George Reeves. According to co-producer Bernard Luber, mid-way through production, Reeves asked for more money. "His lawyer threatened that he'd walk off," said Luber. "I placed the whole thing before the Screen Actors Guild which ultimately supported me." Reeves, said Luber, was offered a substantial chunk of the personal appearances income, as well as 3 percent of the profits from the theatrical release of *Superman and the Mole Men*.[210]

The increase in salary helped mollify Reeves, but the long hours and six-day weeks were still hard on the cast and crew. George Reeves and Phyllis Coates had their own way of dealing with the pressures. "Every day at four o'clock George and I reached for a little nip," said Coates. "The production manager used to descend upon us, but we'd say, 'If you want us to finish the day's work, then you've got to let us have a few minutes.' It all worked out. We never got so sloshed we couldn't finish, and I was young enough then, my eyes never got red...! To this day, I've never recognized one that we did without being a little tipsy."[211]

After alternating on more episodes, Tommy Carr filmed the final five shows of the season beginning October 1, 1951.[212] The final episode filmed would be the first broadcast: "Superman on Earth," which told how Jor-El and Lara sent their son to earth, where he was reared by the Kents until, as a young man, he went to Metropolis and landed a job at *The Daily Planet*. The show's opening—basically a filmed version of the opening narration of the radio program—was then filmed, with George Reeves standing in front of the earth, hands on his hips and jaw jutting defiantly.

Music for the program came courtesy of Mutel, a company formed by David Chudnow to provide packaged music for television. Much of the music was originally composed for two feature films: *Open Secret* (PRC, 1948, composer Herschel Burke Gilbert) and *The Guilty* (Monogram, 1947, composer Rudy Schrager). There was also music believed to have been originally composed for a documentary about American Indians, orchestrated by Jack Shaindlin and composed by one of his two ghostwriters, Lan Adomian or Richard Mohaupt. All of the music was re-recorded in France and attributed to bogus composers to get around a ban on the performance of canned television music in America by the American Federation of Musicians.[213]

The composer of the show's main theme is a mystery. Though credited to Leon Klatzkin, whose work also included the popular Western *Gunsmoke*,[214] David Chudnow claimed that Klatzkin worked as a music cutter on the show, where he simply picked cues from Chudnow's Mutel catalog. The "Superman Theme" was orchestrated and recorded in New York in 1952 by Jack Shaindlin, and may have been written by one of his ghostwriters.[215] The feature film *Superman and the Mole Men*, on the other hand, was scored by Darrell Calker, best known for composing the theme song of Woody Woodpecker.

Filming ended on Saturday, October 13, 1951.[216] Two and a half months after they began shooting, the producers had 26 episodes in the can, including the two created from the *Superman and the Mole Men* feature film. The cast thought it was just another job, that ultimately no one would see it and they would move on to other roles in other films and other TV shows.

The following month, Lippert Pictures—an independent company known for its output of low-budget fare—released *Superman and the Mole Men* as a second-feature attraction,

George Reeves, with shoulder and muscle pads, strikes a familiar pose in *Superman and the Mole Men* (1951). After beginning his career with a small role in *Gone With the Wind* (1939), Reeves felt that the Superman television series was bottom-of-the-barrel work. However, it made him an international celebrity and—after his untimely death—a Hollywood legend (Motion Pictures for Television Inc./Photofest, © Motion Pictures for Television Inc).

playing the bottom half of double-bills. The film came and went with little fanfare. The actors' careers seemed safe. Reeves and Coates returned to film work, and Jack Larson finally went to New York, where he presented his plays in loft readings.[217]

Initially, *Variety* reported that the Superman series would be ready for broadcast by January 1952. As it happened, it wasn't aired until a year later; it premiered in Los Angeles on February 9, 1953.[218] National Periodical Publications, the publishers of the Superman comic book and owners of the character, were not entirely happy with the way the character was portrayed in the first season episodes. According to Gary Grossman, producer Robert Maxwell hoped for an adult time slot, so he made Superman an adult show, with death scenes and rough violence.[219] The comic book company had expected a kid's show.

The actors who felt they had just participated in a sponsorless program that would never be seen failed to count on one thing—the resourcefulness of Flamingo Films' young go-getter David L. Wolper. After two years of trying to sell the Superman program, Wolper approached venerable cereal maker Kellogg's with the program. Admittedly, this wasn't exactly a new idea, considering Kellogg's had sponsored the radio series.

The sale of *Adventures of Superman* was also aided by the Federal Communications Commission. In 1948, the FCC put a freeze on the licensing of any new television stations until they could devise a fair and equitable system for the distribution of TV service among cities and states. In July 1952, the freeze was lifted. New television stations began popping up around the country like dandelions. And, with the growth of the TV industry, there was also a resultant growth in the demand for product.[220]

Eventually, Flamingo Films was removed from the picture entirely when National Periodical Publications bought out their interest in Superman. In its first season, the program aired on ABC, but the Leo Burnett Agency, who handled the Kellogg's advertising account, felt they'd do better buying spot time on local stations, so Kellogg's began syndicating the programs themselves.[221]

When the program did finally hit the airwaves, Phyllis Coates told Walter Ames of *The Los Angeles Times* that her four-year-old daughter didn't find her entirely convincing as Lois Lane. "Chris just can't understand why I can't see through Superman's disguise in the telecasts," Coates said. "She thinks I'm quite stupid about the whole thing."[222]

Within two weeks of the series airing, Phyllis Coates had to change the color of her hair to keep from being mobbed. She recalled that grown women would stop her on the street to ask how it felt to be held in Superman's arms.[223] In New York, Jack Larson was having breakfast with friends at a diner when a crowd began to form outside. Soon, hundreds of schoolchildren had gathered, having discovered that Jimmy Olsen was eating inside. They began pressing against the window, standing on each other's shoulders to get a glimpse of the actor. Larson had to be escorted out by police, who hid him in the Metropolitan Museum of Art until the crowd subsided.[224]

In May of 1953, script conferences began for the second season of *Adventures of Superman*. The program was now under the supervision of a new producer. Robert Maxwell was out, National Comics' editorial director Whitney Ellsworth was in. It was Ellsworth who had championed Superman when Siegel and Shuster first sought to have it published in 1938, and later became the editor of the *Superman* newspaper strip. Born in Brooklyn, New York on November 27, 1908, Frederick Whitney Ellsworth attended Brooklyn's Polytechnic Preparatory Country Day School, graduating in 1926. After taking a cartooning course at the Y.M.C.A., he began working as a gag writer at King Features, working on newspaper comic strips such as *Tillie the Toiler* and *Dumb Dora*. He later worked as a reporter and feature writer for *The Newark Star-Eagle* and *The Newark Ledger*. By the mid–'30s, he was writing for pulp magazines. After writing the play *Maiden Voyage* in 1935, Ellsworth went to work for Major Malcolm Wheeler-Nicholson's fledgling comic book company. In 1937, Ellsworth moved to California, writing for pulp magazines and dime novels. While there, he married Jane Dewey, a young actress under contract to Paramount. The couple eventually moved to New York, where Ellsworth was hired as an artist by Detective Comics (which merged with National Allied Publications to form National Comics in 1944). He quickly moved up the ladder, becoming an editorial director in January 1940.[225] "I was with the company at the time the Superman cartoons were made," Ellsworth told author Gary Grossman. "Max Fleischer's studios were in Miami, and I purchased a few rail tickets South to keep tabs on the production.... Paramount studios took a considerable financial bath on the deal, and we abrogated the contract by mutual consent long before the full projected number of cartoons had been made." In 1941, Ellsworth began writing the *Superman* newspaper strips after Jerry Siegel was drafted. The comic book company later sent Ellsworth to Hollywood to consult on the movie serial adaptations of Superman, Batman and Congo Bill (a character Ellsworth created).[226]

Now that he was in charge of the Superman TV show, Ellsworth made a concerted effort to tone down the hard-edged violence of the program's first season. "I honestly tried not to violate the tenets of good taste," said Ellsworth. "For example, in all the shows that I made, there was only one murder, and that was off-screen ["The Defeat of Superman," 1953]."[227] Ellsworth had, in fact, begun his own editorial code at Detective Comics more than a decade before the Comics Code of 1953 was instituted. Ellsworth, who saw comic books as being entertainment for children, saw to it that DC's stories were light-hearted, clean, and mostly non-violent.[228]

Quoted in Gary Grossman's *Superman: Serial to Cereal*, Jack Larson said, "Because Bob Maxwell and his wife Jessica had done Superman on radio, he created the television show with a tough kind of dialogue and heavily characterized gangsters. Whit, on the other hand, had come out of the comic book industry exactly when comic books had been under fire for violence and sadism. At National, he had been partly responsible for the disappearance of hard-edged drawings and sexuality, and the introduction of a different kind of comic hero. The emphasis was on 'comic' and 'comic villains,' and when Whit took over for Maxwell he leaned heavily in that direction."[229]

Ellsworth's daughter, Patricia Ellsworth Wilson, told Chuck Harter, "My father's approach was that the character Superman on television should reflect the character in the DC comics. That it was a translation to the screen of that character. He always felt that comics magazines were aimed at children and teenagers and so he conceived that the TV show was also aimed at children and teenagers, and he would not have been in favor of very dark, blood-thirsty plots."[230]

Bernard Luber wanted to continue his association with the show, co-producing with Ellsworth as he had with Maxwell. Ellsworth, however, felt he could go it alone. He soon had his hands full, acting as story editor, producer, legal advisor, and company liaison.[231]

Ellsworth was immediately faced with a formidable challenge—finding a new Lois Lane. In the time since production ended on the first season of Superman episodes, Coates had been approached by producer William Asher to co-star with Jack Carson and Allen Jenkins in the pilot for a new show, *Here Comes Calvin.* "I felt badly when I had to leave," said Coates. "We had a rhythm, and we kidded each other an awful lot. It was very hard work, but we liked each other an awful lot. We were really good buddies ... George, Jack and I had a tight little unit, and we worked for the best crew in television, the very best." Whitney Ellsworth offered to double her salary, but Coates had made up her mind. As it happened, *Here Comes*

Calvin was passed over by the networks.[232] Coates kept busy nonetheless, with numerous parts in other TV series, a starring role in the serial *Panther Girl of the Kongo* (1955), and a part in the cult classic *I Was a Teenage Frankenstein* (1957).

After *Adventures of Superman* ceased production in 1951, George Reeves returned to his film career with roles in *Bugles in the Afternoon* (1952), *Rancho Notorious* (1952), and *The Blue Gardenia* (1953). When he reported to the Superman set, he had just finished filming *From Here to Eternity* (1953), the highly anticipated adaptation of James Jones's best-selling novel.

With Coates unavailable, Ellsworth contacted Noel Neill, who had played Lois Lane in the Sam Katzman serials opposite Kirk Alyn. According to Noel Neill's authorized biography, *Truth, Justice and the American Way* by Larry Thomas Ward, when Ellsworth called Neill, she listened attentively, paused for a moment, and then accepted the offer.[233] Since Ellsworth and National Comics were familiar with her characterization from the serials, a screen test was not required. Neill did not meet Reeves until she showed up for the first day of filming. Though he was sad to see Coates go, Reeves struck up an immediate rapport with Neill. During the rehearsal, director Tommy Carr wasn't satisfied with the actress's delivery of a line, and had her do the scene over and over, until she shed a tear in frustration. Reeves asked for a break, then confronted Carr, telling the director to give Neill a break. Neill was grateful to Reeves for sticking up for her. Reeves, she said, "let me do it my way, and I've been doing it my way ever since."[234]

"George was a gentle, kind-spirited guy," Neill told *Los Angeles Times* reporter Rip Rense in 1994. "That was his charm. That was him. He was like a Southern gentleman on the set. Always in a game of gin rummy."[235] Under Ellsworth's guidance, the characters of Superman and Lois Lane were less hard-edged than in the first season episodes. It was a change well suited to the amiable personalities of Reeves and Neill.

With his cast in place, Ellsworth began instituting cost-cutting measures. To begin with, he moved the production from RKO-Pathé to the less expensive California Studios on Santa Monica Blvd. He also made sure the major characters had stock outfits that they wore almost all the time: Clark Kent's double-breasted gray suit, Jimmy Olsen's bow tie and sweater, and Lois Lane's two-piece suit and hat. Clark Kent's office was also re-dressed and re-used as Lois Lane's. Tommy Carr returned as director, now alternating shows with George Blair instead of Lee Sholem.[236] Blair was a veteran director of B-movie crime dramas and Westerns, as well as multiple episodes of Roy Rogers's and Gene Autry's TV programs.

The second season episodes began filming in early June with "Five Minutes to Doom." Ellsworth put the crew on a slightly more relaxed schedule. Instead of filming four episodes every two weeks, they now filmed five episodes every three weeks.[237] The second season yielded an episode considered by many to be the best of the series, "Panic in the Sky," in which Superman suffers amnesia after attempting to deflect a giant asteroid on a collision course with Earth. It was such a sure-fire story that it was later remade as an episode of the 1990s series *Lois & Clark: The New Adventures of Superman*; it also inspired an episode of the *Superboy* series (1991).

The filming of the second season episodes went mostly without incident, except for one memorable special effects snafu. The effects supervisor, Thol "Si" Simonson, had prepared a wall for Superman to burst through. The wall was made of adobe, and Reeves, as Superman, was supposed to crash through it within hours of its completion. However, on this occasion, the crew fell behind in the schedule, and it was decided to film the breakaway wall the next day. As the cameras rolled, Reeves ran full force toward the wall, and slammed into it. But only one arm and one leg got through; the wall had hardened overnight. After a few seconds, the stunned actor pulled his arm and leg out of the wall, stepped back, and announced, "Good day. See you all tomorrow!"[238]

With the series growing in popularity, Reeves was regularly asked to appear at high-profile events. On July 6, 1953, he was on hand when Los Angeles TV station KECA increased its power from 29,000 to 118,000 watts. Reeves was called upon to toss the switch, as Danny Thomas looked on.[239] However, his newfound recognition as Superman also had negative repercussions. When Reeves landed a small role as Sgt. Maylon Stark in *From Here to Eternity*, screenings of the wartime romance were reportedly ruined by people saying "Superman" whenever Reeves came on-screen. For years, a persistent rumor suggested that Reeves's role in the film was cut back as a result, but Superman expert Jim Beaver's research has revealed that Daniel Taradash's original script has only the scenes for Reeves's character that are presently in the film, and in Beaver's interviews with Taradash, director Fred Zinnemann, and editor William A. Lyon, all denied that any of Reeves's scenes had been cut.

Filming for the season ended on September 30, 1953, with the shooting of the episode "Around the World with Superman" and a special episode made for the US Treasury Dept., "Stamp Day for Superman," in which the Man of Steel encouraged boys and girls to buy savings bonds and stamps.[240] During the next year, the *Adventures of Superman* TV show grew in popularity, even as other acting assignments dried up for George Reeves. With the burgeoning success of the show, and no other acting offers, he now had more clout to renegotiate his contract, and more need to do so. Consequently, as the 1954 season began, Reeves demanded more money. In a September 27, 1954, article, *Variety* reported that as a result of Reeves's salary demands, producer Whitney Ellsworth was looking for a new actor to take over the role of Superman (it was presumably at this point that Kirk Alyn was approached and advised the producers to give Reeves his salary increase). As the impasse dragged on, Reeves took his grievances public. He told Walter Ames of *The Los Angeles Times* that for some time he had wanted to do a new youth series with a Mexican and Hawaiian background. He also complained of the hazards of doing personal appearances, where his young admirers kicked him in the shins, slugged him in the back and even punched him in the eye to see if he would flinch. Aside from salary demands, Reeves was also said to have asked officials of National Periodical Publications to halt the sale of Superman capes and other merchandising that he thought might be harmful to youngsters (though they were mostly apocryphal, Reeves was upset by stories that his young fans were injuring themselves trying to perform Superman-like feats, such as leaping from great heights). Whitney Ellsworth responded by saying, "Reeves' agents served an ultimatum on me. It called for a salary increase I was unable to meet. My relations with Reeves are still amiable. I wish him luck."[241]

A month later, the trade journal announced that Reeves and Ellsworth had reached agreement on a new contract. The actor was said to have received a pay raise, but less than he originally demanded.[242] It has been reported that Reeves settled for $2,500 per episode plus a lucrative residual package, in return for a guarantee to star in fifty-two more episodes to be filmed over four year (thirteen each year).[243] Kellogg's bought the original first run and limited rerun rights of the program from National Comics for a fixed price, reportedly ponying up part of George Reeves's renegotiated salary.[244]

Meanwhile, Jack Larson's peak salary was $350 an episode, while Noel Neill's was $225 per episode.[245] Neill's residuals were $35 for the first and second runs of an episode, $45 for the third, fourth and fifth, and $35 for the next two. The residuals ran out in 1962.[246]

When filming resumed on November 15, 1954, there were some dramatic changes in the series. Most significantly, from this point on, the episodes were filmed in color, despite the fact that no homes at the time could receive color broadcasts. This was a far-sighted move on the part of the producers. A decade later, when color TV sets became more common, syndicated programs that were filmed in color were more desirable than those that were only available in black-and-white. The switch to color meant that George Reeves's brown-and-gray Superman costume would now be replaced by a proper red-and-blue one, and the sets would have to be repainted with both black-and-white and color viewing in mind.[247]

The change to color also signaled a change in the show's tone. In part, this was a reaction to the furor that erupted with the publication of *Seduction of the Innocent: The Influence of Comic Books on Today's Youth* by Fredric Wertham, M.D., a psychiatrist who specialized in the treatment of juvenile delinquents. Besides writing that Superman "has long been recognized as a symbol of violent race superiority" and equating him with the Nazis, Wertham also questioned Batman and Robin's sexuality. Needless to say, he was reading much more into the comics than young readers were getting out of them, but his attack led to hearings in the U.S. Senate. By the time the comic book industry formed a self-censoring body, the Comics Code Authority, to head off such criticism, many comics had bitten the dust, victims of the bad press and subsequent flagging sales.[248] Superman remained, but his exploits—both in comic books and on television—were decidedly more juvenile, aimed at a younger "kiddie" audience.[249] One reflection of this can be seen in the method Superman used to dispatch criminals. In the first season episodes, Superman engaged in knockdown, drag-out fights with the bad guys, punching them full in the face. When the show switched to color, Superman simply karate-chopped the criminals' necks, knocking them out with one swift chop.

A new director came on-board for the third season: Harry Gerstad. An editor who had worked on *High Noon* (1952) and who knew Whitney Ellsworth from service in the Signal Corps in World War II, Gerstad directed the first five episodes of the new season,[250] with George Blair returning to direct the remaining eight. For this and the following three seasons, the number of shows filmed would be thirteen instead of twenty-six.

The prior season's episodes, meanwhile, were being released to theaters. Ellsworth put together five feature films, each comprised of three episodes from the 1953 season. The features were released by 20th Century–Fox under the titles *Superman's Peril, Superman Flies Again, Superman in Exile, Superman and Scotland Yard* and *Superman and the Jungle Devil* (all released in 1954).

The following year, the show changed locations again for the fourth season, moving to the La Brea Street studios of Charlie Chaplin (later A&M Records, and as of this writing the home of Jim Henson Productions). Harry Gerstad directed some of the fourth season episodes, alternating with Phil Ford, who was the nephew of legendary director John Ford.[251]

On April 6, 1955, George Reeves made two personal appearances as Superman in Los Angeles. At the downtown Los Angeles Broadway store, Reeves drew a crowd of fifteen thousand youngsters. At his next stop, another Broadway store on Crenshaw Boulevard, he attracted twenty thousand. The personal appearances were to publicize Little Helpers, a children's organization working in behalf of the City of Hope medical center.[252]

Reeves made an appearance on the Multiple Sclerosis telethon in Los Angeles in July, 1956, where he sang and played his guitar.[253] The following month, he flew to New York for an appearance as Superman on the children's program *Romper Room*, and appeared as himself on NBC's *Tony Bennett Show*, again with his guitar.[254] Also in 1956, Reeves was honored by the Myasthenia Gravis Foundation for his efforts on behalf of victims of the neuromuscular disease (he became involved in the Foundation after learning that producer Whitney Ellsworth's daughter was afflicted with the disease). This was all a reflection of the actor's generosity of spirit. When on public appearance tours, he was known to visit the children's wards of hospitals. He also sponsored underprivileged youngsters from the barrios of East Los Angeles, something he began doing even before he landed his TV role. Noel Neill and Jack Larson often recall in interviews that George Reeves had a sign on his dressing room door that read, "Honest George, the People's Friend." It was a persona that Reeves radiated both in and out of the Superman uniform; off-screen as well as on, George Reeves *was* a Superman.[255]

When filming began for the 1956 season of the show, production moved again, this time to ZIV Studios, formerly known as Eagle-Lion.[256] The show was at its peak, garnering its highest ratings.[257] *Billboard* reported that the series ranked sixth among all syndicated shows, and had ranked number two among syndicated shows in New York in December 1955.[258] Since the show had begun filming in 1951, the number of homes with television sets had more than doubled, from 15,300,000 to 38,900,000.[259] *Gone With the Wind* had its first TV broadcast in 1956; fifty-two percent of households with TV tuned in to see the film in which George Reeves had made his big-screen debut.[260]

At the end of the season, Reeves was asked to appear on one of TV's biggest hits, *I Love Lucy*, in an episode in which Lucy promises Little Ricky that Superman will attend his birthday party. In the show, broadcast on January 14, 1957, Reeves arrives at the party to find Lucy, in a Superman tunic, on the ledge of the building, in the rain. He gets to deliver the show's punchline after Ricky, Lucy's husband, scolds her, saying it's the most ridiculous thing she's done in the fifteen years they've been married. Reeves interjects, "You mean to tell me you've been married to her for fifteen years? And they call ME Superman!"

In August of 1957, Noel Neill joined Reeves, his friends Natividad Vacio and Gene LeBell and a troupe of musicians for a tour of state fairs. The show began with Reeves appearing as Superman, saving Lois Lane from Mr. Kryptonite (LeBell). Afterwards, Reeves—out of the Superman uniform—joined Vacio, Neill and the musicians onstage for a program of songs. The tour ended in September, just before filming was to start up on another season of thirteen Superman episodes.[261]

Script conferences began on September 18, 1957.[262] There were a couple of changes. The show was now co-sponsored by Sweets Co. of America,[263] and it moved from syndication to network broadcast, returning to ABC.[264] Tommy Carr, who had directed half of the first season episodes, returned to direct his only color episode, "The Last Knight." George Blair returned to direct four episodes, Phil Ford directed two, and three new directors came onboard. One was Howard Bretherton, whose Superman episode "The Gentle Monster" was the final directing credit in a career that began in the 1920s and included countless Westerns (including 1935's *Hop-Along Cassidy*) and crime dramas (including *The Trap*, the 1946 Charlie Chan feature that had Kirk Alyn in a small role). Another newcomer to Superman was director Lew Landers (aka Louis Friedlander), a former serial director who helmed 1935's *The Raven* with Boris Karloff and Bela Lugosi, and Lugosi's ersatz Dracula film, *The Return of the Vampire* (1944). Lastly, preparing for a career beyond Superman, George Reeves got his Director's Guild of America card and directed the last three episodes filmed, "The Brainy Burro" (in which his friend Natividad Vacio appeared), "The Perils of Superman" (a homage to movie serials) and "All That Glitters."

In 1958, Reeves began looking for a feature film property he could produce and direct. In October of that year, National Comics sent him to New York for a publicity tour. He went without Toni Mannix, and fell into the arms of Lenore Lemmon, a member of New York's cafe society with a notorious past. Reeves brought Lemmon back to Los Angeles, and moved her into his home in Benedict Canyon—a home purchased for him by Toni Mannix. By all accounts, Toni was jealous of Lenore; Reeves' personal life became a roller coaster.

Reeves made headlines on April 12, 1959, when he was in an automobile accident that resulted in a concussion and head gash. The actor was taken to Cedars of Lebanon Hospital, but his condition was hushed up, reportedly because his sponsors didn't want his young fans to think that Superman could get hurt and have to stay in a hospital.[265]

In May of 1959, *Los Angeles Times* reporter Ron Tepper interviewed George Reeves. The article proclaimed that each year some 35 million viewers tuned in to *Adventures of Superman*, and that 48 percent were adults. According to the newspaper, it was also one of the top-rated programs in Japan. Reeves claimed that he had received a letter from the Emperor of Japan telling him how much he enjoyed the series. In the interview, Reeves expressed no embarrassment at portraying the Man of Steel, saying it was a good against evil fantasy and was as American as ham and eggs.[266] Reeves said that his viewers eventually grew out of the Superman age bracket and turned to Westerns, but that they eventually came back to Superman. Realizing that their primary audience was young viewers, he said the show's scripts were carefully screened to minimize violence, though he himself felt that kids were absorbing things quicker than ever before and were learning more in an hour of TV watching than his generation learned in months.

Having tried his hand as a director, Reeves said that is what he'd like to do, adding, "A good director must understand the script and actors. He must give the actors a chance to create; ask him how he would like to play a scene. This is what made *From Here to Eternity* such a success. The director, Fred Zinnemann, gave all these opportunities to the actors."[267]

National Periodical Publications ordered a new series of twenty-six *Superman* episodes in 1959. Producer Whitney Ellsworth personally called Noel Neill and asked her to show up at the ZIV Studio on Santa Monica Boulevard to see if her old suit still fit. She arrived on the stage on June 14 to find George Reeves and director George Blair sitting at a card table playing gin rummy. Reeves was in a buoyant mood, and said he was looking forward to directing half the episodes of the upcoming season.[268]

But just a few days later, on June 17, 1959, newspaper headlines across the country announced the unimaginable: Superman had killed himself.

The banner headlines all told a similar story, that an actor disillusioned by typecasting which caused a slump in his career took his own life. The 45-year-old actor was found naked in his bedroom, a bullet wound in his head, a Luger pistol at his feet. Even in death, Reeves could not escape the typecasting; few of the headlines included his name, most said only that Superman was dead.

Reeves's funeral service was held at 3 P.M. on July 1 at the Gates, Kingsley & Gates Mortuary in West Los Angeles. Among the pallbearers were *Superman* producer Whitney Ellsworth, director George Blair, and actors Alan Ladd and Gig Young (who would also end his life by suicide). Another pallbearer, Reeves's friend Gene LeBell, told Joseph Dalton of *The Los Angeles Herald Examiner*, "At George Reeves' funeral, there were hundreds of people, Caucasians, Mexicans, blacks. Grown men crying. You don't see that much in this world."[269]

To this day, many people find the official verdict of suicide a hard one to accept. Though some said Reeves was discouraged over his Superman typecasting, others said he was looking forward to filming another season of the show, and that he was preparing a science fiction film he planned to direct. Those who believe Reeves was murdered point the finger at two prime suspects—the woman he was then sharing his home with, Lenore Lemmon, and his former lover, Toni Mannix. Reeves's mother was so convinced that he didn't take his own life that she left her home in Galesburg, Illinois, and traveled to California, where she hired famed attorney Jerry Geisler to investigate. The investigation continued until her death in

1964, without producing any verifiable proof of murder. Lenore Lemmon, meanwhile, returned to New York, where she appeared on David Susskind's panel discussion program *Open End* on September 10, 1961, joining Joe E. Lewis, Jackie Gleason, Ernie Kovacs and Toots Shor to talk about Frank Sinatra and the Rat Pack.[270]

What actually happened in George Reeves's home in the early morning hours of June 16, 1959 is a riddle lost to the sands of time. The major players who were there are now all gone. Whole books have been devoted to Reeves's demise, the most definitive being Jan Alan Henderson's *Speeding Bullet: The Life and Bizarre Death of George Reeves* (Michael J. Bifulco, 1999). Writers Sam Kashner and Nancy Schoenberger took up the subject in their book *Hollywood Kryptonite* (St. Martin's Press, 1996). Screenwriter Paul Bernbaum and director Allen Coulter explored the tragedy with the feature film *Hollywoodland* (2006), with Ben Affleck portraying George Reeves. *Hollywoodland* offered several possible solutions to the mystery, but the truth of what happened remains the biggest mystery of all.

"It's the great Hollywood 'What If...,'" said Steven Kirk, curator of The George Reeves Memorial. "What if George Reeves had lived past June 16th, 1959? Would he have become one of the few successful actor-director hyphenates to come out of the 50s? Would he have gone on to appear in a cameo in Richard Donner's *Superman: The Movie*, playing Jor-El? Would he still be greeting his throngs of fans around the world with that million-dollar smile? Sadly, we'll never know what life had in store for this incredibly talented and giving person."[271]

After George Reeves's demise, National Periodical Publications gave serious thought to producing a Jimmy Olsen TV series. Kellogg's had already put up the money for a new season of *Adventures of Superman*; if they didn't find a way to produce a show, the money would have to be returned. Mort Weisinger of National Periodical Publications had come up with a way to keep the money: they would film new stories with Jack Larson, mixed with recycled footage of George Reeves from the *Superman* series. After traveling through Europe, Larson was called to a meeting in New York with Weisinger, Jack Liebowitz and Jay Emmett of National. "They had figured out how to make thirteen programs to salvage the money from Kellogg's," said Larson, "and we had a very unhappy meeting over it, which upset them more than it upset me. I didn't want to do it, and I didn't do it. I said to Jack Liebowitz, 'The show's over.'" Liebowitz hinted that Larson had a contractual obligation, and could be held in breach of contract if he didn't comply. Distraught and agitated, Larson left the meeting. Liebowitz was angry. Jay Emmett caught up to Larson on the street and expressed his concern that Larson seemed disturbed by the discussion and said, "We don't want another tragedy on our hands." They were afraid that Larson, like Reeves, was so unsettled he might commit suicide. "I met with Whitney Ellsworth, and he said he didn't want to do the show either," said Larson, "and so it never proceeded."[272]

To this day, over half a century since *Adventures of Superman* first began production, the show is still on television stations around the world. In 1987, in preparation for Superman's 50th Anniversary, select episodes of the program were released on videotape. That same year, the original theatrical version of *Superman and the Mole Men* was pulled from a bonded warehouse of DC Comics and released for the first time since its original 1951 theatrical run. In 2005 and 2006, Warner Bros. released box sets of the series on DVD, with commentary from Noel Neill and Jack Larson, as well as Superman experts like Gary Grossman and Jim Nolt. The Season 1 box set also included the feature version of *Superman and the Mole Men*, and Kellogg's commercials starring George Reeves.

When *Adventures of Superman* ceased production, Jack Larson appeared in guest spots on a handful of TV programs in the early 1960s before deciding to finally pursue his ambition of becoming a playwright. While in his 30s, he received the first grant awarded to a playwright by The Rockefeller Foundation. With a talent for rhymed verse, he wrote the libretto for composer Virgil Thomson's opera *Lord Byron* and adapted Stravinsky's *L'Histoire du Soldat* as the chamber opera *The Astronaut's Tale*, with a score by Charles Fussell. He also became a film producer, with credits ranging from *The Paper Chase* (1973) to *The China Syndrome* (1979) to *Urban Cowboy* (1980) (all directed by his long-time domestic partner, James Bridges).

However, despite all those accomplishments, Larson knows he is destined to be remembered as Jimmy Olsen. When the premiere of *Lord Byron* was held at the Juilliard School in 1972, Virgil Thomson was struck by Larson's immediate popularity when he arrived for rehearsals. Thomson said the Juilliard students, who had master classes with Callas and Heifetz and Casals, were hard to impress, "but, oh boy, were they excited when Jimmy Olsen showed up."[273]

By 1979, Jack Larson had made peace with the role that sidelined his acting career. "We never made any money out of it, but we were part of a classic," he said, "a classic of American television."[274] In a 1998 interview, he told Anthony Tommasini of *The New York Times* that no matter where he went, he always got warm feelings from people about Jimmy Olsen. "They love him," said Larson, "and I grew to feel that I could never have done anything more special than be Jimmy Olsen." Indeed, the specialness of the character was recognized by the Smithsonian Institution, where the bow tie Larson wore as Jimmy Olsen is now displayed next to Archie Bunker's easy chair and Dorothy's ruby slippers. "I've done much I'm proud of in my life," said Larson. "But I know my tombstone will say, 'Here lies Jimmy Olsen.' And that's okay with me."[275]

Typecast as Lois Lane, Noel Neill retired from acting when the series ended and went to work in public relations. In the early 1970s, when the nostalgia boom hit America, Neill began touring college campuses. At one personal appearance, a young man told her that when he was a kid, he used to run home from school and crawl under the TV to try and look up her dress. Young women praised her as a role model. Speaking to *Los Angeles Times* reporter Rip Rense, Neill said that a lot of the young women at the colleges would tell her that they were inspired growing up by seeing Lois Lane working alongside men. "They said that's how they got into journalism," said Neill. "It was very flattering that the character inspired them."[276]

In the 1980s, Neill became a celebrity assistant to actor Tom Selleck. In August 2004, when Neill was honored by the Golden Boot Awards, an annual celebration of TV and movie cowboys benefiting the Motion Picture and Television Fund, Selleck introduced her to the audience. She still makes personal appearances, showing up at comic book conventions, autograph shows and Superman-related events. In 2003, she wrote an autobiography, *Truth, Justice and the American Way*, with Larry Thomas Ward. In 2006, she and Jack Larson continued their associations with The Man of Steel when they both appeared in *Superman Returns*. The city of Metropolis, Illinois christened Neill "The First Lady of Metropolis" and announced plans to erect a life-sized statue of her as Lois Lane in the town square, near their giant-sized statue of Superman.

And what of George Reeves? More than fifty years after he first donned the Superman uniform, the life and legacy of George Reeves is still being celebrated. A fan magazine dedicated to Reeves and *Adventures of Superman* called *The Adventures Continue* was begun by Dr. Don Rhoden of Omaha, Nebraska in 1988. After the first two issues, Rhoden asked Jim Nolt to take over the magazine. It continued publication until 2001, when issue #16, a 50th anniversary tribute, went to press. Nolt brought *The Adventures Continue* to the Internet beginning in 1994. He served as editor of the site (www.jimnolt.com) until the end of 2005, when he turned over the reins to Lou Koza. The website, designed as a tribute to George Reeves and the cast and crew of *Adventures of Superman*, continues to be the premier source of information concerning the show on the internet. And, continuing the charity work of George Reeves, Nolt and his readers have, since 1989, raised more than $15,000 for the Myasthenia Gravis Foundation of America.

Reeves' birthplace of Woolstock, Iowa, held The George Reeves Memorial Festival on June 16, 2006. Over five hundred people from around the globe came to the tiny town for the three-day event, which included screenings of the Superman TV show and *Superman and the Mole Men*, a presentation of Superman memorabilia and a panel discussion with George Reeves experts Carl Glass (who, with his wife Leslie, runs the website www.GlassHousePresents.com, internet home of the George Reeves Hall of Fame), Chance McFadden, Dennis Lark and Steven Kirk.

When asked about the lasting impact of Reeves, Steven Kirk, the curator of the George Reeve Memorial, responded, "George Reeves is frozen in time, like fellow Hollywood icons Marilyn Monroe and James Dean. He will forever be TV's Superman. And for almost half a century, that was the end of the George Reeves story. But fortunately 'Honest George' has a legion of dedicated fans, writers and historians in his corner. He is not destined to be remembered as 'The guy who played Superman and killed himself,' but as George Reeves, actor-director and philanthropist whose untimely death may have robbed the world of a true Superman, but left an indelible legacy. Even now, plans are underway in his hometown of Woolstock, Iowa to restore the home he was born in and build a museum honoring his life and career.

"Like a certain Man of Steel, George Reeves endures. His fans will make certain of that."[277]

6

The Middle Years

Superpup and Superboy

As if the final season of *Adventures of Superman* wasn't juvenile enough, in 1957 Whitney Ellsworth began searching for a way to make Superman appeal to an even younger audience—the toddler, preschool demographic. His solution was a rather bizarre one, *The Adventures of Superpup*. The idea was to create the equivalent of a live-action cartoon. Collaborating with writer Cal Howard, Ellsworth developed a script in which the city of Pupopolis was threatened by the villainous Professor Sheepdip and his sidekick Wolfingham. In the end, Professor Sheepdip was vanquished by Superpup, a superhero who disguised himself as mild-mannered reporter Bark Bent. Bark worked at *The Daily Bugle*, with fellow reporter Pamela Poodle and editor Terry Bite. Acting as narrator was Montmorency Mouse, who lived in Bark's desk.

All of the major characters would be portrayed by little people in dog masks, except for Montmorency Mouse, who was a hand puppet. With a script completed, Ellsworth took the concept to National Comics, who—amazingly—gave their approval. He then contacted the Allen-Shaw design firm, the company that had created the Howdy Doody puppet, to fabricate the character heads, which were made of lightweight fiberglass and weighed about four pounds each.[278]

As filming was winding down on the George Reeves Superman series, several of the crew on the ZIV lot were told that they would be kept on the payroll to work on a new pilot. Shooting began just one week after production of "All That Glitters," the final episode of *Adventures of Superman*, was finished. To save money, *Superpup* filmed on the same sets used for Superman, and—like the series that inspired it—it was filmed in color. Ellsworth, sure the series would catch on, augmented the budget with money from his own pocket.

Billy Curtis was hired to play the lead role of Superpup/Bark Bent. Curtis was no stranger to the Superman universe. In 1951, he was one of the mole men in *Superman and the Mole Men*, and in a 1956 episode of *Adventures of Superman*, he played Mr. Zero, a Martian. Curtis was a show business veteran; one of his earliest roles was in 1939's *The Wizard of Oz*, in which he appeared as a Munchkin.[279] Newspaper editor Terry Bite was played by Angelo Rossito, whose most high-profile roles paired him with Hollywood bogeyman Bela Lugosi in *Spooks Run Wild* (1941), *The Corpse Vanishes* (1942) and *Scared to Death* (1947). The villain, sheepdog Professor Sheepdip, was played by Harry Monty. The cast was rounded out with other little people brought in by Billy Curtis. His friend Frank Delfino played

Sergeant Beagle (the Inspector Henderson equivalent), while Sadie and Ruth Delfino played Wolfingham and Pamela Poodle.[280] The performers in the canine masks did not actually provide the voices for their characters; those came courtesy of voice actors sitting on the edge of the set, speaking the lines as the costumed actors acted them out.[281]

Working at the same pace as the parent production, filming of *Superpup* was completed in less than a week. The next step was to find a sponsor. Ellsworth had a black-and-white print prepared, and held a surprise screening in a Los Angeles theater to judge the audience reaction. To his disappointment, the screening was a flop; the audience saw the pilot for the abysmal misfire it was. The West Coast sponsors in attendance were unenthused, so the program was sent to National Comics in New York. There was no interest there, either, so the show was put into the vaults and forgotten.[282]

The idea of a Superman-like program aimed at very small children did not die, however; in fact, such a program had already been around for more than a decade. In early 1942, Izzy Klein, a writer working for Paul Terry's Terrytoons company, pitched the idea for Super Fly, an insignificant insect with Superman-like powers. Terry didn't go for that idea, but he could see it had promise. Shortly thereafter, he put his own spin on it and developed Super Mouse, a combination of Superman and Mickey Mouse. He immediately set his animators to work, and on October 16, 1942, the character was introduced to theater audiences in a short color film called "The Mouse of Tomorrow." A follow-up, "Frankenstein's Cat," was released on November 27.[283]

At roughly the same time, another character called Super Mouse made his debut in Nedor Comics' *Coo Coo Comics*, published in October 1942. To save confusion, Terry renamed his rodent hero Mighty Mouse. In his earliest appearances, Mighty Mouse had a costume with the same coloring as Superman's, blue and red with a yellow belt. As the series of color cartoon shorts progressed, the costume changed to yellow and red. In 1945, Terry decided to go back to making cartoons where the characters sung their lines opera-style instead of speaking them, a formula that had proven successful for him in the late 1930s. On January 12, 1945, "Mighty Mouse and the Pirates," the first operatic Mighty Mouse cartoon, was released. Thereafter, Mighty Mouse would fly into action singing "Here I come to save the day!" On August 3, 1945, the Mighty Mouse short "Gypsy Life" was released; it would be nominated for a Best Short Subject Oscar (it lost to "Quiet Please!," a *Tom and Jerry* cartoon produced by Fred Quimby).[284]

Paul Terry sold his studio to CBS in 1955, and the network packaged the catalog of Mighty Mouse cartoons as *Mighty Mouse Playhouse*. The program aired on Saturday mornings from 1955 until 1967.[285]

A more direct descendant of *Superpup* was Leonardo Productions' *Underdog*, which debuted on NBC on October 3, 1964. Voiced by milquetoast character actor Wally Cox, Underdog was a small dog with a potbelly and ill-fitting uniform who flew to the rescue saying, "There's no need to fear, Underdog is here!" (Underdog only spoke in four beat iambic verse). Underdog's Lois Lane was a poodle named Sweet Polly Purebread; his primary villain was a mean-looking gangster dog named Simon Bar Sinister, but he also saved Polly from the clutches of Overcat and Fearo the Ferocious. When not performing heroic deeds, Underdog masqueraded as a humble shoeshine boy named Shoe Shine Boy.[286]

Though *The Adventures of Superpup* had failed to interest sponsors, Whitney Ellsworth was not finished with his attempts to bring another Superman-related series to television. In 1961, he hired producer/writer Vernon Clark to help him co-write episodes of a proposed series based on DC Comics' spin-off series, Superboy. Clark, the head writer at ZIV Studios, had been a producer of such shows as *Highway Patrol* and *Rough Riders*. He wrote three stories with Ellsworth, who wanted to develop thirteen stories and have them ready to go into production immediately if the series was picked up. Another script was written with Paul Harber, and the remaining nine were co-written with Robert Leslie Bellem, who had worked with Ellsworth on several scripts for the *Adventures of Superman* series.[287]

One of the Vernon Clark scripts, "Rajah's Ransom," was chosen to be the pilot episode. Chuck Harter, author of *Cult Movies Presents Superboy & Superpup: The Lost Videos*, noted that an eight-page story called "The Saddest Boy in Smallville," which was nearly identical to the "Rajah's Ransom" script, appeared in issue number 88 of the Superboy comic book in April 1961. Given that Ellsworth was still employed by National Comics, this was likely more than just a coincidence.[288]

With the pilot scripts completed, Whitney Ellsworth began contacting crewmembers from the *Adventures of Superman* series to see if they would be available. Ben Chapman, who had been production manager on Superman, took time off from his duties on the *Flipper* series to come and work on the pilot.[289] Another Superman veteran, George Blair, was hired to direct.[290] Only one thing was missing: Superboy.

From his office at ZIV Studios, Ellsworth announced that he was auditioning actors for Superboy. John Rockwell, a 23-year-old actor on the lot, went to Ellsworth's office while on a break, and found the producer playing gin with the studio head. "You don't have to look any further," Rockwell said, "I can fly." Rockwell said he would take on the winner of the gin game, and ended up playing against Ellsworth. He won the game, and after a brief screen test, won the role. He later said that he felt like he got the role because he was a good gin player.[291] To play Lana Lang, the romantic interest of the teenaged Superboy, Ellsworth hired a young blonde actress named Bunny Henning, who was awarded the role over three other finalists, Trudy Ellison, Marlo Ryan and Mary Ann Roberts.[292] Another Superman veteran, Richard Reeves (no relation to George), was hired to play one of the heavies.[293]

Since the series was to be filmed in black-and-white, John Rockwell was sent to Western Costume to be fitted for a gray and brown Superboy uniform. Shooting began with location work in Griffith Park on April 4, 1961.[294] A natural athlete with gymnastic ability, Rockwell had no trouble executing Superboy's take offs and landings. When he took flight, he ran toward the camera and dived over it, without the aid of a springboard. His landings, like those of George Reeves, were accomplished by having him jump off an out-of-camera-range stepladder.[295]

On April 5, interior scenes were filmed at ZIV on sets of the Kent home, a Smallville High School classroom and the office of Police Chief Parker. On the third day, the crew moved to the Aero Theater in Santa Monica to shoot all of the scenes involving a movie theater.[296]

All of the flying scenes were filmed the following week. Rockwell was suspended on wires and filmed in various flying poses from different angles. These shots were then electronically superimposed over background plates with the use of a video generator. The end result was rather primitive, but allowed for a greater variety of flying shots than those seen in *Adventures of Superman*.[297]

Everyone involved in the production of the show felt they had a winner. Ellsworth held a screening for potential sponsors at ZIV, and Wheaties offered to sponsor the show. However, Kellogg's didn't want a rival cereal company sponsoring a program that was so similar to *Adventures of Superman*, which was still going strong in syndication, so the deal fell through. The print of the show was sent to National Comics in New York, where it was locked away in a vault, never to be seen again.[298] In recent years, both *Superpup* and *Superboy* have surfaced on DVDs traded among private collectors, and in 2006 Warner

Bros. included *The Adventures of Superpup* on the *Ultimate Collectors Edition Superman* boxed set DVDs.

The Singing Superman

By the mid–60s, America was deep in the throes of pop culture. In years past, anything that had mass appeal was looked upon as lowbrow. Now, highbrow intellectuals had learned to enjoy comic books. Roy Lichtenstein's paintings of comic book panels celebrated the urban consumer experience, as did the works of Andy Warhol and Jasper Johns. At the height of this movement, artist, playwright and novelist Jules Feiffer published the book *The Great Comic Book Heroes* (The Dial Press, New York, 1965), which legitimized the reading of comic books for adults as well as children. He argued that comic books are junk, but necessary junk, providing good, solid entertainment for the masses.

The mid–60s were also a time when the word "camp" was being used to describe much of popular culture. Camp derives from the French word "camper," which means "to pose in an exaggerated fashion." Things that were given a camp interpretation were exaggerated, outlandish and—most of all—fun. "You can't camp about something you don't take seriously," Christopher Isherwood wrote in his 1954 novel *The World in the Evening*. "You're not making fun of it; you're making fun *out* of it. You're expressing what's basically serious to you in terms of fun and artifice and elegance."

What was serious to David Newman and Robert Benton was their commitment to Broadway songwriters Charles Strouse and Lee Adams. Strouse and Adams literally scored hits in 1960 with the Elvis Presley spoof, *Bye Bye Birdie* and with the 1964 musical version of Clifford Odets' play *Golden Boy*. Looking for a follow-up, the dynamic musical duo approached former *Esquire* writers Newman and Benton (Newman was the magazine's editor, Benton the art director, when they decided to begin collaborating on articles for other magazines).[299] According to an article Newman and Benton wrote for *The New York Herald Tribune*, Strouse and Adams came to them and asked if, having done okay in magazines, they'd like to get rich. The writing partners felt there was only one answer.[300]

Benton and Newman began looking for an idea to adapt into a musical. They didn't just want to adapt an old movie, so what would it be? The answer came when Newman's wife picked a Superman comic book up from their child's bedroom floor and asked, "How about this for a musical?"[301] Newman and Benton went to Strouse and Adams with their new idea. "It sounds crazy," they said to the songwriters, "But it's Superman." The songwriters found it an inspired choice. It usually took them two years to write a show; *It's a Bird ... It's a Plane ... It's Superman* took them only thirteen months.[302] "Strouse and Adams took a big chance on us," Newman said. "They put up the money for the stage rights to the comic strip and they staked us while we wrote the play."[303]

When the draft was completed in the fall of 1965, Strouse and Adams took it to Harold Prince, one of Broadway's brightest star producer/directors. Prince wasted no time agreeing to stage it.[304] Six years earlier, Prince had produced a musical called *Fiorello!*, about former New York mayor Fiorello LaGuardia. The lead role was played by Tom Bosley, who two decades later would become a TV star as the dad on *Happy Days*. The mayor's assistant was played by a Broadway newcomer, Bob Holiday, who never missed a performance during the Pulitzer Prize–winning show's two-year run.[305] Now, Holiday was about to become Superman.

Bob Holiday was born in 1932 in Seagate, Brooklyn, New York. When he was two years old, his parents moved to New York City. As a child, Holiday enjoyed reading Superman comic books, and listening to the radio show with Bud Collyer. He also enjoyed singing; when he reached high school, he joined the glee club, becoming a soloist.[306] After graduation, he began entering talent contests. When he appeared on *Ted Mack's Original Amateur Hour*, he came in second with his impersonations of movie stars. Soon after, he joined the army. After basic training, he was sent to Germany, where he became a DJ for the Armed Forces Network.[307]

Holiday left the army in 1954. Deciding to pursue a showbiz career, he landed an agent and was soon performing in Manhattan nightclubs as an MC. Two years later, he went on the road, performing in clubs all over the country, including Jack Ruby's Dallas, Texas nightclub, the Colony Club.[308] By 1959, Holiday was back in New York, where he auditioned for the part in *Fiorello!* After that show ended, Holiday returned to night club and dinner theater work, performing with Jayne Mansfield and Mamie van Doren.[309] He then joined the touring company of *Camelot*, playing Lancelot opposite Howard Keel's King Arthur. From there, it was on to the touring company of *Lady in the Dark* with Jane Morgan.[310] After that show closed in August of 1965, Holiday once again went back to nightclub and commercial work. When he heard that Harold Prince was developing a new show for Broadway, he called Prince's casting director, who told him that auditions would be held soon, but wouldn't divulge the title of the musical. Holiday found out soon enough; a few days later, he saw in the newspaper that Prince was looking for an actor to play Superman. Holiday knew this was a once-in-a-lifetime opportunity. After reading Jules Feiffer's *The Great Comic Book Heroes* for inspiration, he went to the audition.[311]

Fifty-one other hopefuls showed up. Prince narrowed the field down to three: Holiday, Charles Rydell, and Don Bragg. Rydell had appeared in off–Broadway productions of *The Threepenny Opera* and *The Secret Life of Walter Mitty*. Bragg was a pole-vaulter who competed in the 1960 Olympics and had once been touted as a potential movie Tarzan. But whereas Rydell had the voice, and Bragg had the body, Holiday had the entire package: he could sing, he had Broadway experience, and he had the kind of body that would look good in blue tights. After a couple of callbacks, the 6'4" performer was told he had won the role.[312] Now that he was Superman, he gave up his two pack a day smoking habit.[313]

Holiday was fitted for a costume that would be worn over a leather flying harness he would wear for the duration of the play. In his book *Superman on Broadway*, written with Chuck Harter, Holiday wrote, "When I put it on for the first time, it was quite something to look in a full length mirror, and see 'Superman' looking back at me."[314]

Although Holiday had some reservations about the way some portions of the play portrayed Superman, he was determined to be the best Superman he could be. DC Comics gave him a tour of their offices, and he received some pointers from none other than Joe Shuster, one of Superman's creators.[315] The rest of the cast quickly fell into place. Joan Hotchkiss, who had appeared for two years as Myra Lake in the soap opera *Secret Storm*, was cast as Lois Lane. Tony winner and Broadway veteran Jack Cassidy was given star billing as gossip columnist Max Mencken, a parody of Walter Winchell. Linda Lavin (later the star of the 1970s TV series *Alice*) played Sydney, and Michael O'Sullivan, an Obie Award Winner, was hired to play the villain, Dr. Abner Sedgwick, a scientist driven to evil after being repeatedly passed over for the Nobel Prize.[316] Sedgwick almost defeats Superman by using psychology; he convinces the Man of Tomorrow that he's an egotist who performs his deeds out of a deep need to be loved, and breaks the superhero's heart when he turns the citizens of Metropolis against him. David Newman said the plotline was suggested by reading the Superman comic books, where he and Benton noticed that the two great dangers that kept repeating "were Superman being destroyed and Superman being unmasked. So we combined them."[317]

Holiday, with his pleasing baritone voice, had three solo songs in the show. "Being Good" opened the musical. "The Strongest Man in the World" was an ironically titled song in which the Man of Steel laments how the strongest man in the world can be the saddest man in the world. "Pow! Bam! Zonk!" closed the show, as Superman beat the heck out of a gang of Chinese acrobat criminals.[318]

While the show was in rehearsals in Philadelphia, the ABC network decided to begin broadcasting a program that was originally slated to kick off the Fall season, but with the network's season going down in flames in the ratings, they came up with a gimmick they called the "Second Season," and decided to premiere one of their new hopefuls early, on January 12, 1966. The show was *Batman*. Airing twice a week, with a cliffhanger episode on Wednesday that was concluded on Thursday, *Batman* quickly became a media sensation, and added a new word to the nation's vocabulary: Batmania. The overwhelming success of the Caped Crusader would have adverse effects on the upcoming Man of Steel musical.

It's a Bird ... It's a Plane ... It's Superman was set to preview in Philadelphia on February 12 and 14, 1966.[319] Audiences for the previews responded with standing ovations, but when the show began its Philadelphia run on the 15th, the critics came down on it like a load of Kryptonite bricks. Ron Snyder of local station KYW-TV proclaimed, "It's a bird, It's a plane, It's a bomb."[320]

Harold Prince felt the Philadelphia critics just didn't get the show. He hoped that by the time they reached Broadway, the problems could be ironed out. He ended the previews a week early.[321] One of the casualties of the harsh reviews was Joan Hotchkiss, who was replaced in the role of Lois Lane by seasoned Broadway veteran Patricia Marand, who had appeared with Jack Cassidy in a 1952 production of *Wish You Were Here* (and prior to that, both had had bit parts in *South Pacific*).[322] Two songs that had been written for Hotchkiss, "A Woman Alone" and "I'm Too Young to Die," were also dropped from the show. Two new songs were introduced, "It's Superman" and "I'm Not Finished Yet." "The Superman March" was also scrapped; in its place, Jack Cassidy was given another song, "So Long, Big Guy." There was a lot riding on the show; Columbia Records had put up $250,000 to stage it, while private investors had kicked in another $400,000.[323]

As rehearsals began for the show's Broadway opening, a decoration appeared outside Bob Holiday's dressing room at the Alvin Theatre. It was a poster of Batman, but written on it were the words, "This looks like a job for Superman!"[324] For the moment, however, Batman had the upper hand. Bob Holiday, as Superman, was supposed to grace the cover of *LIFE* magazine's March 11, 1966 issue. At the last minute, however, he was replaced by Adam West as Batman, a reflection of the Caped Crusader's enormously growing popularity.[325]

The show was set to open at the Alvin on March 29, with previews beginning March 17.[326] On March 21, Holiday, as Superman, appeared on *I've Got a Secret*, a game show hosted by Steve Allen. Holiday's secret was "I'm going to teach Steve Allen to fly like Superman tonight." After the celebrity panel guessed his secret, Holiday joined Steve Allen on the stage, where both were rigged to wire harnesses. The resulting brief bit of video is perhaps the only existing footage of Holiday as the Man of Steel, and he cuts a fine figure in his Superman uniform, with a very authoritative "Up, up and away!" as he takes to the air. The clip can now be seen on Holiday's website, www.supermanbobholiday.com.[327]

By opening night, the cast was ready to win over the tough New York critics. They felt their show was a winner, and they were anxious to prove it. Bob Holiday played Superman to the hilt, Jack Cassidy and Michael O'Sullivan were appropriately slimy and evil, Patricia Marand was a winning Lois Lane, and Linda Lavin, as Sydney, nearly stopped the show with her rendition of "You've Got Possibilities," sung to Holiday's Clark Kent. When the show ended, the audience rose in a standing ovation. Harold Prince, Strouse and Adams, Benton and Newman and the cast all felt they had pulled it off. They knew they had a hit. They stayed up celebrating until the early morning hours, anxiously awaiting the reviews in the morning papers.[328]

The reviews were glowing. Stanley Kauffmann of *The New York Times* wrote, "It is easily the best musical so far this season, but, because that is so damp a compliment, I add at once that it would be enjoyable in any season."[329] Norman Nadel of *The New York World Telegram and Sun* said, "This must be said for 'Superman': you leave the theater smiling, and the smile lasts all the way home."[330] Whitney Bolton of *The New York Morning Telegram* praised the show's star: "Bob Holiday, tall, wide of shoulder, slim of waist, the embodiment of Superman, makes the show come alive and sparkle. His portrait of a ponderous human miracle, in love with good deeds and unabashed virtue, is delightful."[331] John McClain of *The*

Brawny baritone Bob Holiday as Superman and Patricia Marand as Lois Lane in the 1966 Broadway production *It's a Bird ... It's a Plane ... It's Superman.* To promote the show, Holiday made an appearance on *I've Got a Secret!* with Steve Allen. Clips of Holiday teaching Allen how to fly can be seen at Holiday's website, www.supermanbobholiday.com (Photofest).

New York Journal-American said, "The whole story makes very little sense ... [it] is a wild interpretation of the adventures of this towering do-gooder who works part-time on a newspaper but who is never too busy to take off in flight to stamp out evil, wherever he hears about it. 'Superman' is a crazy conception, but it has style and speed."[332]

One dissenting voice came from Cecil Smith, the Broadway correspondent of *The Los Angeles Times.* In his review— in which he erroneously referred to the show's lead as Tom Holiday—Smith wrote that knocking Superman was like knocking the Easter Bunny, adding, "the new Broadway musical wrought from the old comic strip is only sporadically amusing and tends to grow tiresome ... Prince has staged the show with a nice brisk pace and an open vaudeville look. But the whole doesn't seem to have the POW! BAM! BANG! it needs."[333]

Not surprisingly, the matinee performances drew large numbers of children. Holiday remained in his Superman costume after the matinees and invited the kids backstage for autographs. Towering over his young fans, the 6'4" actor signed their programs and admonished them to drink their milk and be good.[334]

As the show progressed, the inevitable happened—Bob Holiday experienced a George Reeves moment. During one performance, as he was flying in on an entrance, the shackle of his flying harness broke. Holiday fell about six feet to the stage. Without breaking character, he sprang to his feet, puts his hands on his hips, looked into the audience and said, "*That* would have hurt any mortal man!" "The audience," Holiday wrote in *Superman on Broadway*, "screamed, cheered and gave me a standing ovation."[335]

In May, the show's cast album was released. Holiday made a personal appearance at Macy's, where he was mobbed by kids. He signed their albums "Up, up and away!"[336] By the following month, however, the audience was declining. Since there were more kids attending, producer Harold Prince added another matinee; after its initial success, it seemed now that the show's real audience was the kids.[337] By July, it was clear to all involved that the show had run its course. It closed on July 17, 1966, after the Sunday matinee performance, having run for 129 performances.[338] Charles Strouse said later that while they thought they would ride the crest of the Pop Art wave with the show, Broadway audiences didn't seem to be aware of the trend. Since *Batman* was at the top of its popularity by the time the show opened, David Newman had another explanation—he said the Broadway Superman was killed by "capelash."[339]

Capelash or no, it also didn't help that the Superman tuner opened in a Broadway season that saw strong musicals such as *Man of La Mancha, Mame* and *Sweet Charity*. Harold Prince, it seems, learned the inevitable lesson; his next Broadway venture was the decidedly less campy *Cabaret*.[340]

In *Superman on Broadway*, Bob Holiday wrote, "Over the years, I have thought about any reasons why the show closed after 129 performances. The incredible pop phenomenon of the *Batman* TV show with Adam West must have been a factor, but I've never been able to pinpoint the exact impact it had. There had to have been other reasons as well but I've never been able to really understand them."[341]

When it came time for the announcement of Tony Award nominations on June 1, 1966, *It's a Bird ... It's a Plane ... It's Superman* was not forgotten. Jack Cassidy, Michael O'Sullivan and Patricia Marand were all nominated. Marand won the 1965–1966 Tony for Best Actress in a Supporting or Featured Role in a Musical for her performance as Lois Lane, beating out contenders Beatrice Arthur (for *Mame*), Helen Gallagher (for *Sweet Charity*) and Charlotte Rae (for *Pickwick*).[342]

After the show ended its run, Bob Holiday went to Los Angeles, where he made some commercials and did some tests for Screen Gems. In early 1967, he was asked to once again put on the blue tights and cape and take the show on the road to St. Louis and Kansas City. He leapt at the opportunity.[343] The play was produced at the Municipal Opera in St. Louis, which was an outdoor venue. Since there was no ceiling over the stage, there was nowhere to secure the pulley for the wires that lifted Superman into flight. The problem was solved when a construction crane was situated behind the stage, allowing Superman to soar much higher than he ever did on Broadway.[344] At the play's climax, for the scene where Dr. Sedgwick and the Flying Lings are awaiting a helicopter to fly them to Red China, an actual helicopter hovered over the stage. It was the weather helicopter from St. Louis radio station KMOX, and is thought to have been the first time an actual helicopter was used in a stage production (take THAT, *Miss Saigon!* BAM! POW!).[345]

Holiday was the only member of the Broadway cast to go on the road. In St. Louis and

Kansas City, Charles Nelson Reilly played the part of the villainous Dr. Abner Sedgewick; years later, Reilly would become the court jester of Burt Reynolds' rat pack, and a director at Reynolds dinner theater in Jupiter, Florida.[346] On opening night, the Municipal Opera had the largest opening night audience it had ever experienced, with kids and adults all cheering the heroics of Superman. The enthusiasm carried over to the local critics, who praised the production.[347]

The show was equally successful in Kansas City, and after it ended, Bob Holiday hung up his Superman uniform for good ... well, sort of. He was back in the recording studio to supply the voice of Superman for a kids' album called "The Official Adventures of Superman," recorded for Leo the Lion Records, a children's division of MGM.[348] Then he returned to Hollywood, hoping to capitalize on his Superman success. He appeared in more TV commercials, and tested for several pilots. Finally, his patience was rewarded when he landed the role of the father in the pilot for a new series producer Sherwood Schwartz was preparing for ABC called *The Brady Bunch*. This was just the break Holiday had been waiting for. But it was not to be. At the eleventh hour, the network overrode Schwartz's casting choice and replaced Holiday with veteran TV actor Robert Reed. Dispirited, Holiday again left Hollywood. He toured in more musicals, including stints in *Mame* with Ann Miller and *Promises, Promises* with Tony Roberts. Eventually, the one-time Man of Steel settled in Hawley, Pennsylvania, and started his own home design business, Bob Holiday Homes.[349] He reconnected with his Man of Steel past in June 2003 when he appeared at the 25th annual Superman festival in Metropolis, Illinois. That same year, he published *Superman on Broadway*.[350]

As for the play, it arrived on television as a hastily produced entry of ABC's late-night *Wide World Special*, opposite NBC's *Tonight Show*, on February 21, 1975. Produced by Norman Twain and directed by Jack Regas, who had been the choreographer of two Elvis Presley films and TV's *The Flip Wilson Show* (1970), *It's a Bird ... It's a Plane ... It's Superman* was shot on video over the course of three days on what appeared to be a shoestring budget. Many fans consider this one-shot program to be a bomb, with its camp humor, cheesy effects, and less-than-stirring song-and-dance numbers, but it is the closest thing that exists to a video record of the 1966 Broadway show. The play was adapted for TV by Romeo Muller, who began his career in the days of live television with episodes of the anthology series *Studio One*. In the early 1960s, he became a writer for puppet animation producers Arthur Rankin Jr. and Jules Bass, penning such Rankin-Bass holiday classics as *Rudolph the Red-Nosed Reindeer* (1964), *Frosty the Snowman* (1969) and *Santa Claus Is Comin' to Town* (1970).[351]

To make the program seem more timely, Muller discarded the Flying Lings, replacing them with Roaring 20s-style gangsters (a nod to the then-popular *Godfather* films), one of whom was played by Al Molinaro, better known as Al Delvecchio on the hit TV series *Happy Days* (1976–1982). The gangsters were given a new production number, "It's a Great Country." To squeeze the production into a 90-minute slot, the songs "Doing Good," "It's Super Nice," "So Long, Big Guy," and "We Don't Matter at All" were dropped from the TV presentation.[352]

In keeping with the spirit of the Broadway production, the sets were made to look as if they were drawn instead of built, a conceit that worked considerably better on Broadway than in the broadcast.

The part of Dr. Abner Sedgwick, played by a relatively young man in the Broadway production, was essayed by venerable actor David Wayne, who relished being evil—a marked departure from his good-guy chores on the *Ellery Queen* TV show (1975); this role was more of a throwback to his portrayal of The Mad Hatter on the *Batman* TV series (1966–68). Lois Lane was played with perky ditziness by Lesley Ann Warren (billed here as Lesley Warren), who first gained prominence in a 1965 televised version of Rodgers & Hammerstein's *Cinderella*. Max Mencken, the role Jack Cassidy played in the original, was played by Kenneth Mars, fresh from his duties in Mel Brooks's *Young Frankenstein*. Loretta Swit played Sydney, showing singing talents she never displayed as "Hot Lips" Houlihan in the TV series *M*A*S*H* (1972–1983), and Allen Ludden, host of the TV game show *Password* (1961–1975) was a Perry White without bite.

And then there was Superman....

David Wilson did his best to look like Superman but was hampered by the cheapest Superman outfit ever assembled and a bushy 1970s haircut that made him appear more like singer/actor Mac Davis. Wilson handled some of the duties capably; the scene where a despondent Superman opines about how the strongest man in the world has the heaviest heart in the world was nicely rendered, with his voice dropping octaves *à la* Bud Collyer as he shifted personas from Clark Kent to Superman and back again when Professor Sedgewick dropped in unexpectedly. It was as Clark Kent that Wilson failed miserably. He was more than meek—he was somnambulistically mousey; no wonder Lois kept failing to notice him when he was right in front of her. Ultimately overplaying the camp, the miscast actor never seemed to hit his stride in the dual role.

In recent years, *It's a Bird, It's a Plane, It's Superman!* has been dusted off and restaged. The Goodspeed Opera House in East Haddam, Connecticut revived it in 1992 with a cast that included Gary Jackson as Superman, Kay McClelland as Lois Lane, Gabriel Barre as Dr. Abner Sedgewick, Jamie Ross as Max Mencken and Jan Neuberger as Sydney. With the shifting political climate, the Flying Lings were now the Flying Fahzumis, an Arabian tumbling troupe. In his *New York Times* review, Stephen Holden noted that Jackson's Superman did not have a voice to match his looks, and said the supporting roles "are overplayed vaudevillian cartoons in a production that has been staged like a traveling circus."[353]

The musical was scheduled for the 2002 season of the New York City Center's *Encores! Great American Musicals in Concert* series, but since the first act concludes with Dr. Sedgewick blowing up Metropolis's City Hall, it was thought best to cancel the production in the wake of the events of September 11, 2001.[354] It eventually took flight on the West Coast in October 2006, when the Showtimes Theater Company in Kirkland, Washington presented a concert version of the musical, with composer Charles Strouse giving a talk afterwards.[355]

Saturday Morning Superman

Even before *It's a Bird ... It's a Plane ... It's Superman!* opened on Broadway, plans were being made to bring a new version of the superhero to television. On December 30, 1965, *The Los Angeles Times* announced that CBS and National Periodical Publications, Inc. had made a deal to produce *The New Adventures of Superman*, a half-hour color cartoon series that would begin airing on Saturday mornings beginning in September of 1966.[356]

The New Adventures of Superman was the first program produced by Filmation Studios, an animation company formed in 1963 by two animators, Lou Scheimer and Hal Sutherland, and former radio announcer Norm Prescott. After a couple of years of producing TV commercials and documentaries, Filmation won the rights to make an animated Superman series.[357]

The New Adventures of Superman was one of the first Saturday morning series to feature human (and Kryptonian) characters instead of cute animals or exaggerated comic characters like Popeye. In order to cut costs, Filmation's animators relied on Max Fleischer's innovative rotoscoping technique. In Gary Grossman's *Saturday Morning TV* (Dell Publishing

Co., Inc., 1981), Norm Prescott explained, "To rotoscope, first we shoot the action with live actors in black and white, directing them to run, swim, jump or whatever it is that we need. Next we blow up those little 35 mm frames. Then we trace them, taking just the perimeter line of the action, and draw into those lines the animated character's face and features. Finally, we ink, paint, and photograph those scenes and they really look fully animated."[358] Well ... sort of. Filmation used limited animation—fewer animation cels used per second of finished film—and used wide background cels that the camera would pan across very slowly, thus requiring less actual animation. But what the cartoons lacked in animation technique, they compensated for with imaginative stories, many written by the same writers who were providing stories for the *Superman* comic books. "*Superman* pulled animation out of the barnyard and gave viewers far-out plots," said Prescott.[359]

Allen Ducovny of National Periodical Publications, who had supervised the production of *Superman* on radio, became executive producer of the animated series. One of the first challenges was finding an actor to provide the voice of Clark Kent and Superman. For Ducovny, it was a no-brainer. He simply called Bud Collyer.

Not only did Collyer, the one-time radio Superman, return to voice the lead, but radio's Lois Lane and Jimmy Olsen—Joan Alexander and Jack Grimes—also signed on (although for about half the episodes, the voice of Lois Lane was actress Julie Bennett). Ted Knight, who would later gain fame as addle-brained newscaster Ted Baxter on TV's *The Mary Tyler Moore Show*, was the voice of Perry White, and Cliff Owens was the voice of Lex Luthor. The half hour series featured three cartoons per episode, with one *Superboy* cartoon sandwiched between two *Superman* adventures. For *Superboy*, Bob Hastings provided the voice of the young Clark Kent and Superboy and Janet Waldo voiced Lana Lang. The announcer for the series was another veteran of radio's *Adventures of Superman*, Jackson Beck.[360]

The program premiered on September 10, 1966. For the first season, Filmation produced eighteen *Superboy* and thirty-six *Superman* adventures.[361] The show was a hit, and typecast Filmation as "the superhero company."[362] By the time the second season kicked off on September 9, 1967, the show had expanded to one hour, and was now called *The Superman-Aquaman Hour of Adventure*. There were still two *Superman* episodes bookending a *Superboy* episode, but now the time slot was filled out with *Aquaman* cartoons. Marvin Miller provided the voice of Aquaman for 36 eight-minute adventures. There were also cartoons featuring other superhero characters—*The Atom* (three cartoons), *The Flash* (three cartoons), *Green Lantern* (three cartoons), *Hawkman* (three cartoons), *Justice League of America* (three cartoons), and *Teen Titans* (three cartoons). Sixteen new *Superman* cartoons and eight new *Superboy* cartoons were produced for the new season.

By the third season, the show changed its title again. When it premiered on September 14, 1968, it was now called *The Batman/Superman Hour*, alternating a new season of *Superboy* and *Superman* cartoons with thirty-four *Batman* cartoons. The voice of Batman was provided by veteran character actor Olan Soulé, who, though he had a great voice for the Caped Crusader, was hardly the superhero type. Physically, he was very slight of build and looked like your average, bespectacled church choir director—a role he played in several episodes of *The Andy Griffith Show* in the early 1960s. Ted Knight, besides providing Perry White's voice for *Superman*, also became the voice of Alfred the Butler and The Riddler. Robin was voiced by Casey Kasem of *American Top 40* fame. "The first thing that I ever did in voice-over in Hollywood was the audition for Robin," said Kasem, "and I got the part, and we did 75 shows for Filmation. That was the beginning of my career in voice work, and cartoons and commercials and being the voice of NBC for four or five years."[363]

After the 1968–69 TV season, Filmation produced no new Superman adventures, but the Man of Steel appeared in an episode of another Filmation series, *The Brady Kids*, on October 7, 1972. The episode, entitled "Cindy's Super Friends," had Superman helping Cindy Brady foil a bank robbery planned by Toulouse La Trick.[364] The voice of Superman was provided by Keith Sutherland,[365] who was also the voice of Jackie Turner on Filmation's *Lassie's Rescue Rangers* series (1973) and voiced several characters for the animated *Star Trek* series (1973).[366] Filmation also animated Superman for a segment of the popular PBS educational series *Sesame Street*, with the superhero teaching kids about the letter "S."

During 1973, the rights to DC Comics superheroes passed from Filmation to another powerhouse of Saturday morning animation, Hanna-Barbera. William Hanna and Joseph Barbera made their reputations at MGM, producing award-winning *Tom & Jerry* shorts. When MGM shut down its animation department in 1957, Hanna and Barbera began producing cartoons for the new medium of television. In 1960, they changed their corporate name from H–B Enterprises to Hanna-Barbera Productions, and began producing shows for all three TV networks. In the 1960s, they produced such classics as *The Huckleberry Hound Show, The Yogi Bear Show, The Flintstones, Jonny Quest* and *Scooby-Doo*. After gaining the rights to the DC Comics characters, Hanna-Barbera set about adapting the popular comic book *Justice League of America* for television. Toning down the violence and skewing the show to a younger audience, the concept was called *The Super Friends*.[367]

The first of sixteen one-hour *Super Friends* episodes debuted on ABC on September 8, 1973. *The Super Friends* teamed Superman, Batman and Robin, Wonder Woman and Aquaman with two teenagers, Marvin and Wendy, and their pet Wonder Dog. The plots had a common theme—none of the superheroes was able to solve the problems on their own; they only prevailed through their efforts as a team. Comic book artist Alex Toth was on hand to make sure the cartoon versions of the National Periodical Publications heroes did not stray too far from their comic book incarnations, and National's editors and writers Carmine Infantino, E. Nelson Bridwell and Julius Schwartz acted as story consultants.[368]

With the passing of Bud Collyer, a new voice for Superman had to be found. The producers turned to Los Angeles radio DJ Danny Dark. Born Daniel Croskery in Oklahoma City, Oklahoma on December 19, 1938, Danny Dark was raised in Tulsa and went to Central High School. English teacher Isabelle E. Ronan trained him for a vocal career; among other pupils she had mentored were actor Tony Randall and radio stalwart Paul Harvey. Danny, a musician, was always a part of bands in high school. He eventually led his own band, the DC's, or Danny Croskery Band, in which he played the trumpet. The band recorded a 45rpm record of *The Tijuana Two-Step*. A jazz lover, he once ran away from home to go to Birdland in New York City, where he met Chet Baker and other jazz greats. While attending Drury University in Springfield, Missouri, Dark started his DJ career at the age of nineteen with radio station KICK. "Danny Croskery had been doing hard labor in the humidity of summer when his older brother, Robert Croskery, landed a job in an air-conditioned radio studio as a DJ," said Danny Dark's daughter, Caroline. "So while working in the humid swamps of wherever he was, he thought that his brother's air-conditioned job spinning records was really where he needed to be. He took over this job from his big brother, who went on to be a preacher. Of course the name Danny Croskery was a mouthful, and his first day of radio they kept him on the air, changing his name every hour or so until they settled on Danny Dark."[369]

After moving on to other stations in Tulsa, Cleveland, New Orleans, Miami and St. Louis, he migrated west and landed at KLAC in Los Angeles in 1963. With the help of L.A. radio pioneer Chuck Blore, he broke into the lucrative voice-over market. He began lending his voice to TV commercials and became an indelible part of pop culture with lines like

"This Bud's for you," "Raid kills bugs dead" and—for Starkist tuna—"Sorry, Charlie." His commercial success led to his becoming the voice of NBC before he was chosen to be the voice of Superman.[370] "He had the most beautiful voice," said Casey Kasem. "You couldn't have made that voice more beautiful than God did."[371]

One *Super Friends* episode told the origin story of Superman. Olan Soulé and Shannon Farnon, who were the voices of Batman and Wonder Woman on the program, provided the voices of Jonathan and Martha Kent. Casey Kasem and Sherry Alberoni were the voices of Jor-El and Lara.

Kasem had known Danny Dark for over a decade when they were both hired for *The Super Friends*. "I met Danny Dark on a street corner in Cleveland, Ohio in 1960, when we were both disc jockeys," said Kasem, "and we spent some time talking and he said, 'You know, I don't really want to be a disc jockey.' And I said, 'what do you want to do?' And he said, 'I want to do voice work. I want to be doing commercials.' And, son of a gun, if that didn't all come true in Hollywood. So we knew each other, and had great respect for one another's talent."[372]

The Super Friends proved to be a popular format, and would reappear in several incarnations over the next decade. In 1977, Hanna-Barbera produced *The All-New Super Friends Hour*. For this series, Marvin, Wendy and Wonder Dog were dropped from the roster. Superman, Batman, Robin, Wonder Woman and Aquaman were now joined by two shape-altering aliens, Wonder Twins Zan and Jayna, and their alien monkey, Gleek. Zan could turn into any kind of liquid or ice, Jana could turn into any animal. Gleek was comedy relief.

Dark's youngest daughter, Sydney Croskery, recalled that the rehearsals for *Super Friends* were often more entertaining than the final programs. "Danny loved to work hard, play hard, laugh a lot," she said. "The group sat around a round table with microphones and practiced lines. We know that the bloopers that happened were one his favorite parts of the experience. They were raucously funny and crude, speaking in their superhero voices yet saying off the wall and crude remarks. One of the smaller parts in the show was truly a star at rehearsals, Michael Bell, the voice of Gleek, the Wonder Twin's monkey. The only joke I can recall is of Michael Bell telling Catwoman he could see she farted as there was a bubble in her skin-tight cat suit."[373]

The following year, the show became *Challenge of the Super Friends*. In this version, the Justice League of America was pitted against the Legion of Doom, a group of thirteen super villains led by Lex Luthor operating out of The Hall of Doom, a secret lair hidden in a swamp. The Wonder Twins were absent from these adventures; in their place were a trio of new heroes created to provide a sense of ethnic diversity: Apache Chief, Black Vulcan and Samurai. However, their tenure was short-lived; by the next year, Apache Chief, Black Vulcan and Samurai were given the boot, and Wonder Twins Jayna and Zan and Gleek the alien monkey returned. The show was again renamed; it was now called *The World's Greatest Super Friends*, and mixed a handful of new episodes with earlier repeats.

When the 1980–81 season began, the title of the show was *The Super Friends Hour*. When the last of these programs was produced, the SuperFriends ended their five-year run. But you can't keep a good superhero down....

In September of 1984, the Super Friends were back on Saturday morning TV with sixteen new half-hour episodes broadcast under the title *Super Friends: The Legendary Super Powers Show*. Danny Dark was back as Superman, a role he would continue to play with the following year's *The Super Powers Team: Galactic Guardians*. "It's nice when they last a long time," said Casey Kasem, "and not all of them do, but *Super Friends* is one that did."[374]

As a voice actor, Danny Dark enjoyed his anonymity. "No one knew his face," said

Caroline Croskery, "though as soon as he spoke, people immediately recognized his voice and would ask what he did. Danny loved children, and he would never hesitate to perform the 'Up, up and away!' line to watch the wonder on children's faces." As Sydney Croskery recalled, "I have so many memories of being a child and standing with my neighborhood friends and making him say over and over again, 'Up, up and away!'"[375]

Like George Reeves before him, Danny Dark was very philanthropic, especially when it came to children. Caroline Croskery remembered, "At certain times in his life he was not only sponsoring children but actually donating time. Around the time of *The Super Friends* he volunteered at Vista Del Mar and set up a community garden for the kids that live there, which he often went over to and worked in.

"Danny Croskery, Danny Dark, was one of those truly charismatic, shining stars in your life. He stood out, he was not a wallflower, he had star power. At a party, he was the one you wanted to hang out with, and I am speaking even if the party consisted of just members of the family."[376]

Danny Dark died at age 65 on June 13, 2004, in Los Angeles from a pulmonary

Danny Dark, the voice of Superman in *Super Friends*. Before becoming the voice of the Man of Steel, Dark was known for his commercial catchphrases, like "This Bud's for you" for Budweiser and "Sorry, Charlie" for Starkist tuna (Photograph courtesy of JoBee Croskery, (c) JoBee Croskery).

hemorrhage. But as long as new generations of children enjoy *The Super Friends*, his legacy will live on. "He had a way of making everyone feel that they were the most special and fantastic person," said Sydney Croskery, "whether they were his children, best friends, or waiter at his favorite restaurant. Not only did he know everybody by name, he had affectionate crazy nicknames for all his loved ones. All were important for Danny Dark, just in the way that any random civilian was important and saved by Superman. I can say that Danny loved life, and loved people with an unmatched intensity."[377]

As America prepared to celebrate the Bicentennial in 1976, Superman seemed blasé, an old-fashioned character from a simpler time who was no longer relevant in an age of disco and sitcoms. He had become the stuff of kids shows and late-night parody, unhip and uncool ... but that was about to change.

7

You'll Believe a Man Can Fly

Superman: The Movie

The Bicentennial Year arrived with celebrations of old-fashioned American values and a resurgence of patriotism, something the country was hungry for after the tragedy of the Vietnam War and the scandals of Watergate. The values that were celebrated were the ones that Superman had always represented—truth, justice and the American Way. But jaded, cynical American film and TV producers couldn't see it. To them, Superman was kid stuff. It took a young film producer in Europe to understand the character's magical appeal.

In the 1930s, Jerry Siegel and Joe Shuster based Superman partly on Zorro, the swash-buckling Robin Hood of Spanish-era Los Angeles created by Johnston McCulley and brought to life in two silent films by the dashing Douglas Fairbanks. And in 1973, after the first of his two films based on Alexandre Dumas' warhorse novel *The Three Musketeers* was in release, film producer Ilya Salkind was walking down the Avenue Victor Hugo in Paris when he spotted a billboard for a *Zorro* movie (Salkind has said in interviews that it was the 1974 version starring French hearth-throb Alain Delon; in his book *The Making of Superman: The Movie*, David Michael Petrou writes that it was a re-release of the 1940 Tyrone Power version of *The Mark of Zorro*).[378] Salkind had come to Paris to discuss with his father, Alexander, ideas for their next film venture. Looking at Zorro, he decided their next movie should be about a hero, and not just any hero, but the ultimate superhero: Superman.[379]

Ilya remembered Superman from his childhood days in New York, where he had lived for a year while his parents, Russian-born film producer and financier Alexander Salkind and Mexican-born poet and playwright Berta Dominguez, tried to reconcile their volatile marriage. During that time, young Ilya began reading comic books, and watching *Adventures of Superman* on TV.[380]

Ilya was educated in the family business. His grandfather, Mikhail, was a Russian lawyer who left the country in 1922 after the Bolshevik revolution. Settling in Berlin, he gave up the legal profession and entered the relatively new business of cinema, producing director G.W. Pabst's *The Joyless Street* in 1925. The film featured a little-known Swedish actress named Greta Garbo.[381] Eight years later, his adaptation of *Don Quixote* (1933), starring Feodor Chaliapin, won the Gold Medal in Venice. Mikhail and his son Alexander fled Europe during World War II, landing first in Cuba, then in Mexico, where Alexander helped his father produce the Buster Keaton film *El Moderno Barba Azul* (*Boom in the Moon*, 1946). Alexander became his father's financial manager; together, they produced Abel Gance's *Austerlitz* (1960), and later Orson Welles's adaptation of Franz Kafka's *The Trial* (1962).[382] According to Ilya Salkind, when he was very young, producer Harry Saltzman came to see his father seeking financing for a proposed series of movies based on the James Bond novels of British author Ian Fleming. Alexander Salkind turned Saltzman down, thinking no one would be interested in a spy character; Saltzman later teamed with Albert R. "Cubby" Broccoli, and the rest is movie blockbuster history.[383]

When Ilya was in his early 20s, he joined his grandfather and father to make *The Light at the Edge of the World* (1971) and *Bluebeard* (1972). When the trio filmed their next movie, *The Three Musketeers* (1973), they discovered that they had enough footage to cut the film in half and release it as two features; the second part, *The Four Musketeers*, was released in 1974. The actors who had contracted to do only one film felt cheated and sued the producers. Afterwards, the Screen Actors Guild introduced contractual language specifying that an actor or actress would be paid for each film that he or she was making; this became known as "the Salkind clause."[384]

Between the releases of the two Three Musketeers films, Mikhail Salkind died, so Ilya, the youngest Salkind of the triumvirate, became the creative guiding force of the family business. Having made up his mind that Superman should be their next project, he now had to convince his father, who controlled the purse strings. Alexander Salkind had never heard of Superman, but his buyers and financial contacts had. Alexander agreed to go along, but Ilya's friend and producing partner Pierre Spengler balked. Spengler didn't believe they would ever be able to make a man fly convincingly on-screen.[385]

Despite Spengler's misgivings, the Salkinds pressed forward, contacting National Periodical Publications (DC Comics) for the film rights to Superman. National had recently been purchased by media conglomerate Warner Communications, who also owned Warner Bros.[386] Warner Bros. had no interest in pursuing a Superman movie, perhaps because after the campy *Batman* series (1966–68), TV was considered the domain of superhero adaptations like *Wonder Woman* (1975–79), *The Amazing Spider-Man* (1977) and *The Incredible Hulk* (1977–82); also, when pulp-novel favorite *Doc Savage: The Man of Bronze* became a big-screen Warner Bros. movie in 1975, the film flopped.

After negotiations with National stalled over issues of creative control, Alexander Salkind suggested they go to the higher-ups. They contacted Warners' publishing division and quickly concluded a deal which gave them the rights to produce Superman films and TV series for 15 years.[387] The renewable options would eventually cost the producers $6 million, but the initial payment was less than half of that amount.[388] Under the terms of the deal, Warners would have budget and casting approval and the right of first refusal for Superman films made by the Salkinds, but otherwise the financing and production of the films was up to the producers.[389]

To show that they were taking the project seriously, the Salkinds announced a budget of $20 million—an astronomical figure at the time—and approached one of the industry's most respected screenwriters, William Goldman. Goldman was very interested in writing the script, but couldn't get a grasp on how to approach the material, so he declined. Undeterred, the Salkinds went to their second choice, novelist Mario Puzo. A few years earlier, Puzo's Mafia novel *The Godfather* had become an Academy Award–winning Best Picture, nabbing Puzo and writer-director Francis Ford Coppola Oscars for the screenplay adaptation.[390] On March 21, 1975, Puzo signed a contract with Alexander Salkind that gave him $300,000 for the screenplay, plus 5 percent of the domestic rentals.[391] As Puzo's writing took up the spring and summer of 1975, the producers gave up on their original ambition to have the film in release by November of that year.[392] On February 29, 1976 (Superman's leap-year birthday, according to legend) the producers took out a full-page ad in *Variety* saying, "Happy Birthday, Superman. Sorry we couldn't be with you." They also arranged for a laser show in New York's Battery Park, projecting "Coming soon—*Superman: The Movie*" onto a huge balloon.[393]

As Puzo was coming up with a storyline that would transcend Superman's comic book origins, the producers were looking for a director. According to Ilya Salkind, William Friedkin, director of *The Exorcist* (1973), was approached, as were Francis Ford Coppola and *The Wild Bunch* (1969) director Sam Peckinpah.[394] Peter Yates, best known as the director of *Bullitt* (1968), was interested, and so was a brash young newcomer named Steven Spielberg whose agent kept calling the Salkinds. Ilya was keen to hire Spielberg, who had just begun working on *Jaws* (1975). Alexander thought they should wait to see how the "shark picture" turned out. As soon as it hit theaters, *Jaws* was a monster hit, and Spielberg was suddenly the most in-demand director in Hollywood—and no longer interested in *Superman*.[395]

Eventually, a director was chosen. With their long-term option, the Salkinds intended from the start to produce a series of Superman films, and they patterned their approach on the most financially successful film franchise of all time, the James Bond films. Thus, it was natural that they hired Guy Hamilton, a director who had helmed four 007 movies, including the trend-setting *Goldfinger* (1964) and the films that had introduced Roger Moore as Bond, *Live and Let Die* (1973) and *The Man with the Golden Gun* (1974).[396] "*Superman* will be the natural successor to the Bond films," Ilya Salkind told reporter Roderick Mann.[397]

Puzo's script, meanwhile, had grown to over 300 pages, enough for two movies, which is exactly what the Salkinds intended. Puzo had exhausted himself with the material, so new writers took over—Robert Benton and David Newman, who had written the book for the 1966 Broadway play *It's a Bird, It's a Plane, It's Superman*. David Newman later recalled that the part of Superman was written for a young Burt Reynolds. They were afraid a clean-cut, Boy Scout character would be laughed off the screen; Reynolds, said Newman, was the only name actor they could think of who could be a good, believable action character and yet have a twinkle in his eye.[398] Newman's wife, Leslie, was hired to write the Lois Lane scenes. The Newmans wrote the famous scene where Superman meets Lois Lane for an interview on her balcony, and she asks him to tell her what color underwear she's wearing. When they finished their drafts, Guy Hamilton brought in British novelist George MacDonald Fraser, who had worked with the Salkinds on the Musketeer movies. Fraser went through the separate scripts for *Superman I* and *II*, editing them down to a more manageable length.[399]

The production had first been based in Paris, but then moved to Rome's Cinecitta Studios, where some of the world's largest soundstages were located. To secure financing for what was expected to be an epic production, the filmmakers needed commitments from name actors. Olympic decathlon gold medalist Bruce Jenner was tested for the lead, but despite his gifts as an athlete, he was no actor. Robert Redford was approached, but turned the part down because he felt it would take too much time out of his life. Sylvester Stallone, who had scored a box-office knockout with *Rocky* (1976), was considered, but the producers felt he did not have the right kind of all–American look for Superman. James Caan wanted too much money, and James Brolin voluntarily withdrew. Paul Newman not only turned down the role of Superman, but he also said no to Jor-El and Lex Luthor. Pop singer Neil Diamond asked personally to be considered, and Denny Miller, a former Tarzan who had appeared as Superman in Air Force recruiting commercials, sent in a photo of himself in Clark Kent hat and glasses.[400] George MacDonald Fraser remembers Alexander Salkind suggesting Muhammad Ali for the role; after a few minutes' consideration, it was decided that the fans and public would not go for a concept as radical as a black Superman[401] (though

DC Comics did publish a special collectors issue in 1978 called *Superman Vs. Muhammad Ali*).[402] In the end, Perry King, the star of *The Lords of Flatbush*, was very close to being cast.[403] So, apparently, was Arnold Schwarzenegger, who told Jennifer Seder of *The Los Angeles Times* that he was considered for the role, but lost out in the final round because of his thick Austrian accent.[404]

As flying tests were underway and sets were being built at Cinecitta, Alexander Salkind had an inspiration. Why worry about casting a name actor as Superman? After all, if Robert Redford or Burt Reynolds were playing the role, the audience wouldn't see Superman on screen, they'd see Redford or Reynolds in a funny suit. Better, he thought, to cast an unknown, whom the audience would accept only as Superman, but this unknown could be surrounded by big-name actors in the supporting roles. Marlon Brando, already a legend even before his Oscar-winning turn as the star of *The Godfather*, was offered the role of Superman's father, Jor-El, and a $3.7 million salary against 11.3 percent of the movie's domestic gross and 5.6 percent of the foreign gross for two weeks' work. It was an offer he couldn't refuse.[405] With Brando on board, Gene Hackman, another Oscar-winner for his turn as the tough-guy cop of *The French Connection* (1971), agreed to play Superman's nemesis, Lex Luthor, for a salary of $2 million.[406] Hackman approached the producers as they were about to offer the role to Dustin Hoffman[407] (Hoffman and Hackman had both been students at George Reeves's old alma mater, the Pasadena Playhouse; both were considered least likely to succeed).[408] The hirings were announced at the annual Cannes Film Festival with a giant banner flown over the beach behind an airplane.[409]

Christopher Lee and Oliver Reed, who had appeared in the Salkinds' *Three Musketeers* films, were both interested in playing the film's other major villain, General Zod. Ilya Salkind felt that Zod's all-black costume would be too reminiscent of Dracula if Christopher Lee, who had played the vampire in a series of Hammer Productions horror films, took the role. As for Oliver Reed, he worried that the actor's often out-of-control drinking would be too much of a disruptive influence on the set.[410] Instead, the role went to Terence Stamp. Soon, the whole industry was buzzing about *Superman*.

The rest of the crew was quickly assembled. Derek Meddings, another veteran of the James Bond films, came on board to do model effects. Roy Field was hired as special effects supervisor, Wally Veevers to supervise flying effects, and Yvonne Blake to do costumes. But with the hiring of Brando, who could not shoot in Italy due to an obscenity lawsuit arising out of *Last Tango in Paris* (1972), the production was forced to relocate to England. Other economic factors also influenced the decision. For one thing, there were union problems in Rome; for another, if the production moved to England, part of the budget overruns could be offset by the availability of Eady Levy monies, production funds the British government took from the sale of movie tickets and made available to filmmakers if they shot a significant portion of their film in England with a majority English crew.[411] As the planned start date of March 1977 neared, the film took up space at Shepperton Studios, occupying eight stages.[412]

With the move to England, tax exile Guy Hamilton had to bow out, so the film was once again without a director. Mark Robson, the director of *Earthquake* (1974), was very keen to take the helm of *Superman*. But Ilya Salkind's wife, Skye Aubrey, suggested that her husband see *The Omen* (1976), a horror thriller directed by Richard Donner, whom she knew. Salkind and his father went to see the film and were impressed by its energy. The choice was now between Robson and Donner. The studio had no preference. Neither did Marlon Brando. In the end, Donner won out.[413] The director told Susan Heller Anderson of *The New York Times*, "This picture is the biggest Erector set given to the biggest kid in the world."[414] Instead of simply making a comic book movie, Donner wanted to approach the material with respect and make the fantastic story seem real. On the wall of his office was a plastic figure of Superman in flight, trailing a banner that read "Verisimilitude."[415] Donner told reporter Roderick Mann, "We're dealing with American literature here. The British have their Shakespeare. We have our Superman. So it's got to be good."[416]

Donner had his work cut out for him. In the eyes of the industry, the film was becoming something of a joke. The original start of production date had come and gone, the director had been replaced, and the production had moved to a different country—and all of that before an actor had even been hired to play the title role. During the Cannes Film Festival in May 1976, the producers tried to boost confidence in the upcoming film with an ambitious publicity stunt. A helicopter was hired to take a huge Superman billboard out to one of the big boats in the harbor. Just as the helicopter was hovering over the boat, the wind changed direction, nearly causing the aircraft to crash in the bay. The billboard was sliced in two. The next day, the local newspaper carried the headline, "Superman Makes Big Splash at Cannes Festival."[417]

Meanwhile, the revolving door of screenwriters continued. After Marlon Brando was hired, the producers decided to improve and expand the role of Jor-El, so George MacDonald Fraser was brought back to write new dialogue.[418] When Richard Donner read the Superman scripts, he found that while they were epic in scope, they were also steeped in the kind of jokey campiness that he intended to avoid. So, he brought in his own writer, Tom Mankiewicz, yet another veteran of the James Bond series. Since Writer's Guild rules at the time only allowed for four writers to be credited, Mankiewicz was listed as a "Creative Consultant."[419]

As they overhauled the mammoth script, Donner and Mankiewicz realized that at its core, the Superman myth that had developed over the years was fundamentally a retelling of the story of Jesus Christ (one wonders what Jerry Siegel and Joe Shuster—both Jewish— would have made of that observation!). Like Jesus, Kal-El comes to earth from the heavens as a baby. Moreover, he is sent by the wise, god-like Jor-El, who is sending to earth his only begotten son. He is reared by a humble family, and Kal-El/Clark Kent/Superman performs miraculous deeds. Where Jesus was crucified, but rose from the dead and ascended into Heaven, Superman is weakened with kryptonite, but is resurrected after Eve Teschmacher removes the deadly meteorite from around his neck, and flies into the sky. And like Jesus reviving Lazarus from the dead, Superman revives Lois Lane, though he has to spin the world backward and reverse time to do it. In the last shot of Superman in the film, he is soaring back into the heavens from whence he came.

With the script for the planned two movies taking shape and the budget now being reported as $26.5 million,[420] the producers continued their search for an ideal Superman. In the same way that she'd recommended Richard Donner to direct the movie, Ilya Salkind's wife, Skye Aubrey, now had a recommendation for the lead role—her dentist. Salkind was skeptical, but agreed to see him. After auditioning so many candidates who didn't measure up, the dentist, Don Voyne, did indeed seem like an ideal choice ... in person. On screen, however, the 38-year-old appeared too old.[421] (Interestingly, Voyne did his screen test opposite Jeff Corey as Lex Luthor; Corey had played "Luke Benson," the leader of the lynch mob, in *Superman and the Mole Men* in 1951).

After that, Ilya Salkind found himself getting increasingly depressed. The producers had seen over two hundred actors, and tested about ten, and had still come up short. Finally, Salkind looked back through the photos of actors they'd already interviewed and came across one which he'd previously dismissed. It was Christopher Reeve's. After Salkind and Richard

Donner met with the actor in New York, Donner had expressed to Salkind that he was too young and too good-looking. Now, however, Salkind was desperate. He decided to give him a screen test anyway.[422] Reeve was flown to London and tested in the full Superman uniform. Though he looked terribly skinny, he exuded a natural air of calm command that sat well on the shoulders of the Man of Steel. Producer Pierre Spengler's wife told her husband that she thought Reeve was really sexy.[423] Ilya Salkind recalled that when the test was shown to Warners, the executives stood and clapped. At that point, Salkind knew everything would be just fine.[424] Christopher Reeve's casting was announced at Sardi's restaurant in New York on February 23, 1977. The planned start of production was only one month and five days away.[425]

Reeve later admitted to reporter Roderick Mann that before he signed the contract to do the first Superman film and a sequel, he sought the advice of Sean Connery, who had experience acting in a blockbuster series as the screen's first James Bond. According to Reeve, Connery told him, "One—be damn good in the first film, or you don't have a problem anyway. Two—be in Outer Mongolia when they try to reach you for the sequel. Three—if you really get in trouble, go see my lawyer."[426]

"I'm still stunned that, after the screen test and all the interviews, they've chosen me," Reeve told Albin Krebs of *The New York Times*. "But somehow I feel ready for it. I feel I could fly—not literally, like Superman—but emotionally."[427] Unlike George Reeves, who portrayed Clark Kent and Superman both as take-charge characters, Christopher Reeve approached the dual role as two distinct personalities. He said that Clark was "really Superman acting like a schlepper and having a good time at it;" he later wrote that he patterned his performance on Cary Grant's against-type turn as a nebbish in *Bringing Up Baby* (1938).[428] Superman, on the other hand, was played with great earnestness; Reeve said it was how he used his powers that made him a hero, and to him, the key to playing the part was that it was about believing, instead of being cynical. He told Dan Carlinsky of *The New York Times* that Superman was a pacifist and very laid back, but he saw Clark Kent "as a deliberate put-on by Superman. Clark's a tongue-in-cheek impression of who we are. There's some of him in all of us. I have a great deal of affection for him—it's not just that he can't get the girl, he can't get the taxi."[429]

Born in New York on September 25, 1952, Christopher Reeve grew up in Princeton, New Jersey, the son of noted translator and poet F.D. Reeve and writer Barbara Johnson. Reeve's family did not own a television, and he didn't read the *Superman* comic books, but he was aware of the character through his friends; with a last name similar to *Adventures of Superman* star George Reeves, he was often asked if he was related to the TV actor. At the age of nine, Reeve became interested in acting. By the time he was thirteen, he was seriously committed to it, appearing in productions at Princeton's McCarter Theater. As a boy, he had asthma as well as Osgood-Schlatter's disease, a painful condition that strikes active boys in their early teens, usually during a growth spurt, marked by microfractures of the lower leg bone where it meets the tendons of the knees. The condition made Reeve awkward; he was 6'2" by age fourteen and moved, he once said, "like a building."[430]

When he entered college at Cornell, Reeve majored in English and music theory, though he often joked that he majored in skiing.[431] After Cornell, he became a student at Juilliard, where one of his classmates and closest friends was Robin Williams, and one of the instructors was legendary actor/director/producer John Houseman, known to movie and TV viewers as the imposing Professor Kingsfield of *The Paper Chase* (1973). One day, Reeve was called in to see Houseman, who told him, "Mr. Reeve. It is terribly important that you become a serious classical actor.... Unless, of course, they offer you a shitload of money to do something else." In his autobiography, *Still Me*, Reeve wrote, "I loved John Houseman from that moment on."[432]

While at Juilliard, Reeve landed a role on the daytime soap opera *Love of Life*. Then, in the fall of 1975, he auditioned for and won a role in Enid Bagnold's play *A Matter of Gravity*. His co-star was Katharine Hepburn. Reeve learned a lot working with the seasoned Hollywood and Broadway veteran, who often said to him, "Be fascinating, Christopher, be fascinating."[433]

When Reeve went to Los Angeles in 1976 looking for film work, he was indeed given a chance to be fascinating when he was offered the lead role in the science-fiction TV series *Man from Atlantis*. When he was told the part would require green contact lenses and webbed feet, he passed; the role went instead to Patrick Duffy, who later became a major TV star as Bobby Ewing on *Dallas* (1978–1991). After much pavement pounding, Reeve eventually landed a film role, playing a sailor in *Gray Lady Down* (1978). The film, which starred Charlton Heston and Stacy Keach, concerned the efforts to rescue a sunken nuclear submarine. By October, a disillusioned Reeve was heading back to New York and theater parts.[434] It seemed that Reeve's career in movies and TV was over before it had begun. But then, in January 1977, his agent Stark Heseltine called to tell him that a major studio was interested in him for the lead role in a big movie.[435]

Casting director Lynn Stalmaster had been pleading with Richard Donner to meet Reeve. Three times Stalmaster put Reeve's photo on the "in" pile; three times the producers put it back on the "out" pile. Reeve went to meet Donner and Ilya Salkind at the Sherry-Netherland Hotel on Fifth Avenue partly because he was intending to catch a train at Grand Central Station—a straight shot down from the hotel—to visit his father. In *Still Me*, Reeve wrote that if the meeting had been held in another part of town, he wouldn't have gone.[436]

When Reeve told his father that he had been cast in *Superman*, his father immediately asked who was going to play Ann. He thought Reeve meant that he was going to be playing Jack Tanner in George Bernard Shaw's play *Man and Superman*. Reeve later told Wayne Warga of *The Los Angeles Times* that this was the beginning of a tense time; his family wrote him off, thinking he'd "gone Hollywood." "It was pretty clear that if I turned typically Hollywood my father and I would break off relations," said Reeve. "He thought it was the ultimate sellout."

Reeve's father, who had leftist political leanings and once worked as a professor of Slavic languages by day and as a laborer unloading banana boats in Hoboken at night, considered himself a worker in the masses. Imagining his son involved in the ultimate commercial venture troubled him. "He was afraid I'd be overwhelmed," said Reeve. "Well, I wasn't—and the reason I wasn't is because of the example my father has set for us all our lives, because of his integrity and because of his intelligence.... It's because of him and what he's taught me that I haven't fallen to pieces."[437]

Once cast as the Man of Steel, Reeve decided that instead of relying on a uniform with fake muscle padding sewn in, he would transform his own lanky physique into something more befitting of a superhero. Under the supervision of British bodybuilder and actor Dave Prowse (best known for playing Darth Vader in the *Star Wars* films), Reeve began weightlifting, eating an extra meal a day, and taking a host of vitamins.[438] The ninety-minute workouts paid off; in just a few weeks, Reeve went from a slender 189 pounds to a robust 202 pounds.[439]

The high-profile role and new physique made Reeve a very desirable eligible bachelor. It wasn't long before he'd found a girlfriend, British modeling executive Gae Exton. Gae might have become his wife, but Reeve had a fear of marital commitment, stemming from his childhood memories of his parents' difficult divorce.

After finding their Superman, the next challenge for the producers was finding Lois

Lane. Numerous actresses tested with Christopher Reeve, including Stockard Channing, Deborah Raffin, Susan Blakely, Lesley Anne Warren (who had played the role in the ABC-TV version of the Broadway play *It's a Bird, It's a Plane, It's Superman*), Holly Palance (daughter of Jack Palance) and a Canadian actress named Margot Kidder. Kidder had an instant on-screen chemistry with Reeve. Her tough, spunky tomboyishness was the perfect complement to his shy, bumbling Clark Kent, and when she appeared opposite Reeve's Superman, her Lois Lane melted into infatuated giddiness. "Lois is very together. She's out to be the best reporter in the world and she doesn't have time for anything else," said Margot Kidder.[440] Two days after her screen test, Kidder was informed that she had won the role.[441]

The daughter of a mining engineer, Margot Kidder was born in Yellowknife, Northwest Territory, Canada on October 17, 1948, and reared in Vancouver until she was 16. Her burning desire to act led her to early jobs in Canadian TV. Noticed by Canadian director Norman Jewison, she was given a part in his film *Gaily, Gaily* (1969) opposite Beau Bridges. She hoped this would open the doors of Hollywood to her, but found other work difficult to come by. She returned to Canadian TV, until she landed a role working with Gene Wilder in *Quackser Fortune Has a Cousin in the Bronx* (1970). When that ended, she became an editor at the Canadian Broadcasting Company. Deciding to give Hollywood another try, she landed a role in the short-lived James Garner TV series *Nichols* (1971). More film work came her way, including roles in *Sisters* (1973), *The Great Waldo Pepper* (1975) and *The Reincarnation of Peter Proud* (1975).[442]

To fill out the supporting roles, Ned Beatty was chosen to play Lex Luthor's assistant, Otis, while former Las Vegas showgirl Valerie Perrine, who had earned an Academy Award nomination for her role in *Lenny* (1975), was chosen to play Luthor's moll, Eve Teschmacher. The role of Jimmy Olsen went to Marc McClure, who had made his film debut in Disney's *Freaky Friday* (1976) and had appeared in episodes of *Happy Days* and *Eight is Enough* in 1977. McClure projected just the right note of youthful eagerness as the *Daily Planet* photographer. The rest of the cast was made up of well-known actors from England and America appearing in small roles. British actress Susannah York played Lara, Superman's mother on Krypton (Joanne Woodward and Anne Bancroft passed on the role),[443] while the Kryptonian elders were played by distinguished European actors Trevor Howard, Harry Andrews and Maria Schell. General Zod's cohorts, Ursa and Non, were played by Sarah Douglas and former boxer Jack O'Halloran (O'Halloran also played professional football with the Philadelphia Eagles). Glenn Ford projected earthy integrity as Jonathan Kent, while Phyllis Thaxter, who was Ilya Salkind's mother-in-law, portrayed Martha Kent.

Shooting began March 28, 1977, with scenes filmed at Shepperton with Marlon Brando draped in black velvet, delivering an instructional speech to his son, Kal-El. Brando had arrived in England with a cold, and two days into shooting, it was getting the better of him. He asked Richard Donner if he could finish the day early. Donner was stunned. As he later told reporter Roderick Mann, knowing how little time they had with Brando and how much he was costing, the director had been calculating how much it cost the production every time the actor went to the bathroom. But instead of arguing, Donner played to the superstar's ego, telling him that since he was, after all, Marlon Brando, if he wanted to go, they couldn't stop him. In return for leaving early, Brando offered to give them an extra day. Realizing that this would give him ample time to shoot all the material he needed with Brando, Donner happily sent him home.[444]

By May, the production was running two weeks behind schedule. It was also growing beyond the limitations of Shepperton Studios, so the decision was made to shift it to Pinewood, home of the James Bond films and the fabled 007 Stage, one of the world's largest, which had been built to house the interior supertanker set for 1977's *The Spy Who Loved Me*. In his autobiography, Christopher Reeve recalled that shortly after the production moved to Pinewood, he was wearing his full Superman outfit, complete with red cape and boots, when he ran into actor John Gielguld, whom he had met once before. Gielguld shook his hand and said, "So delightful to see you. What are you doing now?"[445]

Shooting began at Pinewood on E Stage, where the set representing the interior of *The Daily Planet* had been built. Two weeks were scheduled for filming the newspaper scenes; in the end, shooting on the stage stretched out to five weeks. Part of the delay was due to the difficulty in casting the role of editor Perry White. Walter Matthau, Jason Robards, and Ed Asner were considered; Jack Klugman was eventually cast. But just as flight arrangements were being booked for Klugman, word came that he was, in fact, declining the role. The producers next went to Eddie Albert, who accepted, but then back-pedaled with higher salary demands. After more scrambling, Keenan Wynn agreed to take the part. It was decided to shoot his initial scenes the morning after his arrival in England. The actor arrived for make-up tests, costume fittings, and still photo sessions, after which he complained of chest pains. He was rushed to London hospital, where he collapsed from a case of extreme exhaustion. In desperation, the producers again began searching for an actor to portray the gruff newspaper editor, and hired actor/director Jackie Cooper, who proved ideally suited to the role. Cooper had begun his career as a child, appearing in the *Our Gang* shorts and costarring with Wallace Beery in *The Champ* (1931).

Despite the setbacks and the challenges associated with such a large, special-effects-heavy production, Richard Donner persevered, though relations between the director and his producers were beginning to sour. The producers kept complaining that Donner was going over budget, while Donner claimed that he had never been told what the exact budget was, so he had no way of knowing if he was going over. He told Roderick Mann that that appeared to be the way the Salkinds worked, and it was making his job difficult.[446] In an interview on the *Superman Cinema* website, Ilya Salkind said that Donner had a hard time choosing takes, adding that he shot the red sun of Krypton three hundred times, then used take 3. According to Salkind, even in non-effects shots, like the scenes inside *The Daily Planet* newsroom, Donner did take after take.[447]

Fearing that Donner's methodical pace would doom the picture, the producers threatened legal action. Shouting matches became common between the director and the producers. Alexander Salkind claimed that Donner was in breach of his contract. Ilya Salkind stopped visiting the set. Pierre Spengler refused to be seen with Donner. On the set, the crew began to split into pro–Donner and pro–Salkind camps. In an effort to step up the pace, the producers contacted a director with a reputation for working quickly—Richard Lester, who had helmed the Salkinds' *Musketeers* films.[448] In the end, Alexander Salkind chose not to fire Donner, but Lester was kept on board as an additional producer; he basically acted as a mediator between the producers and Donner, and tried his best to keep a low profile.

Midway through the lengthy filming schedule, Donner was asked if he would make another Superman film. He replied that he didn't think he would; the rigors of flying a human being around and making it look real were just too tough.[449]

Indeed, millions of dollars and months of time had been spent on flying tests, to no avail; no matter what they tried, there seemed to be no way to make Superman fly without visible wires. Finally, Pierre Spengler found a man who claimed that he held the answer to their prayers. Zoran Perisic came to the U.K. from Yugoslavia after working on Columbia's Viking picture *The Long Ships* (1963) and later as a special effects cameraman on Stanley

Kubrick's *2001: A Space Odyssey* (1968). In the mid–1970s, Perisic invented the Zoptic system, a front projection camera rig that would resize the projected image based on the focal length, pan and tilt of the camera lens. Perisic constructed his first rig with equipment he acquired at a clearance sale at Shepperton Studios. When he was brought into *Superman*, he was given six weeks to prove that Zoptic could achieve flying effects with no visible wires. Under the terms of his contract, if the producers were not satisfied with the results of his system, he would have to return his salary advance. When the producers screened Perisic's footage, they were ecstatic. The flying problem was a problem no more.[450] Perisic's system could seamlessly match helicopter footage with Christopher Reeve mounted in a static flying position. As the film camera zoomed in on Reeve, making it look like he was flying past the camera, the Zoptic system would simultaneously zoom the projected aerial footage in perfect synchronization. It looked like Superman was simply flying past a camera mounted on a helicopter. For the first time in the history of the character, Superman's most amazing ability was being captured believably onscreen.

At the beginning of July, the production moved to New York City, where the *Daily News* building was transformed into *The Daily Planet*. Shooting on location meant dealing with crowds of onlookers, who were prone to yelling things at Christopher Reeve like, "Hey, Superman, where's your phone booth?" Said Reeve, "It's funny the first two hundred times."[451] After months in the studio, with lots of time being spent trying to work out the flying effects, Reeve was beginning to have his doubts. However, when he arrived on location on 57th Street in full Superman regalia, the crowd cheered. As he hooked his flying harness up to the crane and was hoisted up into the air, the onlookers roared even louder; it was as thought they couldn't see the cable—all they saw was Superman. That, wrote Reeve in *Still Me*, is when he knew the film would work.[452]

During night shooting on July 13, 1978, there was a massive power blackout in Manhattan. The *Superman* unit was able to keep shooting thanks to the generators they were using for their movie lights, which gave off so much illumination that *The Daily News* was able to go to press the next morning. However, the crew was sent home early that evening, as looters and rioters ran rampant.[453] Another evening's shooting was delayed by rain, putting the film even more behind schedule.

After a couple of weeks, the crew moved on to Calgary, Canada for an additional four weeks of location filming.[454] Calgary had been chosen to substitute for the fictional town of Smallville, Kansas. With Calgary's wheat fields and Bill Brodie's inspired art direction, Richard Donner was able to film scenes that looked straight out of a Norman Rockwell painting. One shot of Martha Kent standing in her doorway looking at Clark walking through the field far in the distance seemed inspired by a similar shot in director John Ford's Western classic, *The Searchers* (1956). In the end, the Smallville scenes were a perfectly nostalgic evocation of a romanticized, sanitized America that never was.

Jeff East, who had starred as Huck Finn in musical adaptations of *Tom Sawyer* (1973) and *Huckleberry Finn* (1974), portrayed the teenage Clark Kent, with the aid of a black wig, a prosthetic nose and Christopher Reeve's dubbed voice. Gene Hackman, Ned Beatty, and Valerie Perrine arrived for three weeks of shooting scenes involving Lex Luthor sabotaging a missile on a convoy. The shooting was continually delayed by rain in an area that had been chosen because of its reputation for beautiful weather.[455]

As a promotional gimmick, DC Comics sponsored the Great Superman Movie Contest. The winner had to collect coupons from comic books to spell out "Superman" and send in the entry. A drawing was then held, with Christopher Reeve selecting two first-place winners. Five thousand second-place winners had a choice of either a book or a subscription to the *Superman* comic book. The two first-place winners, 13-year-old Tim Hussey and 14-year-old Ed Finneran, were chosen to appear as football players in the brief scene with Clark (Jeff East) and Lana Lang (Diane Sherry); unfortunately, they did not get to meet Christopher Reeve, who remained behind in London continuing to film flying sequences. As a consolation, when the teenagers finished filming their scene in Calgary, they were flown to New York for a tour of the DC Comics offices.[456]

After the scenes involving Glenn Ford and Phyllis Thaxter were completed, the crew moved on to scenes involving Clark Kent outracing a train. David Michael Petrou, in his book *The Making of Superman: The Movie*, reports that the crew was amused by the back-and-forth banter between *Superman* serial stars Kirk Alyn and Noel Neill, who were making cameos as Lois Lane's parents.[457] Alyn and Neill were told they would be needed for two days at the most, but because of rain delays, they were on location for a week. The rain had the extra-added bonus of giving most of the crew, including director Richard Donner, head colds.[458]

The crew returned to Pinewood weeks behind schedule and millions of dollars over budget. Completing both films simultaneously as originally planned now seemed like an impossible task, so Richard Lester suggested that all efforts be concentrated on finishing the first film. The second, he reasoned, could be finished at a later date. The ending of the second part—in which Superman reverses the effects of an earthquake and resurrects Lois Lane—would now become the ending of Part I, which was originally supposed to end with a cliffhanger—Superman diverting a missile into space, where it explodes and releases the Phantom Zone villains, General Zod, Non and Ursa. Richard Donner and the producers agreed with Lester.[459] Before the new edict took full effect, crucial scenes for *Superman II* involving Gene Hackman were completed.[460]

The next phase of filming concentrated on scenes inside Luthor's subterranean lair, a magnificent piece of set design by production designer John Barry, whose previous credits included *A Clockwork Orange* (1971) and *Star Wars* (1977). Despite the tensions of budget and schedule, there were some lighter moments on the set. While filming the scene where Superman throws back the lid of a lead box only to be confronted by kryptonite, Gene Hackman pulled a prank on Christopher Reeve by having the lid nailed shut.[461] After completing the scenes in Luthor's lair, Christopher Reeve celebrated his 25th birthday on the set.

The following week, filming began on the mammoth 007 Stage, which had been turned into an Arctic scene of floating icebergs and the exterior of Superman's Fortress of Solitude. Because of the thousands of pounds of corrosive salt used to simulate snow, the cameras and equipment had to be carefully cleaned every night. And because much of the set was in water, crew members were issued knee-high Wellington boots and, in some instances, full wetsuits. As the shooting dragged on, some of the Pinewood employees threatened to strike, feeling they deserved hardship pay for the conditions they were enduring on the Fortress set. But then, one evening, the crew was invited to see thirty minutes of footage that had been assembled to show to Warner Bros. executives. Even in that truncated form, *Superman* worked its magic; when the screening was over, the workers—most of whom had toiled seven months on the film without having seen any of the results—cheered and applauded. They returned to the set with renewed confidence that they were working on a truly special film.[462]

By the end of October, Hackman, Perrine and Beatty had finished their scenes and were sent back to the U.S. There were still months of work ahead, but the producers had to cut costs, and were eager to give their backers a signal that they were still on schedule to finish shooting by October 28, so two-week notices were sent to many of the crew members. Some were happy to finally be relieved of the ordeal of bringing Superman to life. With time running out, the filmmakers went to work on a set of Lois Lane's rooftop apartment, filming her interview with Superman.[463]

After the wrap party at the end of October, production was suspended for a month. At the end of November, shooting resumed with model work and flying scenes. Main unit filming was in limbo because Richard Donner was in the U.S., meeting with Warner Bros. executives to explain why the film was behind schedule and pleading to be allowed to finish it without compromise. As if that weren't enough, the production was now facing yet another crisis. As the budget ballooned, cash flow slowed to a trickle. Many vendors were still waiting to be paid; one construction company threatened to bulldoze the backlot model of the Golden Gate Bridge unless the producers ponied up what was owed to them. Alexander Salkind scrambled to find money to placate them.

Donner returned to Pinewood in December, and began shooting the scene where Superman intercepts three hoodlums on a cabin cruiser.[464] After a break for Christmas, filming resumed in January 1978 with an accident reminiscent of George Reeves in "The Ghost Wolf" episode of *Adventures of Superman*. While stuntman Paul Weston, doubling for Christopher Reeve, was aloft in the flying harness, the wires snapped. Weston fell forty feet to the floor of the stage, missing the mattresses that were meant to break his fall. Miraculously, he was not seriously injured.[465]

The producers were alarmed and angry when *Variety* carried a front-page story saying that Warner Bros., fearing that problems with the flying effects would delay the planned summer release, had rescheduled the film for Christmas 1978. Privately, however, most of those working on the film knew that if they tried to make the summer release, shortcuts would have to be taken which would ultimately damage the film. The producers were further upset when Rona Barrett, the entertainment correspondent on ABC-TV's *Good Morning, America*, reported that Warner Bros. was in fact taking over production of the picture, which was untrue.[466]

The English weather was now proving to be just as uncooperative as the Canadian weather had been. Sleet and pea soup fog slowed down the shooting of the scene where Superman rescues a cat from a tree; what should have taken a couple of days stretched into an entire week.[467] During the third week of shooting, the crew took time out to celebrate the one-year anniversary of Christopher Reeve signing his Superman contract.[468] After months spent in flying harnesses that at first left him with bruises, then calluses, it was understandable that Reeve was having second thoughts. When he signed for the role, he was paid $250,000 for both *Superman: The Movie* and *Superman II*. Reeve told reporter Roderick Mann that the salary wasn't bad when both films were supposed to have been wrapped in ten months, but given the delays, he'd have made more money doing a TV soap opera. Voicing his frustrations to the reporter, he declared that—despite Ilya Salkind's stated desire to do five Superman movies—he would be finished with the role once he finished the sequel.[469]

One of the last major scenes filmed involved Lois Lane's car being crushed in an earthquake. For Margot Kidder, it meant hours of being inside a car that was being slowly squeezed by a hydraulic machine as bags of dirt were poured over her. There was still some flying work to be completed, as well as model work (the destruction of the dam), and special effects shots (Superman flying through the interior of the earth to counteract the earthquake). Special effects and model units continued filming until early August.[470]

Warner Bros. executives traveled to London in the fall of 1978 to view a four-hour assemblage of *Superman*. When it was over, the executives—feeling there wasn't a dull moment in the entire four hours—gave Richard Donner their blessing to let the film run for as long as he felt necessary.[471]

To score the film, the producers enlisted John Williams, whose music for *Jaws* (1975) and *Star Wars* (1977) established him as the preeminent composer of Hollywood blockbusters. His main theme to *Superman* perfectly captured the heroic spirit of the character. After more than a year of production, the film was finally wrapped. What had begun as a $20 million production had now cost over $70 million.[472] Speaking to Roderick Mann, Ilya Salkind said, "If it works, I'll be wealthy to the point where I need never work again." And what, asked Mann, if it doesn't? "That's easy," said Salkind. "I'll be ruined."[473]

Just three weeks before the film was due to be premiered, producer Alexander Salkind asked Warner Bros. to purchase additional distribution rights for $15 million. One industry insider called the ploy ransom; if Warners wanted to get the film in time to make prints, they had to fork over the money, even though the rights were considered to be worth only a fraction of $15 million.[474] Ilya Salkind told the *Superman Cinema* website, "We were flat broke. We undersold all our rights. We needed the money."[475] Warners quickly concluded the deal.

Marketing *Superman: The Movie* presented its own special problems. How was Warner Bros. going to convey to adult audiences that it wasn't a campy kiddie film? Rob Friedman and Bud Rosenthal, the Warners executives in charge of presenting Superman to the public, began by creating a stylized advertising campaign. The Superman "S" shield was redesigned with a chrome look instead of the familiar red and yellow colors. The teaser trailer consisted of an extended aerial point-of-view soaring through the clouds as the names of the actors flew past; there were no shots of live performers. Indeed, all footage of Superman flying was kept out of public view until opening day. Finally, the movie's advertising line, "You'll believe a man can fly," presented a dare to audiences, one they were only too willing to accept.[476]

Superman: The Movie had its American premiere on December 10 at the Kennedy Center in Washington, D.C. The premiere benefited the Special Olympics, a program sponsored by the Kennedy family. Senator Edward Kennedy and his sister, Eunice Kennedy Shriver, were in attendance, as were the Superman cast and President Jimmy Carter. With tickets costing up to $1,000, the event raised almost $200,000 for the Special Olympics.[477] But what should have been a night of great success was filled with great frustration for Ilya Salkind. As he was going up the steps to the premiere with President Carter, Mario Puzo served him with a lawsuit. After the event, Salkind and Puzo were on the same plane, and the producer asked the writer why he was suing. Puzo responded that everybody sues in Hollywood before a film comes out.[478] Puzo, the creator of *The Godfather*, was taking it to the mattresses. And so was the Godfather himself, Marlon Brando, who filed suit on December 13, 1978, two days before the film opened in Los Angeles.[479] Like Puzo, the actor worried that with the cost overruns on the film, the other creditors would take their money first and he would realize nothing from his gross profit participation deal. Shortly afterwards, Richard Donner also filed suit (Brando was due 11.3 percent of the profits, Puzo 5 percent, and Donner 6.25 percent).[480] *The Los Angeles Herald Examiner* speculated that the suits brought by Brando and Puzo were calculated to position them to renegotiate their shares of the second film. Puzo also claimed that the Salkinds had breached his contract by allowing Warner Books to publish a novelization of his screenplay without his approval.[481] As a result of the lawsuits, a judge blocked the revenues of *Superman: The Movie* before it opened.[482]

At the same time, William Forman, who owned a chain of theaters in Los Angeles, hit the Salkinds with civil lawsuits claiming that Alexander Salkind misappropriated $20 million from him to make a series of movies and buy the film rights to *Superman*. The Forman suit was eventually settled for $23.4 million.[483]

Christopher Reeve takes to the skies in 1978's *Superman: The Movie*, which was promoted with the line, "You'll believe a man can fly." Using special effects that were state-of-the-art for the time, the film delivered on its promise (Warner Bros./Photofest).

The night after its Washington, D.C. debut, the film premiered in New York at the Loews Astor Plaza, again raising money for the Special Olympics.[484] A crowd of 1,300 attended the New York opening, including Patricia Kennedy Lawford, Governor Carey, Mario Puzo, Norman Mailer, soccer star Pelé, Lauren Bacall, Dick Cavett, Walter Cronkite, David Hartman, Gilda Radner, and Alan Jay Lerner. After the screening, 450 guests went to Xenon, which had been decorated with "Superman fabric," for a dinner of pheasant and pasticcio (tortellini en croute). Patricia Kennedy Lawford, chairman of the benefit, said tickets to the screening and the dinner party afterward had been as much in demand as those for the King Tut exhibit.[485] The Los Angeles premiere at Mann's Chinese Theater on December 14, 1978, which was attended by Superman creators Jerry Siegel and Joe Shuster, also benefited the Special Olympics, as did other benefit openings in Boston and Chicago.[486]

There were rampant rumors before the film's release that it would include 3-D scenes of Superman in flight. To the disappointment of filmgoers, the rumors proved to be untrue. Nonetheless, upon its release, *Superman: The Movie* was a bona-fide hit with critics and audiences alike. *New York Times* reviewer Vincent Canby wrote, "In Christopher Reeve, a young New York stage and television actor who plays Superman and Clark Kent, the mild-mannered newspaper reporter who is Superman's cover, the producers and Richard Donner, the director, have a performer who manages to be both funny and comic-strip heroic without making a fool of himself."[487] Charles Champlin, writing in *The Los Angeles Times*, agreed, saying that Christopher Reeve was "the Superman who is *Superman's* pleasantest discovery. As Clark Kent he has a myopic, awkward, amusing ingenuousness that suggests he might well take off in non-flying roles once he hangs up his cape."[488] In *Variety*, James Harwood wrote, "Magnify James Bond's extraordinary physical powers while curbing his sex drive and you have the essence of *Superman*, a wonderful, chuckling, preposterously exciting fantasy guaranteed to challenge world box-office records this time round, and perhaps with sequels to come."[489]

The film opened on 508 screens on December 17, 1978 and grossed $7,465,343 over the weekend. It went on to gross $134,218,000 in the U.S. alone.[490] And Warner Bros. made money on their last-minute $15 million investment in the additional foreign distribution rights; the movie grossed more than $50 million overseas.[491]

The success of *Superman: The Movie* quickly established Christopher Reeve as a bona-fide movie star and quieted the naysayers who had viewed the production as an expensive folly. Along with *Jaws*, *Star Wars* and *Close Encounters of the Third Kind*, it helped to establish the big-budget blockbuster, vindicating the wisdom of using lavish "A" movie budgets to make what would have been previously viewed as little "B" pictures. It also enhanced the reputation of the Salkinds as canny producers, though it would take a sequel to put them in the black.

Superman II

In an interview on the eve of the *Superman: The Movie*'s U.S. opening, Ilya Salkind told reporter Dick Kleiner that most of the shooting for *Superman II* was already completed. Ilya Salkind announced that they only had another year of post-production and the second part would be ready, and that after that, they hoped to have a new Superman film in release every 18 months or so, just like the James Bond films. Salkind said the comparison between Superman and 007 revealed the differences between the two characters. James Bond, he said, was sometimes real and sometimes fantasy. "He goes underwater and comes out with a perfect suit," said Salkind. "We're bigger than life but based in reality. Superman could be real—if we accept the fact that the planet Krypton is real. If we can accept that, then we can accept a guy flying around New York."[492]

Pierre Spengler noted that all of the major actors were signed to long-term contracts, especially Christopher Reeve. He said that although Reeve enjoyed playing the character, they had all agreed that—unlike George Reeves—the actor would never be asked to make personal appearances wearing the Superman outfit.[493]

Reeve did, in fact, make some appearances in the Superman uniform. As he wrote in *Still Me*, he began working with the Make-a-Wish Foundation, visiting terminally ill children who wished to meet the Man of Steel.[494] In a *Time* magazine interview, Reeve said that it was hard for him to be silly about Superman because he had seen the transformative power of the character firsthand. Children dying of brain tumors whose last request had been to talk to Superman went to their graves with a peace derived from knowing that their belief in the character was intact. "I've seen that Superman really matters," said Reeve. "It's not Superman the tongue-in-cheek cartoon character they're connecting with; they're connecting with something very basic: the ability to overcome obstacles, the ability to persevere, the ability to understand difficulty and to turn your back on it."[495] Reeve also joined the board of directors of Save the Children, a charity that helped needy children throughout the world.[496]

With filming now behind him, Christopher Reeve was once again allowed to fly without wires. An accomplished pilot, he was forbidden to get behind the controls of an airplane while Superman was being made, for insurance reasons.[497] He also escaped the media blitz resulting from the first film's release with another of his passions—sailing.

Ilya Salkind and Richard Donner had predicted that when *Superman: The Movie* opened, Christopher Reeve would emerge as a major new star. They were right. The young actor was now much in demand. He was offered the lead role in *American Gigolo* after John Travolta turned it down; it would have paid him $1 million.[498] Reeve passed. He also turned down the lead role in *Body Heat*, thinking he wouldn't be convincing as a seedy lawyer.[499] Instead, against the protests of his advisors, he accepted $500,000 to do a movie that set the tone for most of his later non–Superman roles—a character-driven period piece filmed on a low budget. *Somewhere in Time*, a fantasy romance directed by Jeannot Swarzc and co-starring Jane Seymour, performed only modestly at the box office upon its release, but eventually became a highly regarded romantic film. Reeve told Aljean Harmetz of *The New York Times* that in the three months after *Superman* opened, he was advised to take the big money because he might never be so hot again. "They said *Somewhere in Time* was uncommercial," said Reeve. "If the movie is a failure, I might not be hot. But I can honestly live without having to be hot. I'm not burning to be boffo at the B.O. I want to last 50 years—not five months."[500]

Though Reeve had left *Superman* on good terms with the producers, he was now in a dispute with them. He told Roderick Mann that after finishing *Superman* in September, he didn't hear a word from Ilya Salkind or Pierre Spengler, no congratulatory notes about his reviews, no word about when he was supposed to finish the sequel, nothing. So after five months of waiting, he accepted the role in *Somewhere in Time*. Twelve hours after his casting was announced, he received a note telling him to be ready for *Superman II* on July 16— five days after filming was due to finish on *Somewhere in Time*. Then came word that the producers had brought suit against him, alleging that he had walked out of the sequel. Part of the problem was that Reeve had never signed a long-form contract; all the producers had was a three-page deal memo providing for the making of two films at once. Reeve said he had no intention of holding the producers to ransom. "Some people have said, 'Stick it to them; they can't finish the film without you.' And it's true—they can't," said Reeve. "But I wouldn't do a thing like that." In fact, said Reeve, not signing the contract cost him a fortune because he wasn't getting a percentage of the film's gross or any of the merchandising, which could have been worth millions. Worth more to the actor was his freedom; he didn't want to be bound to make the films whether he liked them or not, but rather wanted to be able to choose whether he would participate on a film-by-film basis.[501]

During the renegotiation of his contract, Reeve agreed quickly to the financial terms, but held out for more artistic control. He was upset when the producers announced near the end of March 1979 that Richard Donner had been fired and would not be completing *Superman II*. Donner, whose relations with the Salkinds and Pierre Spengler had been tense throughout the filming of *Superman: The Movie*, told *Variety* in January that he had given the producers an ultimatum to negotiate in good faith for the sequel. "They want me to do it," Donner said, "but it has to be on my terms, and I don't mean financially, I mean control."[502] The Salkinds tried to mend fences, but, according to Ilya Salkind, Donner disappeared during this time.[503] (In January 1979, *Variety* reported that Donner was about to embark on a tour of France, Italy, West Germany, Belgium and Holland to promote the foreign openings of *Superman*).[504] Reportedly unable to find him and work out terms for *Superman II*, they again asked Guy Hamilton to take over the reins, since Richard Lester was busy finishing his Sean Connery drama, *Cuba* (1979).[505]

Nonetheless, Lester, still acting in his capacity as an associate producer, reached out again to George MacDonald Fraser, who recalled "Dick Lester rang me up, and he said, 'We've finished *Superman I*.' I said, congratulations, and he said, 'Now we've got to do *Super-*

man II.' He said, 'I've used the end of *Superman II* on *Superman I*.' And I said, 'You mean the business of Superman flying through the earth's core and all that?' And he said, 'Yes.' So I said, 'Well how are you going to end *Superman II*?' And he said, 'I was hoping you would tell me.' And we finished up at Pinewood Studios looking at all the outtakes from *Superman I* and additional stuff that had been done for *Superman II*. Endless shots of Gene Hackman in a hot-air balloon.... We looked at this, there was about two-and-a-half hours of it, and then Guy Hamilton was back on the scene and he and I went through it in Paris piecing together as much as we could of the stuff that hadn't been used so far, and trying to make a coherent story for *Superman II*."[506]

At the end of March, Reeve met with the Salkinds in London and cleared up the issues that prompted them to file suit against him. According to *Variety*, Reeve was assured that Richard Donner's original concept of the sequel would be carried out.[507] He told Roderick Mann, "The mind boggles at the prospect of doing it with someone else, because Dick [Donner] was so marvelous to work with."[508] In a separate interview with Aljean Harmetz of *The New York Times*, he said he waited to find out whom the eventual director would be to make sure "it wouldn't be a rip-off movie held together with chewing gum."[509]

Reeve was enthused by the script of *Superman II*, which he felt was better than the first film, with a stronger villain in General Zod, who was Superman's equal in terms of strength and ability. Though a lot of the film had been shot during production of *Superman: The Movie*, there was still a major sequence in which Superman battled the Kryptonian villains in Metropolis still to be done, as well as a new opening sequence involving Superman rescuing Lois Lane from terrorists at the Eiffel Tower.[510]

By the time *Superman II* was ready to roll, Richard Lester had completed *Cuba* and was available to direct the new installment. So, for the second time in his career, director Guy Hamilton walked away from Superman.[511] The new director seemed an appropriate choice; like the film itself, he was an American transplant based in England. He was also already very familiar with the material, and familiar with directing sequels. But his background as a director of satirical films that lampooned institutions—the opposite of the Richard Donner approach—gave some observers pause.

Richard Lester was born in Philadelphia, Pennsylvania, in 1932, and was a CBS station manager by the age of 20. At 23, he went to Europe, deciding to make England his home. He established himself as a quick-cutting comedy director with *The Running, Jumping and Standing Still Film* (1960), which led to his directing *A Hard Day's Night* (1964) and *Help!* (1965), both starring The Beatles. The droll humor that Lester injected into those films helped define the public personas of the superstar rock-and-roll band. Lester followed up those successes with *A Funny Thing Happened on the Way to the Forum* (1966) and *Petulia* (1968), and then he became affiliated with the Salkinds as director of *The Three Musketeers* (1973) and *The Four Musketeers* (1974) before being called in to keep *Superman: The Movie* on track.[512]

Filming of *Superman II* commenced in late September 1979. Tasked with carrying out Richard Donner's blueprint, Lester tried to complete the film in the same style with which his predecessor had begun it, though he approached the material from a very different place than Donner. In his book *Still Me*, Reeve said of Richard Lester, "I liked him tremendously, but I thought it was unfair to ask such an accomplished director to imitate the tone and style of someone else's work. Nevertheless, he succeeded in bringing his own brand of humor to it." [513]

At first, the producers were not sure if they would give Lester credit as a director. Christopher Reeve didn't understand why it had to be such a big secret; he said, "The fact is he's the fellow who's calling 'action' and 'cut'—and to my mind that makes him the director."[514] The producers hoped that enough of the footage shot along with the first *Superman* could be used to keep the production schedule short; they hoped to be finished by Christmas. "There's not a chance of that happening unless they start tearing pages from the script," said Reeve. "And Dick Lester's not about to allow that. I must say he's great to work with."[515]

Reeve was dismayed to learn that the scenes Marlon Brando filmed for *Superman II* would now be dropped and reshot with Lara (Susannah York) giving her Kryptonian son advice instead of Jor-El. The reason was economic; if Brando's scenes were used, he would have to be given a percentage of the film's gross.[516] "It's a business decision; not an artistic one," said Reeve. "And that makes me very unhappy. The father-son relationship was very important in Part II, and he's a loss."[517] Dropping Brando meant dropping a scene that had been filmed during production of *Superman: The Movie*. As originally conceived, when a powerless Superman returned to the Fortress of Solitude seeking to have his super strength restored, he appeared before Jor-El, who put out his finger and gave up his spiritual life so his son could regain his powers. Ilya Salkind later claimed that he felt the image of Jor-El and Superman touching fingers like Michelangelo's famous painting of God giving life to Adam was too over-the-top.[518] Admitting that money was obviously a consideration in dropping Brando, he added, "I promise you if it had been a purely artistic decision, without money involved, I'd still have said we didn't need him. The second film is much faster and quicker than the first. In an odd sort of way, Brando's footage slowed it down, and was repetitious. I know Chris Reeve doesn't agree, but there it is." Salkind also reasoned that where the first film needed Brando's star power, the second film had a star of its own—Christopher Reeve.[519]

Despite being threatened with a lawsuit by the producers before filming began, once Reeve was back in the Superman uniform, he was a team player, always putting a positive spin on the situation for interviews. Margot Kidder later claimed that she and Reeve were both unhappy reshooting material for *Superman II* that they had previously done under director Richard Donner, but at the time of filming Reeve told reporter Roderick Mann that morale on the picture was high and he was having a great time.[520] The first few weeks were no cakewalk for Reeve; he had lost weight making *Somewhere in Time*, and had to get back in top physical condition for *Superman II*.[521]

Along with Reeve's professional success came dramatic changes in his personal life. Though he was still reluctant to marry Gae Exton, the couple remained in a committed relationship. During the filming of *Superman II*, Exton gave birth to the couple's son, Matthew, at the Welbeck Street Clinic in Mayfair, London on December 20, 1979.[522]

Any thoughts that money would be saved by using footage shot while *Superman: The Movie* was in production were soon cast aside. To film the climax, in which Superman battles the three Kryptonian supervillains, an 800-foot section of New York's 42nd Street was constructed at Pinewood Studios, at a cost of $4 million.[523] For a brief shot of Superman landing in a rainforest to pick a flower to give to Lois, Reeve and a skeleton film crew were flown to the island of St. Lucia, further escalating the budget.[524]

The Salkinds and Pierre Spengler were worried; despite grosses of $85 million in the U.S. and $60 million in Europe for the first Superman film, they were still in the red. Ilya Salkind announced at the end of the Cannes Film Festival, during which he broke the news that there would definitely be a *Superman III*, that the cost of producing the two superhero epics had exploded from the $20 million originally budgeted to a whopping $109 million—and that was in 1980 dollars! At one point, they entered into talks with Dino De Laurentiis, producer of the 1977 *King Kong* remake, to take over the series. Eventually, the talks fell through, and Superman remained in the hands of the Salkinds, at least for the time being.[525]

Filming ended after eight months of shooting, on March 10, 1980.[526] John Williams was flown to England to score the movie. After showing him the film, Ilya Salkind left the screening room, leaving Williams alone with Richard Lester. The two did not hit it off; when Salkind returned, Williams told him he couldn't work with Lester. Another composer had to be found in a hurry. Ken Thorne, who had composed the background score for *Help!* (1965) and scored *The Magic Christian* (1969), *Royal Flash* (1975) and *Arabian Adventure* (1979) as well as episodes of *The Persuaders* TV series (1971), adapted Williams's music from the first film for the sequel.[527]

The popularity of the Superman films was not lost on American TV networks. On March 18, 1981, a new TV show called *The Greatest American Hero* debuted on ABC. William Katt played a schoolteacher who was given a suit by aliens that gave him amazing powers and abilities—except he didn't quite know how to use them. Warner Bros. felt the idea was too close to their superhero franchise, and took ABC to court, arguing that it infringed on their copyright and was unfair competition. Ultimately, a Manhattan Federal judge rejected Warners' claims, ruling that the bumbling character of *The Greatest American Hero* was almost the opposite of Superman, giving the show a different feel.[528]

With the film finished, Reeve prepared to leave England, but before he did he had lunch with producers Alex and Ilya Salkind and Pierre Spengler. They tried to entice him to do a third Superman film by promising him that they would do their best to come up with a good story for the next installment.[529] He signed his contract for the third film before the end of May; filming was set to begin the following spring for a summer, 1982 release.[530]

When the producers screened the finished film for Warner Bros. executives, the company, hoping to get some of their investment back as quickly as possible, decided to take a gamble and open the movie in every part of the world during each country's peak movie-going period. It opened at Christmastime in France, Italy, Spain, Australia, and South Africa. In England and West Germany, it opened at Easter. It would open in Japan and North America in the summer—six months after its release in other parts of the world. As gambles go, it was a calculated one. Having seen the film, the company felt it was a winner, and that the word-of-mouth coming from other parts of the globe would only be positive.[531]

Superman II flew onto 1,354 American and Canadian theaters on June 19, 1981.[532] Audiences and critics responded to the new Superman with enthusiasm. Sheila Benson of *The Los Angeles Times* said, "Superman with the taste of his own blood in his mouth? Superman *hitchhiking* to his top-of-the-world domain? Superman on the hard end of a haymaker? What goes on here? The most interesting 'Superman' yet.... In his two roles, Reeve is even better than he was in the first film."[533] In *The New York Times*, Janet Maslin wrote that without Christopher Reeve, who was "perfectly suited" to the role, the film would have suffered, saying, "It is Christopher Reeve, of course, without whom this movie would not be remotely possible." She added that Reeve's Superman gave the film "a warmth and energy it might not otherwise have. Mr. Reeve's Clark Kent is even better, because the actor is so delightfully engaged in sharing a private joke with an audience of several hundred million people. He manages to be as sympathetic as he is strong."[534]

Not all the press was so positive, however. Margot Kidder, still upset about the way Richard Donner had been replaced by Richard Lester, openly criticized the Salkinds and Pierre Spengler, saying, "I think they were scummy." The producers countered by saying that perhaps the Superman–Lois Lane romance had gone as far as it could go, hinting that Kidder's character might be dropped from *Superman III*.[535]

On its opening weekend in the U.S., *Superman II* broke box-office records with a first day gross of $4.4 million. The next day, it brought in $5.6 million, which at the time was the highest single box office day in movie history, surpassing the $4.5 million earned by *Star Wars* in 1977.[536] But the film did not generate the kind of repeat business of the original movie. It ended its run with a total domestic gross of over $65 million, almost $20 million less than its predecessor.[537] The film also sparked a new round of super merchandising. By the time of *Superman II*'s release, the Licensing Corporation of America, a Warner Communications subsidiary, had awarded two hundred licenses for more than 1,200 products tied to the two films. There was soap packaged like a telephone booth. There were Superman belt buckles, Superman watches, Superman pillowcases, Superman calendars, Superman pajamas, and a novelization of the first film. Even Bloomingdale's sold Superman sweatshirts.[538]

One part of the marketing campaign would eventually draw fire from the U.S. Congress a decade later. In 1979, before production of *Superman II* began, the Philip Morris tobacco company, maker of the world's number one best-selling cigarette, Marlboro, paid $40,000 for the product to appear in *Superman II*, which explains the prominent Marlboro delivery truck in the fight with the Kryptonian supervillains. A decade later, a Tokyo-based advertising agency paid the producers of the James Bond films $350,000 to feature Lark cigarettes in the 1989 film *Licence to Kill*; Lark's overseas distribution was also controlled by Philip Morris. These acts, among others, caused Congress to pursue legislation that would ban youth-oriented cigarette advertising.[539]

By April 1982, the success of *Superman II* had put the Salkinds back onto the road to financial recovery, and allowed them to finally settle the lawsuits that had been brought against them before the release of *Superman: The Movie* by Marlon Brando and Mario Puzo. The two settlements combined cost the producers $10 million. Another suit over profit participation, brought by Richard Donner, was settled soon after.[540]

Superman III

At one point, the debt amassed by the Salkinds in producing the first two Superman films amounted to over $70 million, most of it owed to a group of Swiss and Dutch banks (one Rotterdam banker even received a screen credit in *Superman II*). As they prepared to make *Superman III*, the budget estimate came in at $40 million. Though the Salkinds were still reportedly $10 million in debt, the banks loaned them the money to make *Superman III*. "They're interested in creating assets, so they can get paid," Alexander Salkind told *The New York Times* reporter Sandra Salmans.[541]

After considering comic book characters Brainiac and Mr. Mxyzptlk as possible villains for the new film,[542] screenwriters David and Leslie Newman began writing a script that took a different tack. They had come up with the basic idea for *Superman III* while working on *Superman II* in Niagara Falls. The bucolic quaintness of Niagara Falls got the Newmans thinking about small towns and the kind of Americana that played such a big part in the films of Frank Capra. After *Superman II*, where the stakes were so big—the destruction of the world—the writers felt they couldn't get any bigger, so they had to get small. Getting small meant taking Clark Kent back to his roots, in Smallville. "We never wanted to do anything more with Lois Lane," said David Newman. "So, we thought, remember that girl that Clark Kent used to like in high school? Wouldn't it be nice if he saw her, his old high school sweetheart, Lana Lang?" To complicate matters, the Newmans decided to make Lana a divorcee with a young son.[543]

Director Richard Lester agreed with the approach. "I think that if you try to do a bigger fight, a bigger battle, it's very difficult," he told Karen Stabiner of *Moviegoer* magazine, adding that instead of having more villains with more rockets against all of America, this time Superman's biggest battle was against himself. Lester hoped that although it was a different kind of fight, it would generate the same kind of excitement.[544]

More excitement was generated with the announcement that Richard Pryor would be co-starring with Reeve in the film. Pryor's involvement began with an appearance on NBC's late-night program *The Tonight Show Starring Johnny Carson*. The comedian, who had made his career with edgy stand-up comedy that attacked racism head-on before landing roles in such memorable films as *Lady Sings the Blues* (1972), *Car Wash* (1976) and *Silver Streak* (1976), had just seen *Superman II* and told Carson, "I love that dude." He then launched into a hilarious demonstration of what he would do if *he* had Superman's powers, saying, "Just give me some of that x-ray vision for one day and I'll be king. Maybe even emperor."[545]

Inspired by the comedian's enthusiasm for Superman, the Newmans and Lester began thinking how wonderful it would be if Richard Pryor were in the new movie.[546] The Newmans wrote the part of Gus Gorman especially for the comedian. Once hired, Pryor flew from his home in Hawaii to Pinewood Studios in London, where filming was about to commence.[547] Later, when asked what had attracted him to the project, he said, "It really was the $4 million."[548]

Before returning to work on *Superman III*, Christopher Reeve starred in *Monsignor* (1982) for producers Frank Yablans and David Niven, Jr. and director Frank Perry. He considered it a significant role that he thought would further establish him as a serious actor, but the film was more melodrama—even high camp—than drama, and did more harm than good to his box-office bankability. At first, Reeve wasn't anxious to step back into the Man of Steel's red boots, but he told reporter Dick Kleiner, "I overcame that attitude during the second week of shooting. There are some inventive things about *Superman III*. I've played the part three times now and it's become easy for me."[549] It also promised to be lucrative. After earning $250,000 for *Superman: The Movie* and $500,000 for *Superman II*, Reeve's deal for *Superman III* gave him a share of the rentals only. Clearly, he expected the new film to be as much of a financial juggernaut as the first two.[550]

Margot Kidder also returned for her third go-round as Lois Lane—but just barely. With a storyline that had Clark Kent returning to Smallville while Lois Lane went on vacation, Kidder's part was almost nonexistent. Some felt this was the Salkinds' way of punishing her for the disparaging remarks she had made to the press after Richard Donner was fired from *Superman II*. "I'm hardly in the film at all," she told Roderick Mann, "but that's all right. It was their decision. I'm not complaining. I owe a lot to Lois Lane. She made it possible for me to take off for Vancouver and play Chekhov for the rest of my life if I choose. And that can't be bad."[551]

To play Lana Lang, Annette O'Toole was brought into the film at the suggestion of David and Leslie Newman, who mentioned her to director Richard Lester after being impressed by her stage work. Her film and TV roles, from being a beauty queen in Michael Ritchie's satire *Smile* (1975) to a zoo keeper in Paul Schrader's 1982 remake of *Cat People*, to her star turn as Tammy Wynette in the TV movie *Stand by Your Man* (1981), showed her to be an accomplished actress able to shine in a wide diversity of roles.[552] As Lana Lang, the Houston, Texas, native was called upon to project small-town sweetness mixed with a sense of regret and longing for what might have been.

O'Toole enjoyed working with Christopher Reeve, who immediately put her at ease by personally taking her around the set on her first day to introduce her to the regular members of the Superman "family" who had worked on the first two films. That evening, Reeve and Gae Exton took O'Toole along with them to a Simon and Garfunkel concert. "My one regret was not getting to fly with Superman," said O'Toole. "But Margot Kidder offered to lend me her rig, and Chris arranged with the technicians to take me up for a brief spin. It was exhilarating."[553]

One of the last actors cast was Robert Vaughn, in a role for which the Newmans had envisioned another actor—Alan Alda. David Newman told an interviewer that they envisioned Ross Webster as the kind of character who, when he's first introduced, is receiving the Humanitarian of the Year award as the nicest guy in the world.[554] Vaughn seemed to relish playing the bad guy for a change; publicly, he was still seen as dashing spy Napoleon Solo, the character he played for four years on the NBC-TV series *The Man From U.N.C.L.E.* (1964–1968) and a 1983 TV movie based on the series. As Webster, he enlists the aid of computer genius Gus Gorman to help him corner the world's supplies of coffee and oil and—oh, yes—destroy Superman.

Among the actors returning to *Superman III* was one who played an integral part in the first film. In the opening title credit sequence, when Clark Kent ducks into a photo booth to change into Superman, there's a blond 8-year-old boy waiting next to the booth with his mother. The boy was played by Aaron Smolinski, a native of Calgary who had appeared in the first Superman film when it shot in Canada five years earlier; Smolinski played Superman as a toddler, emerging from the Kryptonian spacecraft and amazing Ma and Pa Kent by lifting their truck.[555]

Much of *Superman III* was filmed in Calgary, Alberta, Canada, substituting for Smallville, Kansas. In one scene set in a high school gymnasium, Clark sits down at the piano to play "Earth Angel." Annette O'Toole was surprised that Reeve was able to do it for real, instead of faking it. "I didn't know it 'til then," she said, "but he's a terrific pianist. That's Chris you'll hear playing in the scene, instead of the usual dubbing. He's also a writer, skier, speed skater and airplane pilot ... and he speaks several languages. I half expected to see him fly without the rig."[556]

Richard Lester decided to film the scene in one long take. When it was over, instead of calling "Cut," he pointed his finger at Reeve and said, "Bang." He then asked Reeve and O'Toole what movie he was thinking of. Receiving only befuddled looks, he answered, "*Shoot the Piano Player.*" O'Toole remembered, "It was that kind of a set. Always a little fun to cut the tension."[557]

For his part, Reeve had relaxed into the dual roles of Clark Kent and Superman. He told one reporter that since so much of playing Superman was physical, his approach was not to try too hard; a lot of it, he said, was "pure grace and humor. Much of the screen time has to be filled up with presence and that's harder to do, to get up there and simply stay relaxed, and to do that in what could be an embarrassing costume. Those are the challenges of Superman."[558]

In one scene, after Superman rescues Lana Lang's son, Ricky, the Man of Steel flies away but immediately reappears as Clark Kent. The star-struck boy tells the reporter that he's just seen Superman, and when Kent says that he knows the superhero, the boy asks Kent if he can get the Man of Steel's autograph. As he turns to walk away, Kent mutters, "If I had a nickel for every kid who asked me...." According to Reeve, the line was his idea, a last-minute self-reflexive ad-lib.[559]

There were more laughs on the set when the crew returned to Pinewood. One day, Christopher Reeve's old Juilliard classmate, Robin Williams, dropped by. Williams and Richard Pryor launched into an hour-long improvisation of the unabridged version of what happened the night Michael Fagin broke into Queen Elizabeth's bedroom. Pryor, as Fagin, asked, "Where is the Queen's bedroom?" Williams, as Prince Philip, answered, "Oh, don't ask me. I haven't been there in years."[560]

For Richard Lester, however, directing Pryor was a daunting task. Whenever he was working with Pryor on the soundstage, he closed the set to all but essential crewmembers. He was nervous about directing the comedic genius, but Lester was the kind of director who would have been more worried if he had had no worries. He believed that as opposed to the day-to-day worries over meeting the schedule and the budget, a deep-seated sense of anxiety and panic honed his focus. "A genuine sense of 'I don't know what I'm doing' is very good for us, especially as we get older," said the director.[561]

Pryor told Stephen Farber of *The Los Angeles Times* that he enjoyed certain aspects of making *Superman III*. He found it relaxing because he was only a part of the story, and wasn't expected to carry the entire film. However, he found it tedious doing the special effects shots, where much of what was seen on-screen would be added later, and he became bored being in London for three months and spending much of his time in a hotel room, on call. "I liked London," he said. "But after you see the Palace once or twice, it loses its charm. It was a good rest. It was one of those projects where you take the money and run. Don't look back."[562]

Production ended with the filming of a rather mundane scene. On the studio backlot, a replica of the rim of the Grand Canyon had been constructed, over which Robert Vaughn, Annie Ross and Pamela Stephenson would be lifted in hot air balloons held aloft by cranes.[563] In retrospect, it seems a fitting metaphor for a series that was beginning to run out of air.

In the summer of 1983, Superman faced an opponent greater than Lex Luthor and General Zod combined—Darth Vader. *Superman III* would be opening around the same time as the third *Star Wars* film, *Return of the Jedi*, so it was important to get the film on as many of the best screens in the biggest cities as possible. There was one theater it couldn't get booked into, however—a Marin County, California, venue that was the favorite of *Star Wars* creator George Lucas.[564] As it happened, *Return of the Jedi* opened almost a month earlier, on May 25; *Superman III* opened June 17, 1983.

In an interview in *Playgirl* magazine in December 1982, Christopher Reeve had voiced his criticism of President Ronald Reagan, saying, "I think Reagan is absolutely raping poor people in this country. He's frightening. He's got his priorities totally screwed up as to what this country needs and wants." When it came time for the *Superman III* premiere in Washington, D.C. in June 1983 (again benefiting the Special Olympics), Reagan's aides were concerned about whether the President and Reeve should be introduced, fearing Reeve would somehow use the event to voice his outspoken opinions. Consequently, the press and their cameras were kept at bay when the two finally met. The White House aides needn't have worried; Reeve and Reagan discussed the President's physical-fitness program and seemed to get along very well.

With all the restrictions imposed by the White House, Warner Bros., which picked up the tab for the event, were almost frozen out of their own party. Alexander Salkind had planned to present Reagan with one of the Superman capes used in the film, but those plans were nixed. Furthermore, press interviews with the filmmakers and stars were not permitted, but interviews with Reagan-friendly surf rock band The Beach Boys, who had nothing whatsoever to do with the film, were.[565]

As the film was hitting theaters, Richard Pryor made a return visit to NBC's *The Tonight Show Starring Johnny Carson* to promote it, and admitted that he had had some qualms about shooting the film's flying scenes. "I'm afraid of heights," he said. "Maybe you think a man can fly, but I'm still working on how planes get up there." He said that when he donned the flying harness and was lifted aloft for a scene in which Superman flies holding Gus Gorman, "I was still terrified. Then Chris came over to me and smiled his nice Superman smile and said, 'Don't worry, you won't fall. I'll hold you up.' That cat really *believes*."[566]

As the first Superman film fully under Richard Lester's direction, *Superman III* displayed more of the director's quirky humor, which was not necessarily a good thing. The opening title sequence, with an escalating series of slapstick mishaps reminiscent of silent comedies, set the tone for Lester's approach. In *The New York Times*, Janet Maslin wrote, "Anyone who has been following the Superman saga will find this installment enjoyable enough, but some of the magic is missing."[567] Sheila Benson of *The Los Angeles Times* wrote that "even with the dual talents of Christopher Reeve and Richard Pryor, *Superman III* has about half the invention, the sparkle and the originality you might hope for. You could love the earlier works of director Richard Lester and still be flattened by the film." She added that Margot Kidder, in her diminished role, was missed; the Clark Kent–Lana Lang story arc lacked the "fireworks and the eroticism of the first film."[568]

For actor Robert Vaughn, the release of the film had an interesting fallout close to home. "My son was about eight years old and ninety percent of the kids who went to his school were kids of investment bankers so they didn't understand what I did for a living. But when *Superman III* came out, it was, 'Cassidy Vaughn's dad tried to kill Superman!'"[569] However, since Vaughn didn't succeed, his son's stock went up considerably among his classmates.

After seeing the finished film, Christopher Reeve couldn't help but feel that it was a lesser effort. Whereas the first Superman film had taken a fabled view of America, *Superman III* was, in Reeve's opinion, more tongue-in-cheek and less epic. Lester's style, he said, didn't support Superman as a romantic figure.[570] In his book *Still Me*, Reeve said, "I did enjoy the sequence in which Superman has become an evil version of himself and tries to kill Clark Kent in an automobile junkyard. That scene stands alone; I think the rest of *Superman III* was mostly a misconception."[571]

Audiences agreed. When it ended its run, *Superman III* had only brought in $37,200,000 domestically, a little more than half as much as *Superman II* had made two summers earlier.[572] Seeing the handwriting on the wall, Reeve was not enthusiastic about returning for further Superman films. He felt they'd used up all of the character's super powers, and doubted whether the writers could come up with a good enough script.[573] More bluntly, he told Deborah Caulfield of *The Los Angeles Times*, "Look, I've flown, become evil, loved, stopped and turned the world backward. I've faced my peers, I've befriended children and small animals and I've rescued cats from trees. What else is there left for Superman to do that hasn't already been done?"[574] He also voiced his frustration to reporter Richard Freedman, saying, "I've enjoyed playing him. I enjoyed the eighth grade and college, too, but there comes a time when you're done with all that. And I'd have to be a fool to do it just for the money. Once an actor has turned that corner, there's no coming back."[575]

Indeed, Reeves's next two films were of a very high standard artistically. After completing *Superman III*, Reeve took $100,000—a tenth of his usual fee—to join the cast of *The Bostonians* (1984), an adaptation of a Henry James novel produced by Ismail Merchant and directed by James Ivory.[576] Like other Merchant-Ivory productions, it meticulously recreated a bygone era—in this instance, 19th century Boston—with Reeve giving a splendid performance as a Southern writer. Next, he starred in a film that drew upon his piloting skill as well as his acting skill. In *The Aviator* (1985), Reeve co-starred with Roseanne Arquette in a story in which he played an Air Mail pilot who takes on a reluctant passenger and crash lands before reaching his destination. Set in 1928, it was another lovingly crafted period romance that, like *The Bostonians*, failed to generate large box-office returns. But Reeve was still an in-demand actor, and one with a growing family; during production of *The Aviator*, his second child with Gae Exton, Alexandra, was born.

It seemed that after only three films, the series that Ilya Salkind hoped would have the popularity and longevity of the James Bond films had run its course, but the Salkinds were not yet finished with bringing superheroes to the big screen.

Supergirl

While *Superman III* was in theaters, the Salkinds were moving forward with a spin-off project, *Supergirl*. Budgeted at $35 million, much of the cost of the production was raised through presales to foreign distributors, Thorn EMI (who would distribute it on video) and ABC television. Seeing the story as more of a fantasy than an action film, Ilya Salkind called Gary Kurtz, a producer on the first two *Star Wars* films, to ask about a writer named David Odell, who had written *The Dark Crystal* for Kurtz. The screenwriter was brought to London to meet with Salkind, and they began developing a story. After the two of them spent a day at a comic book convention, Odell went away and wrote a treatment—one that would have cost $150 million to produce. The story took place on several planets, and featured not only Supergirl but also her cousin, Superman. To bring the budget to a more modest level, the story was altered so that it took place almost entirely on Earth.[577]

Ilya Salkind and his co-producer, Timothy Burrill, began searching for a director. Salkind wanted someone who had experience with a big-budget, crowd-pleasing film. One name considered was Robert Wise, whose credits included such science fiction classics as *The Day the Earth Stood Still* (1951) and the mega-budget *Star Trek: The Motion Picture* (1979), which had brought the highly popular television series to the big screen.[578] But after seeing *Jaws 2* (1978), Salkind approached Jeannot Szwarc, who had also directed Christopher Reeve's first post–*Superman* film, *Somewhere in Time* (1980). Salkind liked the sweetness of *Somewhere in Time*, not to mention its strong appeal to women, both qualities he hoped Swarzc would bring to *Supergirl*.[579] Szwarc was on the same page; he saw Supergirl as a modern take on *The Wizard of Oz* (1939).[580]

But not all was sweetness behind the scenes. The original script called for scenes of Argo City on Krypton, but Jeannot Szwarc felt it would be too much like *Superman: The Movie* if there were extended scenes on Superman's home planet; he wanted Argo City to be completely separate, with its own look and style. Ilya Salkind recalls that the original script also had Selena, the villain, teaming up with Brainiac. Warner Bros. liked the original, expensive script; they were less enthusiastic about the rewrite. As story discussions between the studio and the producers soured, the studio—feeling the Salkinds were out of sync with them on the project and aware of the diminishing box office returns of the *Superman* films—told the Salkinds to take it elsewhere. The producers approached Tri-Star (a division of Columbia Pictures), who agreed to distribute it.[581]

When it came to casting the lead role, Alexander Salkind, the elder of the producing team, had his heart set on Brooke Shields, a young actress who achieved notoriety playing a teenage prostitute in *Pretty Baby* (1978) before becoming a national icon as the spokesmodel for Calvin Klein blue jeans. Ilya disagreed. He thought the role should be played by an unknown, just as Superman had been.[582] The younger Salkind engaged the services of casting director Lynn Stalmaster, who auditioned hundreds of young actresses, including Demi Moore. Salkind wanted Moore for the role of Lois Lane's younger sister, Lucy, but Moore took a role in the Stanley Donen film *Blame It on Rio* (1984) instead.[583] Helen Slater, a 19-year-old graduate of New York's School for the Performing Arts (immortalized in Alan Parker's 1980 film, *Fame*), impressed Jeannot Szwarc in her screen test. When Ilya showed his father the test, Alexander reluctantly gave in. Helen Slater was signed for $75,000, a fraction of what Shields would have cost.[584]

At first, Dolly Parton was considered for the part of Selena. Ultimately, the role went to Faye Dunaway, who had previously starred in the Salkinds' *Three Musketeers* films.[585] "One of the reasons I took this role is that I loved what Gene Hackman and Ned Beatty did in the first *Superman*," Dunaway told columnist Roderick Mann. "I loved that comic villainy of theirs, so I thought it would be fun to have a go myself."[586]

During casting sessions in New York, Peter Gallagher was seen for the role of the male love interest, but it was Hart Bochner, who would later make a memorable impression in *Die Hard* (1988), who won the role. Rounding out the cast were Peter O'Toole, Simon Ward and Mia Farrow in the Argo City scenes, and Brenda Vaccaro and British comedian Peter Cook in the earthbound scenes. To give the film a sense of continuity with the Superman series, Marc McClure appeared as Jimmy Olsen, with a larger role than some of the Superman films afforded him.[587]

When Szwarc took the helm, Tri-Star asked for changes in the script. Screenwriter David Odell was beginning to feel burned out by the never-ending rewrites, yet more were to come. Christopher Reeve, who (according to Ilya Salkind) had been interested early on, ultimately decided that it wouldn't be right for him, and decided not to appear in the new film. Scenes of Superman and Supergirl meeting and flying together in space, and Superman losing his powers and becoming old, leaving only Supergirl to save the earth from Selena's black magic powers, were now dropped, prompting further revisions.[588]

The film began shooting at Pinewood on a backlot set representing Midvale, Illinois. Some of the technical crew from the Superman films were back, including miniature effects genius Derek Meddings.[589] The filming went very smoothly; maybe too smoothly. Ultimately, Ilya Salkind felt that Szwarc lacked some of the creative fire of Richard Donner and Richard Lester, with whom he had terrific fights during filming. Szwarc, he said, was a little too sweet.[590]

When Szwarc previewed the film for the studio, they were dismayed by its lyrical, fairy tale quality, such as the scenes of Supergirl discovering her new powers on earth, causing a budding flower to open with her X-ray vision, and doing a solo aerial ballet (beautifully shot by cinematographer Alan Hume).[591]

The film was screened for preview audiences in New York and Los Angeles, who felt it was too long, so some scenes were trimmed. It was mostly the lyrical scenes that were excised. The longer version was released internationally, while the shorter version was released in the U.S. In its theatrical trailers and TV spots, *Supergirl* was made to look like an action film; Szwarc felt the studio wanted "Superman in drag," and that they promoted it as such.[592] He feared that audiences who came in expecting fast-paced action instead of a more light-hearted fantasy would be disappointed. He was right. Janet Maslin, writing in *The New York Times*, said the new film "is never as boldly witty as *Superman II*, still the best in the series. Even Miss Dunaway, who seems to be vastly enjoying her witch's role, is constrained by the mildness of the material," adding that Helen Slater was "great fun to look at but hardly a live wire."[593] On the other hand, Roger Ebert of *The Chicago Sun-Times* wrote that Helen Slater was the best thing in the film. He felt she had "the kind of freshness, good health, high spirits, and pluck that would be just right for the character." However, he felt the film as a whole was "an unhappy, unfunny, unexciting movie. Why even go to the trouble of making a movie that feels like it's laughing at itself?"[594]

Financially, the film was an unqualified failure. Audiences stayed away, uninspired by the marketing campaign and their growing disenchantment with a series that had begun on such a high note but quickly went astray with the kind of over-the-top campiness the original tried to avoid. By the time it ended its run, *Supergirl* had brought in only $6 million in domestic rentals, about one-tenth of the rental income from *Superman: The Movie*.[595]

In a 1988 interview, reflecting on the film's failure, Ilya Salkind pointed out that aside from *Wonder Woman* on television, very few films about superheroines had ever been a success, adding, "I guess *Supergirl* was perhaps too campy."[596]

Superman IV: The Quest for Peace

The failure of *Supergirl*, combined with the precipitous drop-off in revenues of the Superman films, gave the Salkinds pause. Each new entry had earned less than the one before it, and the slew of lawsuits that followed the first film insured that the Salkinds had not seen much of a profit on their Superman investment. So when Menahem Golan and Yoram Globus, the principals of Cannon Films, came to them with an offer to buy the Superman license, the Salkinds—who were preparing their $50 million production of *Santa Claus* (1985) for release—were ready to listen.

Menahem Golan (whose last name was originally Globus before he changed it in honor of the Golan Heights) and his cousin Yoram Globus came to America in 1979 and bought a controlling interest in Cannon Films, a company known for minor B-movies. The Israeli filmmakers secured a distribution deal with MGM and immediately began cranking out low-budget exploitation films, scoring an early hit with *Death Wish II* (1982), in which Charles Bronson reprised one of his most famous roles. With aggressive publicity and marketing campaigns, Cannon was able to turn hefty profits on cheaply produced movies, and was soon producing more films annually than even the major studios. As the 1980s progressed and their profits expanded, along with the amounts banks were willing to extend to them in loans, Golan and Globus purchased an international theater chain from Lord Lew Grade, as well as Thorn-EMI, a British company that owned Elstree Studios and a large video library.[597]

On June 18, 1985, Cannon announced that they had purchased the rights to produce *Superman IV* and all further Superman films. The deal had been in the works since the final day of the Cannes Film Festival the month before. Menahem Golan told *Variety*, "It's the biggest deal in our company's history." Production of *Superman IV*, said Golan, would begin the next year with a budget in the $30 million range, and Warner Bros. would release the film in 1987. "We will carefully maintain the spirit of the Superman series," said Golan.[598] In fact, they had not purchased the series outright, but rather had bought an option on it. Their ability to make Superman films would be contingent upon their ability to make on-going payments to the Salkinds.[599]

With the Superman acquisition, Cannon seemed to be cornering the market on big-screen superhero adaptations. They had already snapped up the film rights to *Captain America* and *Spider-Man* from Marvel Comics, and planned on producing both films in 1986.[600] Taking on the high-profile Superman series was part of Cannon's calculated move to change their public image, downplaying their prolific stream of low-budget action films starring Charles Bronson and Chuck Norris. They also produced the John Cassavetes film *Love Streams* (1984), a film version of Sam Shepard's play *Fool for Love* (1985) with Robert Altman directing, and Franco Zefferelli's version of the opera *Otello* (1986). Golan and Globus hoped these ventures would garner them some Academy Awards. "It's important the way the public looks at us," said Golan. "We don't only want to be involved in schlock."[601]

After filming *Superman III*, Christopher Reeve thought he had put the role behind him for good. He told reporter Lawrence Van Gelder, "After *Superman III* I thought, what's the point? This isn't worth it. Then I thought: Rather than complain about the situation, maybe I should take responsibility for this character and do something." While on a skiing vacation in Vermont in 1985, Reeve began thinking about a story in which Superman ends the arms race.[602] The seed of the idea came from another project in which Reeve was involved. "I narrated a documentary made by a group of Boston school children called *A Message to Our Parents*," said Reeve. "These kids had traveled to Washington and Moscow, asking officials in the State Department and Politburo about their future in the nuclear age."[603]

Reeve used Superman as leverage for another project. He had found a strong script that he wanted to make to give his career a boost: *Street Smart*, written by David Freeman. He met with Menahem Golan and Yoram Globus, who said that if Reeve would appear in another Superman, they would produce and finance *Street Smart*.[604] Reeve agreed, on condition that he would be given greater artistic control of *Superman IV*; he wanted to direct the film.[605] A deal was signed with Reeve receiving $5 million for the new Superman film, plus a piece of the profits.[606]

Reeve pitched his Superman disarmament story to Menahem Golan, and was given the go-ahead. With David and Leslie Newman having retired from the Superman business, the writing team of Lawrence Konner and Mark Rosenthal were hired to complete the script for *Superman IV*. Konner and Rosenthal had previous sequel writing experience, having penned *The Jewel of the Nile* (1985), the follow-up to *Romancing the Stone* (1984). At a time when President Ronald Reagan was referring to the Soviet Union as the Evil Empire, Reeve and the screenwriters forged ahead with a story where the Man of Steel rids the world of nuclear weapons.[607] Within three weeks, they had a complete outline.[608]

In *Superman IV: The Quest for Peace*, a 12-year-old boy writes to Superman urging him to fight for world peace. The Man of Steel takes the letter to heart, and takes it upon himself to physically confiscate all the world's nuclear weapons, which he hurls into the sun. But when Lex Luthor escapes captivity, he steals a single strand of Superman's hair, from which he creates an evil clone called Nuclear Man and threatens the now defenseless globe. Reeve wanted to show that Superman was an interplanetary citizen who had made Earth his home and was taking responsibility for what happened on the entire planet. He didn't want Superman to be accused of being American propaganda, adding, "We're living in a global village now, and there has to be a new heightened awareness of our interactions as people on this planet."[609]

Reeve made *Street Smart* before suiting up for *Superman IV*. Directed by Jerry Schatzberg, *Street Smart* began principal photography in New York on April 1, 1986.[610] After a few days shooting in Harlem, the production moved to Montreal to save costs. Playing opposite Reeve was Morgan Freeman, an actor then best known as "Easy Reader" on the children's TV series *The Electric Company*. After his stunning performance in *Street Smart* (which earned him an Academy Award nomination), Freeman soon entered the "A" list of Hollywood actors.[611] Upon its release, *Street Smart* garnered strong reviews, but with Cannon's poor publicity campaign, it failed to generate much heat at the box office.[612]

Privately, Reeve was hurt by the failure of *Street Smart*, but publicly he seemed to take it in stride, saying that doing the occasional Superman film gave him the financial security to be able to take riskier roles. "I don't wake up in the morning and ask myself how I'm going to twist my image around or find ways to prove my versatility," said Reeve. "It makes sense financially for me to continue playing Superman, but I wouldn't do it unless the quality remained high."[613]

Production of *Superman IV* was scheduled to begin in Canada on September 23, 1986.[614] Budgeted at $32 million, the production—like previous Superman films—was based in England, this time at Cannon's Elstree Studios in Hertfordshire.[615]

Not long after Cannon acquired the rights to Superman, director Sidney J. Furie, who had previously helmed *Lady Sings the Blues* (1972), walked into Menahem Golan's office to pitch him an idea. Golan passed on Furie's project, but countered by offering him *Superman IV*.[616] Golan was worried about Christopher Reeve's costly vision of the new film; he hoped Furie, who had just had a hit with the low-budget action film *Iron Eagle* (1986), could bring in a sure-fire action film on a much smaller budget.[617] Furie immediately accepted the challenge. When the director later mentioned to Warner Bros. how bad *Superman III* was, the Warners execs responded that the film brought in fifty million in rentals; if Furie could give them half that, they'd be happy.[618]

Iron Eagle aside, Furie had never been in charge of a mega-budget, effects-driven picture before, and he knew he'd have to learn if he wanted to remain employable. *Superman IV* would give him on-the-job-training. In a *Starlog* magazine interview with Edward Gross, Furie said that since the series had already gone off track once, he felt he had little to lose. "You just jump in," said Furie. "Courage is part of all creative people."[619] His hiring, however, meant that Christopher Reeve was demoted to second unit director.[620] Nonetheless, once filming began, Reeve said, "I have the old enthusiasm back."[621]

The filmmakers decided to bring back Gene Hackman as Lex Luthor. In fact, Sidney J. Furie said he wouldn't have done the film without the actor. He believed that Hackman's Lex Luthor was a wonderful comedic villain, and it was having Hackman opposite Reeve that gave the film its yin and yang.[622]

Furie also fought to bring Margot Kidder back. The actress asked for a large amount of money to return to the role, as Furie felt she should; a man would have been paid the fee without question. Negotiations went on for five months. When it looked like they might go without Kidder, Furie told the producers that without her, there was no picture. Finally, a deal was reached.[623] "The whole idea of a sequel," said Furie, "is to relive the best things of the movie again in a fresh way, but not too fresh. If you really want those same thrills, kicks and things, we had to have those characters." [624]

In a misguided attempt to appeal to the youth market, Jon Cryer, co-star of *Pretty in Pink* (1986), was hired to play Lex Luthor's sidekick, in lieu of Otis. With his punk hairdo and "whoa, dude" surfer-speak, he became an annoying presence who is, thankfully, in few scenes.

Before filming began, Cannon announced a $60 million loss, and immediately reduced the budget of *Superman IV* even farther. The original special effects wizards who had made Superman fly in the first three films were replaced with a new team headed by Harrison Ellenshaw, the founder of Industrial Light & Magic's matte painting department. Ellenshaw raided talent from other effects houses in Hollywood to create an in-house effects company, cleverly named OLW (Olsen Lane and White), after the supporting Superman characters. [625]

The budget cuts dictated that all exterior shots that were supposed to take place on American streets would be filmed on the Elstree backlot or at locations in England.[626] In *Still Me*, Christopher Reeve wrote that for one scene, in which Superman lands on 42nd Street and walks down the roadway to the United Nations to deliver a speech, instead of filming on location with hundreds of extras and vehicles as Richard Donner would have, Sidney Furie shot the scene on a rainy day at an industrial park in England with no cars, only a hundred extras, and a dozen pigeons.[627]

Part of the problem with *Superman IV* is that it tried too hard to recapture the magic of the earlier films. In one scene, Superman goes flying with Lois Lane (a throwback to *Superman: The Movie*), reveals his identity to her, and then gives her amnesia with a kiss (a throwback to *Superman II*). Rather than tributes to the previous films, these "homages" seemed more like tired retreads and furthered the overall feeling that the series had run out of fresh ideas. And as if it weren't bad enough that wires were sometimes visible in the flying shots, in the scene in which Superman and Nuclear Man battle each other on the moon, one can clearly see the folds in the black curtain in the background that's meant to represent the vastness of space. Who's to blame for this? The director? If so, then the blame falls on the shoulders of Christopher Reeve, who reportedly directed the lunar scenes. No wonder that twelve years later, in his autobiography *Still Me*, he wrote, "The less said about *Superman IV* the better."[628]

Of course, no Superman film would be complete if it didn't generate a lawsuit. In March, 1987, Christopher Reeve found himself on the receiving end of a suit filed by writers Barry E. Taff and Kenneth Stoller, who claimed that Reeve had stolen the idea for *Superman IV* from a treatment they had sent to him. Reeve, along with Warner Bros. and Cannon, whom the writers charged went along with Reeve's claims that he came up with the idea on his own, was being sued for $45 million.[629] In documents filed in Los Angeles Superior Court, Taff and Stoller asked for a preliminary injunction to stop the July 17 release of *Superman IV*. The pair claimed that a copy of their treatment outline called "Superman: The Confrontation," which had been registered with the Writers Guild and copyrighted, was sent to Warner Bros. in August 1985. The outline, they said, went to Reeve personally, and the actor promised the writers by phone to take it to the studio. After that, they said, Reeve never called back; the next they heard was when Reeve gave interviews talking about his concept for a new Superman movie, with ideas similar to those in the Taff-Stoller treatment, such as Superman saving the world from nuclear holocaust, hurling the world's nuclear missiles into the sun, addressing the U.N., and Superman's death and resurrection through a device from Krypton that could only be used once.[630] Reeve later filed a cross-complaint seeking damages in excess of $100,000; this was seen as an attempt to recover his attorneys' fees in defending the case.[631] Reeve's attorney said that the treatment written by Taff, a parapsychologist and biomedical researcher, and Stoller, a pediatrician, did not contain material included in *Superman IV*. The writers had signed a standard release that stated if the actor read the script, the duo would not later claim he used the material. The suit dragged on until the end of October 1990, when the writers lost their case. The suit was dismissed.[632]

The original release date of *Superman IV* was Christmas 1987. But in January, Warner Bros. decided it would be better to release it in the summer. The official reason given was that they viewed it as a film that would have great family appeal, so a summer release, when the kids were out of school, was preferable.[633] The real reason is that Warners was disappointed with the finished film, which looked every bit as cheap as Cannon's exploitation films. The flying scenes particularly suffered; without Zoran Perisic's Zoptic system, Ellenshaw had reverted to unconvincing blue-screen opticals. When the film was finally released on July 24, 1987, the studio, after cutting it from 134 to 89 minutes, gave it only the minimum of promotional support; it died a quick death.[634]

Nonetheless, Janet Maslin of *The New York Times* remained supportive, writing, "Christopher Reeve is still giving this character his all, and especially in his bumbling Clark Kent incarnation he remains delightful.... Also back, and also a treat, is Gene Hackman as the gleefully malevolent Lex Luthor. Jon Cryer does a funny turn as Luthor's obnoxious nephew."[635] Most reviewers, though, agreed with *Variety*'s assessment: "Hackman gets a few laughs, but has less to work with than before, and everyone else seems to be just going through the motions and having less fun doing so."[636] When asked if there would be a *Superman V*, Christopher Reeve said that while the current film would be his last, "you never know. To take it one step at a time and not make predictions is the best thing to do."[637] In

Still Me, Reeve wrote, "*Superman IV* was simply a catastrophe from start to finish. That failure was a huge blow to my career."[638]

It was also a blow to Cannon. As with many "mini-majors" of the 1980s, Cannon expanded too fast, and sealed their own doom with the production of high budget movies like *Lifeforce* (1985), *Masters of the Universe* (1987) and *Superman IV: The Quest for Peace* (1987), all of which lost money at the box office. By 1989, the company was facing bankruptcy proceedings and was being investigated by the Securities and Exchange Commission for omissions in its financial records. Golan blamed Globus, causing a rift between the cousins that would take several years to mend. Leaving Cannon, Golan formed 21st Century Film Corporation. After both companies produced competing movies based on the Brazilian lambada dance that were released on the same day, both Cannon and 21st Century faded from the scene.[639]

Had the Salkinds remained involved with Superman, *Superman IV* would likely have been a better film, or at least a better-looking one. Whatever their faults as producers, the Salkinds took pride in their movies. After all, one of the reasons the first two Superman films went outrageously over budget is that the producers spent millions perfecting the flying techniques. Golan and Globus, on the other hand, produced their films so cheaply that they seemed to have contempt for their audiences. As a result, *Superman IV: The Quest for Peace* was a sad end to a once-great series.

Aftermath

During the filming of *Superman IV*, Christopher Reeve was facing personal problems. His relationship with Gae Exton, which began nearly ten years earlier, was deteriorating. When the production ended in February 1987, Reeve moved back to New York, leaving Exton and his children in England[640]; a relationship that began at the time of his first Superman film ended with his last.

Later that summer, working with the Williamstown Theatre Festival in Massachusetts, Reeve met a cabaret singer named Dana Morosini. He was immediately attracted to her, but Dana was no pushover. She thought Reeve would be "an arrogant, stuck-up movie star idiot," whom she wanted nothing to do with.[641] But Reeve wooed her persistently, and within four months they were living together.

The following year, Reeve's relationship with his father broke down. Reeve had been working with novelist and playwright Ariel Dorfman on a screenplay based on Reeve's experiences in Chile, where he had been trying to save the lives of seventy-seven actors threatened with execution by the Pinochet regime. He showed the outline to his father (who was a writer) and asked for suggestions. His father protested, saying he objected to being used in that way, and stormed out of the house. For the next several years, Reeve and his father avoided each other.[642]

On April 7, 1990, *Screen International* reported that the Salkinds were preparing *The New Superman Movie*, with Christopher Reeve again set to star as Superman.[643] Ilya Salkind had developed the script with Mark Jones and former DC Comics writer Cary Bates, who had collaborated with him on the *Superboy* TV series (1988–1992). The story had Superman preparing to marry Lois Lane, until the reporter was kidnapped by Brainiac. It also involved Superman dying and being resurrected in the bottle city of Kandor. According to Salkind, he had lunch with Christopher Reeve at the Carlisle in New York, and Reeve was ready to do it.[644] A *Hollywood Reporter* article in November, 1991, announced that Arnold Schwarzenegger rejected the role of Brainiac in *Superman V*, opting instead to play "the main guy who helps Superman."[645]

However, by that time, Warners had had a phenomenal success with *Batman* (1989), and, according to Salkind, they tried to squelch *Superman V* so they could develop a competing project, *Lois & Clark*, for television. A spate of lawsuits arose. Salkind pressed on; in October of 1992, *The Hollywood Reporter* said that Salkind was moving forward with *Superman—The New Movie*, and that Christopher Reeve had been offered the lead role, with negotiations "dependent on what price he'll accept." The film was to be budgeted at $40 million.[646] As the delays stretched from months into years, Reeve moved on. When it was revealed in 1994 that he was once again being considered to play the role that made him famous, Reeve, at age 42, said he was at least ten years too old for the role. "I think every generation should have a Superman for its own time," he told reporter Dann Gire. "I was the right Superman for the '70s and early '80s."[647] Eventually, Ilya Salkind gave up the fight to get the new film going.[648]

In the meantime, Christopher Reeve had overcome his lifelong fear of marriage and, in April 1992, wed Dana Morosini in Williamstown, Massachusetts.[649] Two months later, their son, Will, was born. Though not the major star he had been when *Superman: The Movie* opened in 1978, Reeve was still a much in-demand actor, appearing in films and TV movies. Reeve wrote that it was a time in which his personal and professional lives seemed perfectly balanced.[650]

Then came the accident.

In 1984, while filming *Anna Karenina* in Budapest, Reeve mounted a horse for a steeplechase scene. Riding alongside the pros, he was bitten by the riding bug. He took up the sport in earnest when he returned to New York, training at a small barn in Bedford. Later that year, when he returned to the Williamstown Theatre Festival in Massachusetts, where he had acted for almost every summer since he was fifteen, he went riding with friends. By 1989, he was competing in combined training events, involving dressage, stadium jumping and cross-country jumping.[651] In 1992, Reeve and his wife Dana moved from the Flatiron district of New York out to the country, which they thought would be better for Will. The move also allowed Reeve to ride six days a week.[652]

From that time on, whenever Reeve traveled to film locations, he found the best trainers in the area and took riding lessons. At the end of May 1995, Reeve was preparing to leave for Ireland, where he was to star in a new film version of *Kidnapped* produced by Francis Ford Coppola and directed by Ivan Passer. He had already rented a house next to a stable and had made arrangements to train with some of the country's best event riders. But before leaving for the Emerald Isle, he wanted to participate in the last event in which he would be able to compete for the season. Originally, he was going to ride in an event in Vermont over the Memorial Day weekend, but at the last minute, he changed his mind. His first riding coach, Bill McGuinness, had called and asked him to join a group going to compete in Culpepper, Virginia. Since Reeve thought it would be more fun to compete as part of a group, he made a last-minute change of plans and agreed to go along.[653]

On May 27, 1995, Reeve prepared to compete with his horse Eastern Express, nicknamed Buck. He had bought the light chestnut gelding in California in 1994, while appearing in John Carpenter's remake of *Village of the Damned*. Reeve competed in the dressage portion in the morning, coming in fourth place. He then went to his nearby hotel room to have lunch with Dana and Will, suited back up and returned to the track. After walking the course, he began his cross-country ride on Buck at 3:01 P.M. Everything went well until Buck came to the third jump, a zig-zag fence just over three feet high. Without warning, Buck came to an abrupt halt. Reeve didn't. The horse put its head down, and as Reeve sailed over the horse's head, his hands became entangled in the bridle, which prevented him from putting his arms out to break his fall. Head first, he struck the top rail of the jump fence. His neck broke. He fell in a heap on the other side of the fence. After gasping "I can't breathe," he passed out. [654]

His first cervical vertebra was shattered. The second vertebra was broken. The broken vertebrae cut and damaged nerves in his spinal cord. Reeve stopped breathing. Paramedics arrived on the scene after three minutes, pumped air into his lungs, immobilized his neck with a collar and took him to the hospital.[655]

The accident was headline news all over the world. Suddenly, both the tabloids and legitimate news outlets were talking about a "Superman curse," pairing Christopher Reeve's tragedy with the memory of George Reeves's suicide.

As the world quickly found out, Reeve was totally paralyzed from the neck down, unable even to breathe on his own. Beyond his medical condition, he suffered overwhelming depression. In those first dark days, envisioning a life of total dependency, he contemplated suicide because he didn't want to be a burden to his family. He said to his wife, "Maybe we should let me go." Crying, Dana said she would support whatever he wanted to do, but stressed that she would be with him for the long haul. "You're still you," she said, "and I love you." Reeve later wrote that those were the words that saved his life.[656]

After six months of rehabilitation, he and Dana returned to their home in Bedford, New York. Reeve had learned how to operate a wheelchair that could be manipulated by puffing or sipping a straw. In the years after his accident, he suffered pneumonia, blood clots, infections, open wounds that took weeks to heal, and autonomic dysreflexia, a dangerous blood pressure condition. But all the while, he used his celebrity status to advocate for research into spinal cord injuries. In 1996, he appeared at the Academy Awards—his first national public appearance after the accident—and later that year spoke at the Democratic National Convention. He remained financially self-sufficient by accepting speaking engagements (reports that Robin Williams paid his medical bills were unfounded). He continued acting, first with a role in the CBS television movie *A Step Toward Tomorrow* (1996), and later in a remake of *Rear Window* (1998). He directed the Emmy award–winning *In the Gloaming* (1997) for HBO. And he accepted an important part on a TV show he greatly admired, *Smallville* (2003).[657]

Reeve advocated for spinal cord research, stem cell research and insurance reform in Washington. He became Chairman of the American Paralysis Association and Vice Chairman of the National Organization on Disability, as well as co-founder (with philanthropist Joan Irvine Smith) of the Reeve-Irvine Research Center in California. In 1996, he created the Christopher Reeve Foundation, which raised research money and provided grants to local agencies dealing with the disabled. Through his efforts, Reeve raised $55 million in research grants and over $7 million for nonprofit organizations dealing with quality of life issues for the disabled.[658]

The accident helped heal Reeve's relationship with his father, who visited him often. In *Still Me*, Reeve wrote, "Out of this disaster has come a new beginning."[659]

Eventually, Reeve regained sensation in his left leg and areas of his left arm, and the ability to move his index finger. He kept a positive outlook about his future, saying, "I'm realistically optimistic. I don't plan to spend the rest of my life like this."[660]

In early October 2004, Dana was in Los Angeles, where she was appearing in the play *Brooklyn Boy*. Reeve, at home in New York, was suffering from a pressure wound, a complication common for people with paralysis. This time, it had become severely infected. Still, there seemed to be no unusual cause for alarm; Reeve had had pressure wounds before. On October 9, he attended his son Will's hockey game. That night, after receiving an antibiotic,

Reeve went into cardiac arrest and fell into a coma. He was rushed to Northern Westchester Hospital. Robin Williams's wife helped Dana board a plane to fly across country. She arrived just before he died on October 10. Their son Will and Reeve's daughter Alexandra were also at his bedside. It was just a few weeks past his 52nd birthday.[661]

Fans around the world were shocked. One particularly poignant editorial cartoon showed Reeve's wheelchair in the lower right of frame, and in the upper left, Superman flying out of frame. That said it all. After years of suffering, Reeve's spirit had taken flight, ascending into the heavens like Superman.

Dana Reeve became the new chairperson of the Christopher Reeve Paralysis Foundation and vowed to carry on her husband's work. Less than a year after her husband's death, she was diagnosed with lung cancer. On March 6, 2006, the 44-year-old passed away.[662]

In *Still Me*, Christopher Reeve wrote, "I think a hero is an ordinary individual who finds the strength to persevere and endure in spite of overwhelming obstacles."[663] By that definition, Christopher and Dana Reeve were real-life heroes whose lives were more inspirational than any comic book creation could ever hope to be.

8

Echoes of the Past

Superman's 50th Anniversary

In 1986, comic book writer John Byrne did a "revamp" of the Superman comic book series. In Byrne's revised version, Clark Kent grew up in Smallville and didn't adopt the Superman persona until he went to Metropolis. Also in the new version, Lois Lane was in love with Clark Kent, but at the same time infatuated with Superman; Clark Kent was no longer the nebbish in Superman's shadow. There was no Supergirl, no Superdog, no Kryptonian horses and monkeys; Superman was the sole survivor of Krypton, period. "All of the debris that has accumulated over the years has been the result of people trying to do something different," Byrne said at the time. "So now I'm taking Superman back to basics, and that becomes different because it hasn't been done in so long. It's basically Siegel and Shuster's Superman meets the Fleischer Superman in 1986."[664]

Two years later, Superman celebrated his 50th anniversary. *Time* magazine featured the Man of Steel on its March 14, 1988, cover. CBS aired a TV special, an unfortunately ill-conceived affair produced by Lorne Michaels, Peter Guber and future *Superman* producer Jon Peters. An odd mix of comedy skits and interview sound bites, the special was a masterpiece of missed opportunities. Jack Larson and Noel Neill appear, but only in comedy bits (Neill plays Lois Lane's mother, questioning her daughter's dating choices); Kirk Alyn, thankfully, gets to give some reminisces about his days as the Man of Steel. Writing about the special in *The New York Times*, John J. O'Connor said that Dana Carvey was a fine host as long as he was presenting clips from the serials, films and TV shows, "but too often he has to introduce labored comedy sketches that, despite the participation of names such as Hal Holbrook, Peter Boyle, Jimmy Breslin and Ralph Nader, are sadly uninspired. At this stage of the pop game, Superman deserves more than a soggy, albeit good-natured sendup."[665]

That same year, Superman returned to Saturday morning TV in a new animated series from Ruby-Spears, a company founded in 1977 by Joe Ruby and Ken Spears, the creators of Scooby-Doo. Ruby-Spears had scored hits with *Thundarr the Barbarian* (1980–1982), *Rubik the Amazing Cube* (1983–1984), a new version of *Alvin and the Chipmunks* (1983–1991) and new cartoons featuring the Looney Tunes characters. For their Superman series, they went to the source, DC Comics. DC artist Gil Kane provided character designs, and writer Marv Wolfman became story editor. The stories followed the John Byrne revamp, portraying Lex Luthor as a billionaire industrialist. The final four minutes of each episode were given over to brief vignettes from Clark Kent's early days in Smallville, with the super-powered youngster learning to deal with issues such as his first day at school, getting his driver's license, and his first kiss.

To voice the Man of Steel, the producers hired Beau Weaver, a veteran voice-over artist who was born in Oklahoma and began working as a radio personality in the 1970s at stations in Los Angeles, San Diego, San Francisco, Houston and Dallas. He became a satellite broadcasting pioneer in the early 1980s, as one of the original on-air talents of Transtar Radio Network, the forerunner to Westwood One. Weaver was also the originator of the idea that geography should be no barrier to talent; in the 1980s, he began doing TV station promos from his location in Colorado utilizing phone patches and overnight courier. By 1990, he was sending his work to clients over digital hookup, faster than a speeding bullet. An aggressive marketer, Weaver was the first voice-over artist with a website, and the first to deliver broadcast audio to clients using MP3 compression.[666]

Though the character was drawn to appear more like the Superman of the comic books, the animation of the Ruby-Spears *Superman* was of the standard cost-effective limited variety. The show's opening sequence was a titillating mixture of old and new: it used the opening narration from the George Reeves TV series of the 1950s, combined with the John Williams "Superman Theme" from the Christopher Reeve films. The show won praise from some Superman purists, but garnered low ratings nonetheless. It disappeared from the CBS Saturday morning schedule after a mere thirteen episodes. Having earned his superhero chops as Superman, Weaver went on to become the voice of Reed Richards in *The Marvel Action Hour: The Fantastic Four* (1994–1995).

Superboy

The John Byrne revamp of the Superman comic books, which was largely in tune with the Salkinds' vision of Superman, left no room for Superboy. In fact, in this new writing of the official Superman history, there never *was* a Superboy. So how, then, did the Salkinds end up producing a *Superboy* TV series?

In 1985, while *Santa Claus: The Movie* was in production, tensions between Alexander and Ilya Salkind reached a breaking point. People who worked on the film were not being paid promptly. Alexander was in charge of the company coffers; Ilya held him responsible for the financial difficulties. By the time the film was finished, Ilya had vowed never to work with his father again.[667] But then someone suggested the idea of a *Superboy* TV series to Alexander Salkind. Viacom, giants in the TV syndication industry, showed interest in the idea, but only on the condition that at least one of the Salkinds be involved. Alexander realized that his strength was in financing, not producing, so he contacted his son. Ilya decided he didn't want to be a partner with his father in the TV show, but he did agree to come aboard as his father's employee, with one proviso: he wanted a lot of money, and he wanted it up front.[668]

When the deal was made, Ilya Salkind waxed enthusiastic to reporters, saying that the company's first television venture would give them a chance to explore areas of the young Clark Kent's life that hadn't been explored in the feature films.[669]

Alexander Salkind, still in cost-cutting mode, decided to save money by locating the series in Florida, away from the jurisdiction of the entertainment unions. Disney had just built a production studio, the Disney/MGM Studios, at Walt Disney World in Orlando, and *Superboy* became the first series filmed at the new facility. Salkind was happy to delegate most of the actual production work to line producer Bob Simmonds, a veteran of the *Superman* film series, and writer/producer Fred Freiberger, whose credits included *Star Trek*

(1966–1969) and *Space: 1999* (1975).[670] Casting was handled by Lynn Stalmaster, the man who had pushed Christopher Reeve for Superman, although Salkind also involved himself in the casting process.[671] Salkind was searching for "very good-looking people," and he found them, beginning with Stacy Haiduk, the actress chosen to play Superboy's romantic interest, Lana Lang. Haiduk, born April 24, 1968, grew up in Grand Rapids, Michigan, where she began dancing when she was four years old. Later developing an interest in acting, she moved to Los Angeles after high school, where her first jobs—appearing in music videos—combined both talents.[672] Commercial work followed, then small roles in soap operas and TV programs.[673] Her red hair and light blue eyes gave her an interesting look; when Salkind saw her, he knew immediately that she was perfect for Lana Lang. Haiduk admitted there were similarities. "Lana is almost exactly like me—a little feisty, a little selfish on the side," she said. "But I see her more as an outgoing person. When she goes after something, she doesn't let anything stand in her way."[674] In an interview with Daniel Dickholtz, Haiduk said she wasn't a comic book reader when she was a child, but she did watch the Superman movies and remembered Annette O'Toole playing Lana. Nonetheless, instead of being influenced by O'Toole's performance, she wanted to create her own original interpretation of the character.[675]

However, when it came to casting the teen-aged Clark Kent/Superboy, Salkind did, in fact, want an actor who was like someone else. Specifically, he wanted someone who resembled a young Christopher Reeve. Lynn Stalmaster sent him John Haymes Newton.[676]

Newton was born in Chapel Hill, North Carolina on December 29, 1965. In school, he was the class clown, always feeling a need to perform and make people laugh.[677] By the time he was a senior, he was thinking seriously about pursuing acting as a career. After graduating from high school, he enrolled in the University of North Carolina at Chapel Hill and studied theater. Within a few months, he moved to New York where he began martial arts training and became more health conscious. He also started studying acting full-time, paying for his classes by working as a bodyguard for celebrities.[678] He received rave reviews for his performance in a production of *Our Town* directed by Robert Allan Ackerman, and after graduating in May 1987 moved to Los Angeles to pursue an acting career. He landed some commercial work, but his big break came not in Hollywood but, ironically, when he went back to North Carolina to visit his family. At that time, Dino DeLaurentiis had just purchased the former Earl Owensby film studio in Wilmington, North Carolina, and Lynn Stalmaster was there casting a movie. When the six-foot-tall 22-year-old with the green eyes and brown hair came in to audition, Stalmaster knew he was just the type Ilya Salkind was searching for.[679] Stalmaster asked Newton if he would be interested in flying down to Florida to screen test for a TV series. When Ilya Salkind saw Newton's screen test, the young actor became his first choice for the role. He was told to darken his brown hair to match that of Reeve's Superman,[680] and within two weeks he had moved to Orlando.[681]

After being cast as Superboy, Newton told David McDonnell and Daniel Dickholtz of *Comics Scene* magazine that the role was incredible because it wasn't about being a superhero, but rather was about a kid going to college who just happened to have superpowers.[682] He later told Edward Gross that he felt a great responsibility playing a character that was an American icon with a fifty-year history.[683]

Although he bore a strong resemblance to Christopher Reeve, Newton chose to vary his portrayal from the approach Reeve had taken with the feature films. Specifically, he wanted to make his Clark Kent less bumbling and nerdy. "He's more of a real guy with real feelings," said Newton, "and he hasn't developed the nerdy facade, which could get very boring on a long-running series. People saw that in four films, and I don't think they want to see it again."[684]

Newton was signed to a four-year contract, for an anticipated run of 104 episodes. He said he wanted to move on to other things after that, and no matter how much money was offered him, he didn't think he would stay with the show more than four seasons.[685] As it would turn out, his tenure in the role was considerably shorter.

James Calvert, who began his career as a child actor with small roles on TV series like *The Jeffersons* (1979), *Eight Is Enough* (1981) and *CHiPs* (1981), was hired to play T.J. White, son of *Daily Planet* editor Perry White. For the young Lex Luthor, Scott Wells, another good-looking actor, was hired. Wells had previously appeared in episodes of the TV series *Emergency!* (1975) and *The Bionic Woman* (1976). Luthor's partner-in-crime, Leo, was played by black-mulletted Michael Manno.

There was some talk early on in the casting process that Pa Kent might be played by serial Superman Kirk Alyn, but in the end the role went to veteran actor Stuart Whitman, an actor who began his career with bit parts in *When Worlds Collide* (1951) and *The Day the Earth Stood Still* (1951), then appeared in over one hundred films and TV shows before signing on for *Superboy*. Salome Jens, an actress whose three decades of film and TV work included episodes of *The Untouchables* (1962–1963), *I Spy* (1967) and *Gunsmoke* (1973), as well as narrating *The Clan of the Cave Bear* (1986) and playing Claudia Chadway on *Falcon Crest* (1987), hid her classic beauty behind a plain apron as Ma Kent. Ilya Salkind made a conscious decision not to have actors from the Christopher Reeve films reprising their roles in the new series, feeling it would "unbalance the show's personality," so Glenn Ford and Phyllis Thaxter were never considered.[686]

The show was announced in February 1988. Throughout the spring, it was being sold to broadcasters. In May, many of the core production personnel were recruited. Shooting began August 15; the premiere date was set for October. Because of a Writers Guild strike, the producers signed an interim agreement with the union that allowed their writers to keep pounding out pages during the work stoppage.[687]

Wishing to exercise some control over this new interpretation of one of their classic superheroes, DC Comics became involved in the writing process. Mike Carlin, then editor of the *Superman* comic books, and his co-editor Andy Helfer conferred on the scripts. Jennette Kahn of DC said the comic book company had approval rights to everything, from the casting of the lead characters to the show's scripts.[688]

The first season episodes chronicled the first year of Clark Kent and Lana Lang as students at Shuster University's Siegel School of Journalism—a nodding reference to Superman's creators. Although placed in a college setting, the stories retained the classic Superman structure: Clark and Lana worked on the school newspaper, where Clark's college roommate, T.J., was the photographer (basically filling the Jimmy Olsen role). Lana was friends with Clark and infatuated with Superboy, who was continually rescuing her from perilous situations. Besides an array of villains played by prominent guest stars, Superboy often had to thwart the plans of another Shuster student, the wealthy and exceedingly smarmy Lex Luthor, portrayed as a handsome (albeit evil) young man with a full head of blond hair.

The TV series showcased a number of prominent guest stars, from former TV stars like Abe Vigoda (episode #3, "Back to Oblivion") and Ray Walston (episode #4, "The Russian Exchange Student"), to former teen idol Leif Garrett (episode #6, "Bringing Down the House"). George Chakiris became a semi-regular beginning with episode #12, "Kryptonite Kills," playing Professor Peterson, a scientist who Superboy often turned to for help, a handsome 1980s version of the nutty professor types played by Sterling Holloway and Phillips Tead in the 1950s *Superman* series.

The show premiered on October 3, 1988, and began its first season run of twenty-six half-hour episodes. In the beginning, it did well in the syndicated ratings, and before long John Haymes Newton was gracing the cover of many teen magazines.[689] It also inspired the creation of the first new *Superboy* comic book series in years; as with the new TV series, the stories centered on Clark Kent's college days.[690]

The show itself was a mixed blessing, however. The writing, particularly in the early episodes, left much to be desired, with Superboy battling petty criminals. And while John Haymes Newton looked good in the Superboy uniform, he wasn't a very charismatic actor. Scott Wells, as Lex Luthor, was even worse; during production, Ilya Salkind sent him to acting classes.[691] The bright spots were James Calvert, who handled the sidekick role with just the right comedic flair, and Stacy Haiduk, who often rose above the call of duty, giving great performances with mediocre material. As Haiduk told Daniel Dickholtz in an interview in *Spectacular* magazine, one of the biggest acting challenges she encountered was keeping a straight face while saying the name "Superboy." "It's not like saying, 'Dean' or 'Jack,'" said Haiduk.[692]

Shot on video, the program lacked the rich look of the feature films, and the flying effects, executed mostly by blue-screen compositing, were not entirely convincing. However, the wire work was very impressive, allowing Superboy to take off and land with seeming effortlessness. Speaking to Edward Gross for *Comics Scene* magazine, Newton said the flying mattes and blue screen shots were frustrating "because we *know* we can do them better."[693] Newton wasn't the only actor who faced the rigors of wire work. For a scene in which Lana Lang fell and was caught in mid-air by Superboy, Stacy Haiduk recalled that she was up on the wires for 45 minutes, twirling around and around until she got sick. [694]

After filming half the episodes for the first season, John Haymes Newton told Edward Gross that he felt some of the show's scripts—like one involving fixing the points of a basketball game—were boring. He was much happier with the thirteenth episode ("Revenge of the Alien"), the first of a two-parter written by DC comic book editors Mike Carlin and Andy Helfer, in which a Predator-type alien comes to earth looking to add another trophy to his collection of conquests. Taking the form of a samurai warrior, he attacks Superboy. Newton hoped to use some of his martial arts skills in the show, but DC insisted that he stick to more traditional fisticuffs.[695] Overall, the actor said that he was pleased with the first thirteen episodes, and he expected the series would improve with stronger writers and higher budgets for the remaining thirteen.[696]

Viacom, however, wasn't interested in syndicating a learning process. They wanted a hit show, and after the initial good ratings, *Superboy* began quickly slipping. Ilya Salkind began getting calls from Viacom, who were hearing complaints from the TV stations that had bought the program that the show was poorly produced.[697] According to Newton, DC Comics was also receiving letters from kids who complained that Clark wasn't as nerdy as he was in the films. This frustrated the actor, who had made a conscious decision to differentiate his portrayal from Reeve's by playing Clark as more of a real person. When he was asked to play the role as more of a nerd, he refused, saying they would just have to fire him.[698]

Besides playing Clark as less of a nerd, Newton wanted to play Superboy as less of the all-powerful Man of Steel. He told Edward Gross of *Comics Scene* magazine that he wanted to make Superboy more vulnerable, and to show the effort that is required to do Superboy's feats. For instance, if Superboy had to lift a fifteen-ton weight, Newton wanted to show that he couldn't just do it with one finger, but rather—as in the Max Fleischer Superman cartoons—he had to struggle with it.[699]

Newton also drew upon his martial arts training, trying to portray a Superboy who operated from a place of peace and calm and awareness of his power, who wasn't showing off just for his own ego. In his interpretation, Clark Kent was the real character, not a put-on, and Superboy was a product of the costume and the character's awareness of his special powers.[700]

Despite his good intentions, Newton's take on the role was failing to resonate with viewers. With the stations complaining, Viacom put pressure on Salkind to improve the program. He became more involved, and brought in Cary Bates from DC Comics as a writer. Bates made the episodes less mundane; whereas before the shows had dealt with Mayan curses and low-rent crooks, Bates introduced characters from the comic books like Mr. Mxyzptlk (episode #16, "Meet Mr. Mxyzptlk"), played by Michael J. Pollard, who gave a decidedly offbeat performance for a very offbeat character, though he certainly looked the part.

Joaquin Phoenix, who would become a major star with his Oscar-nominated roles in *Gladiator* (2000) and *Walk the Line* (2005), made an early appearance as a child actor (under the name Leaf Phoenix) in "Little Hercules" (episode #20), which had a young computer genius hacking into the advanced computer system of a new Navy submarine and accidentally activating a self-destruct mechanism that will explode the sub's missiles (a scaled-down version of the plot of the 1983 film *War Games*, starring Matthew Broderick). Episode #21, "Mutant," co-starred Ilya Salkind's former wife, Skye Aubrey, as Vora. Other first season guest stars included Joseph Campanella (episode #22, "The Phantom of the Third Division"), Doug McClure as a nutty professor who has invented a time-travel machine (episode #24, "Hollywood"), and Sybil Danning as a life-force draining vampire (episode #25, "Succubus").

The final episode of the first season (#26, "Luthor Unleashed") dramatized a bit of Superman lore that dated back to *Adventure Comics* #271 (1960), in which Superboy rescues Lex Luthor from a chemical-caused fire. The fire causes Luthor to lose his hair, turning him into a bald, raving madman vowing revenge on Superboy.

As the end of the season neared, Salkind became disenchanted with his young star. Newton's contract contained a morals clause, and Salkind felt the actor had violated it by being arrested for public drunkenness. When Newton began pushing for a raise, Salkind decided to fire the actor. Salkind had no qualms with how Newton played the role. The actor, he thought, was a terrific Superboy; the producer just had a personality clash with him.[701] Newton, however, spun the story differently, claiming it was his choice to leave the *Superboy* series. He told the *Superman Homepage* website, "I asked for a small raise, twenty percent, which had been previously promised to me and then retracted when the second season was to start. This was due to the amount of dangerous stunts I was performing as well as two serious accidents, one involving a substitute flying rig operator swinging me into some power lines." Luckily for Newton, the power lines were insulated.[702]

Whether by choice or by edict, Newton was out, and while he was at it, Salkind cleaned house. He also got rid of Scott Wells, who he thought was good-looking but a bad actor, and James Calvert, who he felt did not have a strong enough presence. The only major cast member he kept was Stacy Haiduk, and for good reason; Salkind felt she was "dynamite."[703]

Once again, the search was on for an actor to play Superboy. The hunt ended with the signing of dimpled, doe-eyed Gerard Christopher. Despite his youthful appearance, when he signed for the role of the teenage titan, Christopher was thirty-one years old—seven years older than Christopher Reeve was when he signed for the role of Superman.

Christopher told Brian McKernan of *The Adventures Continue* website that he grew up watching George Reeves as Superman. As a young boy, he'd tie a towel around his neck and jump off the garage roof pretending to fly. When he won the role of Superboy, he was so excited he was numb; this wasn't your average acting assignment.[704]

Gerard Christopher seemed to naturally possess the heroic spirit of a young Superman.

In early 1979, while he was living in New York City, he stopped a mugger who was trying to steal a woman's handbag. In August of that same year, just days before the Democratic National Convention began, Gerard pursued and tackled a necklace thief. The incident received national newspaper coverage, and Gerard was given an award by the New York Convention and Visitors Bureau.[705]

Christopher began his career as a model with the prestigious Wilhelmina Modeling Agency. His all–American good looks landed him more than just print assignments. Twice, he was hired by mannequin makers to pose for a mannequin likeness. He also appeared on the covers of romance novels. To finance his college education, he began working in commercials, earning membership in the Screen Actors Guild. After earning a degree in business from the University of Southern California, he studied filmmaking at UCLA. His first television acting role was as a lead in a pilot for CBS called *Welcome to Paradise* (1984), which was filmed in New Zealand.[706] After guest appearances in many prime-time series, he landed a recurring role in the NBC daytime serial *Days of Our Lives*, and in the Aaron Spelling-produced nighttime serial, *Sunset Beach* (1997–1999).[707]

When Ilya Salkind hired Christopher to take over the Superboy role, the show's Nielsen rating was 48; it was on the brink of cancellation. Salkind told Christopher that if the ratings didn't go up immediately, the show would be over, adding, "If you think I'm putting pressure on you, I am."[708] Just a few weeks after the shows with Christopher began airing, the program soared to number 10 in the syndicated Nielsens.

This was partly a reflection of the new dynamics of the show. Mindful of the criticism that his predecessor didn't play Clark Kent as enough of a nebbish, Gerard Christopher's Kent seemed like an escapee from the *Revenge of the Nerds* films; in one episode, he was seen poolside wearing white socks and a long-sleeved shirt tucked into shorts which were pulled high above his waist. His Superboy was more charming in the scenes with Lana Lang, and more assertive in the scenes with the villains—especially Lex Luthor, who had undergone plastic surgery and drank acid to alter his voice and ended up appearing physically bigger, older and more imposing than he had in Season One. Luthor was now portrayed by Sherman Howard who, like Gene Hackman, wore a variety of wigs to hide the follicle-challenged criminal genius's baldness. No longer just a self-satisfied rich kid, this Luthor was initially played for comedy—Gene Hackman times ten. As the series progressed, he became a more multi-faceted character. Stacy Haiduk found Howard a wonderful villain and a wonderful actor, and enjoyed watching his performances.[709]

Haiduk also adjusted quickly to her new leading man, though she admitted it was difficult for him at first when everything was brand new to him. "Gerry is very sensitive," she told Daniel Dickholtz. "John, I think, was much harder. I'm not saying cocky or that type of thing, but he didn't let his sensitive side come out too much. That's kind of the difference between the two. Apart from that, they're great."[710]

To prepare for the dual roles of Clark Kent and Superboy, Gerard Christopher looked at the Kirk Alyn serials, the Christopher Reeve films, and even the 1961 *Superboy* pilot with John Rockwell, who, coincidentally, was a friend of his. Before he got the *Superboy* series, Christopher wasn't even aware that Rockwell had been an actor.[711] Though Christopher's take on Clark Kent was inspired by the Christopher Reeve interpretation, for Superman he harkened back to the actor who had pioneered the role on television. "I have an emotional, sentimental attachment to what George Reeves did," said Christopher. "He just seemed to do Superman the right way, the correct way, the way Superman is supposed to be done."[712]

With the casting of a new Superboy, there was also a change in Clark Kent's college roommate. The T.J. White character was dropped, replaced by young huckster Andy McAllister, played by Ilan Mitchell-Smith. Mitchell-Smith, who studied ballet as a child and won a scholarship to the School of American Ballet, won his first film role in 1983 in the Sidney Lumet film *Daniel*, playing Timothy Hutton's character as a young boy. Film roles in *The Wild Life* (1984), *Weird Science* (1985) and *The Chocolate War* (1988) followed.

There were more changes to the show besides just the cast. The program relocated to Orlando's Universal Studios Florida,[713] and the title changed to *The Adventures of Superboy*. The second season shows also had better production value overall, beginning with better plots. Comic book writers Elliot Maggin, J.M. DeMatteis, Denny O'Neil, Andrew Helfer and Mike Carlin contributed scripts. Cary Bates became a story editor, along with TV writer and Superman fan Mark Jones. Salkind himself wrote a couple of episodes: "Young Dracula" (with Cary Bates) and "Johnny Casanova." More characters from the comic books were introduced, including Bizarro, Metallo, Yellow Peri and the Kryptonite Kid. Plus, Mr. Mxyzptlk returned.[714]

With so many people from the comic book world involved, the new iteration of the show quickly became a favorite among comics fans. However, the constraints of the half-hour time slot meant that the stories were still pretty basic. They were also sometimes lacking in logic. For instance, in episode #36, "Superboy's Deadly Touch," Superboy's X-ray vision allows him to see that a school bus used by a couple of nuns has a bad battery—yet he can't see that one of the nuns is Lex Luthor in drag. Nor, later in the same episode, can he tell that the Luthor he attempts to apprehend is actually an android.

Later in the second season, an intriguing two-part episode, "Abandon Earth" and "Escape to Earth," had Superboy learning of his interstellar origin when aliens claiming to be Jor-El and Lara come to take their long-lost son back to Krypton. In an interesting bit of casting, Jor-El was played by former James Bond George Lazenby (*On Her Majesty's Secret Service*, 1969), and Lara by former Bond woman Britt Ekland (*The Man with the Golden Gun*, 1974). Christopher had fun working with Lazenby, whom he found naturally funny and charming.[715]

By the end of the season, the show was flying high in the ratings. But the producers were not content to stick to the same format for the show's third year. Instead, they decided to move Clark Kent and Lana Lang out of college and into the workforce. When season three began, the duo were now interning at the Bureau for Extranormal Affairs. The Bureau served the same dramatic purpose as *The Daily Planet*: it allowed Clark Kent to find out about breaking stories that required Superboy's special skills, and also provided lots of opportunities for Clark to backpedal away from his co-workers and disappear into a supply closet for a quick change to Superboy. Two new regulars were added to the cast, Robert Levine as C. Dennis Jackson and Peter J. Fernandez as Matt Ritter. C. Dennis Jackson assumed the Perry White function of the frustrated boss sending Clark and Lana out on assignments.

There were cosmetic changes, as well. Clark's demeanor—as well as his wardrobe—was less nerdy, and he and Lana both had new hairdos. Her hair was cut in a shorter bob; his was now blow-dried rather than slicked-down, which one would think would make it even more apparent that he and Superboy were one and the same, but Lana never caught on.

Stacy Haiduk welcomed the third season changes. As she told one interviewer, "How many times can Lana get kidnapped or thrown off a helicopter or pushed off a train? Now I think Lana is much stronger, and very smart. She knows what she wants and when she goes after something, she goes after it."[716] In speaking to Daniel Dickholtz, Haiduk explained the Lana-Clark-Superboy relationship in a way that, in retrospect, seemed to foreshadow *Lois*

& Clark: The New Adventures of Superman. Comparing the show to *Moonlighting*, Haiduk said she'd like to see Lana actually fall in love with Clark, because the actress found Clark charming and actually liked him more than she liked Superboy.[717]

In one of the third season episodes, "Mindscape" (episode #62), Clark throws himself onto an exploding meteorite to protect Lana from the blast. When he stands up and turns around, his shirt is ripped open, revealing a red-and-yellow "S." It confirms what Lana has suspected all along.

"You and Clark—you're the same person. Why did you hide it from me?" she asks.

Clark answers, "Lana, I had my reasons. I wanted to protect people."

"It's too late for that," says Lana. "You don't have to hide it any more. Why not just be Superboy all the time?"

"I need to be Clark."

"Oh, Clark, he's such a geek—I am sorry. I didn't mean that. But Clark, he was only an act, wasn't he?"

"I am Clark, as much as I am Superboy. Sometimes I have to get away from being Superboy."

Of course, it's all a dream.

Another third season episode, "Superboy ... Lost" (episode #63), was a variation of the *Adventures of Superman* episode "Panic in the Sky." The story begins with Superboy flying into space to destroy a meteor on a collision course with earth. Afterward, Superboy—beside a stream in the woods—is awakened by a young woman. He doesn't remember who he is. Even more strangely, SHE doesn't know who he is. She explains that she and her young son have been in their secluded cabin, apparently with no TV, radio, newspaper, or contact with anyone else, for about five years. The amnesiac Superboy finds himself in the midst of a nasty domestic dispute when the woman's estranged husband sends hired goons to kidnap his son back. After rescuing the boy and returning him to his mother, Superboy regains his memory, and flies back to Lana.

As the third season progressed, both Sherman Howard and Gerard Christopher contributed scripts that showed different facets of their characters.[718] Howard's "Mine Games" (episode #74) has Superboy and Lex Luthor trapped in a collapsed mine, with kryptonite. The weakened superhero and the super villain have to put aside their differences momentarily and work together to save themselves. Gerard Christopher's "Wish for Armageddon" (episode#75) had Superboy unknowingly signing a pact with the Devil, who wants to use the Boy of Steel to start World War III.

In the final two episodes of the third season, a two-part adventure called "The Road to Hell" (episodes #77 and #78) had Superboy traveling to other dimensions, where he encountered a very young version of himself (played by Joel Carlson), and an older version, very effectively played by Ron Ely. Gerard Christopher enjoyed working with Ely, who had himself played an iconic character as the star of the *Tarzan* TV series (1966–1969). Christopher was very impressed with Ely, whom he said was one of the most interesting, dynamic, intelligent, and personable individuals he'd ever met.[719]

Christopher continued expanding his behind-the-scenes involvement in the fourth season (1991–92), when he became a co-producer of the program. The series had now hit its stride, turning out consistently superior half-hour adventures. Among them was "Paranoia" (episode #84), which took place entirely at the Bureau for Extranormal Affairs, where a couple of familiar faces were seen among the employees—Noel Neill and Jack Larson. Gerard Christopher recalled that it was exciting for everyone on the crew, since so many of the people who worked on the *Superboy* show grew up with *Adventures of Superman.* During the shooting, said Christopher, "Jack was nice enough to say he thought our show was superior to his, which was sweet of him."[720]

Another standout was "Know Thine Enemy" (episodes #85 and #86), a two-parter in which Superboy was tricked into donning an apparatus that allowed him to relive Lex Luthor's memories. He discovered that Luthor had a horrible childhood, living in poverty with a father who beat him. The episode also revealed that Luthor had a sister, Lena, the only person in the world he loved. When it's reported that she died in a car crash, Luthor decides to destroy the world with nuclear bombs. In the end, it's revealed that Lena had faked her death so she could start life anew under a new identity. Lana Lang finds Lena, takes her to Lex, and the bombs are disarmed. This episode was also notable for being one in which Superboy gives Lana Lang a passionate kiss.

The series wrapped after the 100th and final episode ("Rites of Passage Part 2") was filmed in August 1991; it aired May 17, 1992.[721] Ilya Salkind hoped for a fifth season, but Warner Bros., according to Salkind, didn't; they were about to launch *Lois & Clark: The New Adventures of Superman* in prime-time, and didn't want another competing Superman series on the air at the same time.[722] According to Doug Chambers's *DMWC's Superboy: The Series* website (http://www.geocities.com/dmwc), Warner Bros. actually filed a lien against the series, blocking reruns of the *Superboy* series in North America.[723]

Gerard Christopher recalled that although the crew of 110 had worked for twelve hours a day for almost an entire year, they were sad to see it end. Even though they knew the end was coming and prepared themselves for it psychologically, it was still like saying good-bye to an extended family.[724] Christopher fondly recalls the show as an incredible professional experience which allowed him to work with older, famous actors and wonderful directors, and also afforded him the opportunity to learn more about the craft of filmmaking, earning him credits as a writer, director and producer.[725]

With *Superboy* shut down and his plans for a new Superman movie stalled, Ilya Salkind moved on to a new venture. He joined his father, Alexander, to produce *Christopher Columbus: The Discovery*, which was set for release in 1992, 500 years after Columbus supposedly discovered America. The film was a financial failure, earning only $8 million in box office receipts. In November 1993, Ilya Salkind, Bob Simmonds and Salkind's third wife Jane Chaplin sued Alexander Salkind over monies that were owed them from *Christopher Columbus*, and $7 million that Chaplin allegedly loaned Alexander Salkind to keep the production afloat that was never paid back. The relationship between father and son, already strained, was now shattered. Alexander never produced another movie. After spending much of his later years in litigation, he died in 1997.[726]

After *Superman IV: The Quest for Peace* effectively ended the Salkinds' Superman film franchise, Warner Bros. turned their attention to their next super-hyped superhero franchise: Batman. Tim Burton's *Batman* opened in 1989, and was a huge financial success. However, like the Superman franchise, it ran out of steam by the fourth installment, 1997's *Batman and Robin*. Nonetheless, Superman showed that producing a superhero saga with an "A" level budget could yield generous box office returns, paving the way for other comic book series like *X-Men* (2000) and *Spider-Man* (2002). In an interview with Barry M. Freiman of the *Superman Homepage*, Ilya Salkind said that if he hadn't come up with the idea and his father hadn't come up with the money to make *Superman*, all the other big-budget comic book films that followed wouldn't exist.[727]

But the Superman legacy of Ilya Salkind is not over. Having produced the cinematic adventures of Superman and Supergirl, and having brought Superboy to TV, Salkind's company is now planning to produce a feature film about Superman's creators, Siegel and

Shuster, from a script by Shuster's nephew Warren Shuster Peary and Rick Palacioz.[728] In the fall of 2006, Warner Bros. Home Entertainment released new editions of the Christopher Reeve *Superman* movies featuring, for the first time, commentary from Salkind. The new DVDs, in Salkind's opinion, allowed him to set the record straight after years of Superman fans praising Richard Donner's vision and vilifying Richard Lester and the Salkinds.[729] "So many people have worked on this—and this is what bothers me the most—is when there is kind of this tendency for some people to say, 'I did it all.' Well nobody did it all," Salkind told Freiman. "Everybody deserves credit for what they did."[730]

Giving credit where credit is due, there are some who suggest that the *Superboy* TV series was responsible for influencing one of the defining events of the Superman comic books of the 1990s. As the fourth season of the Superboy series was winding down, according to the *Superboy Homepage*, the idea was for it to culminate in an episode called "The Death of Superboy," in which Lex Luthor finally defeats the Boy of Steel. This—so the story goes—was meant to be followed by a series of TV movies in which Superboy would be resurrected and defeat his arch-nemesis. By that point, *Superman V: The New Movie* was supposed to be in production, with Gerard Christopher graduating to the big-screen role of Superman.

Whatever the true story, "The Death of Superboy" episode of *The Adventures of Superboy* did not actually kill off the character. However, one of the series' writers, Mike Carlin, was involved in "The Death of Superman" storyline in the Superman comic books a year later. When the caped wonder met his demise at the hands of a villain called Doomsday, it became a headline event all over world. The "Death of Superman" comic book became an all-time bestseller, with over 23 million copies flying off the shelves.[731] Superman, who had begun to seem passé, was once again a global phenomenon.

9

Lois and Clark

Capitalizing on the new-found popularity of the Man of Steel, Warner Bros. put a new Superman series into development, *Lois & Clark: The New Adventures of Superman*. As the title suggested, the new series would focus more on the romance of Lois Lane and Clark Kent, instead of emphasizing the heroics of Superman (though there would certainly be no shortage of superfeats in each episode). In omitting Superboy's existence and putting the emphasis on Clark Kent, the show reflected the new direction of the John Byrne "revamp."

After Lorimar Productions sold the idea for a new Superman series to ABC, they went to a writer/producer they had under contract, Deborah Joy Levine, to execute it. Lorimar, said Levine, chose her because they didn't want to just go the action-adventure route with the series, but rather they wanted to make it a relationship show, and Levine was known as a "relationship" writer. Levine had previously produced the TV movies *Murder by Reason of Insanity* (1985) and *Samaritan: The Mitch Snyder Story* (1986), and wrote *Something to Live For: The Alison Gertz Story* (1992). Levine said she didn't want to do a new Superman series, but she wouldn't mind writing a romantic comedy called *Lois & Clark*, with Lois Lane being "the boss of Superman." Once she came up with the title, the rest of the concept naturally fell into place. "The main twist that I did—and the one which people seem to be responding to—is that I wanted a more human Clark," Levine told Edward Gross and Mark Altman. Her focus wasn't on doing a show about Superman, but about two people who worked at the *Daily Planet* who had a love/hate relationship and, oh yes, one of them came from Krypton. Following on from that, instead of Superman creating the Clark Kent persona to disguise himself as a mild-mannered reporter, Levine saw Kent as someone who really wanted more than anything else to be human, to have a family, to be a good writer and to be a good reporter. Co-producer Bryce Zabel said it was pretty clear that they were influenced by the John Byrne revamp, although they tried to put their own stamp on it. "The whole idea that there were a lot of barnacles on the ship of Superman is something we've tried to address and we've done a little scraping here and there," said Zabel.[732]

Lois Lane receiving first billing in the title was a clear indication that she would be receiving as much, if not more, of the focus of the show as Clark Kent. Consequently, the character of Lois Lane was much more developed in this series than in any previous incarnation of Superman. In effect, it was as if the producers were harking back to the more romance-themed *Lois Lane* comic books than the *Superman* comics; it was a fresh, feminist take on the ultimate masculine superhero.

Levine first wrote a two-hour TV movie to act as a pilot for the series. Robert Butler, a director who previously had helmed the pilot episodes of *Batman* (1966–1969), *Hill Street Blues* (1981–1987) and *Moonlighting* (1985–1989), as well as episodes of *Star Trek* (1966–1969) and a series he co-created, *Remington Steele* (1982–1987), was sent the script, which he loved. He spoke to Levine about the script in mid–December, and by mid–January he was on-board.[733]

Since the series was going to center around Lois Lane more so than Clark Kent/Superman, the part of Lois was one of the first cast. The role went to an actress whose first TV appearance had been as a mermaid on an episode of *The Love Boat*, Teri Hatcher. Hatcher, whose father was an electrical engineer, was born in Sunnyvale, California on December 8, 1964. Hatcher claims that she was an unattractive nerd in high school. After graduation, she became a student at De Anza College, where she majored in math and engineering. By age twenty, she was a cheerleader for the San Francisco 49ers. While still in college, a friend asked her to come along to a *Love Boat* audition to lend moral support. Hatcher got the part, appearing as Amy the Love Boat mermaid in the 1985–1986 season. After *The Love Boat*, she landed roles in several other TV series, including a stint as a semi-regular on *MacGyver* (1985–1992), as well as in the films *The Big Picture* (1989), *Tango and Cash* (1989) and *Soapdish* (1991).[734] One of her highest-profile early roles came in a 1993 episode of *Seinfeld* in which Jerry Seinfeld asked his friend Elaine (Julia Louis-Dreyfus) to see if she could determine whether his new girlfriend's breasts were real or if they were surgical implants. The episode ended with Hatcher uttering a line that is still often repeated to her: "They're real, and they're spectacular."[735] She welcomed the role in the new series, saying, "Despite the fact that I have a good-size pair of breasts, in *Lois & Clark* I have the opportunity to show the world they're not my only attribute."[736] She hoped to show that a career woman could be intelligent and smart and still be sensuous, feminine and vulnerable. Hatcher also liked that as opposed to the movies, where Lois was in love with Superman but barely noticed Clark, the series would show Lois falling in love with both men while appreciating their different qualities.[737]

When casting for Clark Kent/Superman began, one of the first actors who showed up was Gerard Christopher. Christopher told Brian McKernan of *The Superboy Homepage* that he read for the show and the casting director didn't like his interpretation. Asked to change it, Christopher did, and the casting director liked it enough to bring him in for a meeting with the producers, who were unaware that he'd previously done *Superboy*.[738] After Christopher read for the producers, one of them said he was perfect for the role. He was excited until they picked up his résumé, looked at the work he'd done, and exclaimed, "You've done this already!" Christopher was thrown out of the room.[739]

Next, the producers went to an actor of Herculean ability—Kevin Sorbo. Sorbo claims that when he went in and tested as Clark Kent with Teri Hatcher, the casting director told him "You've got the part." The actor went home, called up a friend and celebrated that night. The next morning, after he awoke with a champagne headache, the phone rang and he was told that he *didn't* have the part.[740]

The producers eventually decided to go with an actor whom they had auditioned four times—Dean Cain. Since their concept of the character had Clark as a man who'd apparently done a lot of traveling around the world, they were at first thinking of getting a more mature actor. Robert Butler recalled that Dean Cain was the first actor they met, and they were concerned about his youth, though he did possess the ingenuousness and sincerity they were looking for.[741] When Cain came in for his second audition, all the women in the company wanted to come by to check him out; that's when they knew that Cain would become a major sex symbol. Producer Deborah Joy Levine felt Cain had "a smoldering sexiness. Like Clark Kent, he's a mild-mannered guy, but behind it, boy, are you in trouble."[742] The young actor had already developed a following, after appearing as "Rick," the boyfriend of Shannon Doherty's character, in the 1992 season of *Beverly Hills 90210*. What really clinched the role for Cain were the on-screen fireworks when he auditioned with Teri Hatcher. "We had great chemistry from the first read," the actress said.[743] Robert Butler said that after discussing his age and seeing other actors, they finally decided to go back to Cain.[744]

Dean Cain was well aware of the producers' concern that he was too young. He said, "the easiest way to get under my skin is to call this show *Superboy*."[745] From co-producer Bryce Zabel's perspective, Cain's Clark Kent was the kind of engaging, cool guy that most men would want to have as a best friend. He said that although he raised an eyebrow when he heard about the casting, he found Cain to be a totally believable Superman.[746]

Dean Cain was no stranger to the entertainment industry; he had, in fact, been raised in it. Cain, whose father was half–Irish, half–Japanese, was born at Southridge Air Force Base in Mount Clemens, Michigan, on July 31, 1966. His parents divorced before he was born.[747] When he was three years old, his mother, actress Sharon Thomas, moved Dean and his older brother Roger to California, where she met writer/director Christopher Cain. After the couple married, Cain adopted five-year-old Dean, who then grew up in Malibu, California. Growing up, Cain's friends and neighbors were Charlie Sheen and his brother Emilio Estevez, Chris Penn and his brother Sean, Rob Lowe, and Holly Robinson. Cain watched his friends go into acting; Emilio Estevez starred as Billy the Kid in his dad's film *Young Guns* (1988). Dean, meanwhile, pursued athletics. He became a star quarterback at Santa Monica High School and, after graduation, went to Princeton. While in college, he set an NCAA record for most interceptions in a single season, and became the envy of young men everywhere when he dated Brooke Shields for two years.[748] In 1988, Cain graduated from Princeton with a degree in history. He was drafted by the Buffalo Bills football team, where he hoped to play for at least ten years, but during training camp three days before his first preseason game, he sustained a knee injury that permanently sidelined him.[749]

Cain thought about pursuing a career in screenwriting, but an agent who had seen him in a small role in *The Stone Boy*, a 1984 film directed by his stepfather, encouraged him to try acting.[750] "Being a pro ballplayer, having done something else, gave me a perspective to understand it's not that important," Cain later told Mark Olsen of *The Los Angeles Times*. "There are other things out there. But it is a very fun way to make a living."[751]

As casting for *Lois & Clark* continued, the role of Perry White received a make-over. With the masterful acting of Lane Smith, White became more than a blustery old codger. He represented the veteran newsman who worked his way up the ladder of hard knocks, and now saw himself as a mentor to his cadre of reporters. He dispensed love advice to Jimmy Olsen, words of encouragement to Clark, and fatherly wisdom to Lois. And no longer did he shout "Great Caesar's ghost!" Instead, Smith—who was born in Memphis, Tennessee, in 1936 and was twenty years old when Elvis Presley burst upon the national scene—made White a Presley fanatic, prone to using events from Elvis' life to illustrate the life lessons he dispensed, and, in moments of excitement or exasperation, given to shouting "Great shades of Elvis!" Smith decided to make White a totally outrageous character, even though he thought the producers wouldn't go for it. However, when he went in and read for them, they loved his interpretation, and Smith signed his contract that afternoon.[752]

A product of The Actors Studio, where his fellow classmates included Dustin Hoffman and Al Pacino, Smith appeared on Broadway before landing his first film roles in *Man on a Swing* (1974) and *Network* (1976). He moved to Los Angeles in 1977, appearing in the film

Blue Collar (1978). His breakthrough role came when he played Henry Fonda's defense attorney in the TV movie *Gideon's Trumpet* (1980). Later, his portrayal of Richard Nixon in *The Final Days* (1989) earned him a Golden Globe nomination.[753]

After appearing in several high-profile films, including *My Cousin Vinny* (1992), *The Mighty Ducks* (1992) and *The Distinguished Gentleman* (1992), Smith wasn't sure if he should sign on for a TV series. "I call this series 'the golden goose'—it's strictly a money job as far as I'm concerned," he told M.J. Simpson. "That's what television's all about. I much prefer doing movies."[754] Prior to landing the role, Smith wasn't much of a Superman fan, which allowed him to approach Perry White without the baggage of past interpretations. "I just try to create an outrageous character. He's bombastic and two minutes later he's a softie." The main thing he tried to bring to the role, Smith said in an interview on www.MJSimpson.co.uk, was to give Perry White a sense of humor about himself and his view of the world. In Smith's view, since the material was based on a comic book, you could take a lot of license with it; his main focus was to have fun with the part.[755]

The first season set up a dynamic unique to the series, with Clark Kent's becoming infatuated with a Lois Lane who was being wooed, and won by, Lex Luthor. In *Lois & Clark*, Luthor was portrayed as a Professor Moriarty–type character, an ultra-wealthy, respectable industrialist who was secretly behind much of the crime in Metropolis. This Luthor was much the way Sherlock Holmes described Professor Moriarty in the classic short story "The Final Problem": "the organizer of half that is evil and of nearly all that is undetected in this great city. He is a genius, a philosopher, an abstract thinker. He has a brain of the first order. He sits motionless, like a spider in the center of his web, but that web has a thousand radiations, and he knows well every quiver of each of them."[756]

John Shea, who made a memorable impression as Sissy Spacek's husband in the 1982 film *Missing*, was cast as Luthor. "I don't think there has been a character quite like this," Shea said in a 1994 appearance at the Museum of Television and Radio. "This villain is written as a human being, and not just a one-dimensional comic villain or a two-dimensional comic villain, the way he might have been portrayed in the comic books or even other films."[757]

Born April 14, 1949, in North Conway, New Hampshire, Shea began his career as a stage actor. In 1978, he won a role in the TV film *The Nativity*; his first film role came two years later in *Hussy*.[758] Shea appreciated that the science fiction of *Lois & Clark* was treated seriously (one of his earlier roles had been as Romeo in a time-travel episode of *The Man From Atlantis*), but with witty romantic comedy overtones. He said in an interview with Kathie Huddleston on *SciFi.com* that in the real world, the villains were well-dressed power brokers who had a ravenous appetite for the things that satisfied them, and had no regard for the little guy. "They simply go after what they go after without any of the conventional restraints of common morality, which constrains somebody like Clark Kent and well-meaning human beings. Lex Luthor didn't have those restraints, and that's what made him very dangerous."[759]

Jimmy Olsen was played by Michael Landes, who had gone to try out for another pilot when the casting director gave him the script for *Lois & Clark*. He was initially turned off by it, thinking Superman had been done to death. Also, Landes felt he wasn't right for Jimmy Olsen, whom he remembered as being nerdy. His agent compelled him to read the script anyway. In the pilot script, Jimmy Olsen was described as having a pony tail and long hair. Landes had neither, but he did feel like he had the same nervous, hyper energy as the character. When he auditioned, he won the part and was told that if he were older, they would have considered him for Superman.[760] Landes portrayed the *Daily Planet* photographer as less naive, and less of a goof, than previous actors. He also took to calling Clark Kent "C.K.," a change that the writers picked up and continued throughout the run of the series.

In keeping with the John Byrne revamp of the Superman mythos, Clark's parents, Jonathan and Martha Kent, were still both very much alive in *Lois & Clark*. Jonathan was played by veteran character actor Eddie Jones, who was working as a service station attendant in Los Angeles when a friend invited him to attend an acting class. He began working in television in 1958, appearing in *Young Dr. Malone* as Dr. Matt Steele. He didn't enter films until the 1970s, with a role in *Bloodbrothers* (1978), but had been a prolific actor since, with memorable moments in *Prince of the City* (1981), *Year of the Dragon* (1985), *The Rocketeer* (1991) and *A League of Their Own* (1992). He also had recurring roles on the TV series *The Equalizer* (1989) and the short-lived revival of *Dark Shadows* (1991).[761]

Martha Kent was played by K Callan, the "K" being short for Katherine. Callan was born in Texas, where she attended North Texas University until her sophomore year, when she left to act in a theater in Dallas. There, she got married and took a teaching job, finishing her degree while spending eight years as a teacher and working in commercials on the side. She then moved to Oklahoma, where her marriage dissolved. At age thirty-two, Callan decided it was time to make a change in her life, so she moved to New York City, struggling for several years before landing a movie role that got her noticed. She also became a writer, authoring the first book on how to land an agent, as well as *The Script Is Finished, Now What Do I Do?* Callan had no trouble being Clark Kent's mother, since she herself had a son that she thought was pretty super. "My feelings for my son were always present when I was playing with Dean," she told Michelle Erica Green of *LittleReview.com*. "There's no acting—you just put yourself in that place, and it all just comes from there." Callan admitted that although she was never a fan of the Superman comics, she had named her first cat Lois Lane.[762]

Another Texan rounded out the cast of *Lois & Clark*. Playing the part of Cat Grant, the gossip columnist, was Tracy Scoggins. Born November 13, 1959 in Dickinson, Texas, Scoggins studied speech communications and physical education at Southwest Texas State. While working as a Physical Education teacher, she began modeling and, after signing with Elite Modeling Agency, soon became a much in-demand model in Europe. Returning to the U.S., she decided to become an actress and landed roles on *The Dukes of Hazzard* (1981), *The A-Team* (1983) and *The Colbys* (1985–1987).[763]

As filming of the series got underway, Dean Cain and Teri Hatcher discovered that they had a natural rapport on-camera. In a joint interview that they gave to *TV Guide*'s Rick Marin in 1993, Teri Hatcher recalled that the first words she said to Dean Cain were, "You don't like me, do you?" She said that showed how insecure she was; Cain chided her for being hard on herself.[764] He later told *Yolk* magazine's Brett Tam that Hatcher was a fantastic actress who memorized her lines fantastically well and proved to be very durable working a tough job. "They always say the hardest thing to do is hour-long TV," said Cain.[765] John Shea was also enamored of his co-star, saying of Hatcher that there was a distinction between being sexy and being pretty. Being sexy, he said, meant taking what was what going on in your mind and being able to project it through your eyes. "Teri has a love beam that she can turn on and off," said Shea. "You're like a deer in the headlights of a Mack truck and you stand there helpless as it approaches. It's her own super power."[766]

Taking advantage of a larger budget and technological advantages, the pilot episode of *Lois & Clark* showcased some impressive flying effects, from the sublime (Clark Kent floating horizontally up from his bed to the ceiling to fix a light bulb) to the spectacular (Superman flying through the window of the *Daily Planet* with Lois Lane in his arms, a shot which was used in the opening credits for all four seasons of the show). The flying scenes were especially tough on Dean Cain, who had a fear of heights. Being raised thirty feet in the air on a steel cable and dropping back down suddenly in a heroic Superman pose was exhilarating but, the actor said, "At the same time, I'm kind of going, 'I don't want to die in tights!'"[767] He told *People* magazine that dangling over a soundstage with wires attached to his hips was "a pain in the ass."[768] Teri Hatcher concurred. Speaking about the flying scenes, she told *US* magazine, "I have the bruises to prove that it's not all a dream come true. But there's nothing more romantic than flying in a man's arms."[769]

Spending a good deal of his time in a Lycra Superman uniform also meant that Cain had to stay in superior shape. He kept his 6 foot, 190 pound physique fit with a diet of steamed chicken, vegetables and rice, and worked out every other day.[770] Cain told Tom Shales of *The Los Angeles Times*, "I'm stronger right now than I ever was playing football, just because I'm healthy. But I have to be, to fit into That Damn Suit. Boy, that's a tough thing to do, put on that sucker. It's just such an American icon."[771]

Teri Hatcher had her own struggles, performing a lot of what she called "grunt stunts."

Dean Cain and Teri Hatcher redefined Clark Kent/ Superman and Lois Lane as a yuppie couple for the 1990s ABC-TV program *Lois & Clark: The New Adventures of Superman.* The wedding of Superman and Lois Lane on the program coincided with the wedding of the characters in the comics (ABC/ Photofest).

As she told an interviewer for the BBC's *Pebble Mill* program, "grunt stunts" included, "drowning in cement, which we shoot at two o' clock in the morning, when it's freezing cold, and I'm up to here in mud or whatever and falling in the giant cake ... cake frosting all over my body from head to toe. And that stuff dries. It is *not* a great time."[772]

Before the show hit the airwaves, it was publicized with a series of sexy ads that announced to viewers that this was a whole new Superman. One ad had Hatcher with Dean Cain in a tee-shirt and a Superman logo tattooed on his bicep. Hatcher joked, "It's pretty sad when the guy's prettier than the girl."[773] She needn't have worried. Another photo from the same session was taken at the end, at Hatcher's suggestion. After posing for a series of stills in her Lois Lane garb, Hatcher disrobed and wrapped herself in Superman's cape. The image, mixing sex with an American icon, was certainly eye-catching. It became one of the most downloaded photos of the newly-burgeoning technology known as the internet, with over 144,000 hits. It was quite a change of pace for "former nerd" Hatcher, who said, "I didn't have a single request for my wallet-size photo in high school."[774]

When the pilot was completed, it was shown to the advertisers at ABC who, according to Deborah Joy Levine, had a fabulously enthusiastic reaction. However, Levine was still worried about whether the show would live up to the expectations of DC Comics. Her fears were allayed when she received a call from a hotel in Minneapolis where all the Superman writers, artists and illustrators had convened to see the pilot. They were ecstatic. It had been almost a year since Levine first met with the representatives of DC, who seemed wary of doing another Superman series and skeptical about Levine's innovative ideas. To now have the blessing of people who had dedicated their lives to the character meant the world to her.[775]

The network scheduled the *Lois & Clark* pilot for Sunday, September 12, 1993. The 8 P.M. Sunday time slot was one of the most-watched time periods on television, especially among the key demographic of viewers aged 18 to 49 that the network hoped to attract.[776] NBC was going after the same audience with a new series from powerhouse producer Steven Spielberg, *seaQuest DSV*, which featured Stacy Haiduk in its cast. The next morning, the ratings numbers showed a huge audience—for the Spielberg series. Deborah Joy Levine was upset. She had seen the *seaQuest DSV* pilot and felt that it wasn't a very good show. Moreover, since *Lois & Clark* was a new take on the character, approaching Superman from a new perspective, she feared that people who hadn't seen the pilot wouldn't realize what the differences were between the background of their Clark Kent/Superman and the earlier versions. She hoped that audiences who had been lured to the Spielberg series by the advertising and hype would eventually feel that they weren't getting their money's worth and would tune in *Lois & Clark* instead. *SeaQuest DSV* was their Lex Luthor, and—as in the comics—Levine believed that good would win in the end.[777]

Levine's prediction proved correct. By the end of October, *Lois & Clark* was averaging a 10.9 rating/17 share in the Nielsen ratings, slowly catching up with *seaQuest DSV*. In November, *Variety* announced that the series had been picked up for a full run of 22 episodes. However, to boost the action quotient of the shows, ABC shifted the show's creator Deborah Joy Levine to an executive producer position, and brought in another executive producer tasked with raising the ratings, Robert Singer. Singer, who had an overall deal with Lorimar, which by that time had become Warner Bros. Television, was the creator and executive producer of the TV series *Midnight Caller* (1988) and *Reasonable Doubts* (1991) for NBC.[778]

During the early months, when Dean Cain still enjoyed relative anonymity, he had an amusing encounter on Sunset Boulevard in Los Angeles, as he later told *TV Guide*'s Rick Marin. Seeing a lady who'd been in an accident, he pulled his car over to help. Seeing that the fender was bent and stuck on the tire, he got a tire iron and began pulling it free. "Look at you," said the lady, "Like Superman!" Cain responded, "Well, actually I'm not Superman, but I play him on TV."[779]

One-hour episodes of the series began airing September 26, 1993, with the installment "Strange Visitor," which introduced Terrence Knox as Jason Trask, a "Man in Black" government investigator looking into Superman's origin. The third episode, "Neverending Battle" (air date October 3, 1993), had Lex Luthor staging disasters to test Superman's abilities. When innocent people are hurt, Clark feels inadequate, and voices his concern—in a veiled way—to Lois. She tells him that Metropolis needs Superman, but that not even Superman can be everywhere at once. "Then what good is he?" asks Clark. Lois tells him, "Well, what he can't do, it doesn't matter. It's the *idea* of Superman. Someone to believe in. Someone to build a few hopes around. Whatever he *can* do, that's enough. I just wish that I could tell him that." A Superman who could feel self-doubt was something new for television. Writer Dan LeVine told Edward Gross and Mark Altman that the old George Reeves take on the character had very little depth compared to the portrayal of Superman in *Lois & Clark*. LeVine said that with their limited budgets and time constraints, they couldn't invent a new super villain with superpowers every week, but at the same time they didn't want the show to devolve into Lois Lane and Clark Kent solving the types of mysteries that would be more appropriate for *Murder, She Wrote*. The challenge, said LeVine, was to find a middle ground where they could tell stories with imagination that were one second into the future, but still rooted in reality.[780]

Episode #4, "I'm Looking Through You," was the first of the *Lois & Clark* episodes to show Superman doing the sort of things George Reeves did in the 1950s *Adventures of Superman*. Superman stops a crook who shoots at him, with the bullets bouncing off his chest, then he takes the crook's pistol and crushes it in his hands before bursting through a wall to save Lois. It was almost as if the producers were trying to reassure the audience that although this was a more romantic take on Superman, at its core it was still the same old Superman audiences knew and loved.

A more direct connection to the older series came with episode #12, "All Shook Up," which was yet another remake of the 1950s episode "Panic in the Sky." The premise was basically the same. Superman flies into space to destroy a meteor that's hurtling towards earth. His first attempt is unsuccessful, and leaves him with amnesia. Not only is he unaware of his identity, he's also unaware of his super powers. But whereas in the older program Clark became Superman after a visit from Jimmy Olsen, in the new version he becomes Superman after his parents visit and his mother throws him off the top of a building!

The next episode, "Witness," introduced Richard Belzer as Inspector Henderson, the role Robert Shayne had played on the 1950s series. Belzer would play the role in two more first-season episodes, before moving on to a similar role (as Det. John Munch) in the TV series *Law & Order* (1990–present).

Jor-El appeared in episode #16, "The Foundling," as a holographic image projected from a globe Clark found in Trask's warehouse. David Warner, a busy character actor best remembered as Jack the Ripper in *Time After Time* (1979), played Superman's father. The episode also featured a nice bit of demythologizing, when we see that Clark's boyhood tree house has the words "Fortress of Solitude" painted on it.

Throughout the run of the series, Lex Luthor had been wooing Lois Lane, culminating in the two-part season closer, "Barbarians at the Gate" and "The House of Luthor" (episodes #19 and #20). "The House of Luthor" ended with Lois Lane preparing to marry Luthor. When Superman unveiled Luthor's evil schemes, Luthor leapt from a high-rise balcony, committing suicide. A familiar face made a brief cameo in the show—Phyllis Coates, who played Lois Lane opposite George Reeves' Superman in the 1950s series *Adventures of Superman*. Coates played Lois Lane's mother. It was Teri Hatcher's idea to hire the actress. She told Rip Rense of *The Los Angeles Times* that she figured surely Lois Lane's mother would come to her wedding, and if anyone was going to play that role, it should be Phyllis Coates. Coates flew in from Carmel on short notice, happy to have the part. Comparing Hatcher's interpretation of Lois to her own, she said that Hatcher's Lois was a sexy woman of the '90s who also got to play comedy, exhibiting shades of Lois that weren't permitted in the 1950s. In Coates's estimation, Hatcher was the best Lois Lane ever.[781]

Though it was Deborah Joy Levine's fresh take on Superman as a romantic series that made *Lois & Clark* stand out from other interpretations of the mythos and got the program on the air, at the end of the first season, ABC decided to oust her. Though she would still receive credit on the show, Robert Singer was now calling the shots. Under his control, the show changed to more of a standard action series. Lane Smith told M.J. Simpson that in the first year, it was more of a character-driven show, but the change of format to make it more of an action-adventure series really helped it take off in the ratings.[782] Dean Cain told Brett Tam of *Yolk* magazine, "What they're doing is more action, less romance that went nowhere," though he admitted that the action scenes were expensive and more tedious to shoot. Cain said he enjoyed the back-and-forth banter between Lois and Clark, and the show would always have that, but in the new approach, when it happened it would mean more.[783]

There were changes in front of the camera as well as behind the scenes. John Shea, tired of commuting from New York to Los Angeles to film his Lex Luthor scenes, chose not to return after the first season.[784] He asked to be let out of his contract, but the producers were loath to lose him. A compromise was reached where the producers allowed Shea to reduce his participation in the show, returning only for special episodes.[785] He subsequently appeared in only one episode in the second season and two in the third.

No Superman TV series would be complete without at least one major cast change after the first season. For *Adventures of Superman* in the 1950s, Noel Neill replaced Phyllis Coates as Lois Lane. For *Superboy*, Christopher Gerard replaced John Haymes Newton as the title character, and Sherman Howard replaced Scott Wells as Lex Luthor. With *Lois & Clark*, besides the departure of John Shea, Season Two brought a new Jimmy Olsen, Justin Whalin. The reason for the change, according to some accounts, is that ABC hoped to make Jimmy Olsen a teen heart-throb to compete with *seaQuest DSV* star Jonathan Brandis, who was gracing the covers of the popular teen magazines.[786] Lane Smith, having worked out an on-screen relationship with Michael Landes's Jimmy Olsen, took the transition in stride, proclaiming that Justin Whalin was a terrific guy.[787]

Born September 6, 1974, in San Francisco, California, Justin Whalin became an actor for the sake of romance; he signed up for an acting class so he could spend time with a girl he had a crush on. He appeared in a diverse array of TV series, from *General Hospital* (1988) to *Charles in Charge* (1984) to *The Wonder Years* (1989–1990), and had roles in the films *Child's Play 3* (1991) and *Serial Mom* (1994). He became an Emmy-winner at a young age for his work in the TV movie *Other Mothers* (1993). Whalin's Jimmy seemed more eager, and more hip, than Landes's characterization; in his first appearances, he was seen riding a motorcycle and wearing flannel shirts and cowboy boots.[788]

To save on the budgets—and the time it took to film the episodes—there was less wire work in Season Two. From that point on, when Superman took flight, he more often than not spun toward camera and pulled his cape up so that it briefly filled the frame, as the other characters looked skyward and a wind tunnel sound effect was heard.

The second season introduced a couple of characters who would become recurring presences on the show. In Episode #4, Bronson Pinchot, best known for his role as a befuddled foreigner on the buddy sitcom *Perfect Strangers* (1986–1993), played the title role of "The Prankster." The Prankster had been sent to prison as a result of Lois's investigative journalism. When he escaped, he went after the intrepid reporter with elaborate technological pranks, until he was captured by Superman.

The next episode introduced the criminal organization Intergang, run by Bill Church (played by Peter Boyle), which was seemingly inspired by the character of Morgan Edge from the comic books. Trying to bring Church to justice was a beautiful female detective, Mayson

Drake (Farrah Forke), who, much to Lois's chagrin, had designs on Clark. Lois didn't have to fret for long; Drake was killed off by a car bomb in episode #16.

Informant "Bobby Bigmouth," played by prolific character actor Sal Viscuso, made his first appearance in episode #7, "That Old Gang of Mine," which had former criminals being cloned, including Al Capone (William Devane). Episode #17, "Resurrection" introduced Dan Scardino, a government agent who had eyes for Lois. Episode #18, "Tempus Fugitive," a fan favorite, had H.G. Wells coming from the future with Tempus, a man who is tired of the utopia of the future who uses Wells's time machine to go back to Smallville in 1966 to kill baby Kal-El before he's found by the Kents. Bill Church's son, Bill Jr. (Bruce Campbell) was introduced in episode #20, "Individual Responsibility."

Dean Cain, who had ghostwritten screenplays uncredited in the past, finally received screen credit as the writer of episode #9, "Season's Greedings." The show re-teamed Sherman Helmsley and Isabel Sanford, stars of TV's *The Jeffersons* (1975–1985). Helmsley played a toy maker who invented a toy that, although it was ugly, emitted a chemical that made everyone desire it. Cain had been disappointed that the series had not done a Christmas show the previous season, so he intentionally wanted to play up the light-hearted, fantasy holiday elements of this episode, feeling that Metropolis was a very romantic setting for a Christmas story.[789]

Adam West, who had starred as *Batman* in the 1966–69 TV series, made a cameo appearance as a newscaster in episode #21, "Whine, Whine, Whine." In the same episode, Frank Gorshin, who played arch-villain The Riddler on the *Batman* series, played a lawyer who sued Superman.

The season ended with a cliffhanger: Clark proposing marriage to Lois (episode #22, "And the Answer Is..."). Just before she answered, the screen freeze-framed with "To Be Continued..." superimposed. With more action, but a deepening of the Clark-Lois romance, the series ended its second season with stellar ratings. "The show has got so much heat now," Dean Cain told Susan King of *The Los Angeles Times*, adding that when the show wasn't doing well, he lost all pretensions and realized people weren't turning on the TV to see his face. The high ratings at the end of season two were a welcome relief.[790]

The show was also doing great overseas, as Dean Cain discovered when he went on a publicity tour. In summer, 1995, he told Brett Tam of *Yolk* magazine, "It's Warner Bros.' biggest international show. It's the number one American show in ten different countries. It's just huge, it's just gone out of control."[791]

Cain felt the second season started out weakly, because there was no forward momentum in the Clark-Lois relationship. However, with the episode "Tempus Fugitive," things turned around. "There is now a progression in their relationship," he said. "That's the magic of the show, that something goes on between the characters. We ended the season with Clark on his knee proposing to Lois. We shot this great ending last season we didn't use. I pray we start this season with that."[792]

In fact, three possible endings for "And the Answer Is ..." were filmed. One, the one that was used, simply had Lois saying, "Clark...." A second had her saying, "Yes," and a third had her replying, "Who's asking, Clark or Superman?" The latter one was used in the opening episode of Season Three, "We Have a Lot to Talk About," in which Lois surprisingly reveals that she has figured out Clark's secret identity ... and rejects his proposal.

Lois would keep Clark hanging for much of the third season. She also changed her hairstyle to a shorter bob, and Superman's take-offs were once again altered. Now, as he pulled up his cape, he became an animated blur.

The sixth episode of the season, "Don't Tug on Superman's Cape," had Lois fantasizing that she was a Bond woman ("Miss Goodbottom"), with Clark as 007 ("The name is Man. Superman."), complete with a Silver Birch Aston Martin. They're seen leaving a theater with the marquee "The Spy Who Left Me." The show was broadcast on November 6, 1995, just a couple of weeks before the 007 film *GoldenEye* hit theaters. Almost exactly two years later, Hatcher became a Bond woman in real life, acting opposite Pierce Brosnan's 007 in *Tomorrow Never Dies* (1997).

One of the highest ratings ever achieved for *Lois & Clark* came on November 20, 1995, when the eighth episode of the third season, "Chip Off the Old Clark," aired prior to the second installment of *The Beatles Anthology* TV special.

Dean Cain provided another teleplay for episode #10, "Virtually Destroyed," which had Lex Luthor's illegitimate son Jaxon Xavier sending Lois and Clark into a virtual reality world. Lois Lane's parents show up for episode #11, "Home Is Where the Hurt Is," but instead of Phyllis Coates, her mother was now played by Beverly Garland, best known for 1950s sci-fi films like *It Conquered the World* (1956) and *Not of This Earth* (1957) before playing the wife of Fred MacMurray for the final three seasons of *My Three Sons* (1969–1972). And whereas Denis Arndt had played Dr. Sam Lane in the season one episode "Requiem for a Superhero," he was now played by Harve Presnell, a Broadway singer/actor remembered for the film versions of *The Unsinkable Molly Brown* (1964) and *Paint Your Wagon* (1969).

Episode #13, "The Dad Who Came In from the Cold," was another spy story, in which Jimmy Olsen's father, Jack Olsen, was revealed to be a James Bond–like secret agent. James Read played Jimmy's father, and seemed to be having great fun with his scenes of 007-style derring-do.

In episode #14, "Tempus, Anyone?," Lois and H.G. Wells travel to another dimension where Tempus has taken control of Metropolis, and Clark Kent keeps his powers hidden. Lois helps Clark become Superman—while we hear REM's "I Am Superman" on the soundtrack. This segment is notable for being the only *Lois & Clark* appearance of Clark Kent's Smallville girlfriend Lana Lang, played by Emily Procter, who would go on to be Ainsley Hayes on *The West Wing* (1999–2006).

Episode #15, "I Now Pronounce You...," began a 5-episode storyline in which Lois and Clark are finally going to get married—but first they have to stop Dr. Mamba (a campy Tony Curtis) from replacing the President of the United States (Fred Willard) with a frog-eating clone. The next installment (episode #16, "Double Jeopardy"), had Lex Luthor returning, having replaced Lois Lane with a clone just before her marriage to Clark Kent. Meanwhile, the real Lois escapes from Luthor's clutches, only to develop amnesia; she thinks she's "Wanda Detroit," a saucy lounge singer character from a novel she's been writing. Episode #17, "Seconds," had Superman rescuing the real Lois from Lex Luthor. At the end of the episode, Luthor died; consequently, it was John Shea's final appearance in the series. The final two episodes of the Lois clone/amnesia story arc had Lois falling under the spell of Dr. Deter (Larry Poindexter), a psychiatrist who was trying to manipulate Lois to have affections for him. In the end, her memory returned, and the 5-episode story arc, which alienated many fans of the series, was put to rest.

Episode #20 of the third season, "It's a Small World After All," was co-written by Teri Hatcher, and had an old high school rival of Lois Lane's getting revenge on her former tormentors by shrinking their loved ones. A four-episode story arc began with episode #21, "Through A Glass Darkly," which co-starred Jon Tenney, who was Teri Hatcher's husband at the time it was filmed. Tenney and Justine Bateman play Kryptonians who have come to take Kal-El back with them to prevent a war on New Krypton. The ending had Superman saying good-bye to Metropolis and flying into space, telling Lois via telepathy that he loved her.

By the end of season three, the rigors of doing a television series were taking a toll on Teri Hatcher. Speaking to Tim Cogshell of *Entertainment Today*, she said that while she was proud to be part of a show that was a unique part of Americana that families could watch together, and proud that Lois Lane was a role model for young women, nonetheless "doing an hour drama for nine and a half months a year is a lot of your life. And that's the hardest thing about it." Hatcher complained that the heavy schedule put demands on herself and Cain that made it difficult to have a balanced life. "If I could do that show six months a year like on a sitcom," she said, "and have every third week off that would be incredible."[793]

The fourth season began with a two-part episode that resolved the cliffhanger from Season Three, only now the role played by Jon Tenney was played by Mark Kiely. When Lord Nor returns to Earth and tries to take it over, Superman must return and conquer him. With that storyline resolved, the way was paved for episode #3, "Swear to God, This Time We're Not Kidding," in which Clark Kent finally married Lois Lane. This episode was timed to air at the same time as Superman and Lois were wed in the comic books. Tempus (Lane Davies) returned in episode #4, "Soul Mates," in a script that was originally written for John Shea as Lex Luthor.

In episode #5, "Brutal Youth," Jimmy Olsen becomes the victim of a device that ages people. The older version of Jimmy was played by none other than Jack Larson, reprising the role for the first time since the final episode of the 1950s *Adventures of Superman*. Episode #11, "Twas the Night Before Mxymas," introduced Mr. Mxyzptlk to *Lois & Clark*, in the form of Howie Mandel. Tempus returned for episodes #14 and #15, making a run for the Presidency.

A three-episode story arc began with episode #17, "Faster Than a Speeding Vixen," which introduced Patrick Cassidy as Leslie Luckabee, the new owner of *The Daily Planet*. Cassidy was the son of Jack Cassidy, who had played gossip columnist Max Mencken in the 1966 Broadway production, *It's a Bird ... It's a Plane ... It's Superman*. With this episode, *Lois & Clark* moved to Saturday nights, and began dropping in the ratings. After the story arc ended on April 26, 1997, with episode #19, "Voice from the Past," ABC pulled *Lois & Clark* from the schedule. On May 22, the network announced that the program would not be coming back for a fifth season.

Episode #21, "Toy Story," is notable primarily for being the first in which we see Perry White's wife, Alice. Actress Mary Frann, best known as Bob Newhart's wife on the CBS sitcom *Newhart* (1982–1990), played the *Daily Planet* editor's estranged mate. The final episode of the series, "The Family Hour," had Lois and Clark revealing Superman's identity to Lois Lane's physician father to see if it would be possible for them to have children together. By the end of the episode, it's a moot point—a basket arrives on their doorstep, with a baby inside. With that image, *Lois & Clark* went off the air ... in the midst of another cliffhanger.

According to executive producer Brad Bruckner, interviewed by Craig Byrne for *Kryptonsite.com*, the story would have resolved itself in Season Five with the little boy growing at a vastly accelerated rate, becoming a pre-teen in a matter of months. A troubled kid, the boy would develop superpowers, not all of which he would use responsibly. "Turns out he was Kryptonian royalty," said Bruckner, "stashed by his mother to keep him safe from assassins. In the end he had to tearfully leave the only parents he'd ever known—Lois and Clark— and return to save his imperiled people."[794]

In May of 1997, the fate of the show was unclear. The viewership was rapidly declining; popular opinion held that while fans enjoyed seeing Clark pursuing Lois and vice-versa, once the two were married it took all the suspense out of the relationship; there was nowhere for the characters to go. ABC, noting the poor ratings at the end of season four, wanted to dump the show. Warner Bros. wanted to keep it going. The two series stars moved on to other projects. Dean Cain went to Toronto to appear in *Dogboys* (1998), a Ken Russell film for Showtime. Teri Hatcher went to England to film her scenes as James Bond's former flame in Pierce Brosnan's second 007 outing, *Tomorrow Never Dies*.[795]

The actors were not called back to work on *Lois & Clark*, and when the new TV season began, the show was no longer on the schedule. K Callan, in an interview with Michelle Erica Green on *LittleReview.com*, said that given the show's poor ratings in the fourth season, she couldn't fault ABC for canceling it, but she did fault them for not promoting it better to win back the fans that had defected. "For what reason, I don't know," said Callan. "We were there, we *had* to make money. I mean, *Superman*! Come on!"[796]

Dean Cain hoped to segue into feature films at the end of the series' run, but found the transition difficult to make. As with Kirk Alyn and George Reeves before him, casting directors found it hard to see him as anything other than the Man of Steel. "Those guys, they hear you played Superman—and I guarantee you, 90 percent of them have never seen Superman—and they're like 'We don't want him,'" said Cain.[797] Deborah Joy Levine told Eric Messinger of *InStyle* magazine, "I don't think people realize what a fantastic actor Dean is. That's the problem when you play Superman. It's the tights! People typecast you. But Dean's got everything. He's got great comic timing. His dramatic instincts are terrific. Plus, he's incredibly handsome—women just go nuts over him." For her part, Levine later gave Cain a recurring role in a series she produced for the Lifetime cable network, *The Division* (2001–2004).[798]

Nonetheless, Cain stayed active. In 1998, while he was dating country singer Mindy McCready, he directed two of her music videos. McCready dedicated her album, "If I Don't Stay the Night," to him, but the relationship didn't last.[799] In 1999, Cain was approached by TBS to host a new TV version of *Ripley's Believe It or Not!* (2000–2003). Cain not only became the host, but produced the show through his own company. It proved very lucrative for him, though hosting a weekly program of oddities was seen by some in the industry as being the modern equivalent of a carnival barker. "People were saying my career was over," said Cain. "I heard the snickers. But I'm an athlete. You can call me all you want. I've made money every single year since I finished Superman."[800]

Cain remained one of Hollywood's most eligible bachelors, and began dating model Samantha Torres in 2000. After they split, Torres learned she was pregnant. Cain's son, Christopher Dean Cain, was born at Cedars-Sinai on June 11, 2000. Though the couple never married, Cain became a devoted father, sharing custody of his son with Torres.

In 2004, Cain took a role very different from Superman. When the USA Network made *The Perfect Husband: The Laci Peterson Story*, a TV movie based on the headline-grabbing story of Scott Peterson, who murdered his wife Laci just before Christmas 2003, Dean Cain was chosen to play the killer, to whom he bore a striking resemblance. His performance won critical kudos. More recently, Cain has had a recurring role as Casey Manning in the NBC series *Las Vegas* (2003–Present) and played Mormon founder Joseph Smith in the film *September Dawn* (2006), directed by his father, Christopher Cain.

Teri Hatcher, after giving birth to a daughter, Emerson Rose, on November 10, 1997, eventually divorced Jon Tenney in February, 2003.[801] Deciding to concentrate on raising her daughter rather than film and TV work, she chose instead to appear in commercials, and made 75 spots for Radio Shack with football star Howie Long. She also toured in a revival of *Cabaret* as Sally Bowles, to critical acclaim.[802] She returned to television in 2004 to rave reviews as part of the ensemble of the ratings sensation *Desperate Housewives* on ABC.

As much as she was a role model for young women as enterprising reporter Lois Lane on *Lois & Clark*, Teri Hatcher became even more of an inspiration with a real-life act of courage and bravery. In April 2006, Hatcher revealed in an interview with Leslie Bennetts of *Vanity Fair* magazine that she had been the victim of child sexual abuse at the hands of her uncle, Richard Hayes Stone, a secret she had kept for thirty years. She came forward when a recent victim of Stone's committed suicide at age 14. San Jose, California Deputy District Attorney Chuck Gillingham said that without Hatcher's testimony, Stone's case would have been dismissed. Because the actress came forward, he was sentenced to fourteen years in prison. "I have so much respect for what she did," said Gillingham. "This is a person who had nothing to gain and a lot to lose."[803] Within twenty-four hours of the release of the *Vanity Fair* cover story, the district attorney's office in San Jose received over two dozen calls from other victims of sexual abuse who said they were emboldened to come forward as a result of Hatcher's interview.[804]

10

Superman Wings It
to the WB

Although *Lois & Clark* came to an abrupt end, Superman continued to be a TV presence in the 1990s with animated adventures on a new network, the WB. Debuting on January 11, 1995, the WB was a joint venture between Warner Bros. and the Tribune Company, a Chicago-based multimedia company that owned several newspapers and whose subsidiary, Tribune Entertainment, distributed a diverse array of TV programs. One of the earliest hits on the new network was *Batman: The Animated Series*, which began airing on the Fox network in 1992. Unlike the standard animated superhero adventures of the day, *Batman: The Animated Series*, drawing inspiration from the Tim Burton–directed *Batman* films, featured more mature writing and an art–Deco style that harkened back to the Fleischer *Superman* cartoons, with very dark backgrounds and lots of shadows, and characters drawn with blocky bodies and small heads with just the slightest hint of facial features. Series producer Bruce Timm and writer Paul Dini strove to keep the character close to his comic book counterpart, and fans responded; *Batman: The Animated Series* became a hit with adults as well as children. The Emmy-winning series spawned 85 episodes and produced numerous spin-offs, including the direct-to-DVD feature *Batman: Mask of the Phantasm* (1993), before going off the air in 1995.

Bruce Timm, born February 8, 1961, grew up when the Adam West *Batman* series was all the rage. Seeing the show at such a young age, he didn't understand that it was a camp parody; he took the heroics seriously. He told Brian Saner Lamken of *Comicology* that when the cliffhanger of one episode was Robin being eaten by a clam, all the kids at school were talking about it the next day—how could they kill off Robin?[805]

When Timm's family moved to California, he became interested in comic books, especially after a friend gave him a huge box of comic books he no longer wanted. He starved all through junior high, choosing to spend his lunch money on comic books.[806] After high school, he left his job at K-Mart to go to work at a nearby animation facility, Filmation Studios.[807] For Timm, it was just a way of getting paid to draw; at that time—the early 1980s—the level of quality in the animation industry was very poor.[808] Timm started off working on a sword-and-sorcery cartoon called *Blackstar* (1981–1982). Timm found the production-line attitudes disheartening; the emphasis wasn't on doing good drawings, it was just on getting it done.[809] Eventually, Timm left Filmation to go to work for former Disney animator Don Bluth, who was producing a feature-length cartoon, *The Secret of NIMH* (1982), in the classic Disney style. When the feature was completed, he returned to Filmation, where he worked on *He-Man and the Masters of the Universe* (1983–1985). He bounced around between Filmation and Don Bluth Studios for a while, and drew *He-Man* comics that were packaged with Mattel toys.[810] In 1989, he went to work for Warner Bros. animation division, doing storyboards and character designs for *Steven Spielberg Presents Tiny Toon Adventures*. Once at Warners, he worked his way up the ladder until, in the early 1990s, he was promoted to serve as producer on *Batman: The Animated Series*, from 1992 to 1995. According to Timm, there was no interest in doing an animated Superman at that time. [811]

After *Batman* ended its initial run, Timm was contacted by Steven Spielberg, who was a fan of the Batman series and wanted to do something with Timm's team. They pitched an idea he liked, *Freakazoid*, about a teenage superhero. But as Spielberg developed it, it became more humorous, and skewed toward a much, much younger audience. Disappointed, Timm left the project.[812]

At that point, there was beginning to be talk about a new Superman movie. One day, Bruce Timm went in for a meeting with Jean McCurdy, who ran Warner Bros. animation division, and she asked him if he wanted to do Superman cartoons. After his disappointment with *Freakazoid*, Timm enthusiastically said yes. Work on *Superman* began just as *Batman* moved from Fox to the new WB network, which wanted some fresh episodes to attract viewers. For a brief period, Timm and his crew were working on both series at the same time. Just as they were finishing, they also got the order to do *Batman Beyond*, and suddenly were having to produce three shows all at once.[813]

Even after the experience Timm gained on *Batman*, *Superman* proved to be a challenge. Timm felt that, fundamentally, Superman wasn't as cool as Batman, and taking a character that had been around for so long and making him seem fresh and exciting was a considerable challenge. Compared to the *Batman* series, where stories took place mostly at night and the settings were always in deep shadow, the *Superman* stories took place mostly in daytime, with a much more colorful palette. Timm believed that when the Fleischers did their Superman cartoons in the 1940s, they also recognized the intrinsic dullness of the character, and threw in all the film noir elements to compensate. However, he felt the noir elements were a better fit for the nocturnal Batman character than for Superman.[814] To further delineate the two series, he took a different design approach with Superman, making the look of the show more graphic and angular.[815]

Paul Dini, one of the primary writers on *Superman: The Animated Series*, was also aware of the Fleischer *Superman* cartoons, which he first saw in college. The shorts made an impact on him by showing that you didn't need a lot of dialogue to tell a story. "You could rely heavily on stylization and mood and action to convey pretty much all the emotions in a seven-minute short," said Dini. "The emotion is conveyed by the animation, the music and the posing of the characters."[816]

Bruce Timm originally wanted *Superman: The Animated Series* to be a period show set in the 1940s, which would have made it like a continuation of the Max Fleischer cartoons. The original character designs were done in that style,[817] but in the end, they decided it would be better to keep the stories contemporary, although there was still a retro, Art Deco element to the character designs and cityscapes. "The reason why we didn't make it Fleischeresque," said Timm, "is that I didn't want anybody to literally put it side-by-side with the old Fleischer shorts and say, 'They're just doing a third-rate knockoff of the Fleischers.' Because we can't compare with that."[818]

When it came time to cast a voice actor to play Superman, one of the first actors who came in to read for the part was Clancy Brown, an actor whose first film role came in 1983's

Bad Boys. With his portrayal of the monster in *The Bride* (1985), a remake of the horror classic *The Bride of Frankenstein* (1935), Brown embarked on a long career of playing villains, including menacing roles in films such as *Shoot to Kill* (1988), *The Shawshank Redemption* (1994) and *Starship Troopers* (1997). Brown's first child was born around the time that more and more film productions were moving outside of California. Wishing to stay close to home, he began doing voice work.[819] After auditioning for the role of Superman, he was instead offered the role of Lex Luthor. "I thought, Geez, it's like the story of my life," said Brown. "Can't I be the good guy once?"[820]

Producer Bruce Timm thought Brown's delivery sounded like Telly Savalas,[821] who had played the villain Ernst Stavro Blofeld in a James Bond film that Bruce Timm proclaims is one of his all-time favorite movies, *On Her Majesty's Secret Service* (1969). "I watch it about once or twice a year," Timm said.[822] Like Savalas's Blofeld, Timm's Lex Luthor was a thug who was also an incredibly successful businessman. The character was drawn to strongly resemble Savalas. Interestingly, Sherman Howard, who played Lex Luthor in the *Superboy* TV series,

Superman as he appeared in *Superman: The Animated Series* (1996–2000). Producer Bruce Timm originally wanted to set the show in the 1940s, but ultimately decided that would only invite comparisons with the Max Flesicher cartoons of that era (DC Comics/Warner Bros. Television/Photofest, (c) DC Comics/Warner Bros. Television).

had originally auditioned for the role of Lex Luthor in the animated series.[823] Though he lost out to Brown, Howard resurfaced later as the voice of the Preserver in the two-part episode "The Main Man."

The role of Superman went to Timothy Daly, who played the part with great earnestness. Born March 1, 1956, in New York City, Daly was the son of actor James Daly and the younger brother of actress Tyne Daly. While attending Bennington College in Vermont, he studied theater and literature and acted in summer stock.[824] He made his film debut in *Diner* (1982), directed by Barry Levinson, and went on to appear in the CBS-TV series *Almost Grown* (1988–1989).[825] He found long-term success in the NBC sitcom *Wings* (1990–1997), beating out Kevin Conroy for one of the lead roles. Conroy went on to be the voice of Batman, appearing alongside Daly in some Superman-Batman crossover episodes.[826] In an interview with *TV Guide*, Tim Daly was asked if playing Superman brought him a wider range of fans. "I wouldn't say it's *massive*," responded Daly. "It's small but avid. Maybe more than avid. Maybe ... *obsessed*."[827]

Timm knew exactly whom he wanted for Lois Lane: Dana Delany, who calls herself a "Lois freak." Born March 13, 1956, in New York City and raised in Stamford, Connecticut, Delany was a big fan of the George Reeves series, which she claims to have watched religiously. After church on Sundays, her family would go to the drug store, where Delany used her allowance to buy a comic book; she recalled that this was during the time that Lois Lane had her own comic (*Superman's Girlfriend, Lois Lane*).[828] With a long-held ambition to become an actress, Delany moved to New York City after graduating from Wesleyan University. Her first TV role came in the 1979–1980 season of the daytime serial *Love of Life*. After a stint on *As the World Turns*, she moved to prime time with small roles in *Moonlighting*, *Magnum P.I.*, and *thirtysomething*. Her big break came in 1988, when she landed the lead role of Lt. Colleen Murphy in the TV movie *China Beach*. The movie gained enough viewers to become a series, which ran for 62 episodes from 1988 to 1991. When that series ended, she landed meaty roles in the films *Tombstone* (1993) and *Exit to Eden* (1994). In 1993, she provided the voice of Andrea Beaumont, a/k/a The Phantasm, in the animated feature *Batman: Mask of the Phantasm*. Delany was recommended for the role by her friend Arleen Sorkin, who provided the voice of Harley Quinn on *Batman: The Animated Series*.[829]

Producer Bruce Timm was already impressed with Delany's work when he began preparing a *Superman* series in 1996.[830] Her audition tape was the scene where Lois looks at a picture of Superman after he's been spotted for the first time in Metropolis and she says, "Nice S." "And I thought, 'that's just great,'" said Delany.[831] She told Barry Freiman of *The Superman Homepage* website that she enjoyed doing voice work, particularly on the Superman adventures, where the scripts were superior to half the movies and TV shows that she read.[832] Given the retro feel of the Superman animation, Delany patterned her Lois Lane after Rosalind Russell's performance as Hildy Johnson in the classic film *His Girl Friday* (1940). The rapid-fire delivery, she said, was "a character thing more than a voice thing."[833] Asked to compare her Lois to the interpretation of others who have played the role, Delany concluded that, being an animated character, "my Lois will always look good."[834]

In casting other roles in the series, Timm continued to go for actors who weren't necessarily known as voice actors. David Kaufman, who had played Duane Preston in the TV series *Down to Earth* (1984–1986), provided the voice of Jimmy Olsen. Perry White was played by George Dzundza, who played Det. Sgt. Max Greevey on *Law & Order* (1990–1991) and appeared in films such as *The Deer Hunter* (1978), *No Way Out* (1987), *Basic Instinct* (1992) and *Crimson Tide* (1995). He also voiced Scarface and Ventriloquist on *Batman: The Animated Series*. Other actors who lent their vocal talents to the show included real-life couple Shelly Fabares and Mike Farrell as Ma and Pa Kent, Christopher McDonald as Jor-El, Finola Hughes as Lara-El, Joseph Bologna as Dan Turpin (a character created by legendary comic artist Jack Kirby, and drawn to look like Kirby), Brad Garrett as Bibbo and Lobo (a/k/a The Main Man), Malcolm McDowell as Metallo, Michael Dorn as Steel, Edward Asner as Granny Goodness, Joely Fisher as Lana Lang, Bud Cort as The Toyman, Ted Levine as Sinestro, Gilbert Gottfried as Mr. Mxyzptlk, and Lori Petty as Livewire. The casting continued a trend Bruce Timm had begun with the *Batman* series. "I wanted to avoid 'cartoon actors,' for the most part," said Timm, "because every other superhero show I had seen for the last 20 years before that had the same tone and voices to it."[835] Timm didn't want his programs to sound "cartoony," and reasoned that the best way to make them sound natural and convincing was by using actors who weren't traditional voice-over actors.[836]

In other animated series, the vocal performer often records his or her role in isolation, appearing at the studio as their schedule permits, rarely meeting other cast members during production. This was not the case with *Superman: The Animated Series*, where the entire cast got together in one room and recorded the dialogue tracks as if they were doing an old-time radio show.[837] The dialogue was recorded at the Warner Bros. Animation facility, a cavernous space within the Sherman Oaks Galleria.[838]

Superman: The Animated Series premiered on Sept. 6, 1996. The animation was far superior to the limited animation of the 1960s and 1970s series, and the stories—geared for a more mature audience than the Saturday morning kiddie shows—were above average. The first episode, "Last Son of Krypton, Part I" took place entirely on Krypton, and introduced Brainiac as a supercomputer who ran the planet. Brainiac deliberately sabotages Jor-El's efforts to evacuate the planet before it explodes, but the scientist is able to send his son away in a rocketship before the cataclysm. The WB series *Smallville* would later pick up on this idea, portraying Brainiac as a Kryptonian cyborg.

The second episode, "Last Son of Krypton, Part II," was the first time Ma and Pa Kent were shown as a youthful couple (at least, when they initially discovered Kal-El) instead of characters old enough to be Clark's grandparents. After discovering Kal-El's spaceship in a field, Martha walks away cradling the baby in her arms, musing that they could name it "Christopher, or Kevin, or Kirk ..." Superman, of course, had previously been played by Christopher Reeve and Kirk Alyn.[839]

The second episode also had Clark as a teenager conflicted about his superpowers. A later scene where the Kents explain that he is not human, that they found him in a spaceship, is reminiscent of a scene that would later be dramatized on the series *Smallville*, which would also adopt the notion that the young Clark Kent is not, to begin with, unquestioningly accepting of his otherworldly abilities.[840]

The program had a puckish humor; when Perry White shows Clark Kent, Jimmy Olsen and Lois Lane video footage of Superman in action, freeze-framing on the Man of Steel, Lois remarks, "He's strong, he flies, he's the Nietzschean fantasy ideal all wrapped up in a red cape. He's superman." And that is how the character is christened. Also, Superman agrees to be interviewed by Lois Lane after Martha Kent advises, "I don't want anyone thinking you're like that nut from Gotham City."

As in the Fleischer cartoons of the 1940s, the Superman of this series was not all-powerful; you see him actually struggling with some of his super feats, as in the third episode when he stops a damaged jet from crashing into downtown Metropolis (a scene also repeated in 2006's *Superman Returns*). The series performed well enough to stay on the WB schedule for four years; the last of its 54 episodes was broadcast on February 12, 2000.[841]

But an animated Superman was not off the airwaves for long. On November 17, 2001, a new series premiered: *Justice League*. Like *Challenge of the Super Friends*, *Justice League* had superheroes banding together to battle supervillains, although again the storylines and execution were more adult than in the 1970s series. Joining Superman were Batman (Kevin Conroy), Wonder Woman (Susan Eisenberg), Green Lantern (Phil LaMarr), J'onn J'onzz, the Martian Manhunter (Carl Lumbley), Hawkgirl (Maria Canals), and The Flash (Michael Rosenbaum, *Smallville*'s Lex Luthor).

Unfortunately, while this series was being prepared, Tim Daly made a commitment to star in a remake of the 1960s TV series *The Fugitive*. Consequently, the role of Superman went to George Newbern. Born December 10, 1964, Newbern graduated from Northwestern University in 1986 with a degree in theatrical arts. He had a recurring role as Payne McIlroy on the CBS sitcom *Designing Women* (1986–1992), and began doing voice work with the TV series *Dark Water* (1991–1993). He appeared as Dr. Scott Frank in the 1997–1998 season of the medical drama *Chicago Hope*, and played Owen Frank on twenty episodes of the TV series *Providence* in 2002. He also had film roles in *Switching Channels* (1988), which starred Kathleen Turner, Burt Reynolds and Christopher Reeve, and played the son-in-law of Steve Martin's character in *Father of the Bride* (1991) and *Father of the Bride Part II* (1995). Comparing Newbern's interpretation of Superman to Tim Daly's, Dana Delany said, "Tim was more the straight-forward hero, but George is great. To me, the difference is he's a little goofier. It's a different Superman, but equally viable as Tim's."[842]

Superman was redesigned for the new series, drawn with much longer legs, a very squat forehead and a longer, more angular chin. He was also made to appear older, with lines around his eyes, more physical girth, and a shining streak in his hair. Some fans complained that Superman seemed less powerful than he did in his own series,[843] but producer Rich Fogel countered that to make the show work, they had to make it so that the powers of the individual characters would complement each other without a lot of overlap to create a good chemistry for the group. Consequently, the Martian Manhunter was made less powerful than he was in the comics so his abilities wouldn't be too identical to Superman's. "And quite frankly," said Fogel, "there are situations where Superman, if he was really on top of his game, could take care of everything by himself and he wouldn't need the Justice League. So we'd be left with a Superman show, which we've had already."[844] Another of the show's producers, James Tucker, said that Superman was "getting his butt kicked" as much on *Justice League* as he did on his own show, but that on *Justice League*, there were six other heroes who could take up the slack, so the Man of Steel didn't have to finish the job himself. In Tucker's view, it wasn't a matter of *Justice League* portraying him weaker, but rather that they didn't show him doing everything that he could do.[845]

Unlike the *Super Friends* cartoons, *Justice League* did not feature the superheroes with young sidekicks or odd pets, though statuettes of The Wonder Twins were seen in a museum fight scene in the episode "And Injustice For All." The creators intended for the show to pay homage to the original *Justice League* comics, but they also wanted to have a racially diverse cast. Hence, The Green Lantern was portrayed as black (the comic books had featured three different Green Lanterns, including John Stewart, the African-American Green Lantern chosen for this series), while Hawkgirl was voiced by a Hispanic actress. As with the *Batman* and *Superman* series, *Justice League* attracted an impressive array of voice talent, including Powers Boothe as Grodd, Olivia d'Abo as Morgaine Le Fey, Virginia Madsen as Roulette, Robert Englund as Felix Faust, Eric Roberts as Mongul and Fred Dryer as Sgt. Rock.

Beginning with the second season, when the show was retitled *Justice League Unlimited*, fans felt that Superman's portrayal was more consistent with what had come before, especially since the streak in Superman's hair was drastically toned down, making the character appear younger. Dana Delany returned as Lois Lane in the second season, and has continued to play the role since, making her the actress who has played the role the longest on television or in the movies.[846]

Though George Newbern continues to play Superman on *Justice League Unlimited*, Tim Daly returned to the role for the 2002 video game *Superman: Shadow of Apokolips* and the 2006 direct-to-video release *Superman: Brainiac Attacks*.[847] As of this writing, with new episodes of *Justice League Unlimited* on the horizon, it is safe to say that the animated adventures of Superman will continue.

11

Smallville

The success of the Superman animated series showed Warner Bros. that there was still some life left in The Man of Steel. When the popular youth-oriented series *Buffy the Vampire Slayer* (1997–2003) jumped from the WB to rival network UPN, Peter Roth, the president of Warner Bros. TV, needed another drama series to fill the vacant time slot.[848] A possibility was a series being shepherded by Mike Tollin and Brian Robbins, whose Tollin/Robbins production company began developing a script based on the young Bruce Wayne, a/k/a Batman, in the summer of 2000. Because of conflicts with Warner Bros. movie division, that idea was unable to be pursued as a series. So, the development team at Tollin/Robbins shifted their focus, from Batman to Superman.[849] Coincidentally, at the same time, writing partners Al Gough and Miles Millar, who were one year into a deal with Warner Bros. Television, were also pondering a Superman TV series. Thinking that they would be unable to get the rights to the Superman character, they went to the network in the summer of 2000 to pitch a series about Lois Lane, whom they envisioned as a cross between *Ally McBeal* and *Nancy Drew*.[850] Roth met with Gough and Millar, who had scored hits with the TV series *Timecop* (1997) and *Martial Law* (1998–2000) and the movie *Shanghai Noon* (2000), and asked them if they would develop a show that would focus on a teenaged Clark Kent before he became Superman.[851]

Gough and Millar were interested in the idea of doing the series, but they made it clear that they didn't want to just do a remake of *Superboy*. They wanted to create something new and cool. Their basic premise was a very clever one: a program primarily aimed at teenagers about teenagers in which the main character was an alien, an outcast trying to be normal and to be accepted and to fit in with his peers—struggles that all teenagers could relate to. In its early developmental stages, the series was called *The Teenage Clark Kent Project*. In an interview on the *KryptonSite* website, Al Gough said that although *Lois & Clark* was a popular show with a lot of fans, Gough and Millar wanted to do their own interpretation of the character to make him more current and relatable for a youthful audience. To do this, they would show Clark as being as vulnerable as any ordinary teenager, albeit one who is not only dealing with puberty but is also learning to cope with his emerging superpowers.[852] The superpowers set Clark apart from his peers, but he's not boastful or confident about them; he's embarrassed, like any kid who feels different would be. Gough said there could be no better example of a young person trying to come to terms with his identity and find his way in the world than Clark Kent. The fact that no other producers had every really focused on the trials that led Clark to become The Man of Steel was what attracted Gough and Millar to the project.[853]

Gough took at least part of his cue from the *Batman* movies of the 1980s and 1990s, which were dark film noir evocations of the comic book. "Batman had always been considered cool and Superman kind of cheesy," said Gough. Consequently, the producers sought to ground the character in reality and portray him as an angst-ridden teen to give the show a more contemporary feel.[854]

As with all TV versions of Superman, the new show took some liberties with the classic storylines from the comic books. When Kal-El's spaceship arrives in Smallville, Kansas, it comes in the midst of a horrifying meteor shower that brings mayhem and destruction, kills Lana Lang's parents and causes Jonathan and Martha Kent to wreck their truck. The blast from the crash-landing of one of the meteors also causes a very young Lex Luthor to lose his hair, though at the same time it cures his chronic asthma. As the years pass, the contamination of the kryptonite in the soil of Smallville gives rise to a wide array of mutants and strange occurrences; it's like *Twin Peaks* on steroids. One of the most intriguing aspects of the new program was its reinvention of Lex Luthor. Gough liked that in their show, the character was in his early 20s and would first befriend Clark before becoming his mortal enemy. Part of the fun is that while everyone knows where the relationship ends, the producers got to show how it began and developed.[855]

There was an interesting duality at the heart of the show. On the one hand, the series showed how Clark Kent, due largely to the influence of his salt-of-the-earth father, became a force for good despite his awesome abilities. On the other hand, it showed how Lex Luthor was nurtured into being an evil megalomaniac by his ruthless, heartless, industrialist father, Lionel Luthor. Alfred Gough said that Lionel wasn't intended to be in the series for the long run, but the produces became fascinated by how he affected Lex and how his extreme parenting contrasted with Kent. Ultimately, they reasoned, Clark Kent became Superman and Lex Luthor became a villain because of how they were raised.[856]

In an interview with Craig Byrne of *KryptonSite.com*, Gough said that the producers were looking for a Clark Kent who was edgy and filled with angst, but still had the essence of the Superman he grows up to be. To signal that this was a more serious interpretation, it was decided that Clark wouldn't wear the Superman uniform, wouldn't wear glasses, and wouldn't fly.[857] But according to executive producer and writer Miles Millar, quoted in *The Los Angeles Times*, there was another reason for making this a more earthbound Clark Kent: "The kids now can't get past that cape. It is the most recognizable element, yes, but it is also the thing that makes it cheesy."[858] Gough and Millar's vision of the show was one that would become known as the "no tights, no flights" approach. However, even though Clark was never seen in the Superman outfit, he was more often than not seen wearing a blue tee-shirt with a bright red jacket or vice-versa, so he at least wore the iconic colors.

Executive producing the series was the team of Mike Tollin and Brian Robbins, through their Tollin/Robbins banner. In their early days, the pair had produced kids shows for Nickelodeon such as *All That* (1994–2005), *Kenan & Kel* (1996–1999) and *The Amanda Show* (1999–2002). Tollin said that after doing so many shows for pre-teens, it was a natural progression to do a show aimed at teens.[859] Robbins, a former actor with a long history of small roles in episodes of TV series like *The Facts of Life* and *Charles in Charge*, added, "We based the show on Clark Kent's being an archetypal hero and imbuing it with all these values set in mid–America. It wasn't going to be trendy, it wasn't going to be a faddish show and replace *Buffy* in sensibilities."[860]

The Teenage Clark Kent Project was a hot item. Both the Fox Network and the WB Network (a subsidiary of Time Warner Communications) wanted it. Al Gough, Miles Millar and Warner Bros. Television's Peter Roth had pitched the show to the presidents of both companies on the same day, showing up to the Fox and WB conference rooms wearing Superman tee-shirts. Fox offered more money for the pilot commitment and more for each episode in the event the pilot was picked up as a series, but Warner Bros. Television and Tollin/Robbins Productions went with the WB, who made a thirteen episode commitment with a per episode license fee that was thought to be the highest the network had ever paid for a first-year drama series. WB Entertainment president Susanne Daniels said, "The pitch was fantastic. Every character was worked out in depth. They mapped out the story arcs, the specific mysteries. This was one of those pitches you want to work with." The *Teenage Clark Kent Project*, she added, finally allowed the WB to work with DC Comics. "Part of getting into business required it be a substantial commitment," said Daniels. "They weren't going to let Superman go to anybody."[861]

The casting process began in October of 2000, with casting directors fanning out to ten major cities looking for Clark Kent, Lana Lang and Lex Luthor. As with *Superboy* and *Lois & Clark*, the female lead was cast before Clark Kent; *Variety* announced the hiring of Kristin Kreuk as Lana Lang on February 5, 2001.[862] Alfred Gough knew she was the right actress for the part as soon as he saw her audition tape. Struck by her delicate beauty, Gough said, "When you look into her eyes you immediately understand why Clark Kent pines for her."[863]

Born to a Chinese mother and Dutch father on December 30, 1982 in Vancouver, British Columbia, Kristin Kreuk was discovered during her senior year of high school, when her drama teacher told her she should audition for the Fox Broadcasting series *Edgemont*. Kreuk landed the role of Chinese Canadian student Laurel Yeung, and soon after won the lead in a TV movie, *Snow White: The Fairest of Them All* (2001).[864] After being cast in *Smallville*, she pulled double duty, continuing to play Laurel in *Edgemont* at the same time as she was filming the new series.[865]

Her early success as an actress sidetracked her first career choice; she told Gene Geter of *KryptonSite.com* that she originally wanted to be a forensic scientist. "I was interested in the problem-solving aspect to it," said Kreuk.[866]

For *Smallville*, the role of Lana Lang was very different from the sassy, sexy college-age Lana of the *Superboy* TV series. As played by Kristin Kreuk, *Smallville*'s Lana was fragile and uncomfortable in her own skin, which was befitting of a girl who lost her parents at a very young age. "Lana is a good person, who believes in the goodness of people," said Kreuk, who admired the purity and intelligence of the character. While she felt Lana was unlike her in a lot of ways, she said, "I'd like to believe that deep down I'm as good and honest as she is."[867]

Finding an actor to play the young Clark Kent proved more formidable. The challenge for the producers was finding an actor who could be Superman before he was Superman. With casting directors looking all over the country, hundreds of actors were seen in person and on videotape, but to no avail. The search ended when 23-year-old Tom Welling came in to audition. "Not only did he have the right look, but he also had that right sort of spirit—you could see him becoming Superman," said Gough. "There's a gentleness, but also real strength." The producers felt Welling had an indefinable star quality. When they asked him to read opposite Kristin Kreuk, they also saw that their two leads had great chemistry together.[868]

Initially, however, Welling turned the role down, because he wasn't sure what type of series *Smallville* would be. Welling told Robert Falconer of *The Hollywood North Report* that when he was first contacted about the series, everybody connected with it was extremely guarded concerning what the show was about. All he knew was the basic concept, "Superman in high school," which was not something the actor was interested in doing. David Nutter, who had been signed to direct the pilot, had a detailed conversation with Welling's manager. Nutter said that if Welling came in to audition, they'd let him read the script, but they couldn't let him read it unless he auditioned. "So I went in and auditioned, they liked what I did, and they said, 'Come back tomorrow and you can read the script.' And when I read the script I thought, 'Okay, now I get it.' It was amazing, I mean I really thought it was great."[869]

A native of Okemos, Michigan, where he was born on April 26, 1977, Tom Welling graduated from Okemos High School in 1995 and became a model for the Louisa Modeling Agency. His good looks landed him an acting role in the CBS series *Judging Amy* in the 2000–2001 season.[870] As Rob the karate instructor, he proved so popular with audiences that his role, which was originally scheduled for only three episodes, was extended to six.[871] Roles in UPN's *Special Unit 2* (2001–2002) and Fox's *Undeclared* (2001–2002) followed, and then came the audition for *Smallville*.[872]

Welling was not a particular fan of Superman before being cast in the series. "I saw the movies and dressed as Superman for 2 years in a row on Halloween when I was 4 and 5," he told interviewer Haggay Kraus on the website *MichaelRosenbaum.com*. Aside from that, however, Welling didn't really know anything about the character or the story. He believed this helped him in his portrayal: he was learning about Superman just as Clark was learning about his emerging powers. Welling said that, like Clark, he didn't really know who he was supposed to be. [873] In an interview with John Levesque of *The Seattle Post-Intelligencer*, Welling said that he had not re-watched any of the previous Superman movies or TV shows, preferring to come at the character from a fresh standpoint.[874]

The young actor was concerned about the typecasting suffered by other actors who had played the Man of Steel, particularly when, as he told Kraus, he was faced with the prospect of signing a binding five-year contract. He asked his father for advice. His father told him that if he did a good job, people would understand that Clark Kent was just one role he could play, and it might open doors to other opportunities. Welling duly signed his contract.[875]

Although he was a relatively novice actor, Welling hit just the right note in the way he played Clark Kent. In an interview with Frazier Moore of the Associated Press, Welling said that Clark's abilities were like an exaggerated form of puberty. Every kid can run; Clark can run faster. Any kid can pick up things; Clark can lift really heavy things.[876]

Of course, one of the basic tenets of drama is that the stronger the antagonist, the stronger the hero is perceived to be. When it came to casting Lex Luthor, creator/producer Alfred Gough said they looked for "a young Michael Keaton, who had humor and charisma and a sense of danger to him."[877] Michael Rosenbaum, Gough said, "gave us that in spades."[878] Gough told *KryptonSite.com*'s Craig Byrne that Rosenbaum was funny, he was charming, he was charismatic; "He is Lex Luthor."[879] Rosenbaum was cast just two weeks before filming of the pilot was due to begin, after a number of other actors were considered for the role, including Leonard Roberts. "I actually read for Lex in the pilot. I remember thinking, 'I think this is going to be a long shot!'" said Roberts. "But when I went in, I just committed to it. They were totally receptive, which I thought was cool, and that they were interested in what could be brought to it." Roberts lost out on playing Luthor, but the producers remembered him and four years later cast him as the Kryptonian Nam-Ek, who terrorized Smallville in the Season Five opener.[880]

Though he had little time to prepare for the role, Michael Rosenbaum nailed it from the outset. Unlike previous actors who chose to play up the camp value of Lex Luthor,

Rosenbaum made him a slick charmer; he was the seductive serpent in the Eden of Smallville. Instead of adopting the humor of Gene Hackman's portrayal, Rosenbaum told Marc D. Allan of *The Indianapolis Star*, "For me, I'm re-inventing a character. I'm playing him in a way that no one's ever seen him before."[881]

Born on July 11, 1972, in Oceanside, Long Island, New York, Rosenbaum grew up in Newburgh, Indiana. From an early age, he was aware of Superman, as he told Haggay Kraus. He admitted that when he was very young, he had Superman underwear and ran around the house as though he were flying.[882] His earliest ambition was to be a professional hockey player, until a back injury sidelined him. "I was really competitive, probably too competitive," said Rosenbaum. In high school, he performed in a production of *Grease*, and was bitten by the acting bug. Rosenbaum said that he was very short as a child and lacking in self-confidence, which he gained from being on the stage. His grandmother, he said, always told him he had talent, and now he believed she was right.[883]

After high school, Rosenbaum continued acting at Western Kentucky University. One of his earliest TV jobs came on *Late Night with Conan O'Brien* where he was one of the "Amsterdam Kids."[884] Next came roles in the movies *Midnight in the Garden of Good and Evil* (1997) and *Urban Legend* (1998), and more TV work, including appearances on *The Tom Show* (1997–1998) and *Zoe, Duncan, Jack & Jane* (1999–2000). Rosenbaum told Haggay Kraus that because he had appeared on so many comedy series on the WB, the network was reluctant to accept him as Lex Luthor, having pigeonholed him as a comic actor. It was only after he auditioned that they saw a different side of his persona and decided to give him a chance. Then they asked him to shave his head.[885] Rosenbaum's bald pate and swaggering confidence earned him a nickname among the show's female fans: "Sexy Lexy."[886] His family reacted differently to his shorn locks. He told Marc D. Allan of *The Indianapolis Star* that his father laughed and told him he looked like an idiot.[887]

Among the new characters created for the show, one of the most intriguing was the diabolical industrialist Lionel Luthor, Lex Luthor's father. Lex, said Michael Rosenbaum, didn't want to hate his father, he just wanted a father who would listen to him—and Lionel Luthor was not that man.[888] Lionel was the ultimate in charming yet despicable villains. He believed the cruel tests he put his son through would mold him into a ruthless businessman, yet the audience knew that Lionel's machinations were pushing Lex into a life of unrelenting evil.

Playing the part of Lionel Luthor was John Glover, a seasoned film, television and theater actor who once played the Devil in *Brimstone* (1998–1999).[889] "I hope I make Lex's life as bad as he makes mine," said Glover, adding that he had a fabulous time acting opposite Michael Rosenbaum.[890] Rosenbaum said that despite the tensions they displayed on-screen, off-camera he and Glover had a great relationship. He also felt Glover was an underrated actor who deserved an Emmy.[891]

Glover was born in Salisbury, Maryland, on August 7, 1944, and began his professional career in theater. After a decade of stage work, he was cast opposite Jane Fonda in *Julia* (1977), playing a first-class heel. The film's director, Fred Zinnemann (who also directed George Reeves in *From Here to Eternity*) gave Glover an insight that has served him well in playing the succession of nasty characters he's brought to life since. Though Glover was playing a detestable character, Zinnemann told him that the character would see his self as being very noble. The advice gave Glover the insight that an evil character doesn't believe they're doing evil; they have a different mind-set.[892]

Glover sees Lionel Luthor's mind games with his son as tests to strengthen him and prepare him to someday take over the Luthor empire.[893] Despite how it may seem, Lionel

Luthor is not, in Glover's eyes, a totally amoral sociopath, but rather a man with a conscience "deep in his soul. It's all based on strength. It's all for Lex. It's going to make him a stronger person. I have to look at it that way.... There's a conscience in there that's working."[894]

The flipside of fatherhood is represented by John Schneider as Jonathan Kent. Whereas Lionel Luthor is testing Lex and molding him in his own image, Jonathan Kent is nurturing Clark and trying to instill in him a strong sense of morals, values and personal responsibility. Schneider told *The Los Angeles Times* that he felt the time was ripe for a heroic figure. "It is out of such times of national turmoil and concern that came such people as Audie Murphy, Jimmy Stewart and John Wayne," said Schneider. "Now we have *Smallville*. And it's really about the raising and teaching of a true American fictional hero."[895] Producer Al Gough said that Schneider helped to ground the show.[896] For his part, Schneider approached the role from a unique perspective, portraying Jonathan Kent as a man coping with a special needs child. "It really bothers Clark, because he says he doesn't want to go through his entire high school life as a loser," Schneider told John Levesque of *The Seattle Post-Intelligencer*. "He doesn't look at it saying, 'Wow, I've got these superpowers, isn't this great?' He looks at it by saying, 'I'm really strange. There's something wrong with me.'"[897]

John Schneider was born April 8, 1954, in Mt. Kisco, New York. As a child, Schneider collected baseball cards, but he also had his comic books in the '60s. He told Daniel Robert Epstein of *Sci-Fi/Fantasy* magazine that he was a big Captain America fan as well as a fan of the *Superman* TV show.[898] When Schneider heard that a new TV series that was casting was looking for Southern actors, he claimed to be born in Snailville, Georgia, and, consequently, landed one of the lead roles in *The Dukes of Hazzard* (1979–1985).[899] When that show came to an end, Schneider branched out into singing, releasing the Country album "Tryin' to Outrun the Wind." In 1983, Schneider—with Marie Osmond—co-founded The Children's Miracle Network, which raises money for children's hospitals.[900] Schneider said playing Jonathan Kent was "really a position of honor for me. Since we know how Clark Kent is going to turn out, the onus is on the parents to raise him to be that. The assumption is that he must have had some pretty good parents." Schneider felt it would be helpful to parents who watched the show to see how important Jonathan and Martha Kent were in raising Clark, and to see parents who weren't portrayed, as they were on so many other programs, like idiots.[901] Series writer Jeph Loeb noted that Jonathan Kent's paternal dialogue could have come off as corny, but sounded authentic coming from Schneider. "John is so grounded, so honest about his feelings that he's like bedrock," said Loeb.[902]

In previous live-action versions of the Superman story, Jonathan and Martha Kent had been portrayed by actors old enough to be Clark Kent's grandparents rather than his parents. *Smallville* was the first time that they were portrayed as a youthful couple, and it was a welcome change. Martha Kent, particularly, was given much more of a back-story than her comic book equivalent ever had; in *Smallville*, we learn that her father was wealthy and disapproved of her marrying struggling farmer Jonathan Kent. To play this more nuanced Martha, the producers cast Cynthia Ettinger, an actress then best known for her role as Sylvia Rohan in episodes of the TV series *Providence* (1999–2002); she has since gone on to star as Rita Sue Dreifuss on *Carnivále* (2003–2005) and Claudia on *Deadwood* (2004–present).

Rounding out the cast were Sam Jones III as Clark Kent's best friend Pete Ross, a character from the comic books, and Allison Mack as high school reporter Chloe Sullivan, a character created especially for the series. Al Gough felt that Sam Jones III, who played Pete Ross, and Allison Mack, who played Chloe, really lit up the screen.[903] Sam Jones III was born April 29, 1983 in Boston, Massachusetts. After acting in local commercials, he went to Los Angeles and appeared in the TV shows *CSI, ER* and *NYPD Blue*.[904] Allison Mack was born July 29, 1982, in Preetz, Germany. At the age of two, her family moved to Southern California. At age four, she was appearing in commercials and print ads. By age seven, she was studying acting. Prior to *Smallville*, she guest-starred in TV shows like *7th Heaven* and *Providence*, and was in the film *Honey, We Shrunk Ourselves* (1997).[905]

As important as any of the cast members is the setting itself; as the title suggests, the town of Smallville is as much a character in the show as the people who inhabit it. Al Gough said the intention was to keep the show grounded in reality. Like other rural American towns, Smallville was changing. Corporations (in this case, LuthorCorp) and housing developments were encroaching on the farmland; there was a struggle between farmers like the Kents who wanted to hold on to a traditional way of life and progressive thinkers like the Luthors who wanted to bring the community into the 21st century.[906] By the time the show began production in 2000, it was the beginning of an economic downturn in America. Middle class workers were losing their jobs as corporations were outsourcing and downsizing. In the Kent family struggling to keep their farm afloat, viewers saw themselves. In Lionel Luthor building an empire with heartless disregard for his employees and those who stood in the way of his ambition, they saw a personification of the kind of greed and power that led to the Enron scandal. It was exactly what executive producer Miles Millar intended; he didn't want the show to feel like a relic of the 1950s; he wanted this depiction of Smallville to feel contemporary.[907]

Brian Robbins was initially attached to direct the pilot episode[908]; eventually, he would drop out to make room for David Nutter, who had a reputation for directing pilots that

Michael Rosenbaum as Lex Luthor and Tom Welling as Clark Kent, from the Season 3 *Smallville* episode "Phoenix" (airdate October 8, 2003) (Photofest, © The WB/David Gray).

went to series, such as *Roswell* (1999–2002) and *Millennium* (1996–1999). Nutter also had previous experience with Clark Kent; he had directed several episodes of the Salkinds' *Superboy* series. Consequently, he wasn't entirely sure he wanted to take on another Superman project. However, when he spoke to Peter Roth, the president of Warner Bros. Television, Roth's genuine excitement for *Smallville* enthused Nutter. In an interview with Ed Gross as he was about to direct the *Smallville* pilot, Nutter said he intended to do it "in a way that's hip; in a way that's smart, in a way that's fun and also do it in a way that is compelling storytelling. The script is fantastic and I think it's kick-ass, very smart, a lot of fun and very involving for the audience."[909]

For Nutter, the pilot was essentially the story of a young man with a secret he couldn't reveal to other people, a dilemma Nutter felt that a lot of teenagers could relate to.[910] In his approach to the material, he was determined to somehow make Superman as hip as Batman. He wanted to reach a new generation of viewers while at the same time keeping it accessible to older audience members who would be familiar with the Superman myth from previous incarnations. Nutter believed the show could be surprising and exciting and attract a broad audience from across the spectrum. For him, it was the kind of opportunity he'd been waiting for.[911]

Although the series takes place in Kansas, it was filmed in and around Vancouver, British Columbia, Canada, where location scouting began in January 2001. Michael Rosenbaum complained that although the location was beautiful, it rained all the time.[912] Indeed, if one looks closely, there is rain in the background of almost every scene of the pilot. The Government of Canada building in downtown Vancouver was used for the exterior of Lionel Luthor's company, LuthorCorp, until season three, when the Central City mall and office tower in Surrey was used. Vancouver Technical School was used as the exterior of Smallville High initially, with interiors filmed at Templeton Secondary School. Eventually, both exterior and interior school scenes were shot at Templeton. Scenes of Smallville's main streets and town square were filmed in Cloverdale, British Columbia, which was so proud of its association with the show that it erected a sign on its outskirts proclaiming it to be "Home of Smallville." The Kent farm was actually the home of Mario and Karen Anderlini. In season two, Cloverdale's Clova Cinema became Lana Lang's coffee shop, "The Talon."[913]

Filming of the series pilot commenced in March 2001 and lasted for sixteen days of first-unit work and an additional five days of second unit shooting (after the pilot, subsequent episodes were filmed on an eleven day schedule, eight days of main unit and three days of second unit). The filming was book-ended by one of the pilot's most memorable scenes, in which Lex Luthor crashed his Porsche Carrera into Clark Kent and through a bridge, plunging into the river, where Clark rescued him from drowning. One of the first shots filmed was the aftermath of the scene, where Jonathan Kent comes to pick up Clark. The last shot filmed was a second-unit pick-up of Clark Kent ripping open the roof of the Porsche and pulling Lex out. Michael Rosenbaum found the filming of that shot to be particularly challenging, spending take after take at the studio submerged in a car inside a 12-foot tank of water. He later said that all he could hear were echoes and the voice of the director. "I was honestly scared," he admitted.[914] It didn't help that Rosenbaum suffers from claustrophobia.

As the pilot was being filmed, market research showed that the core audience of the WB—mainstream, middle class teenagers—provided almost a blank slate for presenting new adventures of Clark Kent. "What we found is that most of the audience that watch the WB were not familiar with Superman at all," Alfred Gough recalls. "We did a pilot test and in the middle there was a glitch in the tape and the boys had to tell the girls they were watching Superman. The girls had no idea."[915] According to *Variety*, most fans of the *Smallville* series weren't very aware of either the 1970s and '80s Christopher Reeve films or the 1950s George Reeves TV show.[916]

When actor Michael Rosenbaum saw the completed pilot for the first time, he had tears in his eyes. "I said to myself: 'This is it,'" he remembered. "I called my family and told them, 'This is it.' They had never heard me say that before about anything else."[917] Warner Bros. TV president Peter Roth was also pleased, telling *Variety*, "They created the perfect contemporization of one of the great cultural icons of our time."[918]

Well ... almost perfect. When the network screened the pilot, they asked for one major change: recast Martha Kent. Cynthia Ettinger, they felt, looked more like Clark Kent's sister than his mother.[919] A replacement was quickly sought, and Annette O'Toole took over the role. John Schneider and Tom Welling were brought back, and all the scenes involving Martha Kent were reshot. O'Toole had had previous experience with Superman; she played Lana Lang opposite Christopher Reeve in *Superman III* (1983). Born on April Fool's Day of 1952, O'Toole began her career with guest spots on TV shows like *My Three Sons* (1967), *Gunsmoke* (1970) and *The Partridge Family* (1971),[920] and won critical acclaim for her roles in *48 Hours* (1982) and *Cat People* (1982). "Young or old, Martha has always had a certain strength and wisdom," said series writer Jeph Loeb, "and Annette brings that to the character along with a sensuality that is very underplayed, but is always there."[921]

The pilot episode established all the major characters and conflicts that would carry over into the series proper. It begins with the meteor shower that decimates Smallville and masks the arrival of a strange visitor from another planet. The alien baby is given the name Clark and raised by Jonathan and Martha Kent, but by the time he's a teenager in high school, he realizes he has abilities that he must keep secret. He also harbors a not-so-secret crush on his neighbor and schoolmate Lana Lang, literally going weak in the knees whenever he approaches her due to the necklace she wears made from a fragment of the kryptonite meteor that killed her parents. When he stumbles in front of her and spills his schoolbooks, we see that one of them is a book by Nietzsche. Lana hands it back to him, saying, "I didn't know you had a dark side," adding, "So which one are you, Man or Superman?"—a reference to Nietzsche's *Thus Spake Zarathustra*.

Clark's best friends, Pete Ross and Chloe Sullivan, work with him on the school newspaper, the *Torch*, which is apparently named after the high school newspaper for which Jerry Siegel and Joe Shuster worked, *The Glenville Torch*. Clark saves Lex Luthor from drowning after Lex's Porsche rams into Clark and crashes through the guardrail of a bridge. Afterwards, Clark befriends Lex, whose father, millionaire industrialist Lionel Luthor, has sent him to Smallville to head up a small division of LuthorCorp, which is headquartered in nearby Metropolis.

One plot element provided a striking image for publicizing the show. Every year, the jocks at Smallville High pick an unfortunate outcast student to be their "scarecrow," which means they tie him to a cross in a cornfield and paint a red "S" (for Smallville) on his chest. In the pilot, of course, they pick Clark. The image of a shirtless and crucified Tom Welling was the main one used to publicize the show, appearing in print ads and on billboards all over the country. It was an image that—like a nude Teri Hatcher wrapped in Superman's cape—was at once shocking and seductive, and it did the trick.

When the pilot for *Smallville* aired on the WB on October 16, 2001, it drew the best ratings of any pilot in the WB network's seven-year history, with 8.35 million viewers.[922] On the basis of those numbers, one week later, the network ordered another nine episodes to supplement their original 13-episode commitment, making for a full season's run of twenty-two shows.[923] "A lot of people were pretty sure it would be a hit," said Kristin Kreuk. "The scripts were very good, and the network got behind it." On the strength of the show's high ratings, the network felt confident enough midway through the first season to renew it for a second one.[924]

As filming of the first season episodes got underway, Tom Welling found himself in the same situation Kirk Alyn had experienced five decades earlier, with directors seeing him so much as the character that they forgot he didn't actually have super powers. In filming a scene where there was a car explosion and a character was thrown from the vehicle, Welling recalled, "the director comes up and says, 'OK, Tom, I want you to run over, pick him up and carry him across the street.' He wants me to bend down and pick a guy who weighs two hundred pounds off the ground! I go, 'I'm not Clark Kent!'"[925]

When the series began, Clark Kent had super strength and super speed. As the episodes progressed, he developed new powers—heat vision, super hearing, X-ray vision, and the ability to leap tall buildings in a single bound. As each new talent arose, he went through an awkward period of learning to control it. Alfred Gough liked the idea that Clark Kent's powers developed incrementally since childhood; as a child of four, he could have lifted a coffee table, but not a pick-up truck. Gough said that while this borrowed from the John Byrne revamp, the difference in *Smallville* is that—unlike in the comics—Clark is not a well-adjusted kid hiding his powers and pretending it's no big deal. In *Smallville*, Clark's learning to adjust to his emerging powers is a *huge* deal.[926]

The first few episodes pitted Clark against other residents of Smallville who had weird powers as a result of long-term exposure to "the meteor rocks," including a boy who morphed into a bug, a football coach who could cause spontaneous fires, a girl who could shapeshift, a kid with ice in his veins who stole heat from his victims, etc. The formula quickly began to wear thin; fans termed it the "Freak of the Week" approach. As the series progressed, some more intriguing continuing storylines developed, such as Lex befriending Clark while at the same time investigating him, and Lionel Luthor's growing awareness of Clark's abilities. There were also some in-jokes for the die-hard Superman fans, such as in episode #18, "Drone," when Clark runs for class president using the catchy slogan "The Man of Tomorrow," a phrase used to describe Superman in the comic books.

Season 1 ended with a cliffhanger—a tornado strikes Smallville. The natural disaster occurs just as Lana is returning from dropping off her boyfriend, who has joined the Marines; a private investigator struggles with Jonathan Kent after finding the spaceship in Kent's storm cellar; Lex has to decide whether to save his father, who is trapped under a fallen beam; and Clark is at the Spring Formal with Chloe, whom he promptly abandons to go to Lana's rescue.

The second season brought about some changes. Behind the scenes, Jeph Loeb, a writer of the *Supergirl* and *Superman/Batman* comics, became a supervising producer and writer on the series; he would remain with *Smallville* for three seasons. In front of the cameras, Lionel Luthor became more than just an occasional presence. Because of his theater commitments, John Glover was unable to fully commit to the show's first season. In season two, he became a regular cast member.[927] To give Lionel Luthor a new twist, he was now blind, which appealed to Glover, who thought putting a limitation on a character who had a need to be in control and know everything made the mind games between Lionel and Lex even more wonderfully complex.[928]

A new character, Dr. Helen Bryce, was introduced in the ninth episode of the season, "Dichotic." Played by Vancouver native Emmanuelle Vaugier, the character would appear in six more episodes in season two, becoming Lex Luthor's bride at the close of the season. Vaugier had previously played a gypsy doctor on the WB's *Charmed*. "Most of my time on the show is spent working with Michael Rosenbaum," said Vaugier, "and he's definitely very charming and funny. He's always making everybody laugh."[929] Another new cast member was Patrick Cassidy, who portrayed Leslie Luckabee in season four of *Lois & Clark*. Cassidy took on the recurring role of Henry Small, who is revealed to be Lana Lang's still-living father, beginning with episode #7. Jason Connery, who had appeared in the first season episode "Hothead," returned as Lionel Luthor's strong-arm man Dominic Senatori for two episodes of season two. Connery, who once played a TV hero himself as Robin Hood in the British series *Robin of Sherwood* (1986), is the son of former James Bond star Sean Connery.

When cameras rolled on season two of *Smallville*, Tom Welling returned to the set feeling more at ease than the previous year. "The first season, I didn't know how to act," he said. "I just tried to believe in the character. But I think my confusion on-set translated into Clark's confusion as a character. If you watch how Clark is now, he's a bit more comfortable. I'm a bit more comfortable, too."[930]

In the third episode of the season, Pete Ross found Clark's spaceship. In order to protect his secret, Clark was forced to take Pete into his confidence. This new story development meant more air time for Sam Jones III. The change came after fans of the show wrote to Warner Bros. asking to see more of Clark and Pete. Jones was impressed that fans had even noticed him; he felt like he basically just appeared in the episodes to say "hi" to Clark and then he was gone. But when his fans created a website for the actor and began writing to the producers demanding that he get more airtime, the producers listened.[931]

Audiences responded enthusiastically to the new episodes. By February, the show's second season ratings were up by more than a third[932]; it was averaging 7.5 million viewers most weeks.[933] Among the show's fans was one who really knew what it meant to be Superman—Christopher Reeve. From the very genesis of the series, the producers had hoped to entice him to appear in an episode. In season two, they got their wish. When Reeve appeared as Dr. Virgil Swann, a reclusive scientist who offers Clark information about his Kryptonian heritage in the season's seventeenth episode, "Legacy" (air date: February 25, 2003), newspapers around the country heralded the passing of the torch from one generation's Superman to another's.

"When we created the show, Miles and I said the first movie was our gold standard," Alfred Gough recalled. "In the back of our heads, we wanted to get Chris to do the show."[934] The producers called Reeve's agent, pitched the idea for the episode, and asked if Reeve would have any interest. The agent called Reeve, then called the producers back. It turned out the actor was a big fan of the show; his friends told him that Tom Welling looked like a younger version of him. In a 45-minute conversation with Reeve, Gough pitched him the idea for the character, who was to become a wise man/mentor to Clark.[935] To accommodate Reeve, the scenes involving Dr. Swann were filmed in New York City, where the New York Public Library was dressed to become Swann's home. According to supervising producer and writer Jeph Loeb, the only time the show left Canada to film on location was for the Dr. Swann scenes.[936]

As with many youth-oriented series, *Smallville* used music from popular recording artists to underscore the show's action and romance scenes. The show's main theme, "Save Me" by Remy Zero, rose to number 27 on the Billboard Modern Rock Chart.[937] As a winking in-joke, Remy Zero was seen performing the song at the Smallville High School Spring Formal at the close of Season 1. During the show's second season, a soundtrack CD was released on February 25, 2003, the same day the Christopher Reeve episode aired. Called "Smallville Soundtrack: The Talon Mix," the CD featured music by artists whose songs were used in the series, including Sixpence None the Richer, the Flaming Lips, Weezer, Ryan Adams, Lifehouse, Five for Fighting, AM Radio and Phantom Planet. A week prior to its release, in second season episode #16, "Fever," the group Steadman was seen performing at a fundraising event where the CD was being sold. Brian Cohen, senior VP of marking for Elektra, a division of Time-Warner, said, "Bringing in the element of somebody creating a compilation is a great way to gently bring in the idea of a soundtrack within the narrative of the show. It has never been done." The disc used CD key technology to provide buyers with access to online bonuses that included the first issue of DC Comics' *Smallville* comic book, a 3-D interactive map of the town and videos of performances by VonRay and Remy Zero. VonRay's track "Inside Out," the first single from the CD, had been in second season episode #8, which aired November 12, 2002; Elektra released the band's debut album the following spring.[938]

With the success of the *Smallville* series, the comic book version of Superman began to become more like the character seen on the TV series. Jeph Loeb, who is also a writer of the Superman comics as well as a supervising producer and writer on *Smallville*, said that Al Gough and Miles Millar's vision of the character was influencing the way a new generation saw Superman, just as the 1978 film became a gigantic hit and defined the character to such an extent that the comic books were "rebooted" in 1986 to conform more closely to that conception. "It's the mark of a great icon—particularly in pop culture—that a character and his world can be reconceived over and over and still have the same resonance as it had in 1938!" said Loeb.[939]

In viewing *Smallville*, one can see a distinct difference in how TV programming has evolved over fifty years. In 1951, the first season episodes of *Adventures of Superman* were considered too violent for a kids' TV show. By January 14, 2003, when the second season *Smallville* episode "Visage" aired, the shape-shifting character Tina Greer (a creepy Lizzy Caplan) was seen to suddenly and violently beat an off-camera Marine to death with a baseball bat, cackling with laughter as blood splashed back into frame. It was a moment that made the most violent instances of the George Reeves series seem innocently tame.

Near the end of Season Two, a new character was added to the *Smallville* roster. With Sheriff Ethan (played by Mitchell Kosterman) implicated in a plot to frame Jonathan Kent in episode thirteen, "Suspect," the town was left without a Sheriff until episode nineteen, "Precipice," which introduced Camille Mitchell as Sheriff Nancy Adams. Sheriff Adams had a gruff, tough-as-nails, take-no-prisoners John Wayne attitude in a petite body. She added a welcome dose of droll humor to the episodes in which she appeared.

Season Two also introduced caves that were covered with what the residents believe to be Native American hieroglyphics, but which were actually Kryptonian symbols. In the final two episodes of the season, Clark was contacted by his father, Jor-El. In a departure from the comic books and all previous film and TV versions, Jor-El was portrayed not as a wise and benevolent scientist but rather as an apparently evil warlord who sent Kal-El to earth to conquer and rule the planet. But then, how else would Jor-El behave when his voice was provided by Terence Stamp, who had previously portrayed the villainous Kryptonian General Zod in *Superman: The Movie* and *Superman II*?

Red kryptonite, which turns Clark Kent into a supercharged Mr. Hyde, was introduced in episode four of Season Two, "Red." In "Exodus," the final episode, Martha Kent loses the child she's carrying and Clark blames himself. Slipping a red kryptonite ring onto his finger, he becomes a leather-jacketed, motorcycle-riding badass and takes off for Metropolis.

By the end of the second season, Warner Bros. Television was anxious to keep Al Gough and Miles Millar as showrunners on *Smallville*, which ranked as the network's top-rated show in key demographics. The studio signed the pair to a two-year, seven-figure agreement. Gough and Millar were now very much in demand; besides continuing to chart the course of the teenaged Superman, they were also writing the screenplay for a big-screen adaptation of a rival superhero, *Spider-Man 2* (2004). They were also working on an *Iron Man* script for New Line. In signing the writing/producing pair to a new contract, Warner Bros. hoped to keep creative consistency on *Smallville* at least until the show reached its fourth season, when it would have enough episodes for syndication. Warner Bros. TV President Peter Roth told Josef Adalian of *Daily Variety* that it was important for the company to maintain the quality of the series. "*Smallville* is arguably one of the most important assets for this studio," said Roth, "and by signing Al and Miles to a long-term agreement, we've protected the future of this franchise."[940] Al Gough was happy to remain aboard, saying that he and Miles Millar wanted to protect their vision and ensure that it would continue.[941]

Season Three began with Clark living in Metropolis, having become a bank robber under the influence of the red kryptonite ring—only now, Clark was calling himself Kal. To bring him back, Jonathan Kent had to make a deal with Jor-El which temporarily gave him powers equal to Clark's, but ultimately left him with a weakened heart.

The fifth episode of Season Three, which aired October 29, 2003, introduced the *Smallville* audience to a classic Superman character, Perry White. But this was not the Perry White audiences had come to expect. As played by Michael McKean, better known as David St. Hubbins in *This Is Spinal Tap* (1984), this Perry was a down-on-his-luck alcoholic who had gone from prize-winning journalist to tabloid hack. Producer Mark Verheiden chose to also write the episode. Having previously worked for five years at *The Los Angeles Times*, he felt an affinity for the Perry White character; he had met real-life journalists with Perry's characteristics.[942]

McKean, in a rare dramatic turn, nailed the role. "He really caught the spirit of a man who knows he's hit a dead-end road," said Verheiden, "but can't quite figure out how to turn things around ... until he meets Clark."[943] When Perry calls Sheriff Adams (Camille Mitchell) "chief," she says curtly, "Don't call me chief!"—a throwback to Jimmy Olsen's frequent line from the *Adventures of Superman* TV series of the 1950s. "How can you do an episode featuring Perry White without a little callback?" asked Verheiden.[944] The episode was directed by Jeannot Szwarc, who had previously helmed *Supergirl* (1984). Verheiden felt that Szwarc had an innate understanding of the material.

Michael McKean had a couple of Superman connections before he appeared on the show. Eight years earlier, while he was a cast member of *Saturday Night Live*, McKean had played the editor of *The Daily Planet* in a sketch in which Superman refused to save the earth from an oncoming meteor.[945] He was also the real-life husband of Annette O'Toole.

Later in the season, new storylines were set in motion. It was revealed that Chloe Sullivan's cousin was Lois Lane, setting the stage for Lois to join the series later. Lex had a mental breakdown and was institutionalized at the Belle Reve Asylum. And when the producers realized that the Clark Kent–Lana Lang romance was running out of steam, they introduced a new character, Adam Knight, played by Ian Somerhalder. But the hoped-for sparks between Lana and Adam didn't materialize; on-screen, Somerhalder and Kristin Kreuk just didn't have the right chemistry. Their solution was to make the storyline a little darker, which they always planned to do, but instead of having the story arc play out over the entire season, they brought it to an abrupt end.[946] Clark developed a new power—super hearing. It was revealed that Lionel Luthor was dying of a liver disease, and Pete Ross, straining under the burden of keeping Clark's secret, decided to leave Smallville when his parents divorced. In the final episode of the season, a young woman claiming to be Kara from Krypton led Clark into the caves, where Jor-El brought him into another dimension.

When Season Four began, Pete Ross was gone, but two new characters came aboard: Lois Lane (played by Erica Durance) and Jason Teague (Lana's new boyfriend, played by Jensen Ackles). Both were introduced in the first episode of the season, "Crusade," which aired September 22, 2004. Before they could bring Lois into *Smallville*, the producers had to clear it with the movie division of Warner Bros. Though they wanted to use the character for a full season of twenty-two episodes, the studio only allowed them to use her for thirteen.[947]

In an interview in *The New York Post*, Erica Durance said, "Of all the different female leads in comics, Lois Lane was always my favorite because she was so involved ... she's a go-getter, she was really in there, quite tough and kind of a hero in her own right."[948] Durance, born June 21, 1978, had previously appeared in the TV series *Andromeda* (2000–2005), *Tru Calling* (2003–2005) and *The Chris Isaak Show* (2001–2004).[949]

"I think we needed to introduce a new character into Clark's life," said Al Gough, "and it's interesting since this is the woman he will ultimately end up with, who at this point, when he meets her, doesn't like her at all."[950] However, bringing Lois into *Smallville* seemed to push the redefining of the Superman character beyond the beyond; a question as yet unanswered by the producers is how Lois, having met and known Clark as a young man, before he was using eyeglasses as a disguise, won't recognize him years later when he becomes Superman.

As portrayed by Durance, the new, younger Lois had some characteristics of Margot Kidder's Lois Lane, including a penchant for sarcasm and wise-cracks (like the Lois of the WB cartoons, she calls Clark "Smallville"), and craving cigarettes that she knows she shouldn't smoke. In another passing of the torch, former Lois Lane Margot Kidder appeared in the season opener, portraying Bridgette Crosby, an associate of Dr. Swann.

Durance brought a dash of humor to the show; in fact, Season Four had a lighter tone overall than the previous season, which producer Al Gough felt became too dark and a little too adult; with Lionel Luthor becoming a larger presence, the Season Three episodes, in Gough's opinion, became too sci-fi and strayed too far away from the core concept of a teenage Clark Kent dealing with his issues. In Season Four, Gough wanted to return to that, with story arcs like Clark Kent joining the football team, not only because he believed he could control his powers, but also because he needed scholarship money for college.[951]

More characters from the DC Universe were seen in the fourth season episodes, including a teenage version of The Flash (in episode #5, "Run"), and a reinvention of Mr. Mxyzptlk (in episode #7, "Jinx"). Mikhail Mxyzptlk was now a foreign exchange student who came not from another dimension but from Eastern Europe—which, one supposes, is like another dimension to most high schoolers. He was also a bookie fixing Smallville High's football games, with the power to make people do things just by speaking them; for instance, when he whispers "fumble," a player on the field fumbles the football.

Alicia Baker, a character from Season Three, returned and provided a temporary love interest for Clark in episode #11, "Unsafe." When she feared that Clark was going to dump her, Alicia arranged for Chloe to observe Clark in action, catching an airborne car. From this point on, Chloe knew Clark's secret, though it would still be some time before he knew that she knew.

One fourth season episode, "Spirit" (episode #18), gave Annette O'Toole a chance to show she could play more than the dutiful farm mother, when Martha Kent finds her body possessed by the spirit of a ditsy teenager. In a scene straight out of *Freaky Friday* (1976, remade 2003), Martha dances wildly in her kitchen until Clark comes home. When he asks about supper, she offers him ice cream, and gives him an impassioned diatribe about how important it is for him to attend the senior prom.

The season ended with a bang, as another meteor shower struck Smallville. Having acquired all of the "elements"—the three stones whose acquisition had driven the plots of all the season's episodes—Clark put them together and he and Chloe were suddenly transported to the Arctic.

The fourth season episodes continued to click with viewers; the show held its own in the ratings, even when pitted against ABC's hit series *Lost*.[952] However, in season five, the WB network decided to protect it's top-rated show by taking it out of direct competition with *Lost* and moving it from Wednesday to Thursday nights. As a result, the show's ratings climbed; it averaged 5.5 million viewers, a jump of eight percent over the previous year's numbers. Producer Al Gough said they were more than surprised, "we were shocked and relieved."[953]

The increased ratings—setting Thursday night records for the WB—were good news for the sales department; Thursday night was lucrative because the film studios pay top dollar to place ads that attract audiences to their movies that are opening the next day. Peter Roth, president of Warner Bros. Television, said that *Smallville* was one of the biggest hits the subsidiary had produced for the parent company, and since it was a wholly owned Time Warner property, it had been given the full weight and impact of the network.[954]

By the fifth season, Clark and his friends were finally out of high school and pursuing new lives in college and in Metropolis. "This is where Clark starts to step up and take the mantle of Superman," Gough says, "and Lex's descent into evil is accelerated."[955] By this point in its run, the show was also being seen in syndication. In the U.S., it was running on the ABC Family cable channel. Overseas, it was Warner Bros. International Television's highest-rated series since *ER*.[956]

In "Arrival," the first episode of the season, Clark finds himself in the Arctic with the "elements," which he tosses into the snow. A crystal fortress rises from the ice, a Fortress of Solitude that looks almost identical to the one from the Christopher Reeve films. In this and subsequent episodes, the Fortress of Solitude is the place Clark goes to speak with Jor-El. Meanwhile, two Kryptonian "disciples of Zod" are causing havoc in Smallville, looking for the son of Jor-El, until Clark returns and sends them to the Phantom Zone (which is also portrayed as it was in the 1978 film). After doing so, Clark discovers that he has lost his superpowers. In this first episode of the season, Erica Durance makes a brief appearance as Lois Lane. As with Season Four, she was contracted to appear in thirteen of the Season Five episodes as Lois.

The season's second episode, "Mortal," showed the powerless Clark overcoming a threat posed to his family by escapees from the Belle Reve sanitarium. It ended with the now-human Clark getting together with Lana at the Talon. After four seasons of circling in each other's orbit, the two finally collided and consummated their relationship. The next episode, "Hidden," revealed the two of them waking up in Clark's bed, and his parents catching them as Lana tried to sneak out. Before the third episode ended, the now mortal Clark was shot. After dying on the operating table, Jor-El—now possessing Lionel Luthor's body—transported him to the Fortress of Solitude. Jor-El told him that his mortal journey was over, but he would return with all his normal gifts. However, the life of someone close to Clark would be taken in exchange for his.

Another classic DC superhero appeared in *Smallville*'s fifth season—Aquaman. The show's fourth episode, "Aqua," featuring the underwater ace, was one of the season's highest-rated, attracting a viewership of 6.4. million.[957] Aquaman, called Arthur Curry or "A.C.," was portrayed as a crusading environmentalist in green swim trunks and orange tank top, who had a crush on Lois Lane. The popularity of the episode prompted Warner Bros. Television to begin developing an Aquaman series for prime time.[958] Writer-producers Al Gough and Miles Millar were commissioned to produce a pilot that was filmed but never aired; ultimately, it failed to get picked up as a series.[959]

The fourth episode of the season also properly introduced a character that had been glimpsed at the end of episode two—Professor Milton Fine, otherwise known in the comic books as Brainiac. As played by James Marsters, Fine was a more loquacious version of the T-1000 cyborg from *Terminator 2: Judgment Day* (1991). He initially appeared to be a benevolent ally to Clark Kent, filling him in with clues about his Kryptonian heritage. Later in the season (in episode #8, "Solitude"), he was revealed to be a confederate of General Zod, sent to trick Clark into destroying the Fortress of Solitude and with it his link to Jor-El.

"Thirst," episode five of the fifth season, was *Smallville*'s Halloween episode. It began with Chloe facing the hard-bitten editor-in-chief of *The Daily Planet*, Pauline Kahn, played by Carrie Fisher, an actress best known for her role as Princess Leia in the *Star Wars* films. With a storyline that involved Lana Lang becoming a pledge in a sorority of vampires, the episode had the cheeky humor to name the leader of the vampire sorority Buffy, an obvious nod to the former WB hit *Buffy the Vampire Slayer* (1997–2003). Interestingly, when Chloe and Clark went undercover at the sorority's Halloween costume bash, Clark arrived dressed as Zorro—an interesting coincidence, given that Douglas Fairbanks's Zorro was an inspiration for Superman, and a Zorro poster in Paris prompted Ilya Salkind to produce *Superman: The Movie*.

The next episode, "Exposed," contained deliberate in-jokes, with John Schneider's former *The Dukes of Hazzard* co-star, Tom Wopat, cast as Senator Jack Jennings, an old friend of Jonathan's who is up for re-election. When Jennings arrived at the Kent farm, he was seen recklessly driving a Dodge Charger, the same type of car as *The Dukes of Hazzard*'s General Lee. There was also a James Bond reference—when Clark rescued Lois Lane while dressed in a black business suit, Lois greeted him with, "Hey 007, nice of you to show up."

The twelfth episode of season five, "Reckoning," was the hundredth episode of the series—the first time a series based on Superman had reached that milestone.[960] Broadcast January 26, 2006, the episode marked a pivotal turning point, as Clark finally revealed his true powers to Lana, and proposed to her. However, when Lana died in a car chase, Clark had to plead with Jor-El to bring her back to life. His wish was granted, but Clark nonetheless lost someone close to him—his father, Jonathan.[961]

Al Gough said Jonathan's death was always contemplated, since it was part of the mythology. Going into the fifth season, they decided it was time for the boy to become a man. In order for Clark to step up and embrace his destiny, the mentor/father figure had to die. Though sad to leave the show, John Schneider was proud of the way his character's demise was handled. "It was like John Wayne in *The Cowboys*. An empowering death. Which is so important, because if Jonathan Kent had just died, it would have been terrible. It would have been meaningless."[962]

With the death of Jonathan Kent, Martha Kent became more of a foreground character, much to Annette O'Toole's delight. "I do feel bad about John Schneider," she said, "but it did free up this character." Martha Kent, she said, would now be seen as her own character, not just an extension of "Jonathan's fatherly ways."[963] Indeed, since Jonathan had just been elected to the Kansas senate before his untimely death, Martha now stepped in to serve out his term.

Tom Welling, following the example of George Reeves before him, stepped behind the camera to direct one of the final episodes of the season, "Fragile." Michael Rosenbaum told Bryan Cairns of *Smallville Magazine* that he couldn't resist giving Welling a hard time over his directorial debut. "He'd tell me to do stuff and I'd go, 'I'm not listening to you. You are a rookie!'" said Rosenbaum. "Or I'd say, 'Ooooh, look at the big director! Look at me! I'm a director! Hey, I'm an actor.' Then a second later, 'Hey, I'm a director. No, I'm an actor. I'm so cool." Despite his good-natured ribbing, Rosenbaum felt that Welling did a great job.[964] Producer Al Gough agreed, saying, "He's worked with every actor on every set for five years, so he has a real innate understanding of how the production process works, but he was also very good in prep and also in story meetings, when we were developing the script." According to Gough, Welling would be directing another episode in Season Six.[965]

Smallville began its sixth season on a new network, the CW, which was created when the Warner Bros.–owned WB merged with CBS-owned UPN; the initials "CW" take the "C" from CBS and the "W" from Warner Bros. The new network, it was felt, would benefit from broadcasting the ratings winners of both previous networks, including the WB's *Smallville* and UPN's *Veronica Mars*.

Executive producer Al Gough promised that *Smallville*'s sixth season would show the lonely path a hero must take. When Clark Kent returned from the Phantom Zone, so did some of the Zone's Kryptonian villains. Over the course of the season, they would come looking for Clark; after all, it was his father who condemned them to the Phantom Zone.[966] Helping Clark was another DC Comics character, The Green Arrow, played by Justin Hartley, who became a romantic interest for Lois Lane. The Green Arrow also had another mission, according to Gough—trying "to find like-minded people with powers and sort of start a nascent Justice League." Toward that end, heroes who had shown up in past episodes were expected to return, including Aquaman, the Flash and Cyborg.

Chloe Sullivan also had a love interest in season six: Jimmy Olsen, played by Aaron Ashmore. In the season's premiere episode, Jimmy called Clark "C.K."—a callback to *Lois & Clark: The New Adventures of Superman*. The premiere episode also paid homage to *Superman II*, with Lex Luthor, whose body was possessed by the Kryptonian villain Zod, saying to Clark, "Kneel before Zod." Clark does, and extends his hand. But, as in *Superman II*, when Zod/Luthor's hand touches Clark/Superman's, good triumphs over evil (in this instance, Clark slips a medallion which looks like the familiar Superman shield into Lex Luthor's hand, which causes Zod to leave Lex's body and return to the Phantom Zone). The *Smallville* Season Six premiere episode drew an estimated audience of five million viewers.[967]

As of this writing, *Smallville*'s Season Six is still underway, and it has proven to be a ratings champ for the new CW network. Beyond that, *Smallville*, since its first broadcast in 2001, has had a wider cultural impact. The big-screen equivalent was *Batman Begins* (2005), which "rebooted" the moribund Batman film franchise. And whereas in the 1970s Ilya Salkind hoped *Superman* would be his equivalent to the James Bond film series, the James Bond film series had now become equivalent to *Smallville*, "rebooting" 007 with *Casino Royale* (2006). Small-screen examples were less successful; a WB update of *The Lone Ranger* (2003) never made it past the pilot, and a new WB revamp of *Tarzan* (2003) fizzled after only eight episodes. But *Smallville* kept rolling along, and Warner Bros. TV was thrilled with its success. "Advertisers love *Smallville*, and it's been wildly successful for our network in terms of revenue," said WB Entertainment president David Janollari, adding that it had helped expand the network's audience by bringing in young males.[968]

As the series progressed, its young cast became media stars. Michael Rosenbaum began moonlighting, this time on the side of good; besides playing Lex Luthor in *Smallville*, he also provided the voice of The Flash in the *Justice League* animated series.[969] But it was his portrayal of Lex that kept him in the spotlight. In 2004, he told reporter Terry Morrow, "I was at a party and one of my heroes—Quentin Tarantino—yells across the room. 'Hey, it's Lex Luthor! I love your show!' It's awesome."[970]

The good-versus-evil plots, coupled with the romantic complications of its young characters, kept audiences tuning in week after week. "I think that the show appeals to so many different types of people," said Kristin Kreuk. "There are various elements to it. Heart and soul. Romance. The show deals with family relationships that appeal to all different ages and races."[971] Tom Welling had his own theory for why the show continued to perform so well. "I think there's a little bit of all of us in Clark Kent," he said. "So many people, so many different ages, from so many different backgrounds, can associate with him and stay in touch with what he's going through, because we've all been there, or we're going through it now."[972]

As season six got underway, Bill Radford of *The Gazette* asked Al Gough how much longer the show would last. "This year and, God willing, next, and then I think that's probably ultimately when we call it a day," he said. As for the possibility of a seventh season, he said, "We never say never," adding, "we certainly don't want to outlast our welcome."[973] He later told Ian Spelling of *Smallville Magazine* that he and Miles Millar love the series and love being involved and were signed on through season seven. Beyond that, they'll have to play it by ear.[974]

It is anyone's guess how long the series will last, but with its superior writing, directing, production values, special effects and acting, it is safe to say that *Smallville* is, simply put, the best depiction to date of Superman on television.

12

And Now, a Word from Superman

When *Superman Returns* flew into theaters in the summer of 2006, it brought with it the expected wave of toys and tie-in merchandise. Warner Bros. teamed with Burger King and PepsiCo (which included PepsiCo brands Tropicana, Aquafina and Frito-Lay), as well as Mattel toys, Duracell, Samsung, Perfectmatch.com, the "Got Milk?" campaign, and—in their first-ever movie tie-in—Quaker State Oil.[975] It was a continuation of Superman promotion that has existed ever since 1939, when Robert Maxwell, as head of National Comics subsidiary Superman, Inc., began licensing Superman products to toy manufacturers.[976]

Superman has been a presence in TV advertising since the 1950s. A 1954 commercial offered a brief glimpse of an animated Superman with VERY limited animation; Superman is static, but the "S" on his chest flies out as the ad cuts to a kid excited to be receiving his official Superman T-shirt, which Kellogg's offered for a Frosted Flakes box top and fifty cents. Another commercial offered a "flying Superman"—a blue plastic figure with a red plastic cape that looked like airplane wings, which could be launched with a rubber band—for a Kellogg's Corn Flakes box top and ten cents.

During the time that Kellogg's was the sponsor of *Adventures of Superman*, several commercials were made featuring cast members George Reeves, John Hamilton and Jack Larson hawking Sugar Frosted Flakes and Sugar Smacks. For these spots, Reeves appeared as "Clark Kent, star of Superman," using his X-ray vision to spy on kids enjoying the cereals, or else sitting down to breakfast with Perry White and Jimmy Olsen at his home or in White's office.

In the early 1960s, an animated Superman appeared with "the Soaky Kid" and Tennessee Tuxedo in a commercial introducing the new Colgate Soaky Superman (a Superman-shaped bottle of bubble bath). The 1970s saw the Caped One pitching his own brand of peanut butter in an animated ad where a group of kids free him from the clutches of Lex Luthor, who has imprisoned The Man of Steel and is holding him at bay with kryptonite to get Superman to tell him the secret of Superman Peanut Butter's great taste. In 1980, Post Cereals featured an animated Superman, Batman, Robin and Wonder Woman in a commercial touting their "create a villain" contest. The grand prize for the nine lucky winners was a trip to Hollywood, California, for breakfast with the superheroes and the villain they created. A 1986 spot for the AT&T calling card had a cartoon Clark Kent and Lois Lane obviously modeled after Christopher Reeve and Margot Kidder. Another 1980s ad featured a live-action Lois Lane making Ore-Ida French fries for her boyfriend; at the end of the commercial, an animated Superman flies onto her balcony.

On the live-action front, Superman went to work for the United States Air Force in 1974 in a series of recruiting commercials with the tagline, "Join our super team." The gist of the ads was that Superman was glum that the Air Force wouldn't let him play on their team because he was too powerful; the Air Force wanted regular guys. When the Air Force spots began, Peter Lupus—better known as Willie Armitage, the strongman of the popular espionage series *Mission: Impossible*—starred as the Man of Tomorrow. "They called my agent up and wanted to know if I wanted to do Superman," Lupus remembered. "They had got the go-ahead from whoever owned Superman, and they said they were having trouble getting an actor okayed, and they've okayed you. So I said fine."

The 6'4" former Mr. Indianapolis (1954) and Mr. Indiana (1960) had appeared in a number of sword-and-sandal movies in Italy in the early 1960s under the name Rock Stevens. When he was chosen by TV producer Bruce Geller for the *Mission: Impossible* role, Geller convinced him to use his real name. The series was a hit both in the U.S. and internationally, running from 1966 to 1973.

The first of the Air Force commercials Lupus shot was filmed at the Orange Bowl, with a group of pro football players. "It was a thrill to be in that uniform," said Lupus. "I felt stronger. You feel like you want to jump when you first put it on. You see yourself flying through the air. But I always liked it, because growing up, I wore glasses, and a lot of people thought that I looked like Clark Kent.

"I think the world needs to know that there is a Superman. I think generations keep coming along, and they'll keep accepting him, because of his background and what he stands for. He's fighting evil, he's not a bully, he fights for people and doesn't use his strength negatively, doesn't show it off. I think that keeps going."[977]

Lupus, however, did not. After a second commercial was filmed in Los Angeles with Jerry West and a group of pro basketball players, personal appearance conflicts kept Lupus from being available for the next ad. A replacement had to be found in a hurry, and that's how Tarzan became Superman.

Denny Miller, a former UCLA basketball star, made his acting debut playing the title role in MGM's 1959 remake of *Tarzan the Ape Man*. He then went on to a lengthy television stint as "Duke Shannon" on the 1961–64 Western *Wagon Train* (where the producers compelled him to change his professional name to Scott Miller), and spoofed his earlier stint as Tarzan when he played "Tongo the Ape Man" on a 1967 episode of *Gilligan's Island*. A slew of TV guest-starring roles were followed by a high-profile turn as "Wyoming Bill Kelso" in Blake Edwards's *The Party* (1968), where Miller, showing his comic side, held his own alongside Peter Sellers.

The blond, 6'4" actor also brought his sense of humor to the tongue-in-cheek Air Force recruiting spots. "I got the job," said Miller, "and I was flown to Florida during spring training and went to ten different baseball camps. Now, you haven't lived until you go into a locker room full of seventy athletes, and it's hot and muggy, and with the black rinse that they put on you, there's a streak of black sweat running down your nose, and you've got this funny little suit on with an S on your chest, and these Mickey Mouse cowboy boots instead of the boots they should have had. The delight was not in getting there, the delight was in meeting people like Yogi Berra and Walter Alston and other famous, successful baseball managers. They were a delight to talk to while I did the commercial. I managed to pick up a conversation with a few of the stars, like Johnny Bench. It was a very good-paying job, and I'm glad I did it. But if I were to have a choice, I wouldn't have done it in a place that had such high humidity."[978]

Unlike Lupus, Miller did not feel any great responsibility in taking the role. "I've been a clown since high school, so I took that opportunity to try and jump higher than a tall building and not get off the ground ... I would go around and flip the cape around and everything. I didn't feel the presence of any tradition. I wasn't as much of a Superman fan as I was of Tarzan, to tell you the truth. Tarzan was more like an Olympic athlete, and Superman was made out of something I didn't know about, kryptonite. So the 'S' wasn't for me, and it was silly."

Even so, some years later, when word went out that Hollywood was looking for a new Superman for the film that eventually became *Superman: The Movie*, Miller gave the role another go. "I tried," he said. "I got my picture taken by a buddy with the porkpie hat and the horn rim glasses, not in the outfit. And I went on an interview, but I didn't get it. I wasn't right. I have bird legs. I've accused God of having my legs put on backwards. But I think the guy that they picked was marvelous in it."

Lupus and Miller, both of whom are in their 70s and are still fit and trim, now promote health awareness. Lupus has a website, www.peterlupusenterprises.com, through which he offers various health products. Miller recently authored the book *Toxic Waist? Get to Know Sweat!* (available from www.denny-miller.com) which

With black hair rinse, blond Denny Miller was transformed into Superman for a series of Air Force recruiting commercials that ran in 1974. Seen here with Walter Alston, Miller replaced former *Mission: Impossible* strongman Peter Lupus in the spots (Photograph courtesy of Denny Miller, © Denny Miller).

seeks to motivate readers to improve their diet and exercise habits.

Perhaps the most famous of all Superman ads were those featuring an animated Superman interacting with comedian Jerry Seinfeld. Seinfeld, whose eponymous NBC-TV sitcom ran for nine seasons beginning in 1990, was such a long-time Superman fan that he worked a Superman reference into nearly every episode of his series. In the sitcom, he had a Superman figurine on a shelf near his stereo, and a Superman magnet on his refrigerator; he dropped Superman references into his conversation, referring to his friend's enemies as "Lex Luthors;" he picked "Jor-El" as his ATM PIN code; he beats an old school rival in a footrace to the theme from *Superman: The Movie*. Seinfeld also authored a children's book, *Halloween*, in which the main character desires to own a really-for-real Superman suit instead of the baggy store-bought one his mother had gotten him to go trick-or-treating in.[979]

During the NFL playoffs and Super Bowl XXXII in January 1988, an American Express credit card ad was aired that featured a live-action Jerry Seinfeld interacting with an animated Superman, whose voice was provided by Patrick Warburton.[980] Warburton had been a semi-regular on *Seinfeld*, appearing on eleven episodes between 1995 and 1998 as David Puddy, the handsome but lunkheaded car mechanic boyfriend of Elaine (Julia Louis-Dreyfus). Born in Paterson, New Jersey, on November 14, 1964, Warburton studied marine biology at Orange Coast College before embarking on a TV and film career. His TV debut came with a small part in *The Paper Chase: The Third Year* in 1986. By the mid–1990s, he was very busy with roles in numerous sitcoms and TV commercials. He also became an accomplished voice artist, lending his vocal talents to the title character of *Buzz Lightyear of Star Command* (2000–2001), as well as voicing Kronk in the animated feature *The Emperor's New Groove* (2000), Joe Swanson on the *Family Guy* TV series (1999–2006), and Steve Barkin on the series *Kim Possible* (2002–2006).

The commercial had its origin in early October 1997 when Seinfeld, who had just signed an agreement to do an American Express ad produced by filmmaker Gary Streiner for the credit card company's longtime advertising agency, Ogilvy & Mather, arranged lunch with a Warner Bros. executive to see about the possibility of working Superman into the spot. He also asked if Warner Bros. would contact Jack Larson to see if he would appear in the ad, and wondered if the executive could get him an autographed picture of Larson.[981]

"There was a series of phone calls about it," recalled Larson. "They asked me if I would do a cameo. 'What is it that you want me to do?' I asked, and they couldn't tell me. Then I heard from the director who told me that Jerry Seinfeld was a Superman fan and he wanted very much for me to do this. And I said, 'What do you want me to do?' He said, 'I don't know. Jerry knows what he wants you to do. Would you come to the studio Saturday morning?'" Larson arrived to find that the filming location on the Warner Bros. backlot was the same used for the *Lois & Clark* TV series, though it had a different association for him. "Where we shot was just exactly opposite where Ethel Barrymore made her last film in 1957, *Johnny Trouble*, which I was in. At that point, Jerry Seinfeld explained to me what he wanted me to do."[982]

The idea behind Larson's cameo was that one camera would follow him in a tracking shot, while another followed Jerry Seinfeld in a tracking shot. Seinfeld would pretend to be talking to Superman, who would be added later by the Warner Bros. animation department. "The Superman character would see me, and I would look up at the Superman character and say, 'Hiya, pal.'" To get the movements correct, Seinfeld ran through each shot with Warburton, who then stepped off-camera for the actual filming. The animated Superman was added later, courtesy of Warner Bros. Classic Animation division. Despite the careful choreography, getting the timing just right proved impossible. "We shot it and we shot it and we shot it," said Larson, "and they never could get it. They had four monitors, and after each take, everyone would run to the monitors—the director, the Warner Bros. animation people. But I saw right away that nothing counted until Jerry Seinfeld looked at the monitor. Finally, they got it, but the animation people said it wouldn't work, because just at the point where I'm smiling up at him, Superman's cape would have been covering my face."[983]

The producers went to Plan B. "The next day," said Larson, "they decided to have me standing beside a building that said *Daily Planet*, reading a newspaper. And we shot it until it was quite late." Figuring that it would be impossible for them to cut from a tracking shot of Seinfeld to a static shot of himself, Larson figured his cameo would never be used.[984] However, he gave an autographed photo to Seinfeld, as requested, and the comedian asked him if he would come to his dressing room and watch an *Adventures of Superman* episode with him. Seinfeld, who had all of the programs on videotape, popped in the "Panic in the Sky" episode, and peppered Larson with questions as they watched.[985]

Viewing the episode apparently gave Seinfeld a new idea about how to end the commercial. Since he was determined to keep Larson in the spot, Seinfeld had the editors optically remove his own image from the shot where he walks past a building as Larson looks up at Superman. They then added an encroaching shadow at the bottom of the frame, so that instead of looking at the Man of Steel, Larson appeared to be looking up at an approaching comet. The commercial then ended with Seinfeld—who had just rescued Lois Lane by using his American Express card—looking up at the comet and saying to the animated Superman, "I think you better get this one."[986] Lois Lane was played by Audrey Kissel, who appeared in a ninth season episode of *Seinfeld*, "The Blood," as Tara, the girlfriend of George (Jason Alexander).[987]

The ad, which presented Superman and Seinfeld as old friends, as though Seinfeld had moved on from George, Kramer and Elaine and was now hanging out with a superhero, featured some clever dialogue. When Superman asks Seinfeld if he signs a lot of autographs, the comedian says, "Oh, yeah. You?" "Some," says Superman, adding, "They ask me to bend stuff a lot."

Seinfeld asked that Superman be drawn in the style of comic book artist Curt Swan, who illustrated the Superman comics from the 1950s until the 1970s. It took 56 artists creating over 12,000 drawings to bring Superman to life. The live-action and animation were then composited together to create the final product. From start to finish, the brief ad took nearly four months to complete.[988]

The commercial was a hit, and in 2004, American Express decided to follow it up with a more ambitious ad campaign, *The Adventures of Seinfeld and Superman*, which would include two seven-minute episodes, "A Uniform Used to Mean Something" and "Hindsight Is 20/20," that would debut on a special website set up by American Express. Since they premiered on the "web," the episodes were called "webisodes" in the press.

Ogilvy & Mather again turned to Gary Streiner to produce the spots, both of which were written by Seinfeld with Christian Charles. Charles wrote and directed "The Greatest City on Earth" segment of the post-9/11 TV special, *The Concert for New York* (2001), and also directed *Comedian*, a documentary about Seinfeld. Charles did not direct the webisodes, however. That task fell to an "A" list director, Barry Levinson, who had an illustrious career as a writer before becoming an award-winning director. Levinson began his career coming up with skits for *The Carol Burnett Show* in 1967, was one of several writers on the Mel Brooks films *Silent Movie* (1976) and *High Anxiety* (1977), and contributed to the screenplay of *... And Justice for All* (1979). In 1982, he made his feature directing debut with the critically acclaimed *Diner*, which he followed up with *The Natural* (1984), *Young Sherlock Holmes* (1985), *Good Morning, Vietnam* (1987) and *Rain Man* (1988), the latter netting him an Oscar for Best Direction. His career since has been equally marked by hits, such as *Bugsy* (1991), and misses, such as the critically-maligned *Sphere* (1998). He also executive produced the acclaimed TV series' *Homicide: Life on the Street* (1993–1999) and *Oz* (1997–2003).

Unlike the previous spot, which was shot on the Warner Bros. lot, Levinson shot the two new pieces on location. "A Uniform Used to Mean Something" was filmed in New York in November 2003, while "Hindsight is 20/20" was shot shortly after in Death Valley. Despite the big names attached, the two spots were filmed on a modest budget, with Canon XL-1 DV cameras outfitted with a professional lens package.[989]

Instead of animating Superman in the traditional way, the new commercials used computers, animating with Macromedia Flash and compositing in Apple Shake, which took much, much less time. Unplugged Studio in Toronto was given the task of bringing Superman to life, and they began by analyzing the 1998 commercial. To prove how quickly they could turn the product around, they then took test footage of Seinfeld ad-libbing with an off-camera Levinson and, using Flash, were able to deliver a minute of animation in two days. The producers were amazed with the speed, low cost and quality of the animation, especially as compared to the "old-school" animation of the 1998 commercial.[990]

In "A Uniform Used to Mean Something," Seinfeld chats with Superman in a diner, the witty banter being reminiscent of that in the *Seinfeld* TV series. Superman complains that too much mayonnaise on his tuna fish sandwich makes him queasy, wipes his lip with his cape, which is "impervious to stain," and speaks of the joys of Surround Sound before the pair go out on the street. A thief snatches a package from underneath Seinfeld's arm, and the comedian exclaims, "Hey! That guy just stole my new DVD player!" Superman says, "What, am I not here?," and gesturing to the "S" on his chest, "How do you miss this?" Superman flies off to apprehend the criminal. He lands in front of the astonished thief, hands on his hips and chest thrust out. The thief throws the DVD player, which bounces off Superman's chest and falls to the ground, wrecked. When Seinfeld later asks, "Why didn't you just catch it?" Superman answers, "I don't do that. I do this"—and thrusts out his chest. He offers to fly around the earth at super speed to reverse the rotation and go back in time to before the DVD player hit the ground. "I don't know," says Seinfeld, "it's quite a production, don't you think?" Thankfully, Seinfeld's American Express card gives him product protection against theft, damage or bouncing off a superhero's chest within 90 days of purchase. The spot ends with Superman being unable to hook up the DVD player in Seinfeld's apartment, so the two go see the new hit play *Oh, Yes, Wyoming!*

"Hindsight Is 20/20" finds the two on a road trip in the middle of the desert. When they get out to take some photos, Superman accidentally locks the keys in the car. He offers to rip off the door, melt the lock, peel back the roof, even spin the world around and go back in time. Seinfeld declares, "No going back in time! Do you know how many people you annoyed with the back-in-time thing?" Luckily, Seinfeld has his American Express card, and can call for roadside assistance.

In the behind-the-scenes footage on the American Express website, Seinfeld said, "When you're reading the Superman comic book as a kid you don't think, 'Maybe some day he and I will hang out,' but I'm doing it!" He told *Time* magazine that he thought it was time to refurbish the Superman character, saying. "I thought that they kind of botched it up. The last series of films really lost the whole essence of the appeal of the character." [991]

Noel Neill had a cameo in "Hindsight Is 20/20." She landed the role after making an appearance at an autograph show. The organizers told her that Jerry Seinfeld would be in town in a few days, and asked her if she would sign a photo for him. Remembering that Jack Larson had been in the first Seinfeld-Superman commercial, when she signed the photo, she wrote at the bottom, "You know, I do commercials, too." A short while later, she was contacted about being in the new American Express spot. "I was flown out to Las Vegas," she said, "and driven out to Death Valley for the shoot. And when I got there, as I was waiting in the car, I saw Seinfeld approaching, wagging his finger. So, I rolled down the window, and he said, 'You see! I saw your note!'"[992]

The campaign had three objectives: branding, getting people to sign up for American Express cards, and helping those with cards understand what features were available to them.[993] They accomplished this by luring visitors to an American Express website, www.americanexpress.com/jerry, where they were presented with the living room of a New York apartment. A poster for the documentary *Comedian* is on the wall; a table in the foreground has film reels, a program for *Oh, Yes, Wyoming!*, and an American Express card. Clicking on the film reels, visitors could see the webisodes, behind-the-scenes footage, and videos about American Express Card membership.[994]

"A Uniform Used to Mean Something" premiered on the website on March 29, 2004. "Hindsight Is 20/20" premiered two months later, on May 20.[995] The day that the first webisode premiered, Seinfeld and Superman were interviewed by Matt Lauer on NBC's *Today Show*.[996] When Lauer asked how they met, Superman said, "We got to know each other after I heard I was referenced on some TV show. I was flattered."

The spots were an enormous success. According to American Express, from March 29 to April 12 there were over a million visits to the sub-site. The credit card company promoted the webisodes with TV teasers (one of which had Superman avoiding calls from The Green Lantern), links on Google, postcards, and newspapers ads. Beginning April 16th, thousands of LidRocks, tiny DVDs of the commercials atop soda lids, were distributed in New York movie theaters for four weeks.[997]

On May 20, the day that "Hindsight Is 20/20" made its web debut, the first webisode was aired in its entirety on NBC, preceding the encore presentation of the final episode of *Friends*.[998] It also aired on the cable network TBS June 15–19, 2004, immediately following syndicated repeats of *Sex and the City*.[999]

The spots were praised in *Time* magazine, which said, "Seinfeld's Superman, who gets too much mayonnaise on his sandwich and can't figure out a DVD player, may be the most credibly human version yet."[1000] In reviewing the first webisode on *Slate.com*, Seth Stevenson said it was "pretty good," with "several helpings of that trademark Seinfeld humor-of-the-quotidian, which we've all come to know and sometimes enjoy," adding, "The whole thing—with its brew of animated superhero, live-action celebrity, and fiercely mundane conversation topics—owes a lot to *Space Ghost: Coast to Coast*, a late-night Cartoon Network favorite."[1001] In 2005, the ads won a National Silver ADDY Award from the American Advertising Federation.[1002]

13

Reviving Superman

The Dearth of Superman

By the turn of the 21st century, comic books and comic book heroes were no longer kid stuff. Whereas in the 1950s, the average comic book reader was 12 years old, by the 1990s, the average comic book reader was 20. A mere decade later, in 2001, the average age of comic book readers was 25. As the consumer of the stories matured, so did the stories themselves. Comic books became darker in tone, and more adult in their plots and character development, a change that was reflected in the film and TV adaptations of comic book heroes, from *Smallville* to *X-Men* (2000) to *Spider-Man* (2002).[1003] However, while the age of the average reader climbed, the sales of comic books dropped, as did the number of outlets that sold them. During a brief comic book boom in the 1990s, sales reached 48 million per month. By 2001, only 6 to 7 million comic books were sold every month. In the 1990s, the number of comic book stores increased from about 3,500 to more than 12,000. By 2001, there were fewer than 3,000.[1004]

Despite the drop in comic book sales, comic book characters were more abundant at the movies than they had been since the heyday of the serials. By 2005, Marvel had seen their characters *Spider-Man*, *X-Men*, *The Hulk* (2003), *Blade* (1998) and *The Fantastic Four* (2005) adapted to big-budget movies. DC and Warner Bros. had reinvigorated the Batman series with *Batman Begins* (2005), but stumbled badly with a misguided interpretation of *Catwoman* (2004). Meanwhile, the biggest superhero in the DC galaxy languished in development hell.

Thoughts of resurrecting the Superman franchise began in the early 1990s, after the big-screen reinvention of *Batman* (1989), under the direction of Tim Burton, became a monster hit for Warner Bros., spawning a successful sequel, *Batman Returns*, in 1992. Together, the first two Batman films grossed $696 million worldwide, and brought in millions more in merchandising. By 1993, the film rights to Superman reverted to Warner Bros. from the Salkinds. Eager to capitalize on a new franchise, the studio entrusted *Batman* producer Jon Peters with bringing Superman back to movie screens.

Peters was a controversial figure in an industry over-populated with controversial figures. A one-time hairdresser with a knack for self-promotion, he was said to be the model for the character played by Warren Beatty in *Shampoo* (1975). His second wife was actress Lesley Ann Warren, who played Lois Lane in the TV adaptation of *It's a Bird, It's a Plane, It's Superman* (1975); their union lasted from 1967 until 1977. Peters became Barbra Streisand's hairstylist on the film *For Pete's Sake* (1974), and used his affiliation with the superstar to leverage himself as a producer on the hugely successful 1976 remake of *A Star Is Born*, which starred Streisand and Kris Kristofferson. In 1980, Peters teamed with Peter Guber and Neil Bogart, the cofounders of Casablanca Records and Filmworks (which gave the world KISS, Donna Summer and The Village People), to form Boardwalk Entertainment. When that company dissolved, Guber and Peters formed the Guber-Peters Company in 1982. Guber-Peters produced some of Hollywood's most profitable hits, including *An American Werewolf in London* (1981), *Flashdance* (1983), *The Color Purple* (1985), *Rain Man* (1988), *Batman* (1989) and *Batman Returns* (1992). With Lorne Michaels, they also executive produced a 1988 TV special, *Superman's 50th Anniversary*. Guber and Peters also briefly ran Sony/Columbia Studios beginning in 1989, but after two years, Peters, who reportedly never felt comfortable as a studio manager, resigned to start his own production company. In 1994, he signed a joint venture deal with Warner Bros. to develop motion pictures for the studio, which resulted in a diverse slate of pictures, including *My Fellow Americans* (1996), *Rosewood* (1997) and *Wild Wild West* (1999).

The new Superman movie had its roots in the enormously popular DC Comics story "The Death of Superman." The storyline, begun in 1992 and winding through several issues of different DC Comics titles, was developed as a response to the flagging sales of comic books in the early 1990s. Mike Carlin, who was then editor-in-chief of the four Superman titles DC published every month, said that at that time the measures the publisher had to take to get people to read the comics was very drastic and calculated.[1005] But, as calculated moves go, "The Death of Superman" paid off in a big way. When newspapers and TV newscasts began reporting that Superman was about to be killed off, the public responded by making "The Death of Superman" one of the year's highest-selling comics. The comic book series was later collected into a paperback that became the best-selling graphic novel of all time[1006]; according to DC Comics president Paul Levitz, it sold 700,000 copies in one month in 1993.[1007] Carlin said that the bottom line was that in the eyes of younger readers the character had become passé after fifty years, so in order to show that Superman still had something to offer the world of the 1990s and beyond, they first had to show how awful it would be if he were no longer around. That gave them the impetus for the storyline.[1008]

The storyline involved Superman's epic battle against an alien monster appropriately named Doomsday. When the battle ends, Doomsday is dead, but so is the Man of Steel. This set in motion further storylines about Superman's funeral and the emergence of four new characters: a cyborg Superman; a teenage clone called The Metropolis Kid who hated being called Superboy; The Last Son of Krypton, who has no compunction about killing criminals; and John Henry Irons, a/k/a Steel, a black ironworker and ex-military weapons designer who fashioned an outfit of steel and vowed to carry on the Superman legacy. Eventually, the one and only original Superman was, of course, resurrected, though for a while he was seen in revamped metallic red and blue suits, with no cape.

Steel made his way to movie screens in 1997, in the form of 7'1" Los Angeles Lakers basketball superstar Shaquille O'Neal. In real life, O'Neal, a Superman fanatic, had a Superman tattoo on his left biceps, and the Superman symbol was etched into the glass of the front doors of his mansion in Beverly Hills as well as the headlights of his Mercedes. During basketball games at the Staples Center, the Lakers' home court, the Superman theme was often played over the loudspeakers when O'Neal slammed the basketball through the hoop. He thought of himself as having a dual nature—Shaquille the soft-spoken corporate businessman, and Shaq the dominant champion athlete—much like Clark Kent and Superman. In 2002, he told *The New Yorker*'s Rebecca Mead that he would like his final resting place to be a mausoleum, "all marble, with Superman logos everywhere."[1009] Wishing to be a force for good like his favorite superhero, O'Neal wants to be a police officer when he retires from basketball; during the off-seasons, he has worked with both the Los Angeles and Miami police departments.

Produced for Warner Bros. by Quincy Jones–David Salzman Entertainment, *Steel*, while only tangentially a Superman movie, was an entertaining film that was modestly budgeted and quickly filmed over a ten-week period in the fall of 1996.[1010] Written and directed by Kenneth Johnson, who had previously brought *The Incredible Hulk* to television in a series that ran from 1978 to 1982, the film told the story of ex-military man John Henry Irons, a weapons designer who, with the help of his Uncle Joe (played by Richard Roundtree, star of the *Shaft* movies and TV series in the 1970s), and wheelchair-bound friend Susan Sparks (Annabeth Gish), takes on industrialist villain Nathaniel Burke (Judd Nelson). *Variety* said "he's the nicest superhero on the block," but called the film "strictly kid's stuff."[1011] Though the major actors were contracted for a sequel, none materialized due to the film's poor box-office performance. Budgeted at $16 million, *Steel* brought in less than $1.7 million at the U.S. box-office.

Meanwhile, by 1996, Jon Peters was putting together his Superman package.[1012] Warner Bros., hoping for an Independence Day release of July 4, 1998 (The Man of Steel's 60th anniversary year), had hired Jonathan Lemkin, a writer under contract to the studio, to pen a screenplay based on the "Death and Rebirth of Superman" comic book arc. Lemkin, a writer whose credits included episodes of the TV series *Hill Street Blues*, *21 Jump Street* and *Beverly Hills 90210*, and the Al Pacino–Keanu Reeves movie *The Devil's Advocate* (1997), had just finished a draft of *Lethal Weapon 4*. He felt the fantasy elements of *The Devil's Advocate* and the action of *Lethal Weapon 4* combined to convince the studio that he was the writer for Superman. After mapping out the plotline for a script that would be titled *Superman Reborn*, Lemkin and Jon Peters had to present their ideas to the CEOs of Warner Bros. Lemkin told Edward Gross of *Cinemania* magazine that he realized he had been entrusted with a huge corporate asset, and consequently the process of writing the script was different than any other project he'd ever worked on.[1013] Warner Bros. was concerned about the new film's marketing potential; with the Batman movies, they made more from the merchandising of toys tied to the films than from the films themselves.

Lemkin launched into writing the script with the purpose of reintroducing the Man of Steel to a movie-going public that hadn't seen a new Superman movie in almost a decade. The challenge was how to bring the character into the '90s and keep him fresh. One thing Lemkin didn't want to change was Superman's Boy Scout quality; he admired that the hero always wanted to do the right thing and enthusiastically and courageously faced whatever challenges confronted him. Told to "shake things up," Lemkin delivered a script that made bold changes to the Superman mythology. In *Superman Reborn*, Superman, an alien, is unable to give his love to Lois Lane, a human. But as he lies dying in her arms after defeating Doomsday, he professes his love and his life-force jumps into her, impregnating her. Lois then gives birth to a child who grows twenty-one years in three weeks and becomes the new Superman. The challenge for Lemkin was how to treat the legendary elements of the character's story with respect while at the same time putting a fresh, unique spin on it.[1014]

Warner Bros. was not bowled over by Lemkin's script, and, as so often happens on mega-budget Hollywood blockbusters, decided to go with another writer. Jon Peters already had his next scribe in mind: Gregory Poirier, who penned the screenplay to the historical drama *Rosewood* (1997), which Peters produced. Poirier retained Doomsday as a villain, but also included Brainiac, a character from the comic books that was first introduced as a super-intelligent alien in 1958, but later changed into a super-intelligent humanoid computer. In Poirier's script, which used Lemkin's as a basis, Brainiac was a galactic conqueror who destroyed planets, after first collecting a representative specimen. Arriving on Earth, Brainiac falls in love with Lois Lane, and decides that she will be the specimen he will save from the planet's destruction. Superman, meanwhile, is having such a hard time reconciling his alien and human personas that he seeks the advice of a psychiatrist. When Brainiac unleashes his creation Doomsday, a monster with kryptonite-laced blood, Superman engages the beast in battle and the two fight to the death. After Superman's funeral, where Batman makes a brief appearance, Brainiac attempts to steal Superman's body to harvest its genetic material. He's stopped by an intergalactic bounty hunter named Cadmus, who revives Superman. When his powers return, Superman eventually defeats Brainiac.

Like Lemkin's script, the Poirier script didn't exactly have Warner Bros. execs jumping up and down. Other writers were contacted, including comic book enthusiast Kevin Smith, who partly financed his first movie, the 1994 hit independent film *Clerks*, by selling his comic book collection. By this point, Smith had made two more films, *Mallrats* (1995) and *Chasing Amy* (1997), and had written for both DC and Marvel Comics. Warner Bros. offered him his choice of three scripts to re-write: a sequel to *Beetle Juice* (1988), a feature film version of the 1960s *Outer Limits* TV episode "The Architects of Fear," or *Superman Reborn*.

Smith told *Cinemania* magazine's Edward Gross that he was intrigued by Superman for two reasons—his love of comic books, and because he had read the Poirier script and hated it. He felt Poirier missed the boat in trying to give Superman angst. "Batman is about angst; Superman is about hope," said Smith. "Superman's angst is not that he doesn't want to be Superman. If he has any, it's that he can't do it all; he can't do enough and save everyone." Smith made his feelings known to the executives at Warner Bros, telling them not just that the script was bad, but that it would be a disservice to Superman fans and to the character himself. Smith's point-of-view was that just by the fact that it was a Superman movie, enough people would show up for the studio to gross a hundred million, but if they were going to make a movie, why throw it away? Why not make a good one? [1015]

With those comments, Smith figured he had talked himself out of a gig with Warner Bros., but he was asked to repeat his views to more Warner Bros. executives until he finally met with Lorenzo Di Bonaventura, the co-head of Warners' theatrical production, and Superman producer Jon Peters. After becoming the third writer to work on the project, now titled *Superman Lives!*, Smith found that Peters was the classic Hollywood "writer-killer," a term for a producer who is unsure of what he wants and continually asks for changes that may not be in the best interest of the story. There were, however, two things that Peters was adamant about: there would be no scenes of Superman in flight, and Superman would not be seen in the familiar red-and-blue uniform. Smith eventually decided that, consciously or not, Peters was trying to force Superman into a Batman mold. He incorporated some of Peters's ideas, and hedged on others, like the producer's resistance to seeing Superman in flight. In Smith's conception, whenever Superman flew, all viewers would see was a flash of red accompanied by a sonic boom. As for the costume, Smith at first tried to sidestep the issue by simply not describing it, saying only that the character was seen from the boots up. In a meeting with Warner Bros. executives, one of them asked Smith if he could describe the costume. Smith insisted that everyone knew the costume, and it was the job of the costume designer to come up with a concept that was hopefully close to the uniform everyone knew and loved. The executive wasn't satisfied; he asked if Smith could say that it was "90's style." In his next draft, when Superman first appeared, Smith wrote, "we see Superman in the red and blue costume, '90s style."[1016]

Peters also insisted that the third act have a scene where Superman battles a giant spider. The spider became a major headache for Smith, who had to find a way to make it work even though it had nothing to do with the rest of the script. To make it even more challenging, Warner Bros. didn't want it to be a spider, so it had to be called something else.

More dispiriting for Smith was the studio's attention to how much merchandising the film could inspire. "That's *all* they talk about," Smith said. At one point, Smith had written a scene with Superman and Lois Lane that took place on Mount Rushmore and contained what Smith considered to be the best dialogue in the screenplay, revealing much about their interpersonal relationship. The studio insisted the script was too long, and ordered him to cut the scene. Smith argued that he could cut some lines, but he needed the scene—it was the heart of the story. The studio kept asking to cut it, and Smith almost quit twice in frustration. Finally, a studio executive told the writer that he had to understand that this was a corporate movie; it wasn't about the quality of the dialogue between Superman and Lois Lane, it was about how many toys they could sell. "That was real soul-killing, man," said Smith.[1017]

As 1997 dawned, Warner Bros. was already looking for promotional partners for what they hoped would be their big summer hit of 1998. Disney had sewn up an exclusive ten-year deal with the nation's number one fast food hamburger chain, McDonald's, so Warners entered into negotiations with Burger King. In announcing the deal, *Variety* said that the Jon Peters production intended to be in pre-production in June for a fall start; all that existed at that point, according to the trade paper, were production sketches.[1018]

While Smith was continuing to hone the screenplay, Peters was looking for his Man of Steel. His choice was one that sent ripples of dismay throughout the entertainment community and comic book fandom. On February 21, 1997, *Variety* broke the news that Nicolas Cage was seriously considering taking the lead role in *Superman Reborn*.[1019]

Nicolas Cage was born in Long Beach, California, on January 7, 1964, as Nicolas Coppola. His father, August Coppola, a comparative literature professor, was the brother of famed film director Francis Ford Coppola. When Nicolas Coppola finished high school and decided to pursue a career as an actor, he decided to change his name to escape any appearance of nepotism. Looking to comic books as an inspiration, he took the last name "Cage" from the Marvel Comics character Luke Cage.[1020] His first film role came with a brief appearance in *Fast Times at Ridgemont High* (1982), the film that also launched Sean Penn's career. The following year, he scored a hit with his role in *Valley Girl* (1983), and went on to a career marked by always interesting performances in films as diverse as *Birdy* (1984), *Raising Arizona* (1987), *Moonstruck* (1987), *Honeymoon in Vegas* (1992), *Guarding Tess* (1994), and *Leaving Las Vegas* (1995), for which he won an Academy Award for Best Actor. Beginning in 1996, Cage re-invented himself as an action hero with a trio of films, *The Rock* (1996), *Con Air* (1997) and *Face/Off* (1997), all of which grossed more than $100 million at the U.S. box-office. A comic book aficionado, Cage sports a tattoo of the character Ghost Rider, and when he and his third wife Alice Kim had a son on October 3, 2005, they named their child Kal-El.[1021] However, despite Cage's irrefutable acting chops, Superman fans were concerned that he didn't match the part physically; although he had added considerable musculature to his lean frame for his role in *Con Air*, his face did not have the chiseled contours one normally associates with Superman; Cage appeared too ethnic, too identifiably Italian, for the white-bread Man of Steel.

By March of 1997, Kevin Smith had completed two drafts, and felt that the script "was 90 percent there, perhaps there was another 10 percent to go to make it the movie they wanted to make."[1022] But Smith never got the chance to take it that extra ten percent, owing to Warner Bros. and Jon Peters's choice of director. On April 4, 1997, *Variety* announced that Tim Burton had entered into talks with Warner Bros. about directing *Superman Lives!*[1023] Burton had helped the studio redefine and relaunch Batman with the successful films *Batman* and *Batman Returns*, both of which were produced by Jon Peters, and had most recently directed *Mars Attacks!* (1996) for the studio. Though *Mars Attacks!* earned only a little over half of its $70 million budget in the U.S., it grossed a respectable $101 million worldwide. For Burton, however, it was a disappointment, and he wanted the next picture he directed to be a sure thing. The studio offered him a choice of a live-action version of the 1970s animated cartoon *Scooby Doo*, or Superman. Burton chose the latter. "It was great for the studio because they had a script they liked and had worked on for a while," said Kevin Smith, "and they had a director who had made them over half a billion dollars previously on a super hero franchise."[1024] According to Smith, although he had been assured by Jon Peters and Warners executives that he would remain with the project until the end, his tenure effectively ended as soon as Burton was hired. As Smith later recounted the events, Tim Burton told the studio that he wanted to go a different way, and—since he had a shortlist of writers that he preferred working with—he wanted Wesley Strick to do the redraft. Smith claims he didn't talk to Jon Peters after that, but he did ask Warner Bros. to arrange a meeting between himself and Burton. The meeting never materialized, and Smith moved on to other projects, while Strick set about putting his own spin on *Superman Lives!*[1025]

Strick, a former lead guitarist and singer with the New York City band The Commotion, emerged on the scene as the sole screenwriter of the 1989 film *True Believer*, starring James Woods and Robert Downey, Jr. He followed that up with *Cape Fear* (1991), *Wolf* (1994) and *The Saint* (1997), among others. His affiliation with Tim Burton began in 1992, when he did some uncredited work on the script of Burton's *Batman Returns*.

As Strick began drafting a new version of the Superman screenplay—in which he merged Brainiac and Lex Luthor into a single villain, Luthiac—trouble was brewing in Metropolis. Within days of Nicolas Cage's announcement for the role of Superman, *Variety* reported that he was also committed to star with Will Smith in *Snake Eyes*, a Paramount film to be directed by Brian De Palma. Smith left the film when his salary demands weren't met, delaying its start date. This was problematic for Cage, who was scheduled to begin *Superman Lives!* around the first of November, as soon as *Snake Eyes* finished.[1026] The situation came to a head at the end of May, with Cage apparently committed to two films whose schedules were overlapping. Both Warner Bros. and Paramount believed they had Cage locked for the dates they needed him; now Cage's representatives at Creative Artists Agency and Brillstein-Grey were claiming otherwise. At issue was whether Cage's commitment to *Superman Lives!* took precedence over his commitment to *Snake Eyes*; Warner Bros., naturally, believed that it did. Paramount believed CAA had waived Cage's Superman commitment after Will Smith dropped out of *Snake Eyes*. High-ranking executives from Warner Bros. and Paramount and Cage's agents scrambled to find a solution before the brouhaha ended up in legal proceedings.[1027]

Variety later reported that the trouble began when Richard Lovett, the president of Creative Artists Agency, who represented both DePalma and Cage, made promises to both studios that they had Cage locked in for their shooting dates when, in fact, they didn't. Lovett then tried to smooth things out behind the scenes. CAA contended that the communication problem rested with Paramount, saying that the entire time they were negotiating for Cage, his deal was always contingent on the start date for *Superman Lives!* Ultimately, an agreement was reached—Cage would first film *Snake Eyes*, which would shoot for twelve weeks beginning July 21. Immediately after that, he would begin *Superman Lives!*, whose start date had been postponed one week to October 6. In the event October 6 arrived and Cage was not finished with *Snake Eyes*, he would resume filming it after he had completed his work on *Superman Lives!*[1028] After the dust had settled, the issue of Cage's availability became a moot point anyway, when Warner Bros. decided to move the start date of *Superman Lives!* from October 1997 to January 1998, for a projected release date of Christmas rather than summer 1998.[1029] By October, 1997—when *Superman Lives!* was originally supposed to begin shooting—its start date was again pushed back, this time until late spring 1998, to give Tim Burton more time to nail down the screenplay. The release date was also moved again, to an undetermined 1999 date.[1030] By now, the studio had given up hopes of releasing the new film in time to coincide with the superhero's sixtieth anniversary.

Undeterred, Jon Peters and Tim Burton began looking for an actor to play the villain in the new film. On March 3, 1998, *Variety* reported that Kevin Spacey was being courted by Warner Bros. to play Lex Luthor in *Superman Lives!* Spacey, who gained wide exposure as bad-guy Mel Profitt in the TV series *Wiseguy* (1987–1990) before jumping to the big screen with roles in *Rocket Gibraltar* (1988), *Glengarry Glen Ross* (1992) and *The Usual Suspects* (1995), was coming off a critically-acclaimed role in *L.A. Confidential* (1997).[1031]

The script had now gone to another writer, Dan Gilroy, a co-writer and producer of the 1992 movie *Freejack*, which starred Mick Jagger as a time-traveling bounty hunter; he was also the co-writer of the 1994 Dennis Hopper-directed comedy *Chasers*. Gilroy began writing using Strick's script as a foundation. It was in Warners Bros.' best interest to keep moving the project forward; both Nicolas Cage and director Tim Burton had pay-or-play deals, which meant they would be paid their contracted salaries whether the film got made or not. Warner Bros. co-president of production, Lorenzo Di Bonaventura, said the studio looked forward to introducing the world to the new Nicolas Cage Superman, adding that the actor was passionate about the character. By that point, the studio was in serious talks with Kevin Spacey to play Brainiac instead of Lex Luthor, and comedian Chris Rock to play Jimmy Olsen. But when Gilroy turned in his script draft, the studio realized that it would take a budget of more than $100 million to bring it to the screen.[1032]

The poor performance of several Warner Bros. films had the studio in cost-cutting mode. Over a period of eighteen months, they had seen disappointing box office returns on *Fathers' Day* (1997), *Midnight in the Garden of Good and Evil* (1997), *Mad City* (1997), and *The Postman* (1997), a film starring Kevin Costner that became an industry joke.[1033] Wary of similar failures, they pulled the plug on *I Am Legend*, which Ridley Scott was to direct with Arnold Schwarzenegger starring, which had a budget of more than $100 million. Two final big-budget extravaganzas were already in the pipeline and too far along to stop, adaptations of the 1960s TV series *Wild, Wild West* (1999) and *The Avengers* (1998).[1034] Warners decided to scale back their output from 28 films per year to 20, particularly cutting back on the big-budget "event" pictures to concentrate on more mid-sized budget films.[1035] At the same time, other studios were also cost-cutting. Universal put the brakes on a $100-million-plus version of *The Hulk*, and Fox 2000 shut down Jan De Bont's sci-fi Western, *Ghost Riders in the Sky*, which also had a $100-million-plus price tag. "Every studio is acutely conscious of how much the negative cost of their films are," said Di Bonaventura. "We're not alone."[1036]

On April 17, 1998, Di Bonaventura announced that production of *Superman Lives!* would be delayed. He told *Variety*'s Paul Karon and Chris Petrikin, "We have decided to postpone the start of Superman till such a time as the budget is appropriate and the script realizes its potential."[1037] More candidly, Di Bonaventura told *The Los Angeles Times*' Amy Wallace that the screenplay simply wasn't good enough, although he stressed that Warners was "very happy" with Tim Burton and his current writing team. "When you're trying to live up to something that is such an important asset to this company, you set a very high standard. We felt we had to raise the bar," said Di Bonventura.[1038] Another factor influencing his decision was that the projected budget had ballooned to more than $125 million.[1039] The studio worked with Tim Burton to reconfigure *Superman*, but by summer, the film had been officially removed from the Warner Bros. slate.

Variety reported that *Superman Lives!* was cancelled because the script didn't work and the budget had soared to $140 million. When the plug was pulled, Nicolas Cage—having finished *Snake Eyes* (1998)—went to work for director Martin Scorsese in *Bringing Out the Dead* (1999), while Tim Burton went to direct Johnny Depp in *Sleepy Hollow* (1999).[1040] Burton regretted not bringing Superman to fruition. "That was extremely painful," he told *Entertainment Weekly's* Christopher Nashawaty. After months spent in one meeting after another and scouting locations, Burton said, "I don't think those people realize how much of your heart and soul you pour into something. I was pretty shell-shocked by the whole situation." When the project fell apart, the director was careful about choosing his next script, not wanting to do a terrible film just to move on. When *Sleepy Hollow* was offered, he felt he'd found the right piece. "Who knows," he said, "maybe it was because of my previous year [on *Superman Lives!*] that I related to a character with no head."[1041]

Although the project was officially dead, Dan Gilroy kept working on the *Superman* script, and in September 1998 turned in a draft to producer Jon Peters that got Warner Bros. and Nicolas Cage excited again. The new script had a greater emphasis on characters, and was budgeted at less than $100 million.[1042] Nonetheless, by June of 1999, Gilroy was out, replaced by Bill Wisher, who co-wrote the script for *Terminator 2: Judgment Day* (1991) with director James Cameron. Wisher met with Nicolas Cage to pitch him his ideas.[1043] After Wisher's script was turned in, the project lay dormant until April of 2001, when Warner Bros. began courting Paul Attanasio for a Superman rewrite. Attanasio, the former film critic of *The Washington Post*, had just been hired by Steven Soderbergh and George Clooney's Section Eight Productions to script *The Good German*. A writer with a strong pedigree, Attanasio had been nominated for Oscars for his scripts for *Quiz Show* (1994) and *Donnie Brasco* (1997).[1044]

By August 7, the Superman saga began to take an odd detour. While *Superman Lives!* was going through its continuing game of musical chairs with writers, Warner Bros. announced that Andrew Kevin Walker, the screenwriter of *Se7en* (1995) and Tim Burton's *Sleepy Hollow*, had been commissioned to write a script that would pit Superman against Batman, with Wolfgang Petersen attached to direct. This film would be made in addition to the Jon Peters-produced Superman movie and the latest Batman film, which had just been announced with Darren Aronofsky, director of *Pi* (1998) and *Requiem for a Dream* (2000), attached to direct.[1045]

Andrew Kevin Walker's script for *Batman Vs. Superman* had the two superheroes coming to blows over a difference in philosophies. Petersen told *Variety* it was a clash of the titans, with noble and good Superman battling dark, obsessive Batman. Besides directing, Petersen was also slated to produce the film with Diana Rathbun. Lorenzo Di Bonaventura, who was overseeing the project, said "We are very pleased that Wolfgang Petersen is bringing his considerable talents to this newest episode of two of our most important franchises. In his hands, *Batman vs. Superman* will carry forward the Warner Bros. superhero tradition; we look forward to starting this project as soon as possible."

Petersen was looking at early 2003 as a start date, with plans for five or six months of shooting.[1046] "As a European, it is challenging to do a project about these two American icons together in one movie," he said. "Growing up with American comics, to make a movie based on two of them is fascinating. I love it." In Andrew Kevin Walker's script, the two crime-fighters not only teamed up against evildoers, but each also experienced their own inner conflict. Superman's unwavering belief in right and wrong was challenged, while Batman went down a path of self-destruction.[1047] Petersen was also attached to several other projects for the studio, including the Trojan War epic *Troy*. In interviews, he said that he always had a handful of projects cooking, but he was excited about doing *Batman vs. Superman*.[1048]

By February 13, 2002, Warner Bros. was announcing that McG (the professional name of Joseph McGinty Nichol), the director of their hit film *Charlie's Angels* (2000), had closed a deal to develop and direct the new Superman film.[1049] McG came to prominence as a director of music videos; when his video of the Smashmouth song "Walkin' on the Sun" won Billboard's Pop Video of the Year Award in 1997, the young director—who has a degree in Psychology from the University of California, Irvine—began being courted by the studios. After *Charlie's Angels* grossed over $40 million in its opening weekend in the U.S. and went on to gross $258 million worldwide, Warner Bros. felt comfortable entrusting their most valuable franchise to the relative novice.

The script duties were now in the hands of J.J. Abrams, the creator of the TV series *Felicity* (1998–2002) and *Alias* (2001–2006). Lorenzo Di Bonaventura, now promoted to head of worldwide production for the studio, vowed to revive the Superman film as part of the studio's endeavor to create franchises based on its DC Comics characters. By this stage, Nicolas Cage had followed Tim Burton's lead and permanently exited the project, allowing McG and Abrams to start from scratch.[1050]

In July 2002, casting began for *Batman Vs. Superman*, with Matt Damon mentioned as a possibility to play one of the heroes. "We are not going to go with typical action stars, but great actors who will do an action-oriented part," said Wolfgang Petersen.[1051] That same month, Warner Bros. announced a deal valued at $200 to $600 million with Mattel for five properties: Batman, Superman, Looney Tunes, Baby Looney Tunes and Justice League. Mattel snagged the deal when number two toymaker Hasbro walked away because the price was too steep.[1052]

By August of 2002, Wolfgang Petersen had decided to give *Troy* precedence over *Batman Vs. Superman*, announcing that *Troy* would begin production in spring 2003. Petersen said, "Of these two projects I have developed at Warner Bros., I had hoped to make *Troy* first and am pleased that the scheduling worked out that way. I'm looking forward to directing *Batman Vs. Superman* in the future."[1053] Lorenzo di Bonaventura said, "We decided that *Batman Vs. Superman* is like a good wine—it will find its time and only get better. Wolfgang instinctually saw the opportunity in both pictures and decided that *Troy* was the one to go with first. It will be a full-tilt movie, an epic adventure." The decision to move on *Troy* and delay *Batman Vs. Superman* was influenced by the fact that other studios were developing similar projects—like Revolution Studios' *Hannibal* and Universal/20th Century-Fox's coproduction *Alexander the Great*.[1054]

Meanwhile, the continued delays on *Superman Lives!* forced McG off the project in August of 2002. The studio now wanted the Man of Steel movie for summer 2004. McG, in the meantime, had to prep *Charlie's Angels 2: Halo* (a title later changed to *Charlie's Angels: Full Throttle*) for its planned June 27, 2003 release. The studio began negotiations with Brett Ratner, director of *Rush Hour*, the surprise 1998 action comedy hit that paired Hong Kong superstar Jackie Chan with comedian Chris Tucker, and its equally successful sequel, *Rush Hour 2* (2001).[1055] Speaking to *The Hollywood Reporter's* Zorianna Kitt, Ratner—who has a framed copy of Superman's Action Comics debut framed in his house—said he'd always wanted to do a superhero movie, adding, "There are certain choices I make that I know will affect the rest of my life, and I feel that I was born to direct Superman." Ratner had just finished *Red Dragon* (2002), based on the Thomas Harris novel that introduced the world to cannibal killer Hannibal Lecter, and after making such a dark movie, "I wanted to do something positive, uplifting and spiritual and emotional that people around the world can identify with." As for the casting, Ratner knew that he wanted a Superman in his 20s, and said he'd love to hire his *Red Dragon* star, Anthony Hopkins, for Jor-El.[1056]

The J.J. Abrams script, called *Superman I* and meant to be the first of a trilogy (à la *Lord of the Rings*, the surprise hit of 2001) took some creative liberties with the established Superman mythos. As Abrams explained in an interview with *Entertainment Weekly*'s Jeff Jensen, while the original *Superman* lived up to its promise of making viewers believe that a man could fly, two decades later movies, TV shows and commercials were filled with flying men. Now it would take more than spectacle to win over an audience; it would also take an emotionally rich story.'

In Abrams's version of the story, Jor-El sends Kal-El to earth in a rocketship not because the planet is about to explode, but because a rogue Kryptonian named Kata-Zor has staged a coup d'état of Krypton's government, which is led by Jor-El. A Kryptonian prophecy says a son of Krypton will face great trials on another world before returning to Krypton as its savior. Kata-Zor feels Jor-El is trying to bring about the prophecy by sending Kal-El away, and imprisons Jor-El and Lara. The rocket lands in Smallville, where Jonathan and Martha Kent discover the alien child and rear it as their own. As he matures, Clark discovers a canister that arrived with his rocket. When he opens it, the Superman costume emerges, standing on its own before it jumps onto Clark and attaches itself. Instead of his meeting Lois Lane in Metropolis, she is introduced as a high school classmate of Clark's. As young Clark learns to use his powers, the scene shifts back to Krypton, where Kata-Zor and his son, Ty-Zor, torture Jor-El and Lara to find out where they've sent Kal-El. Ty-Zor carries the torture too far, killing Lara.

Back on earth, we see that Clark Kent and Lois Lane are now reporters for *The Daily Planet*. Lois has been following a CIA agent named Lex Luthor who claims he can prove the existence of a Kryptonian on earth. Perry White assigns Lois to interview the President of the United States on Air Force One. As the interview is in progress, the plane is damaged, and Clark opens the canister containing the outfit. He rescues the plane and Lois, effectively making his debut to the world. The event is noticed on Krypton, and Kata-Zor sends Ty-Zor to earth to destroy Kal-El. Ty-Zor and his army arrive on earth and lure Superman to an airplane hangar made of lead, where Lois Lane is drowning in a water tank chained to kryptonite. Superman saves her, then dies. Back on Krypton, Jor-El senses his son's death, and commits suicide. His spirit travels to earth, where it informs Kal-El that he cannot die until the prophecy is fulfilled. Superman's body rises from the grave, and meets with leaders of the United Nations. Under Superman's leadership, U.N. warplanes armed with kryptonite missiles take on Ty-Zor and his army, and defeat them. Superman then goes to Lois, and tells her he must return to Krypton to save the planet. He is then confronted by Lex Luthor, who is revealed to be a Kryptonian. The two battle until Lex Luthor is defeated and imprisoned, and Superman leaves for Krypton.[1057]

The J.J. Abrams script took a beating on September 23, 2002, when the *Ain't It Cool News* website featured a scene-by-scene critique by "Moriarty" (Drew McWeeney) which savaged it. "You'll Believe a Franchise Can Suck!!," wrote McWeeney, who lambasted the script's Krypton elements and questioned Jimmy Olsen's heterosexuality. Abrams told *The Hollywood Reporter*'s Gregg Kilday, "Primarily, I feel that Superman means a lot to a lot of people, so I was not surprised by the reaction to this and to the script." A couple of days later, the website's proprietor, Harry Knowles, urged mass protests at Warner Bros. and at a Los Angeles book signing where Abrams was scheduled to appear. Abrams felt Knowles's remarks were out of bounds, given that Knowles hadn't actually read the script, so he put in a call to the webmaster. The following Saturday, Knowles wrote about the two-hour conversation on his website, saying that Abrams was a Superman fan who knew his stuff and wanted to make a positive contribution to the character's legacy, though he conceded this didn't mean that the movie still wouldn't suck. Abrams, who was polishing the controversial screenplay, told Kilday that he wanted Knowles to know that he loved Superman and respected the audience, but added, "There is no one document that defines that character—there have been so many permutations, additions and changes along the way." Abrams said that he understood that people were afraid the movie would turn out badly, but that he and Ratner and everyone else involved were desperate to make it good.[1058]

By mid–October 2002, *Superman I* got a boost when Lorenzo Di Bonaventura, who had championed the rival studio production *Batman Vs. Superman*, left Warner Bros. Alan Horn, the president and COO of Warner Bros., had championed the J.J. Abrams script; with Di Bonaventura's departure, *Batman Vs. Superman* was put on the back burner indefinitely. To fill Di Bonaventura's position as president of production, Horn hired former ICM agent Jeff Robinov.[1059]

By December 2002, even *The Times of London* was abuzz with casting rumors, saying the next Superman could be a British actor. According to an article by Sam Lister, forty British drama students and young actors had been tested to play the Man of Steel in *The Death of Superman*, the first of a projected three-part trilogy. Casting agents had also been dispatched to Sydney and New York. While the filmmakers were testing actors from drama schools like Guildhall, the London Academy of Dramatic Art and the Royal Academy of Dramatic Art, Jude Law's agent contacted them to remind them of his client's availability. Ian Hart, who had most recently played Dr. Watson in new British TV adaptations of the Sherlock Holmes stories, said, "I can see me in the tights and a cape. That would be something else." Welsh actor Christian Bale was also reportedly auditioned; he would later win the role of Batman in *Batman Begins* (2005). *The Times* said that Sir Anthony Hopkins had signed on to play Jor-El, and that twelve screen tests of British actors were taken back to Los Angeles for Ratner to see. Asked for his opinion, Jim Hambrick, proprietor of The Super Museum in Metropolis, Illinois, said, "If an unknown Briton comes out as best for the role, that would not be a problem. Superman should be considered more of a worldly character." The film, according to *The Times*, was scheduled to begin shooting in April 2003 at Pinewood Studios.[1060]

During the Christmas holiday of 2002, Brett Ratner expressed his passion for the Superman project by sending out Christmas cards with his face superimposed on a flying Superman. Little did he know the Christmas cards would be his only Superman production.[1061] The new year dawned with rumors flying on the internet that Ratner was out and Michael Bay was in as director of *Superman*. *Variety's* Michael Fleming cut to the chase, and called Bay, who proclaimed the rumor 100 percent false. For his part, Ratner wondered why Warners was still paying him such big paychecks if he was off the film. Ratner said the rumors were based on internet gossip; the biggest hiccup in getting the project started was finding the right actor to play Superman. According to other rumors, the new picture's budget was over $200 million, with Warners insisting that it not exceed $180 million. There was also speculation that Ratner's top choice for the role was Josh Hartnett, who wouldn't sign a deal that came with two pre-negotiated sequels (even though all three pics would have earned the actor $100 million), which led Ratner to set up tests with Ashton Kutcher, Brendan Fraser and Jude Law. Ratner told Fleming that it was a lie the budget had exceeded $200 million; in fact, the film's budget wouldn't be completed for another few weeks. However, he did acknowledge that his top choices for the lead role were reluctant to sign long-term agreements, and that he'd "warned them of the consequences of being Superman. They'll live this character for ten years because I'm telling one story over three movies and plan to direct all three if the first is as successful as everyone suspects."[1062]

On February 9, 2003, *Variety* reported that one of the top contenders for Superman was 30-year-old Victor Webster, star of the syndicated TV show *Mutant X* (2001). The Canadian actor was also a regular on the daytime soap *Days of Our Lives* (in the 1999–2000 season).[1063] A month later, the trade journal was reporting that the competition for Superman was down to two choices, Brendan Fraser and Matthew Bomer, after Paul Walker, star of *The Fast and the Furious* (2001) opted out of consideration. The trio had done screen tests with director Brett Ratner; Walker was the only one who had an option to remove himself from the running, which he did because of reservations about making a seven-year commitment to the role.[1064] Fraser had prior experience playing square-jawed heroes, with his star turns in *George of the Jungle* (1997), *The Mummy* (1999) and *Dudley Do-Right* (1999). Bomer had appeared in the 2000 season of the venerable soap-opera *All My Children*; he later played the part of Luc on the 2003–2004 TV series *Tru Calling*. On a more spurious note, *Variety* claimed that, according to talent agents, the reason actors were passing on the plum role was their fear of the "Superman Curse." Victims of the curse included George Reeves, a suicide; Clayton "Bud" Collyer, who died of a circulatory ailment after returning to voice the role for the 1966 animated series (never mind that he died three years later, in 1969); Christopher Reeve, paralyzed from his riding accident; and Margot Kidder, who suffered a breakdown.[1065]

Whatever the real reasons, the difficulty of casting the role led Brett Ratner to drop out of the project on March 19, 2003. The director released a statement saying that he had chosen to withdraw as director of *Superman*, a decision prompted by his inability to cast the lead role. Nonetheless, he said, "I appreciate the efforts of Warner Bros. and the entire production team during this process." Warners production president Jeff Robinov released his own statement: "We have tremendous regard for Brett's creativity and passion for this project and we understand this was a very tough choice for him. We are disappointed but wish him the best in his future pursuits." Apparently, the final straw for Ratner was the unwillingness of Warner Bros. executives to accept his choice for Superman, soap opera star Matthew Bomer, after the choice for the role came down to a decision between Bomer and Brendan Fraser.[1066] Ratner's six-month option expired on a Saturday, and on the following Monday, the remaining two actors excused themselves from contention.[1067] Frustrated, Ratner walked away. According to *Variety*, Warner Bros. had been uneasy about the tensions existing between Ratner and Jon Peters (according to rumor, the pair had almost come to blows at one point), and a budget that had reportedly grown to over $225 million.[1068]

Unwilling to give up on Superman, the studio and Jon Peters went back to McG in September 2003, after the director had completed *Charlie's Angels: Full Throttle* (2003). The studio had just received a new draft of the screenplay, and although they had no deal officially in place with McG, they were ready to go ahead if they could get a budget that worked and an actor in place. The studio hoped to have the new Superman movie in theaters in 2005 or spring 2006.[1069] Nine months later, McG was still testing actors, hoping for a late 2004 start date. Warners, having effectively sidelined Jon Peters, who had been shepherding the project since its Tim Burton-Nicolas Cage incarnation, were now negotiating with Gilbert

Adler and Neil Moritz to come aboard as producers. Adler had produced 63 episodes of *Tales from the Crypt* between 1991 and 1996, and produced the horror films *Bordello of Blood* (1996), *House on Haunted Hill* (1999), *Thir13en Ghosts* (2001) and *Ghost Ship* (2002). Moritz, the producer of *I Know What You Did Last Summer* (1997), *The Fast and the Furious* (2001) and *xXx* (2002), was unable to come to terms with the studio. Location scouting was set to begin in Australia, and the J.J. Abrams script had been streamlined to a budget around $200 million. The story still revolved around Superman's battle with Lex Luthor and a mysterious killer from Krypton who had come to hunt the Man of Steel. Though still not officially signed, McG had tested six actors for the role, including Jason Behr (of the 1999–2002 TV series *Roswell*), Henry Cavill (a British actor who played a key role in 2002's *The Count of Monte Cristo* as the son of the villain, but who is revealed to actually be the son of the hero), Jared Padalecki (who portrayed "Dean Forester" on 68 episodes of *Gilmore Girls* from 2000 to 2005) and Michael Cassidy (who portrayed Zach Stevens on the hit series *The OC* in the 2004–2005 season). Warner Bros. chairman-CEO Alan Horn and production president Jeff Robinov were expected to decide on whether any of McG's candidates would get the starring role.[1070] In a BBC interview in November 2003, Brendan Fraser said he hadn't ruled out the possibility of playing the part, saying, "I'm thinking about it. The big, dangling question is: is the studio thinking about it?" He added, "Who knows if they'll make the movie, but they've got my number."[1071]

By July 2004, McG, who was still not officially on the picture, was now officially off the picture. The breaking point was the director's inability to come to an agreement with the studio over where the film should be shot. Warners was reportedly already building sets at Australia's Fox Studios, feeling that shooting outside the U.S. would save tens of millions in production costs. McG, however, wanted to shoot in North America. He said in a statement that when he scouted locations in New York, "I became enamored with our greatest American city. It was clear to me that this was Metropolis. As a filmmaker, I felt it was inappropriate to try to capture the heart of America on another continent. I look at Superman as a character that embodies all that is beautiful about America."[1072] The actual reason McG wanted to shoot in the U.S. is that the director had a fear of flying over open water. The studio insisted that shooting in Australia would shave $30 million off the picture's budget, and—aware of McG's fear—they offered to buy out the entire first-class cabin of a Qantas commercial jet to get McG down under. When McG refused, they next offered the corporate jet.[1073] On a Friday afternoon near the end of June, the day before McG and Warners executives were scheduled to fly to Australia for location scouting, Warner Bros.' president of production Jeff Robinov received a call from Patrick Whitesell, McG's agent at Endeavor. Whitesell told Robinov that McG would not be boarding the flight the next day. On Saturday, the Warner Bros. corporate jet sat on a runway at Burbank Airport, ready to fly to Hawaii and then on to Australia. The Warner Bros. executives were on-board. All that was missing was the director. True to his agent's word, he never showed up.[1074]

In an interview later with *The New York Times*, Robinov said that Whitesell met with him at Warner Bros. in early spring and assured him that McG would go to Australia. Based on that assumption, in May, Warners began hiring special-effects teams and costume designers and rented sound stages in Australia.[1075] In a *Los Angeles Times* interview with John Horn, Robinov commented, "When you go down the road with movies that are this expensive, you have to believe in the people, in the process and in the direction you are taking, and honestly, we have not been comfortable."[1076] Robinov told *The New York Times'* Laura M. Holson, "We haven't got it right yet; it's that simple."[1077] According to *The Los Angeles Times*, by this point, with all the payouts to producers, directors, writers and actors, Warner Bros.

had spent between $20 million and $40 million trying to relaunch the Superman franchise.[1078]

As June came to a close, Warner Bros. president Alan Horn agreed to meet with McG in Horn's studio office. McG made a final pitch for filming in Canada, presenting financial figures and photographs he had taken on a recent trip illustrating how Canada could substitute for American farmland. But Horn could not be swayed; the movie would shoot in Australia.[1079]

Robinov said that if McG had gotten on the plane, they would have made the movie. "But once he didn't, we had a decision to make," said the production chief. As news of McG's dismissal spread, the studio began receiving phone calls from other directors who were interested. Among them was Bryan Singer, director of the phenomenally successful *X-Men* (2000), who had first expressed interest in Superman a year earlier. At the time, Singer was developing a remake of the 1976 sci-fi film *Logan's Run* for Warners. Over the weekend of July 10–11, he met with Horn and Robinov and told them his vision of Superman. The executives liked what they heard. McG was fired, and Singer was hired on July 16. As Robinov told *The New York Times*, "It's hard to have the appearance that we don't know what we are doing, but we are committed to Superman and we will continue trying until we get it right."[1080]

And Finally ... Superman Returns

For his part, Bryan Singer hoped that he would be able to break a new Superman curse, one that over the course of a decade had consumed three directors and eight writers without resulting in a finished film. "My interest in Superman dates back many, many years," said Singer. "In fact, it was the Richard Donner classic film that was my day-to-day inspiration in shaping the X-Men universe for the screen. I feel that Superman has been late in his return and it is time for him to fly again."[1081] He told Daniel Restuccio of *Post Magazine*, "I've been a fan of the character since the George Reeves television show and the Donner movie. I was negotiating to do *X-Men 3* when the director fell out of Superman. I felt it was a rare opportunity. It was a very tough choice because I love the X-Men universe."[1082]

Singer felt a certain kinship to the Big Blue Boy Scout, as he told *Empire Magazine*: "I am adopted. I'm an American and an only child. Superman was these three things. Except what interests me is that he is the ultimate immigrant and he carries what makes him different with pride."[1083]

Born Bryan Jay Singer in New York City on September 17, 1965, Bryan Singer is a distant cousin of actors Marc Singer and Lori Singer. Growing up as an adopted child, Singer said, "I loved the notion that Superman was the adopted son of this bucolic farm-dwelling family. Even though my parents were wonderful and great and I absolutely love them, I think as a kid I fantasized that I had some special royal alien heritage. I identify with the character on that level."[1084] The only Jewish kid on a block full of Catholics, he often felt like an outsider, especially after his parents divorced when he was 13; Catholic families, he noted, did not get divorced. Instead of doing his schoolwork, he wrote stories and made 8mm films. One night, he saw a profile of director Steven Spielberg on the TV newsmagazine *20/20*, and saw in the director's life a parallel of his own—Jewish kid, suburbs, divorce, and avid 8mm filmmaker. When it came time for his class to graduate from West Windsor-Plainsboro High School in New Jersey, Singer just barely squeaked by. Though he was a self-professed nerd, he was hardly a model student; he claims his cumulative GPA was about 1.9.[1085] To further his education in filmmaking, Singer first went to the School of Visual Arts in New York, and then applied to and was accepted at USC, the alma mater of Francis Ford Coppola and George Lucas.[1086]

While at USC, Singer directed the short film *Lion's Den* (1988), starring his childhood friend, actor Ethan Hawke. The following year, he graduated from USC, and began the long road to making his debut feature. He teamed up with high school friend Christopher McQuarrie, and the result was the low-budget *Public Access*, which won the Grand Jury Prize at the 1993 Sundance Film Festival. Where most new directors stumble on their sophomore effort, Singer shone, producing and directing *The Usual Suspects* (1995), which won a Best Supporting Actor Oscar for Kevin Spacey, and a screenplay Oscar for McQuarrie.[1087] He built upon that success with *Apt Pupil* (1998), based on a Stephen King novella, *X-Men* and *X2: X-Men United* (2003). *X-Men*, filmed on a budget of $75 million, brought in $294 million worldwide, becoming one of the biggest hits of 2000. *X2* was an even bigger hit; filmed for an estimated $110 million, it reaped $406 million worldwide. Singer was now firmly on the Hollywood "A" list.

Thoughts of directing Superman had been dancing in Singer's head for some time before the job was officially offered to him. Both *X-Men* and *X2: X-Men United* were produced by Lauren Shuler Donner, whose husband, Richard Donner, directed *Superman: The Movie*. While in Austin, Texas promoting a DVD release, Singer talked to Richard Donner about how he would approach a Superman movie if he got the chance. Donner was impressed with his ideas. At that instant, Singer told *Premiere* magazine, he felt he had Donner's blessing. "I don't think I would have felt comfortable making a Superman movie without that," said Singer.[1088]

Singer was about to board a plane for a short working vacation to Hawaii with his *Logan's Run* scriptwriters, Michael Dougherty and Dan Harris, when he was asked to formally pitch his ideas for *Superman* to the studio. The focus of the Hawaii trip now shifted to Superman, as the trio set about coming up with a story outline.[1089]

Singer's first move was to totally scrap the J.J. Abrams script, which he felt was problematic in its concept. Singer didn't want to do a retelling of Superman's origins, he wanted to do a return story.[1090] This had been the brilliance of his pitch to Warner Bros. Instead of reinventing Superman for the new millennium, Singer wanted to make a film that would be a continuation of the Christopher Reeve films. Dougherty and Harris, already employed to write *Logan's Run*, felt there wasn't a lot of pressure on them to bring Superman back to movie screens. Given how many other scripts had come and gone, they felt they were working in an atmosphere of diminished expectations. The writers knew they'd never be able to satisfy the expectations of all their prospective audience members, but figured that since they and Singer were Superman fans, they knew what *they'd* like to see in a new Superman movie, and they used that as a jumping-off point. Going back to Donner's Superman, they determined the three key ingredients were action, romance and humor.[1091]

The approach that the writers took was rather like the mantra adopted by *GoldenEye* writer Bruce Feirstein when he helped reintroduce James Bond to movie audiences in 1995 after a six-year absence: The world has changed, 007 has not. Speaking of *Superman*, Dougherty and Harris wrote, "The character himself is unchanged—only the world around him has moved forward."[1092]

Working with Singer, the writers developed a story in which Superman has been absent for five years, having rocketed into space to investigate a remnant of the planet Krypton discovered by astronomers. When he returns, he finds that Lois Lane has moved on; she is now living with Perry White's nephew, Richard, and the couple has a son. Furthermore, she was so hurt by Superman's abandonment that she wrote an article entitled "Why the

World Doesn't Need Superman." When Superman makes a very public reappearance—rescuing a jet on which Lois Lane is a passenger and depositing it in a baseball stadium during the midst of a nationally telecast game, demonstrating why the world *does* need Superman—Lex Luthor takes notice, and vows to get his revenge on the Man of Steel. Superman defeats Luthor, but apparently dies in the process, though he is resurrected before the end of the script, thus preserving the "Death and Rebirth of Superman" arcs of the unfilmed screenplays. The new screenwriters struggled with a problem that the writers of 1978's *Superman: The Movie* had faced: how to make a hero created during the Depression relevant to modern audiences. In an *Entertainment Weekly* interview, Dougherty said their idea was to address the perceived irrelevancy of Superman head-on by crafting a story around the theme of his irrelevancy.[1093]

Dougherty and Harris didn't see *Superman Returns* as a direct sequel to any particular film, but rather as another chapter in the hero's story, much as the James Bond films continue the story of 007 but aren't necessarily direct sequels to each other. From the standpoint of the screenwriters, although they were definitely following on from the origin of Superman as presented in Donner's 1978 film, they weren't saying that the events of *Superman II* through *Superman IV: The Quest for Peace* didn't happen, but they weren't acknowledging that they DID happen either.[1094]

Of course, the script had to have certain expected elements. The writers created a checklist of things they felt were absolute requirements, including "save Lois from disaster" and "show bullets bouncing off Superman's chest." In a sequence where Superman prevents a bank robbery, they decided that instead of pistols or automatic weapons, Superman would face a heavy artillery machine gun. But still, the shells bouncing off the Man of Steel's chest didn't seem enough; audiences had seen Superman get shot before. "Then Bryan interjected, 'But never directly in the eye,'" Dougherty and Harris wrote in *scr(i)pt Magazine*. "All of a sudden, we found a way to make the classic 'bouncing bullets' scene unique."[1095]

The action sequences, however, were window-dressing to a story that dealt more with the emotional core of Superman. "How does a man who's nearly invulnerable deal with heartache?" the writers wondered. They perceived that when Superman saw Lois, Jason and Richard together as a family, it presented the sort of normal life that he wanted but that had always escaped him; even superheroes long to have a family life.[1096]

Early drafts of the script included references to a post-9/11 world, but ultimately Singer chose to cut them, feeling it was too soon for Superman to address such a big issue. One change Singer definitely wanted to make was that he wanted his Superman to be a universal hero, not just an American hero, hence the alteration of the classic "Truth, justice and the American way" line in the final film, where Perry White asks if Superman still stands for "Truth, justice ... all that stuff."[1097] Singer told *Empire Magazine* that it was a good time to reintroduce Superman; at a time when cinema screens were filled with angst-ridden superheroes, Superman would stand out by being a genuinely good character in an angst-ridden world.[1098]

In a sharp departure from the previous concepts, one thing Singer made clear from the beginning was that audiences would see Superman fly, and they would see him in the familiar uniform of blue suit, red cape, and an S on his chest. He told *Entertainment Weekly*'s Jeff Jensen, "If you're going to make *Superman*, make *Superman*. Don't be afraid of it."[1099]

On the return flight to Los Angeles from Hawaii, Singer and his writers decided there were only two actors who could play Lex Luthor and his assistant, Kitty Kowalski (a character who is almost a carbon copy of *Superman: The Movie*'s Eve Teschmacher): Kevin Spacey and Parker Posey.[1100] Spacey, who had been considered for both the Lex Luthor and Brainiac roles in earlier incarnations of *Superman*, had one of his meatiest roles in Singer's *The Usual Suspects*.

Back in Los Angeles, Singer and the writers presented their pitch to Warner Bros., and the studio promptly bought it.[1101] Warner Bros. president of production Jeff Robinov told *Entertainment Weekly* that the smart thing would have been to put the project on the back burner and consider what to do next, but when they heard Signer's pitch, they knew they were finally in business.[1102] The studio greenlit the film after Singer spent what he later called a "terrible, terrible night" of budget-cutting to bring the price tag down to $184.5 million. Slashed from the budget was a $20 million-plus full-scale set of downtown Metropolis that would have eventually become part of an Australian theme park.[1103] In taking the reins of *Superman*, Singer had to excuse himself from directing the third entry in the X-Men series. Consequently, one-time *Superman* director Brett Ratner took up the reins of *X-Men: The Last Stand* (2006).

Warner Bros. wanted Singer to stick to McG's original release date of June 2006, so the director immediately set to work scouting locations in Australia and began casting. Kevin Spacey, eager to work with Singer again, readily accepted the part of Lex Luthor. When Spacey was originally offered the role by director Tim Burton and later Brett Ratner, he was coming off his high-profile baddie roles in *The Usual Suspects* and *Se7en*; during that time, said the actor, "all anyone ever thought of me was dark and evil." Nine years later, he had broadened his resume, with roles in *Midnight in the Garden of Good and Evil*, *American Beauty* (1999), for which he won his second Academy Award, *The Shipping News* (2001), *The Life of David Gale* (2003) and *Beyond the Sea* (2004), a labor-of-love biopic of singer Bobby Darin which Spacey had long wanted to make, and which he directed as well as starred in. Spacey had no qualms about shaving his head for the role of Lex Luthor, having shorn his locks previously for *Se7en*. For that film, *Se7en* director David Fincher also shaved his head in a show of support. Spacey mentioned that fact to Bryan Singer, but Singer didn't take the bait.[1104]

While Singer was going through McG's audition tapes of potential Superman actors and casting directors were scouring the globe for unknowns, it was rumored that Jim Caviezel, who had just played the part of Jesus in Mel Gibson's controversial and hugely profitable Biblical epic *The Passion of the Christ* (2004), was in talks with Warner Bros. about accepting the Superman role, though the actor's agent denied it.[1105] In October 2004, the actor told website *IESB.com* that the role appealed to him a great deal, "but I haven't seen a script yet. I like to play iconic characters, and I see the role of Superman as a big responsibility. Playing Superman would be a great challenge. I have had no direct, face-to-face talks with Bryan Singer. All talking has been done through mediators." In an interview on the *Ain't-it-cool.com* website, Singer said that although Caviezel was a wonderful actor, he was committed to casting an unknown.[1106] In fact, Singer had already met with a young actor named Brandon Routh, and had decided that the Iowa native who was one of the five finalists for McG's *Superman* would be his Man of Steel.

When McG left the project and Singer took over, Routh—who had heard nothing from the studio—kept checking internet sites to keep tabs on what Singer was doing. He knew the director had his audition tape, and fretted about whether or not he would call. Finally, on the morning of August 13, 2004, Routh's phone rang. It was Singer, and he wanted to meet the actor as soon as possible.[1107] The director had, indeed, seen Routh's prior screen test tapes, and liked what he saw. When he arrived at a Coffee Bean and Tea Leaf outlet on Sunset Boulevard for a face-to-face meeting, Routh was seated, waiting. After Singer introduced himself, Routh asked if he'd like to eat at a table outside. As Singer later related to

Harry Knowles in an interview on the *Ain't It Cool News* website, "He stood up and up and up and up...." As they talked, Singer kept thinking about how Routh would photograph, and what would possibly rule him out as Superman. But in the end, he could find no flaws; the more they spoke, the more Singer felt that Routh was a thoroughly unique individual. "I felt literally from that meeting that I had my Superman, even though it was several months later that I officially made the decision and told him."[1108]

On October 20, 2004, *Variety* announced that Bryan Singer had cast Brandon Routh in the role of Superman in *Superman Returns*. The trade journal noted that 25-year-old Routh was from Norwalk, Iowa, a town situated just one hundred miles south of Woolstock, the hometown of original TV Superman George Reeves.[1109] Routh was actually born in Des Moines on October 9, 1979, but was reared in nearby Norwalk. A fan of Superman from an early age, he told *Premiere* magazine that when *Superman: The Movie* was going to be shown on television, "I was five or six years old and dressed up in my Superman pajamas. I was so excited to see it, I gave myself a migraine. I was puking through half of the movie."[1110] Known as "B.J." to his friends, Routh was a high school athlete who participated in swimming and soccer, and also appeared in some school plays. After spending a year at the University of Iowa, he headed to Hollywood looking for his big break.[1111] He got it in 1999, with a role in the sitcom *Odd Man Out*. Next, he became an MTV heartthrob, appearing in four episodes of MTV's nighttime soap *Undressed* (1999–2002), and a Christina Aguilera video, "What a Girl Wants." After a role on the popular WB series *Gilmore Girls* (2000–present), he settled into the role of Seth Anderson on the ABC soap opera *One Life to Live* in the 2001–2002 season. One-off guest-starring parts on TV shows like *Cold Case* (2003–present), *Will & Grace* (1998–2006) and *Oliver Beene* (2003–2004) followed, as well as a role in the low-budget movie *Deadly* (2005).[1112]

In 2003, the young actor's destiny was foreshadowed when he attended a Halloween costume party as Clark Kent, complete with black horn-rim glasses and a Superman tunic underneath his shirt and tie. After screen testing for McG and eventually being cast as the Man of Steel by Bryan Singer, Routh was eager to take on the iconic role. "The spirit of Superman is great to have around. I'm really excited to be a part of it and sharing the legacy," Routh told *DarkHorizon.com*'s Paul Fischer.[1113] To get in shape for the role, which he knew would require lots of wire work, Routh did rope yoga, which he described as a mix of Pilates and yoga, to help him stay flexible. Once on location in Australia, he rose at 4:30 A.M. to lift weights, adding an extra ten pounds of muscle to his 6'3" frame; at his heaviest, he wavered between 218 and 220 pounds.[1114]

With the lead role settled, Singer began filling out the rest of the cast. In January, *The Hollywood Reporter* announced that Singer had cast James Marsden, who played Cyclops in the *X-Men* films, as Richard White, nephew of *Daily Planet* editor Perry White. For Perry, Singer chose another actor whose work he was very familiar with—Hugh Laurie, who was making a splash on TV as the star of the medical drama *House*, which Singer produced.[1115] A couple of weeks later, Sam Huntington was announced for the role of *Daily Planet* cub reporter and photographer Jimmy Olsen, and negotiations were on-going for Kate Bosworth to play Lois Lane; by early February, she was firmly on-board.[1116] Bryan Singer later told Harry Knowles that Bosworth hadn't expected to take on a role that would give her such instant visibility on such a wide level so early in her career. For Bosworth, who made her film debut at age 15 in 1998's *The Horse Whisperer*, playing Lois Lane meant she would be reunited with her *Beyond the Sea* co-star and director, Kevin Spacey; Bosworth had played Spacey's wife in the 2004 film.[1117] It was, in fact, Spacey who recommended Bosworth to Singer.[1118] The director was pleased; he said he was looking for youthful actors for

Superman and Lois Lane who would age well into the expected sequels. Though she was only 23 years old, he felt Bosworth could convincingly project Lois Lane's heartbreak over Superman's long absence. It helped that, prior to the start of shooting, Bosworth broke up with her boyfriend, *Lord of the Rings* actor Orlando Bloom. She told *Entertainment Weekly* that it was an interesting time in her life.[1119]

Of course, no Superman movie would be complete without a Zorro connection. When scheduling conflicts precluded Hugh Laurie from playing Perry White, Singer turned to an actor who had once played Zorro in a 1974 ABC-TV remake of *The Mark of Zorro*, Frank Langella. In a distinguished Broadway and film career, Langella had starred in the 1979 film adaptation of the hit Broadway play *Dracula*, was Sherlock Holmes in the 1981 TV movie *Sherlock Holmes: The Strange Case of Alice Faulkner*, an evil chief of staff to the U.S. president in the 1993 comedy *Dave*, and made an oily Clare Quilty in a 1997 remake of *Lolita*. In contrast to John Hamilton and Jackie Cooper, Langella played a more toned-down version of the newspaper editor, one who exuded quiet authority instead of comically barking orders.

One of the last roles cast was that of Ma Kent, and to fill it, Singer turned to another film and Broadway veteran, Eva Marie Saint. Saint's first TV role was in a 1947 DuMont Television Network production of *A Christmas Carol* that starred John Carradine as Scrooge. Her film debut came seven years later, when she starred opposite Marlon Brando in the classic *On the Waterfront* (1954) This was later followed by another memorable role as Eve Kendall in the Alfred Hitchcock classic, *North by Northwest* (1959). The actress felt that the time was right for a new Superman movie; in an interview with Elliot V. Kotek of *Moving Pictures Magazine*, she said that with things so bad in the world today, Superman could help people escape, saying he represented "someone who can take care of things, and help the needy. I wish he'd been around at the time of [Hurricane] Katrina. It sounds silly to think that way, but part of us wants somebody to lead us and make things better, not just in New Orleans or Iraq, but everywhere."[1120]

Brandon Routh as Superman and Kate Bosworth as Lois Lane in *Superman Returns* (2006). After numerous starts and stops that began a decade earlier with the announcement that Tim Burton would direct Nicolas Cage in a new *Superman* film, fans and critics alike were pleased that director Bryan Singer treated the character with respect and reverence (Warner Bros./Photofest, © Warner Bros.)

In a move that generated

much press, Marlon Brando was also slated to be in the film as Jor-El, despite the fact that he had died at age 80 on July 1, 2004. Since Singer and his writers viewed the plot of *Superman Returns* as a continuation of *Superman II*, the director planned to use footage of Brando that was shot for *Superman II* but never used; the footage had been discovered years later in a Kansas warehouse.[1121]

As 2004 ended, Warner Bros. and Singer could take solace from a poll conducted in the United Kingdom by the UCI cinema chain that asked 4,985 moviegoers to determine the top five superheroes. Superman was the top choice. The others were Spider-Man (number 2), Batman (number 3), The Hulk (number 4), and Mr. Incredible of *The Incredibles* (number 5). It bears mentioning that the poll was a publicity stunt for the release of the Disney-Pixar animated movie *The Incredibles* (2004), which—like *Superman Returns*—also involved themes of identity and the relevancy of superheroes in a modern world.[1122]

Superman Returns would not only be modern, but cutting edge. It was the first major motion picture shot with Panavision's Genesis digital camera.[1123] Singer had contemplated shooting the film in 70mm, but his cinematographer Newton Thomas Sigel mentioned the new camera and how it recorded the image to a single chip, and was meant to look more like film than other digital cameras.[1124] Released in 2004, the Genesis camera's recorder was a detachable Sony SRW-1 VTR that was made to look like a Panavision film magazine and—the biggest selling point for Singer—was capable of using all existing 35mm lenses.[1125] This meant that Singer could use the exact same lenses he had used to shoot *Apt Pupil* and *X2: X-Men United* (he would have used them for *X-Men*, but that was shot with anamorphic lenses). Jimmy Jensen, Singer's focus puller, kept the lenses on retainer at Panavision; nobody but Jensen ever used them.[1126] Singer and Sigel tested the new digital camera in daylight, half light, sunlight, artificial light, and night light. They filmed vistas, and they filmed human actors. All the tests were conducted with a Super 35 camera shooting film mounted next to the Genesis camera. "The two of us looked at it and thought we can gain a unique look and not sacrifice anything by using this camera. The question then was how many cameras can [Panavision] build, and will there be enough cameras in time for us to shoot?" By the time they had finished, the production had used fifteen Genesis cameras.[1127]

Superman Returns began filming in Tamworth, 250 miles north of Sydney, Australia on March 21, 2005, the first day of a planned 118-day shoot. The first scenes shot were those involving Clark and Ma Kent on the Kent Farm, and flashbacks involving a teenage Clark Kent, played by Stephan Bender. When filming moved to the Fox Studios in Sydney, where it would eventually occupy every stage on the lot, two more familiar faces appeared. To play a dying millionaire who leaves her fortune to Lex Luthor, Singer chose Noel Neill, the screen's very first Lois Lane. Neill's *Adventures of Superman* co-star, Jack Larson, was given the small role of Bo the Bartender for an early scene with Clark Kent and Jimmy Olsen.

One day, Larson was standing with Singer on a set representing the roof of *The Daily Planet* when he saw a familiar sight. "There HE is!," he told Singer. Singer didn't know what he was talking about, until he turned and saw Brandon Routh in his Superman uniform.[1128]

The whole world got to see HIM on April 22, 2005, when Warner Bros. released a photo of a stern-looking Brandon Routh, hands on his hips, in the new Superman uniform. As designed by Louise Mingenbach, there were some distinct differences from earlier incarnations; the "S" shield was smaller and upraised, the red trunks were now more like a Speedo, the "S" shield was repeated in the belt buckle, and his cape and boots, more a deep burgundy than bright red, seemed to have a leathery texture. Still, it was less of a dramatic license than Singer had taken with *X-Men*, replacing the comic book's blue-and-yellow spandex with dark leather uniforms. "With X-Men, although they had extraordinary powers, they also had physical weaknesses," Singer told *USA Today*. "The suits were for protection as well as costume. Superman is the Man of Steel. Bullets bounce off him, not the suit." According to Singer, Superman's more modern costume showed that "he's not afraid."[1129] Singer said he looked at models and went through various sizes and styles of uniform until he found the one that his gut told him, 'This is SUPERMAN.'[1130] Singer told Harry Knowles that he was disappointed that people saw the uniform as being a dramatic departure, because he felt that he was respecting the essence of the comic book character in a way that worked on film with Brandon Routh.[1131]

As filming progressed, Routh suffered through what every Superman actor before him had endured: the perils of flying. While filming the scene where Superman reunites with Lois Lane on the top of the *Daily Planet* building, Routh was outfitted with a harness under his suit. When a crew member pushed a button, the computerized rigging system hoisted the actor up into the rafters of the soundstage. During a retake, Routh was lifted up too far, and banged noisily into a rafter. Luckily, he was unharmed. Routh told *Entertainment Weekly*'s Jeff Jensen that everyone on set assumed he was injured because he didn't say anything, but he had kept quiet because he could see Kate Bosworth down below with the camera still filming her and he didn't want to disturb her.[1132]

Singer and Routh strove to make Superman's flying look as graceful as possible, with "the movement of the character being very regal," said Routh.[1133] As an actor, Routh found that an important part of the flying scenes was to always have an intention in his mind. When he was up on the wires, he concentrated on where the character was going, who he was going to save. "There's so much that needs to be conveyed through just the image of my face on screen," he said.[1134]

For his part, Kevin Spacey seemed to be having a grand time reveling in Lex Luthor's villainy. Eschewing the affability of Gene Hackman's interpretation, Spacey played an angrier, bitterer Lex Luthor. Looking at the early versions of the script, Spacey decided to tone down Lex Luthor's outrageous costumes and wigs, and he and Parker Posey decided that their Lex Luthor-Kitty Kowalski banter would have the edgy bite of Richard Burton and Elizabeth Taylor in *Who's Afraid of Virginia Woolf?* (1966). Screenwriter Dan Harris said that Spacey's take was scarier than the writers intended, but also better. Bryan Singer was very pleased with the underlying menace projected by Spacey, repeating the cardinal rule of storytelling: your hero is only as strong as your villain.[1135]

One of the film's set-piece scenes, showing Superman rescuing a space shuttle and then guiding a jetliner to a safe landing inside a baseball stadium, was a constant work-in-progress, with shots for it being filmed throughout the production. But that was just a primer for the difficulties the cast and crew faced filming the climactic action inside three giant water tanks. Besides the emotional challenges she faced as Lois Lane, Kate Bosworth had to deal with days spent submerged in water waiting for her rescuer to come. She told *Entertainment Weekly* that every day she spent in the water she wondered what the hell they were doing. Singer was beginning to wonder the same thing. With his cast and crew exhausted from their months of hard labor, he asked the studio for a three-week recess. To the relief of Bosworth and the rest of the cast and crew, the studio agreed.[1136] Singer used the time to edit footage, reevaluate the budget, and to make sure that the film was coalescing as he hoped. He knew there was a lot of expectation for the film, and because of his own love for the character, wanted to be sure that he wouldn't do Superman any kind of disservice.[1137]

Before filming wrapped, Singer took a couple more breaks. He visited the set of Peter Jackson's epic remake of *King Kong* (2005), where he reportedly helped out with the scene where Kong fights a T-Rex,[1138] and in mid–July he visited the 36th annual Comic-Con in

San Diego, California, where he debuted a brief sampling of footage. "This is Comic-Con, and it is *Superman*," said Singer, pumping up the crowd. "If there was ever a time to make the long flight for a short visit, this was it." After the footage was screened, some 6,500 comic book fans jammed into a hall at the San Diego Convention Center gave the assemblage a standing ovation.[1139]

Learning a lesson from the surprise hit *The Blair Witch Project* (1999), which built up tremendous interest in the film through a website long before it premiered, Warner Bros. joined with the fan website The Blue Tights Network (www.bluetights.net) to premiere Bryan Singer's video journals from the making of the film, allowing fans to check the progress of the shooting through video blogs. The video journals were later seen on the official movie website, www.SupermanReturns.com. Feeling the pressures of shepherding the mammoth production to its ultimate conclusion, Bryan Singer joked that if viewers took a close look at the blogs, "you'll see me aging and becoming more gaunt and more wasted."[1140]

To compose the score for *Superman Returns*, Singer turned to his frequent collaborator John Ottman, whom he first met while at USC film school. Ottman composed the scores for five of Singer's films, beginning with the 1988 short film *Lion's Den*, which Ottman and Singer co-directed. Singer was thrilled with Ottman's music for *Superman Returns* (which Ottman also edited, with Elliot Graham). Singer liked that Ottman wasn't afraid to incorporate John Williams's music in his score, including areas where Singer didn't expect it.[1141] Ottman not only used Williams's "Superman Theme," he also echoed the melody of "Can You Read My Mind" for a scene in which Superman takes Lois Lane flying above Metropolis.

After shooting for about eight months on locations and sets in Australia, *Superman Returns* wrapped principal photography in mid–August 2005. Completing the special effects, which involved hundreds of computer generated imaging (CGI) shots, continued for another four months. Singer told *Empire* magazine that while making the film was a great experience, it was a much more involved production than anything he'd had to contend with making the *X-Men* films.[1142] When it was all over, extra effects shots and the expense of filming the big set-piece action scenes had pushed the budget to $204 million, according to Warner Bros. Without the Australian tax credits, the final cost would have been around $223 million. As filming came to a close, Warners struck a deal with Legendary Pictures, an independent film company, to share some of the burden and, eventually, some of the revenue. Given the anticipated $100 million in marketing and promotion costs, it was estimated that the film would have to gross more than $600 million worldwide to turn a profit, which meant it also needed the widest audience possible. Actor James Marsden wasn't worried. "If somebody gave you $200 million to make a movie that could reach the most people you could," he said, "who would it be about? The answer is either going to be Superman or Jesus."[1143]

There were, in fact, overt parallels between the Man of Steel as presented in *Superman Returns* and Jesus Christ that were apparent in the teaser trailer released to theaters and the internet on November 17, 2005—in time for the Thanksgiving holiday. The trailer, highlighted by John Williams's music and voice-over from Marlon Brando, was reassuring to fans of the Christopher Reeve films. Singer said the idea was to do something very elegant that would say, very simply, "We're here and we're coming."[1144] The Superman-Christ connection was reinforced by Brando intoning, "They can be a great people, Kal-El, they wish to be; they only lack the light to show the way. For this reason above all, their capacity for good, I have sent them you, my only son."

As the release date neared, there was much debate in the press about the Superman-

Christ connection. In an article entitled "Is the New Superman Meant to Be Jesus?," Finlo Rohrer of *BBC News Magazine* pointed out the similarities between *Superman Returns* and the Christ story: Superman was shown as having the weight of the world's suffering on his shoulders; his five years in space were an echo of the Ascension; Superman said the world needed a savior; when he returned to earth, he was cradled in his mother's arms (an image reminiscent of Michelangelo's Pieta); he hovered above the earth with arms outstretched, a visual that recalled Christ's crucifixion (the image was also used on the film's posters); Lex Luthor stabbed the dying hero in the side with a shard of kryptonite, just as Jesus was stabbed in the side with a spear while dying on the cross; the nurse discovering the empty hospital room was equivalent to Mary discovering Jesus's empty tomb; and lastly, both Superman and Jesus rose from the dead. Stephen Skelton, author of *The Gospel According to the World's Greatest Superhero* (Harvest House Publishers, 2006), even prepared a guide for pastors who might have wanted to use *Superman Returns* in their sermons. Skelton told the BBC, "You would have to be blind to miss what they are doing in terms of the Christ imagery." On the other hand, Giles Fraser, parish vicar at Putney in London, felt that using *Superman Returns* "as evangelism for adults is completely ridiculous. It is making Christianity into this rather wholesome nicely, nicely affirmation of American values, the morphing of Jesus into the American hero."[1145]

Christians were not the only ones who saw religious parallels in Superman. Rabbi Simcha Weinstein, author of *Up, Up and Oy Vey!: How Jewish History, Culture and Values Shaped the Comic Book Superhero* (Leviathan Press, 2006), noted the Jewish influences in Superman: both his creators were Jewish; both Superman and his father's Kryptonian names end with El, the Hebrew name for God; Superman being sent to Earth in a rocket was similar to Moses being sent away in a basket; just as Jews were condemned by Nazis during World War II, so was Superman—Goebbels wrote an anti-Superman diatribe in the April 1940 edition of the SS newspaper *Das Schwarze Korps*; and lastly, Superman, an alien trying to find his place in human society, evoked the story of Jews immigrating to other lands and assimilating with other cultures. An article by Shen Shi'an on *The Buddhist Channel* website (www. buddhistchannel.tv), "'Superman Returns' to His Bodhisattva Career," posited that Superman was a Bodhisattva, a great being who aspires to unconditionally help others to become free from any suffering.[1146]

When asked about the film's Biblical implications, Bryan Singer said, "I think Jews and Christians who've seen the film have gotten quite a thrill out of it. Remember these Judea Christian stories, these biblical stories, have been told in many different ways.... For goodness sake, one of the biggest pop stars in the world is called Madonna!"[1147]

When the film was released in the U.S. on June 28 and in the U.K. on July 13, 2006, it was mostly met with critical praise. Writing in *Variety*, Todd McCarthy called it a "grandly conceived and sensitively drawn" film that, while being aware of what came before, was "never self-consciously hip, ironic, post-modern or camp. To the contrary, it's quite sincere, with an artistic elegance and a genuine emotional investment in the material that creates renewed engagement in these long-familiar characters and a well-earned payoff after 2½ hours spent with them."[1148] In his review, *BBC News* entertainment reporter Neil Smith wrote the long, chaotic process of bringing Superman back to movie screens "...only showed how tough it was to escape Reeve's looming shadow. Singer's solution is not to dodge that association, but to embrace it. Picking up where Reeve's first two Superman movies left off, the *X-Men* director presents an irony-free action adventure that merges state-of-the-art technology with dewy-eyed nostalgia."[1149]

There were some notable dissenters, however. Kenneth Turan of *The Los Angeles Times* called the film "a hummingbird in reverse. The tiny beast shouldn't be able to fly but does, while the massive movie should soar but only sporadically gets off the ground." As one of the chief deficits, he cited the performances, which he felt were weak throughout the film, writing, "When the ghost of Marlon Brando (as father Jor-El in a vintage hologram) gives one of your most memorable performances, you're in trouble."[1150] Anthony Lane of *The New Yorker* echoed the feeling of many reviewers when he wrote, "The latest actor to don the cape is Brandon Routh, who—whether on his own initiative or not—offers not so much his personal interpretation of Superman as his best impersonation of Christopher Reeve playing Superman."[1151] In a review that highlighted the Christian parallels, Manohla Dargis of *The New York Times* wrote that every era got the superhero it deserved, "or at least the one filmmakers think we want. For Mr. Singer that means a Superman who fights his foes in a scene that visually echoes the garden betrayal in *The Passion of the Christ* and even hangs in the air much as Jesus did on the cross." [1152]

For Bryan Singer, however, the review that was the most meaningful was the one given by Richard Donner, director of *Superman: The Movie*. After attending the U.S. premiere, Donner heaped praise on the new movie. He felt that Singer used CGI wisely, saying that his Superman was made with all the cutting edge special effects advantages that were available to him at that time, but "what Bryan Singer has done with what is available to him now is a miracle to me." He also had high praise for the film's star. "Routh is wonderful," said Donner. "He's brought his own identity to the role, and he is Superman." More bittersweet for Donner was Routh's uncanny resemblance to Christopher Reeve. Sitting in the theater and thinking of Reeve made Donner very emotional. "I still can't believe that he's not around," he said.[1153] *Superman Returns* was dedicated to the memory of Christopher and Dana Reeve.

Although the film was not set to officially open until Wednesday, June 28, 2006, about 2,500 of the 3,915 theaters in the U.S. that were showing *Superman Returns* began having "preview" screenings at 10 P.M. on the 27th. The previews brought in an estimated $3 million. On opening day, *Superman Returns* had the 11th biggest Wednesday debut of all time, with a U.S. gross of $18 million. It also set a single-day record of $1.2 million from 76 Imax theaters, where the film screened with roughly 20 minutes of its digital footage presented in 3-D.[1154] In its first five days, the film took in $84.2 million. While still a respectable amount, it was a disappointment for such a costly blockbuster; by comparison, Singer's previous film, *X2: X-Men United*, had captured $122.9 million in four days.

In its second weekend, Superman faced a foe even more formidable than Lex Luthor: Johnny Depp as Capt. Jack Sparrow in Disney's sequel to *Pirates of the Caribbean: The Curse of the Black Pearl* (2003), the much-anticipated *Pirates of the Caribbean: Dead Man's Chest* (2006). The Disney film set a new box-office record when it earned $132 in its first three days. By that point, *Superman Returns* had brought in $141.7 million, but it had taken twelve days to do so, and was running out of steam.[1155] By the time it ended its run, *Superman Returns* had earned over $389 million worldwide, with just over $200 million coming from its U.S. box office returns. For any other movie, this would have been a triumph; for one whose budget topped $200 million, it was less than super. Nonetheless, Warner Bros. and Bryan Singer have announced that there will be a sequel, set to fly into theaters in 2009.

Afterword

Will there be another Superman movie? Of course there will. It's inevitable, because Superman is too much a part of our culture. He has been celebrated in song by Jim Croce, Barbra Streisand, The Kinks, REM, Five for Fighting, and 3 Doors Down. He has been a video game fixture since the dawn of the computer revolution. The comic books are still selling steadily, and the yearly Superman Celebration in Metropolis, Illinois continues to attract thousands of visitors each June.

From the pages of the comics to radio's theater of the imagination, from the intimacy of television to the majesty of the movies, there has always been and will perhaps always be a Superman for every medium and every generation.

Appendix I: Superman Books

A Job for Superman! by Kirk Alyn (Self published, 1971). A first-person account by the first person to play Superman onscreen, this paperback offers a breezy overview of the career of Kirk Alyn, with the first third of the book devoted to the making of the Superman serials.

Cult Movies Presents Superboy & Superpup: The Lost Videos by Chuck Harter (Cult Movies, 1993). A thoroughly researched and very interesting account of the two *Adventures of Superman* spin-offs.

The Illustrated History—Superhero Comics of the Golden Age by Mike Benton (Taylor, 1992). A terrific guide to comic book heroes of the 1930s and 40s and their creators.

The Making of Superman: The Movie by David Michael Petrou (Warner Books, 1978). This paperback gives wonderful insight into the making of the first Superman film.

Men of Tomorrow: Geeks, Gangsters and the Birth of the Comic Book by Gerard Jones (Basic, 2004). A fascinating, exhaustively researched account of the rise of the comic book industry, with captivating chapters on Jerry Siegel, Joe Shuster and the guiding lights of National Comics.

Speeding Bullet: The Life and Bizarre Death of George Reeves by Jan Alan Henderson (Michael J. Bifulco, 1999). As the title suggests, this book concerns itself more with the circumstances of George Reeves' death than with the production of the Superman TV series, and gives one of the best examinations of the events surrounding the actor's demise.

Still Me by Christopher Reeve (Random House, 1998). Christopher Reeve's touching memoir, written after his tragic riding accident.

Superman on Broadway by Bob Holiday and Chuck Harter (Bob Holiday and Chuck Harter, 2003). A good bio of Holiday, with lots of information on his performance in *It's A Bird...It's A Plane...It's Superman.*

Superman on Television by Michael Bifulco (Michael J. Bifulco, 1998). A great episode guide of the George Reeves TV series, with a good selection of black-and-white photos.

Superman: Serial to Cereal by Gary Grossman (Popular Library, 1977). One of the first books to chronicle Superman in mass media, this book looks at the Fleischer cartoons and Kirk Alyn serials but concentrates primarily on the George Reeves TV series *Adventures of Superman.* Grossman interviewed almost everyone connected with the series, and presented a great account of its production.

Superman, The Complete History: The Life and Times of the Man of Steel by Les Daniels (Chronicle, 1998). With eye-catching design layouts by Chin-Yee Lai, this book presents an exhaustive history of the first sixty years of Superman, concentrating primarily on the comic books, with only passing references to Superman in movies and TV.

Truth, Justice, and the American Way: The Life and Times of Noel Neill, the Original Lois Lane by Larry Thomas Ward (Nicholas Lawrence, 2003). An entertaining look at the life of Noel Neill, with some fun anecdotes about filming *Adventures of Superman* and working with George Reeves.

Appendix II:
Superman-Related Websites

The Adventures Continue: www.jimnolt.com. A great website for information about George Reeves and *Adventures of Superman*.

The Blue Tights Network: www.bluetights.net. A fan website that was chosen by Bryan Singer to host his video journals from the making of *Superman Returns*, which were later released on the official Warner Bros. *Superman Returns* website, www.SupermanReturns.com.

Bob Holiday's Website: www.supermanbobholiday.com. Bob Holiday's website, which presents the latest information about the Broadway star and video clips of his appearance on *I've Got a Secret!*

The Christopher Reeve Homepage: www.chrisreevehomepage.com. A good source of information about Christopher Reeve's life and career.

Don Markstein's Toonopedia: www.toonopedia.com. A great resource for fans of animated cartoons, with an exhaustive A–Z listing of practically every cartoon ever made.

DMWC's Superboy: The Series website: www.geocities.com/dmwc. Episode guides, interviews, and video and audio clips about the *Superboy* TV series.

Glass House Presents: www.GlassHousePresents.com. Home of the George Reeves Hall of Fame, a premier George Reeves website.

Kryptonsite.com: A terrific website for fans of *Smallville*, with interviews, episode guides, and all the latest news about the program.

Superboy Home Page: www.superboyhomepage.com. A good source for news about Superman as well as information about the Superboy series.

The Superman Homepage: www.supermanhomepage.com. If it has anything to do with Superman, you'll find it here. One of the best one-stop sources of Superman information.

The Superman Supersite: www.supermansupersite.com. Another great Superman website with a variety of Superman resources.

Appendix III:
Superman Cast

The Adventures of Superman (radio): SUPERMAN/CLARK KENT (Clayton "Bud" Collyer [1940–1949]; Michael Fitzmaurice [1949–1951]); LOIS LANE (Rollie Bester [early shows], Helen Choate [early shows], Joan Alexander); JIMMY OLSEN (Jackie Kelk); PERRY WHITE (Julian Noa); INSPECTOR HENDERSON (Matt Crowley, Earl George); JOR-EL AND LARA (Ned Wever & Agnes Moorehead [1940])

Superman cartoons (1940s): SUPERMAN/CLARK KENT (Clayton "Bud" Collyer); LOIS LANE (Joan Alexander); PERRY WHITE (Julian Noa);

Superman (serial, 1948): SUPERMAN/CLARK KENT (Alan Dinehart III [Clark Kent as a small boy], Ralph Hodges [teenage Clark Kent], Kirk Alyn [adult Superman]); LOIS LANE (Noel Neill); JIMMY OLSEN (Tommy Bond); PERRY WHITE (Pierre Watkin); MA & PA KENT (Edward Cassidy & Virginia Carroll); JOR-EL AND LARA (Nelson Leigh & Luana Walters)

Atom Man vs. Superman (serial, 1950): SUPERMAN/CLARK KENT (Kirk Alyn); LOIS LANE (Noel Neill); JIMMY OLSEN (Tommy Bond); PERRY WHITE (Pierre Watkin); LEX LUTHOR (Lyle Talbot)

Superman and the Mole Men (1951): (George Reeves); LOIS LANE (Phyllis Coates)

The Adventures of Superman (TV 1951–1957): SUPERMAN/CLARK KENT (George Reeves); LOIS LANE (Phyllis Coates [1951]; Noel Neill [1953–1957]); JIMMY OLSEN (Jack Larson); PERRY WHITE (John Hamilton); INSPECTOR HENDERSON (Robert Shayne); MA & PA KENT (Tom Fadden & Frances Morris [Season 1]); JOR-EL AND LARA (Robert Rockwell & Aline Towne [Season 1])

The Adventures of Superboy (TV pilot, 1961): SUPERMAN/CLARK KENT (Johnny Rockwell); LANA LANG (Bunny Henning); MA KENT (Monty Margetts)

It's a Bird, It's a Plane, It's Superman (Broadway play, 1966): SUPERMAN/CLARK KENT (Bob Holiday); LOIS LANE (Joan Hotchkiss [Philadelphia try-outs]), Patricia Marand); PERRY WHITE (Eric Mason)

The New Adventures of Superman (1966 animated series): SUPERMAN/CLARK KENT (Bob Hastings [Superboy] Bud Collyer [Superman]); LOIS LANE (Joan Alexander); LANA LANG (Janet Waldo); JIMMY OLSEN (Jack Grimes); PERRY WHITE (Ted Knight); LEX LUTHOR (Jackson Beck)

The Superman/Aquaman Hour of Adventure (1967 animated series): SUPERMAN/CLARK KENT (Bob Hastings [Superboy]); LOIS LANE (Joan Alexander, Julie Bennett); LANA LANG (Janet Waldo); JIMMY OLSEN (Jack Grimes); PERRY WHITE (Jackson Beck); LEX LUTHOR (Jackson Beck);

The Batman/Superman Hour (1968 animated series): SUPERMAN/CLARK KENT (Bob Hastings [Superboy] Bud Collyer [Superman]); JIMMY OLSEN (Jack Grimes); PERRY WHITE (Jackson Beck); LEX LUTHOR (Jackson Beck)

Super Friends (1973): SUPERMAN/CLARK KENT (Danny Dark); LEX LUTHOR (Stan Jones)

It's a Bird, It's a Plane, It's Superman (1975 TV special): SUPERMAN/CLARK KENT (David Wilson); LOIS LANE (Lesley Ann Warren); PERRY WHITE (Allen Ludden); MA & PA KENT (George Chandler & Irene Tedrow)

The All-New Super Friends Hour (1977–78): SUPERMAN/CLARK KENT (Danny Dark); LEX LUTHOR (Stan Jones)

Challenge of the Super Friends (1978): SUPERMAN/CLARK KENT (Danny Dark); LEX LUTHOR (Stan Jones)

The World's Greatest SuperFriends (1979): SUPERMAN/CLARK KENT (Danny Dark); LEX LUTHOR (Stan Jones)

Superman: The Movie (1978): SUPERMAN/CLARK KENT; (Lee Quigley [baby Kal-El], Aaron Smolinsky [toddler Kal-El], Jeff East [young Clark Kent], Christopher Reeve [adult Superman]); LOIS LANE (Margot Kidder); LANA LANG (Diane Sherry); JIMMY OLSEN (Marc McClure); PERRY WHITE (Jackie Cooper); LEX LUTHOR (Gene Hackman); MA & PA KENT (Glenn Ford & Phyllis Thaxter); JOR-EL AND LARA (Marlon Brando & Susannah York)

Superman II (1980): SUPERMAN/CLARK KENT (Christopher Reeve); LOIS LANE (Margot Kidder); JIMMY OLSEN (Marc McClure); PERRY WHITE (Jackie Cooper); LEX LUTHOR (Gene Hackman); LARA (Susannah York)

Superman III (1983): SUPERMAN/CLARK KENT (Christopher Reeve); LOIS LANE (Margot Kidder); LANA LANG (Annette O'Toole); JIMMY OLSEN (Marc McClure); PERRY WHITE (Jackie Cooper)

SuperFriends: The Legendary Super Powers Show (1984): SUPERMAN/CLARK KENT (Danny Dark); LEX LUTHOR (Stan Jones)

The Super Powers Team: Galactic Guardians (1986) SUPERMAN/CLARK KENT (Danny Dark);

Superman IV: The Quest for Peace (1987): SUPERMAN/CLARK KENT (Christopher Reeve); LOIS LANE (Margot Kidder); JIMMY OLSEN (Marc McClure); PERRY WHITE (Jackie Cooper); LEX LUTHOR (Gene Hackman)

Superman (animated series, 1988): SUPERMAN/CLARK KENT (Beau Weaver); LOIS LANE (Ginny McSwain); JIMMY OLSEN (Mark L. Taylor); PERRY WHITE (Stanley Ralph Ross); LEX LUTHOR (Michael Bell); MA & PA KENT (Alan Oppenheimer & Tress MacNeille)

Superboy (1988–1992): SUPERMAN/CLARK KENT (John Haymes Newton [1988–1989]; Gerard Christopher [1989–1992]); LANA LANG (Stacy Haiduk [1988–1992]); LEX LUTHOR (Scott Wells [1988–1989], Sherman Howard [1989–1992]); MA & PA KENT (Stuart Whitman & Salome Jens); JOR-EL AND LARA (George Lazenby and Britt Ekland [fake Jor-El & Lara] [2nd Season]; Jacob Witkin & Kathy Poling [3rd Season, "Mindscape"])

Lois & Clark: The New Adventures of Superman (1993–1997): SUPERMAN/CLARK KENT (Dean Cain); LOIS LANE (Teri Hatcher); LANA LANG (Emily Proctor [1995]); JIMMY OLSEN (Michael

Landes [1993–1994], Justin Whalin [1994–1997]); PERRY WHITE (Lane Smith); LEX LUTHOR (John Shea [1993–1994]); INSPECTOR HENDERSON (Richard Belzer [1993]); MA & PA KENT (Eddie Jones & K Callan); JOR-EL (David Warner [1993], Francois Giroday [1996])

Superman (animated series, 1996–2000) SUPERMAN/CLARK KENT (Jason Marsden [Teenage Clark Kent], Timothy Daly); LOIS LANE (Dana Delany); LANA LANG (Kelly Schmidt [episode 2], Joely Fisher); JIMMY OLSEN (David Kaufman); PERRY WHITE (George Dzundza); LEX LUTHOR (Clancy Brown); INSPECTOR HENDERSON (Mel Winkler [as Commissioner Henderson]); MA & PA KENT (Mike Farrell & Shelly Fabares); JOR-EL AND LARA (Christopher McDonald and Finola Hughes)

Justice League / Justice League Unlimited (animated series, 2001–Present): SUPERMAN/CLARK KENT (George Newbern); LOIS LANE (Dana Delany); LEX LUTHOR (Clancy Brown); PA KENT (Mike Farrell)

Smallville (2001–Present): SUPERMAN/CLARK KENT (Tom Welling); LOIS LANE (Erica Durance [2005, 2006]); LANA LANG (Kristin Kreuk); PERRY WHITE (Michael McKean [Season 3]); LEX LUTHOR (Michael Rosenbaum); MA & PA KENT (John Schneider [2001–2005] & Annette O'Toole [2001–2006]); JOR-EL (Terence Stamp as the voice of Jor-El [Seasons 2–6]);

Superman Returns (2006): SUPERMAN/CLARK KENT (Stephan Bender [young Clark Kent], Brandon Routh [adult Superman]); LOIS LANE (Kate Bosworth); JIMMY OLSEN (Sam Huntington); PERRY WHITE (Frank Langella); LEX LUTHOR (Kevin Spacey); MA KENT (Eva Marie Saint); JOR-EL (Marlon Brando)

Chapter Notes

Chapter 1

1. *The Illustrated History—Superhero Comics of the Golden Age* by Mike Benton (c) 1992 Mike Benton, published by Taylor Publishing Company, Dallas, TX, p. 7.
2. "Jerry Siegel, Superman's Creator, Dies at 81" by Robert McG. Thomas Jr., *The New York Times*, Jan. 31, 1996, p. B6.
3. *Men of Tomorrow: Geeks, Gangsters and the Birth of the Comic Book* by Gerard Jones, (c) 2004 Gerard Jones, published by Basic Books, New York, NY, p. 35.
4. "Jerry Siegel, Superman's Creator, Dies at 81" by Robert McG. Thomas Jr., *The New York Times*, Jan. 31, 1996, p. B6.
5. *Men of Tomorrow: Geeks, Gangsters and the Birth of the Comic Book* by Gerard Jones, (c) 2004 Gerard Jones, published by Basic Books, New York, NY, p. 23
6. *Ibid.*, 38–39.
7. *Ibid.*
8. *Ibid.*
9. *The Illustrated History—Superhero Comics of the Golden Age* by Mike Benton (c) 1992 Mike Benton, published by Taylor Publishing Company, Dallas, TX, p. 8.
10. *Ibid.*, 9.
11. *Ibid.*
12. *Ibid.*
13. *Ibid.*, 10.
14. *Ibid.*, 10–11.
15. *Ibid.*, p. 137.
16. "Lois Lane = Torchy Blane" by Jerry Siegel, *TIME Magazine*, May 30, 1988, p. 6–7.
17. "Created Famed Character 47 Years Ago: Superman's Originators Warm Up After Long Freeze-Out," by John L. Mitchell, *The Los Angeles Times*, June 18, 1981.
18. *The Illustrated History—Superhero Comics of the Golden Age* by Mike Benton (c) 1992 Mike Benton, published by Taylor Publishing Company, Dallas, TX, p. 12.
19. *Ibid.*, 13.
20. *Ibid.*, 15.
21. *Ibid.*, 14.
22. *Ibid.*, 15.
23. *Ibid.*
24. *Ibid.*
25. *Ibid.*, 16.
26. *Ibid.*, 17.
27. *Men of Tomorrow: Geeks, Gangsters and the Birth of the Comic Book* by Gerard Jones, (c) 2004 Gerard Jones, published by Basic Books, New York, NY, p. 125.
28. *Ibid.*, 172.
29. *The Illustrated History—Superhero Comics of the Golden Age* by Mike Benton (c) 1992 Mike Benton, published by Taylor Publishing Company, Dallas, TX, p. 17.
30. *Men of Tomorrow: Geeks, Gangsters and the Birth of the Comic Book* by Gerard Jones, (c) 2004 Gerard Jones, published by Basic Books, New York, NY, p. 145–146.
31. *Ibid.*, 171.
32. *Ibid.*, 158.
33. *Ibid.*, 171.
34. *Ibid.*, 172.
35. *Ibid.*, 177–179.
36. *Ibid.*, 179–180.
37. *Ibid.*, 184.
38. *Ibid.*, 185.
39. "The Man of Tomorrow and the Boys of Yesterday" by Dennis Dooley, *Superman at Fifty! The Persistence of a Legend!* edited by Dennis Dooley and Gary Engle, p. 33, (c) 1987 Octavia Press, Cleveland, Ohio.
40. "'Superman,' 'Dick Tracy' et al Here to Stay, Educators Find in an Evaluation of Comics" by Catherine MacKenzie, *The New York Times*, Dec. 15, 1944.
41. *Men of Tomorrow: Geeks, Gangsters and the Birth of the Comic Book* by Gerard Jones, (c) 2004 Gerard Jones, published by Basic Books, New York, NY, p. 216.
42. *Ibid.*, 219.
43. *Ibid.*, 225.
44. *Ibid.*, 226–229.
45. *Ibid.*, 244.
46. *Ibid.*, 245–247.
47. *Ibid.*, 245.
48. *Ibid.*, 248.
49. *Ibid.*, 249.
50. *Ibid.*, 251.
51. *Ibid.*, 268–270.
52. *Ibid.*, 283.
53. *Ibid.*, 284.
54. *Ibid.*, 285–291.
55. *Ibid.*, 307–308.
56. *Ibid.*, 309–310.
57. "Jerry Siegel, Superman's Creator, Dies at 81" by Robert McG. Thomas, Jr., *The New York Times*, January 31, 1996.
58. *Men of Tomorrow: Geeks, Gangsters and the Birth of*

the *Comic Book* by Gerard Jones, (c) 2004 Gerard Jones, published by Basic Books, New York, NY, p. 316.

59. *Ibid.*

60. *Ibid.*, xiii.

61. *Ibid.*, 317–318.

62. "Mild-Mannered Cartoonists Go To Aid of Superman's Creators" by David Vidal, *The New York Times*, Dec. 10, 1975.

63. *Ibid.*

64. "The Life and Exceedingly Hard Times of Superman" by Aljean Harmetz, *The New York Times*, June 14, 1981.

65. *Men of Tomorrow: Geeks, Gangsters and the Birth of the Comic Book* by Gerard Jones, (c) 2004 Gerard Jones, published by Basic Books, New York, NY, p. 320–321.

66. *Ibid.*, 322.

67. "Jerry Siegel, Superman's Creator, Dies at 81" by Robert McG. Thomas Jr., *The New York Times*, Jan. 31, 1996, p. B6.

68. "The Life and Exceedingly Hard Times of Superman" by Aljean Harmetz, *The New York Times*, June 14, 1981.

69. "Created Famed Character 47 Years Ago: Superman's Originators Warm Up After Long Freeze-Out," by John L. Mitchell, *The Los Angeles Times*, June 18, 1981.

70. *Men of Tomorrow: Geeks, Gangsters and the Birth of the Comic Book* by Gerard Jones, (c) 2004 Gerard Jones, published by Basic Books, New York, NY, p. 333–336.

Chapter 2

71. "Radio, It Was Magic!" by Joel Siegel, *The Los Angeles Times*, Sept. 28, 1969.

72. *Men of Tomorrow: Geeks, Gangsters and the Birth of the Comic Book* by Gerard Jones, (c) 2004 Gerard Jones, published by Basic Books, New York, NY, p. 157.

73. "The Ubiquitous Mr. Collyer" by Leonard Bruder, *The New York Times*, Nov. 25, 1945.

74. Interview with Cynthia Collyer, April 25, 2006.

75. "Bud Collyer Dies; Host of TV Shows," *The New York Times*, Sept. 9, 1969.

76. *Whatever Became of ...* Radio program hosted by Richard Lamparski, broadcast in 1966.

77. Interview with Cynthia Collyer, April 25, 2006.

78. *The New York Times*, Sept. 13, 1942.

79. Interview with Cynthia Collyer, April 25, 2006.

80. *Whatever Became of ...* Radio program hosted by Richard Lamparski, broadcast in 1966.

81. *Ibid.*

82. Interview with Cynthia Collyer, April 25, 2006.

83. *Whatever Became of ...* Radio program hosted by Richard Lamparski, broadcast in 1966.

84. *Ibid.*

85. Interview with Cynthia Collyer, April 25, 2006.

86. *Whatever Became of ...* Radio program hosted by Richard Lamparski, broadcast in 1966.

87. "The Ubiquitous Mr. Collyer" by Leonard Buder, *The New York Times*, November 25, 1945.

88. "On the New Superman" by Jack Gould, *The New York Times* April 28, 1946.

89. *Ibid.*

90. Interview with Cynthia Collyer, April 25, 2006

91. *The Tonight Show With Johnny Carson*, NBC-TV, April 22, 1969, and "Radio, It Was Magic!" by Joel Siegel, *The Los Angeles Times*, Sept. 28, 1969.

Chapter 3

92. "Betty Boop" by Don Markstein, *Don Markstein's Toonopedia*, http://www.toonopedia.com/boop.htm

93. *Ibid.*

94. *Ibid.*

95. Skerry, Philip with Lambert, Chris, "From Panel to Panavision," *Superman at Fifty! The Persistence of a Legend!* edited by Dennis Dooley and Gary Engle, p. 70, (c) 1987 Octavia Press, Cleveland, Ohio, p. 64–65

96. "Max Fleischer," *Wikipedia*, http://en.wikipedia.org/wiki/Max_Fleischer

Chapter 4

97. *A Job For Superman* by Kirk Alyn, (c) 1971 by Kirk Alyn, p. 20.

98. *Ibid.*, 41–46.

99. *Ibid.*, 56.

100. *Ibid.*, 61.

101. *Ibid.*, 52.

102. "Virginia O'Brien To Become Mother," *The Los Angeles Times*, Dec. 15, 1944.

103. *A Job For Superman* by Kirk Alyn, (c) 1971 by Kirk Alyn, p. 70.

104. *Ibid.*, 73–79.

105. "Looking at Hollywood" by Hedda Hopper, *The Los Angeles Times*, March 8, 1943.

106. "Child Born to Virginia O'Brien," *The New York Times*, June 22, 1945.

107. *Superman: Serial to Cereal* by Gary Grossman, (c) 1977 Popular Library, New York, p. 19.

108. *Data For Bulletin of Screen Achievement Records*, Academy of Motion Pictures Arts & Sciences.

109. *Superman: Serial to Cereal* by Gary Grossman, (c) 1977 Popular Library, New York, p. 37.

110. Interview with Cynthia Collyer, April 25, 2006.

111. *Whatever Became of ...* Radio program hosted by Richard Lamparski, broadcast in 1966.

112. *A Job For Superman* by Kirk Alyn, (c) 1971 by Kirk Alyn, p. 4.

113. *Ibid.*, 4–5.

114. "Kirk Alyn: Superman Remembers" by Jeff Elliot, *Starlog* Magazine, March, 1979.

115. *A Job For Superman* by Kirk Alyn, (c) 1971 by Kirk Alyn, p. 6.

116. *Superman: Serial to Cereal* by Gary Grossman, (c) 1977 Popular Library, New York, p. 37.

117. *A Job For Superman* by Kirk Alyn, (c) 1971 by Kirk Alyn, p. 6.

118. *Superman: Serial to Cereal* by Gary Grossman, (c) 1977 Popular Library, New York, p. 31.

119. "Noel Neill Set For Superman Serial" by Edwin Schallert, *The Los Angeles Times*, Jan. 10, 1948.

120. *Truth, Justice & The American Way: The Life and Times of Noel Neill, The Original Lois Lane* by Larry Thomas Ward, (c) 2003 by Larry Thomas Ward, Nicholas Lawrence Books, p. 11.

121. *Truth, Justice & The American Way: The Life and Times of Noel Neill, The Original Ibid.*, 13–14.

122. *Truth, Justice & The American Way: The Life and Times of Noel Neill, The Original Ibid.*, 18–20.

123. *Ibid.*, 26.

124. *Ibid.*, 37.

125. *Ibid.*, 40.

126. *Ibid.*, 41–47.

127. *Superman: Serial to Cereal* by Gary Grossman, (c) 1977 Popular Library, New York, p. 31.

128. *A Job For Superman* by Kirk Alyn, (c) 1971 by Kirk Alyn, p. 8.

129. *Ibid.*, 9.

130. Interview with Noel Neill, March 16, 2005.

131. "Kirk Alyn Obituary," *Associated Press*, March 16, 1999.

132. "Kirk Alyn: Superman Remembers" by Jeff Elliot, *Starlog* Magazine, March, 1979.

133. *A Job For Superman* by Kirk Alyn, (c) 1971 by Kirk Alyn, p. 10–13.

134. *Ibid.*, 12.

135. *Superman: Serial to Cereal* by Gary Grossman, (c) 1977 Popular Library, New York, p. 40.

136. *Ibid.*, 17.

137. "OK, Trivia Buffs, Name The Original Superman" by Kerry Webster, *The Los Angeles Herald-Examiner*, Feb. 24, 1984.

138. *A Job For Superman* by Kirk Alyn, (c) 1971 by Kirk Alyn, p. 20.

139. *Ibid.*, 16–17.

140. "Kirk Alyn: Superman Remembers" by Jeff Elliot, *Starlog* Magazine, March, 1979.

141. *Data For Bulletin of Screen Achievement Records*, Academy of Motion Pictures Arts & Sciences.

142. *Superman: Serial to Cereal* by Gary Grossman, (c) 1977 Popular Library, New York, p. 53.

143. "First Runs Book Serial," *The Los Angeles Times*, July 7, 1948.

144. *Superman: Serial to Cereal* by Gary Grossman, (c) 1977 Popular Library, New York, p. 27.

145. "Original Superman Returns for 50th," *The Los Angeles Times*, July 28, 1987.

146. "Simple," *The New York Times*, Jan. 29, 1950.

147. *A Job For Superman* by Kirk Alyn, (c) 1971 by Kirk Alyn, p. 13.

148. "Studio Briefs," *The Los Angeles Times*, Feb. 1, 1950.

149. *Data For Bulletin of Screen Achievement Records*, Academy of Motion Pictures Arts & Sciences.

150. "Kirk Alyn: Superman Remembers" by Jeff Elliot, *Starlog* Magazine, March, 1979.

151. "What A Super Guy! (And The Original, Too)" by b.b. brown, source and date unknown, Academy of Motion Picture Arts & Sciences.

152. *Ibid.*

153. "Film Superman Flies on Wings of Nostalgia" by William Stephens, *The Los Angeles Times*, Sept. 4, 1972

154. *Ibid.*

155. "Original Superman Returns for 50th," *The Los Angeles Times*, July 28, 1987.

156. "Singer Virginia O'Brien Tells Blow, Gets Decree," *The Los Angeles Times*, June 25, 1955.

157. "What A Super Guy! (And The Original, Too)" by b.b. brown, source and date unknown, Academy of Motion Picture Arts & Sciences.

158. "Superman Is Alive and Well and Living in North Hollywood," by Lisa Mitchell, *The Los Angeles Times*, Aug. 12, 1977.

159. *Ibid.*

160. "Superman Is In Demand Again," *Manitowec (Wis) Herald-Times*, July 5, 1972.

161. "Superman Is Alive and Well and Living in North Hollywood," by Lisa Mitchell, *The Los Angeles Times*, Aug. 12, 1977.

162. Interview with Jim Hambrick, February 24, 2006.

163. Interview with Noel Neill, March 16, 2005.

164. *A Job For Superman* by Kirk Alyn, (c) 1971 by Kirk Alyn, p. 29.

165. Interview with Jim Hambrick, February 24, 2006.

166. *Ibid.*

167. "Ex-Superman Has Place of His Own to Hang Up Suit" by Steve Harvey, *The Los Angeles Times*, March 28, 1974.

168. "'Super Schumck' Irks Superman," *Valley News*, April 22, 1977.

169. "People, Etc.," *Syracuse Herald-American*, March 27, 1977.

170. Interview with Noel Neill, March 16, 2005.

171. "What A Super Guy! (And The Original, Too)" by b.b. brown, source and date unknown, Academy of Motion Picture Arts & Sciences.

172. *Ibid.*

173. Interview with Jim Hambrick, February 24, 2006.

174. "Original Superman Returns for 50th," *The Los Angeles Times*, July 28, 1987.

175. "What A Super Guy! (And The Original, Too)" by b.b. brown, source and date unknown, Academy of Motion Picture Arts & Sciences.

176. "CBS Has Super Celebration For Man of Steel" by Kathryn Baker, *Associated Press*, Feb. 28, 1988.

177. "Kirk Alyn: Superman Remembers" by Jeff Elliot, *Starlog* Magazine, March, 1979.

178. Interview with Jim Hambrick, February 24, 2006.

Chapter 5

179. "Radio: It Was Magic" by Joel Siegel, *The Los Angeles Times*, September 28, 1969.

180. *Superman: Serial to Cereal* by Gary Grossman, (c) 1977 Popular Library, New York, p. 114 and *Producer* by David L. Wolper with David Fisher, (c) 2003 by David L. Wolper, A Lisa Drew Book/Scribner, p. 15.

181. *Producer* by David L. Wolper with David Fisher, (c) 2003 by David L. Wolper, A Lisa Drew Book/Scribner, p. 15–17.

182. *Superman: Serial to Cereal* by Gary Grossman, (c) 1977 Popular Library, New York, p. 110.

183. *Ibid.*, 316.

184. "TV Tidbits" by Walter Ames, *The Los Angeles Times*, June 27, 1951, p. 20.

185. *Superman: Serial to Cereal* by Gary Grossman, (c) 1977 Popular Library, New York, p. 68.

186. *Ibid.*, 82.

187. "TV Tidbits" by Walter Ames, *The Los Angeles Times*, July 6, 1951, p. 20.

188. "Video Actress Can't Convince Daughter" by Walter Ames, *The Los Angeles Times*, March 29, 1953, p. D11.

189. Interview with Jack Larson, December 11, 2006.

190. "A 'Superman' of the Literary Set" by David Colker, *The Los Angeles Herald Examiner*, Feb. 16, 1986.

191. *Superman: Serial to Cereal* by Gary Grossman, (c) 1977 Popular Library, New York, p. 136.

192. Interview with Jack Larson, December 11, 2006.

193. "Golly, Jimmy Olsen Writes Librettos!" by Anthony Tommasini, *The New York Times*, May 15, 1998.

194. Interview with Jack Larson, December 11, 2006.

195. "Kay Thompson and Williams Brothers Have Plans for Television Musical Comedy" by Clark Roberts, *The Los Angeles Times*, July 27, 1951, p. 20.

196. "Present at the Creation of Superman and the Mole Men" by Patricia Ellsworth Wilson, *The Adventures Continue # 14*, (c) Jim Nolt 1997.

197. *Cult Movies Presents Superboy & Superpup: The Lost Videos* by Chuck Harter, (c) 1993 by Chuck Harter, published by Cult Movies, Hollywood, CA, p. 3.

198. "Present at the Creation of Superman and the Mole Men" by Patricia Ellsworth Wilson, *The Adventures Continue # 14*.

199. *Superman: Serial to Cereal* by Gary Grossman, (c) 1977 Popular Library, New York, p. 105.

200. *Ibid.*, 113.

201. "Look! Up on the Screen! It's ... Lois Lane?" by Rip Rense, *The Los Angeles Times*, Apr. 5, 1994.

202. Skerry, Philip with Lambert, Chris, "From Panel to Panavision," *Superman at Fifty! The Persistence of a Legend!* edited by Dennis Dooley and Gary Engle, (c) 1987 Octavia Press, Cleveland, Ohio, p. 70.

203. "Metropolis and Mayberry" by Randy Garrett, *The Adventures Continue* website, www.jimnolt.com/fortyacres1.htm, Spring, 2001.

204. *Superman: Serial to Cereal* by Gary Grossman, (c) 1977 Popular Library, New York, p. 111.

205. *Ibid.*, 140.

206. *Ibid.*, 116.

207. *Ibid.*, 120.

208. *Ibid.*, 128.

209. *Ibid.*, 129.

210. *Ibid.*, 316.

211. *Ibid.*, 149.

212. *Ibid.*, 152.

213. *Adventures of Superman Notes* by Paul Mandell, http://members.tripod.com/~davidschultz/superman-music.htm.

214. *Superman: Serial to Cereal* by Gary Grossman, (c) 1977 Popular Library, New York, p. 258.

215. *Adventures of Superman Notes* by Paul Mandell, http://members.tripod.com/~davidschultz/superman-music.htm.

216. *Superman: Serial to Cereal* by Gary Grossman, (c) 1977 Popular Library, New York, p. 157.

217. "Golly, Jimmy Olsen Writes Librettos!" by Anthony Tommasini, *The New York Times*, May 15, 1998.

218. *The Los Angeles Times*, February 9, 1953.

219. *Superman: Serial to Cereal* by Gary Grossman, (c) 1977 Popular Library, New York, p. 114.

220. *Producer* by David L. Wolper with David Fisher, (c) 2003 by David L. Wolper, A Lisa Drew Book/Scribner, p. 19.

221. *Superman: Serial to Cereal* by Gary Grossman, (c) 1977 Popular Library, New York, p. 114.

222. Walter Ames, *The Los Angeles Times*, March 29, 1953.

223. *Superman on Television Tenth Anniversary Edition* by Michael Bifulco, (c) 1998 Michael Bifulco, published by Michael Bifulco, p. 204.

224. *Hollywood Kryptonite: The Bulldog, The Lady and the Death of Superman* by Sam Kashner and Nancy Schoenberger, (c) 1996 by Sam Kashner and Nancy Schoenberger, published by St. Martin's Press, New York, p. 21.

225. *Cult Movies Presents Superboy & Superpup: The Lost Videos* by Chuck Harter, (c) 1993 by Chuck Harter, published by Cult Movies, Hollywood, CA, p. 1.

226. *Superman: Serial to Cereal* by Gary Grossman, (c) 1977 Popular Library, New York, p. 160–161.

227. *Ibid.*, 162.

228. *Cult Movies Presents Superboy & Superpup: The Lost*

229. *Superman: Serial to Cereal* by Gary Grossman, (c) 1977 Popular Library, New York, p. 158.

230. *Cult Movies Presents Superboy & Superpup: The Lost Videos* by Chuck Harter, (c) 1993 by Chuck Harter, published by Cult Movies, Hollywood, CA, p. 3.

231. *Superman: Serial to Cereal* by Gary Grossman, (c) 1977 Popular Library, New York, p. 162–163.

232. *Ibid.*, 150.

233. *Truth, Justice & The American Way: The Life and Times of Noel Neill The Original Lois Lane, An Authorized Biography* by Larry Thomas Ward, (c) 2003 by Larry Thomas Ward, published by Nicholas Lawrence Books, p. 75.

234. *Ibid.*, 82.

235. "A Crush More Powerful Than a Locomotive" by Rip Rense, *The Los Angeles Times*, Aug. 12, 1994.

236. *Superman: Serial to Cereal* by Gary Grossman, (c) 1977 Popular Library, New York, p. 164–165.

237. *Ibid.*, 174.

238. *Ibid.*, 175–176.

239. Walter Ames, *The Los Angeles Times*, July 6, 1953.

240. *Superman: Serial to Cereal* by Gary Grossman, (c) 1977 Popular Library, New York, p. 174.

241. "Superman George Reeves And Producers Disagree On New Television Deal" by Walter Ames, *The Los Angeles Times*, September 27, 1954.

242. *Superman: Serial to Cereal* by Gary Grossman, (c) 1977 Popular Library, New York, p. 224.

243. *Ibid.*, 223–225.

244. *Ibid.*, 254.

245. "A Visit With Lois & Jimmy" by Howard Rosenberg, *The Los Angeles Times*, Feb. 16, 1979.

246. *Superman: Serial to Cereal* by Gary Grossman, (c) 1977 Popular Library, New York, p. 171.

247. *Ibid.*, 227.

248. *Superman: The Complete History* by Les Daniels, (c) 1998 by DC Comics, published by Chronicle Books, San Francisco, CA, p. 131.

249. *Superman: Serial to Cereal* by Gary Grossman, (c) 1977 Popular Library, New York, p. 227–228.

250. *Ibid.*, 225–226.

251. *Ibid.*, 252–256.

252. "Children in Stores Visited by Superman," *The Los Angeles Times*, April 6, 1955.

253. Walter Ames, *The Los Angeles Times*, July 31, 1956.

254. "CBS May Sign Duff, A Producer," *New York Times*, Val Adams, Aug. 7, 1956.

255. *Superman: Serial to Cereal* by Gary Grossman, (c) 1977 Popular Library, New York, p. 84.

256. *Ibid.*, 274.

257. *Cult Movies Presents Superboy & Superpup: The Lost Videos* by Chuck Harter, (c) 1993 by Chuck Harter, published by Cult Movies, Hollywood, CA, p. 5.

258. *Superman on Television Tenth Anniversary Edition* by Michael Bifulco, (c) 1998 Michael Bifulco, published by Michael Bifulco, p. 163.

259. "TV Ratings 1951–1952" and "TV Ratings 1956–1957," www.classictvhits.com/tvratings/1951.htm and www.classictvhits.com/tvratings/1956.htm.

260. "Broadcasting Timeline," www.factmonster.com/ipka/AO151956.html.

261. *Cult Movies Presents Superboy & Superpup: The Lost Videos* by Chuck Harter, (c) 1993 by Chuck Harter, published by Cult Movies, Hollywood, CA, p. 25.

262. *Superman: Serial to Cereal* by Gary Grossman, (c) 1977 Popular Library, New York, p. 293.

263. *Variety*, Oct. 13, 1957.

264. *Superman: Serial to Cereal* by Gary Grossman, (c) 1977 Popular Library, New York, p. 298.

265. "The Week in Review," *The Los Angeles Times*, April 12, 1959, and "Notes on Our Cuffs-Top Secret" by the Section Staffers, *Ibid.*, May 10, 1959.

266. "It's a Bird! A plane! It's Reeves!—A Job for Superman? He Lets George Do It" by Ron Tepper, *The Los Angeles Times*, May 10, 1959.

267. *Ibid.*

268. *Truth, Justice & The American Way: The Life and Times of Noel Neill The Original Lois Lane, An Authorized Biography* by Larry Thomas Ward, (c) 2003 by Larry Thomas Ward, published by Nicholas Lawrence Books, p. 109.

269. "Anniversary for the Man of Steel: Death of First Superman Still a Supermystery," by Joseph Dalton, *The Los Angeles Herald Examiner*, Feb. 28, 1988.

270. "TV: Paar as Symptom" by Jack Gould, *The New York Times*, Sept. 11, 1961.

271. Interview with Steven Kirk, July 21, 2006.

272. Interview with Jack Larson, Dec. 11, 2006.

273. "Golly, Jimmy Olsen Writes Librettos!" by Anthony Tommasini, *The New York Times*, May 15, 1998.

274. "A Visit With Lois & Jimmy" by Howard Rosenberg, *The Los Angeles Times*, Feb. 16, 1979.

275. "Golly, Jimmy Olsen Writes Librettos!" by Anthony Tommasini, *The New York Times*, May 15, 1998.

276. "A Crush More Powerful Than a Locomotive" by Rip Rense, *The Los Angeles Times*, Aug. 12, 1994.

277. Interview with Steven Kirk, July 21, 2006.

Chapter 6

278. *Cult Movies Presents Superboy & Superpup: The Lost Videos* by Chuck Harter, (c) 1993 by Chuck Harter, published by Cult Movies, Hollywood, CA, p. 27.

279. *Ibid.*, 28.

280. *Ibid.*, 29.

281. *Ibid.*, 28.

282. *Ibid.*, 33.

283. "Mighty Mouse," *Don Markstein's Toonpedia*, http://www.toonpedia.com/mightym.htm.

284. *Ibid.*

285. *Ibid.*

286. "Underdog," *Don Markstein's Toonpedia*, http://www.toonpedia.com/underdog.htm.

287. *Cult Movies Presents Superboy & Superpup: The Lost Videos* by Chuck Harter, (c) 1993 by Chuck Harter, published by Cult Movies, Hollywood, CA, p. 71.

288. *Ibid.*

289. *Ibid.*

290. *Ibid.*, 72.

291. *Ibid.*

292. *Ibid.*, 73.

293. *Ibid.*, 74.

294. *Ibid.*

295. *Ibid.*, 79.

296. *Ibid.*

297. *Ibid.*, 81.

298. *Ibid.*, 82.

299. *The Best Plays of 1965–1966*, Edited by Otis L. Guernsey Jr., (c) 1966 by Dodd, Mead & Co., New York.

300. Deutsch, Didier C., *It's A Bird, It's A Plane, It's Superman* CD liner notes, (c) 1992 Sony Music Entertainment Inc. p. 9–10.

301. "That Bird is 'Superman'" by William Peper, *The New York World Telegram*, March 24, 1966.

302. "Rehearsals Begin—4 New Shows Due" by Stuart W. Little, *The New York Times*, Jan. 11, 1966.

303. "That Bird is 'Superman'" by William Peper, *The New York World Telegram*, March 24, 1966.

304. Deutsch, Didier C., *It's A Bird, It's A Plane, It's Superman* CD liner notes, (c) 1992 Sony Music Entertainment Inc., p. 10.

305. *Superman on Broadway* by Bob Holiday and Chuck Harter, (c) 2003 by Bob Holiday and Chuck Harter, published by Chuck Harter, p. 12.

306. *Ibid.*, 7.

307. *Ibid.*, 8.

308. *Ibid.*

309. *Ibid.*, 14–15.

310. *Ibid.*, 16.

311. *Ibid.*, 17.

312. "Superman Toils for Musical Role" by Sam Zolotow, *The New York Times*, Nov. 17, 1965.

313. "Superman! And Eligible!" *The New York Daily News*, June 2, 1966.

314. *Superman on Broadway* by Bob Holiday and Chuck Harter, (c) 2003 by Bob Holiday and Chuck Harter, published by Chuck Harter, p. 20.

315. *Ibid.*

316. *Ibid.*, 24.

317. "That Bird is 'Superman'" by William Peper, *The New York World Telegram*, March 24, 1966.

318. *Superman on Broadway* by Bob Holiday and Chuck Harter, (c) 2003 by Bob Holiday and Chuck Harter, published by Chuck Harter, p. 20.

319. "So I Said to Superman ..." by Joseph F. Lowry, *The Philadelphia Sunday Bulletin Magazine*, Feb. 6, 1966.

320. "Hal Prince Raps Philly as Tryout City; Local Critics 'Post-College Twerps'" by Tom Morse, *Weekly Variety*, April 6, 1966.

321. *Superman on Broadway* by Bob Holiday and Chuck Harter, (c) 2003 by Bob Holiday and Chuck Harter, published by Chuck Harter, p. 25.

322. "By The Way ... with Bill Henry," by Bill Henry, *The Los Angeles Times*, Oct. 2, 1952, p. A1.

323. *Superman on Broadway* by Bob Holiday and Chuck Harter, (c) 2003 by Bob Holiday and Chuck Harter, published by Chuck Harter, p. 21.

324. *Ibid.*, 47.

325. *Ibid.*, 26.

326. "'Superman' Plans Pricing Changes," *New York Herald Tribune*, Jan. 11, 1966.

327. *Superman on Broadway* by Bob Holiday and Chuck Harter, (c) 2003 by Bob Holiday and Chuck Harter, published by Chuck Harter, p. 28.

328. *Ibid.*, 51.

329. "Theater: 'It's a Bird ... It's a Plane ... It's Superman,' It's a Musical and It's Here" by Stanley Kauffmann, *The New York Times*, March 30, 1966.

330. "'Superman,' Airy, Merry" by Norman Nadel, *The New York World Telegram and Sun*, March 30, 1966.

331. "Stage Review: 'Superman' Is Camp And Mostly 'WHAM!'" by Whitney Bolton, *New York Morning Telegram*, March 31, 1966.

332. Deutsch, Didier C., *It's A Bird, It's A Plane, It's Superman* CD liner notes, (c) 1992 Sony Music Entertainment Inc., p. 12. .

333. "Broadway 'Superman': It's a Bird" by Cecil Smith, *The Los Angeles Times*, April 1, 1966, p. C1.

334. *Superman on Broadway* by Bob Holiday and Chuck Harter, (c) 2003 by Bob Holiday and Chuck Harter, published by Chuck Harter, p. 47.

335. *Ibid.*, 62.

336. *Ibid.*, 74.

337. *Ibid.*, 78.

338. *Ibid.*, 80.

339. Deutsch, Didier C., *It's A Bird, It's A Plane, It's Superman* CD liner notes, (c) 1992 Sony Music Entertainment Inc., p. 13.

340. "Obscure Videos: Two By Strouse" by Ken Mandelbaum, *Broadway.com*, http://www.broadway.com/gen/Buzz_Story.aspx?ci-518409.

341. *Superman on Broadway* by Bob Holiday and Chuck Harter, (c) 2003 by Bob Holiday and Chuck Harter, published by Chuck Harter, p. 81.

342. "Nominees Chosen for Tony Awards" by Douglas Watt, *The Los Angeles Times*, June 1, 1966, p. C13.

343. *Superman on Broadway* by Bob Holiday and Chuck Harter, (c) 2003 by Bob Holiday and Chuck Harter, published by Chuck Harter, p. 81, 83.

344. *Ibid.*, 85.

345. "'Superman' Opens Week's Run in Park" by Myles Standish, *St. Louis Post Dispatch*, July 5, 1967.

346. *Ibid.*

347. "'Man of Steel' Looks the Part: 10,026 Enjoy 'Superman' Exploits, Songs at Muny" by Frank Hunter, *St. Louis Globe Democrat*, July 5, 1967.

348. *Superman on Broadway* by Bob Holiday and Chuck Harter, (c) 2003 by Bob Holiday and Chuck Harter, published by Chuck Harter, p. 76.

349. *Ibid.*, 97.

350. *Ibid.*, 99.

351. http://www.imdb.com/name/nm0612239/bio.

352. "Obscure Videos: Two By Strouse" by Ken Mandelbaum, http://www.broadway.com/gen/Buzz_Story.aspx?ci-518409.

353. "Theater: Superman as Dimwit in 1966 Parable" by Stephen Holden, *The New York Times*, June 20, 1992.

354. http://www.broadway.com/gen/Buzz_Story.aspx?ci=518409.

355. "It's Got Possibilities" by Peter Filichia, *Theater Mania*, Oct. 2, 2006, http://www.theatermania.com/peterfilichia/permalinks/2006/10/02/Its-Got-Possibilities/.

356. "New Superman Series Slated," *The Los Angeles Times*, Dec. 30, 1965.

357. http://www.danhausertrek.com/Animated-Series/Filmation.html#Show66.

358. Grossman, Gary H., *Saturday Morning TV*, (c) 1981 by Gary Grossman, published by Dell Publishing Co., Inc., p. 363.

359. *Ibid.*

360. http://www.bcdb.com/cartoon_characters/25361-New_Adventures_of_Superman.html.

361. *Ibid.*

362. Grossman, Gary H., *Saturday Morning TV*, (c) 1981 by Gary Grossman, published by Dell Publishing Co., Inc., p. 363.

363. Interview with Casey Kasem, July 18, 2006.

364. http://www.bradyworld.com/episodes/kids.htm.

365. http://voices.fuzzy.com/actor.idc?actor_id=1875.

366. http://www.imdb.com/name/nm0840127/.

367. "Super Friends," *Wikipedia*, http://en.wikipedia.org/wiki/Superfriends.

368. http://www.bcdb.com/cartoons/Hanna-Barbera_Studios/S/Super_Friends/index.html.

369. Interview with Caroline & Sydney Croskery, July 27, 2006.

370. http://www.supermanhomepage.com/tv/tv.php?topic=cast-crew/danny-dark.

371. Interview with Casey Kasem, July 18, 2006.

372. *Ibid.*

373. Interview with Caroline & Sydney Croskery, July 27, 2006.

374. Interview with Casey Kasem, July 18, 2006.

375. Interview with Caroline & Sydney Croskery, July 27, 2006.

376. *Ibid.*

377. *Ibid.*

Chapter 7

378. Petrou, David Michael, *The Making of Superman: The Movie*, (c) 1978 David Michael Petrou, published by Warner Books, NY, p. 24.

379. "One-on-One Interview with Producer Ilya Salkind" by Barry M. Freiman, *SupermanHomepage.com*, June 30, 2006, http://www.supermanhomepage.com/movies/movies.php?topic=interview-salkind.

380. *Ibid.*

381. "A. Salkind Dead at 76" by Rex Wiener, *Variety*, March 18, 1997.

382. "The Salkind Heroes Wear Red and Fly High" by Sandra Salmans, *The New York Times*, July 17, 1983.

383. "Ilya Salkind Interview: Supergirl" conducted April 13, 2000 by Scott Michael Bosco,(c) 2000 Scott Michael Bosco, http://www.geocities.com/Hollywood/Palace/3454/ilyasupergirl.html.

384. "One-on-One Interview with Producer Ilya Salkind" by Barry M. Freiman, *SupermanHomepage.com*, June 30, 2006, http://www.supermanhomepage.com/movies/movies.php?topic=interview-salkind

385. *Ibid.*

386. *Ibid.*

387. *Ibid.*

388. "The Life and Exceedingly Hard Times of Superman" by Aljean Harmetz, *The New York Times*, June 14, 1981.

389. "One-on-One Interview with Producer Ilya Salkind" by Barry M. Freiman, *SupermanHomepage.com*, June 30, 2006, http://www.supermanhomepage.com/movies/movies.php?topic=interview-salkind.

390. Petrou, David Michael, *The Making of Superman: The Movie*, (c) 1978 David Michael Petrou, published by Warner Books, NY, p. 28.

391. "Yipes! 'Superman' Jackpot Goes Tilt! Or, Lawsuits, Litigation and the American Way," by Gregg Kilday, *The Los Angeles Herald Examiner*, January 28, 1979.

392. Petrou, David Michael, *The Making of Superman: The Movie*, (c) 1978 David Michael Petrou, published by Warner Books, NY, p. 28.

393. *Ibid.*, 30.

394. "One-on-One Interview with Producer Ilya Salkind" by Barry M. Freiman, *SupermanHomepage.com*, June 30, 2006, http://www.supermanhomepage.com/movies/movies.php?topic=interview-salkind

395. *Ibid.*

396. *Ibid.*

397. "Superman Makes the Leap to the Screen" by Roderick Mann, *The Los Angeles Times*, July 31, 1977.

398. "Dialogue on Film: David and Leslie Newman," by Don Shewey, *American Film*, July/August 1983, p. 24.

399. Interview with George MacDonald Fraser conducted by John Cork, August 22, 2006.

400. "Superstar Lineup for Superman" by Lee Grant, *The Los Angeles Times*, Jan. 15, 1977.

401. Interview with George MacDonald Fraser conducted by John Cork, August 22, 2006.

402. *Superman: The Complete History* by Les Daniels, (c) 1998 by DC Comics, published by Chronicle Books, San Francisco, CA, p. 147.

403. "Superstar Lineup for Superman" by Lee Grant, *The Los Angeles Times*, Jan. 15, 1977.

404. "Arnold" by Jennifer Seder, *The Los Angeles Times*, June 22, 1979.

405. "The Life and Exceedingly Hard Times of Superman" by Aljean Harmetz, *The New York Times*, June 14, 1981.

406. Petrou, David Michael, *The Making of Superman: The Movie*, (c) 1978 David Michael Petrou, published by Warner Books, NY, p. 38–39.

407. http://www.supermancinema.co.uk/special_features/interviews/ilya_salkind/ilya-stm.asp.

408. *Superman II* premiere program book.

409. "One-on-One Interview with Producer Ilya Salkind" by Barry M. Freiman, *SupermanHomepage.com*, June 30, 2006, http://www.supermanhomepage.com/movies/movies.php?topic=interview-salkind.

410. http://www.supermancinema.co.uk/special_features/interviews/ilya_salkind/ilya-stm.asp.

411. "One-on-One Interview with Producer Ilya Salkind" by Barry M. Freiman, *SupermanHomepage.com*, June 30, 2006, http://www.supermanhomepage.com/movies/movies.php?topic=interview-salkind.

412. "It's A Bird! It's A Plane! It's A Movie!" by Susan Heller Anderson, *The New York Times*, June 26, 1977.

413. "One-on-One Interview with Producer Ilya Salkind" by Barry M. Freiman, *SupermanHomepage.com*, June 30, 2006, http://www.supermanhomepage.com/movies/movies.php?topic=interview-salkind.

414. "It's A Bird! It's A Plane! It's A Movie!" by Susan Heller Anderson, *The New York Times*, June 26, 1977.

415. Reeve, Christopher, *Still Me*, (c) 1998 Cambria Productions Inc., published by Random House, NY, p. 198.

416. "Superman Makes the Leap to the Screen" by Roderick Mann, *The Los Angeles Times*, July 31, 1977.

417. Petrou, David Michael, *The Making of Superman: The Movie*, (c) 1978 David Michael Petrou, published by Warner Books, NY, p. 93.

418. Interview with George MacDonald Fraser conducted by John Cork, August 22, 2006.

419. "One-on-One Interview with Producer Ilya Salkind" by Barry M. Freiman, *SupermanHomepage.com*, June 30, 2006, http://www.supermanhomepage.com/movies/movies.php?topic=interview-salkind.

420. "Superstar Lineup for Superman" by Lee Grant, *The Los Angeles Times*, Jan. 15, 1977.

421. "Superman Makes the Leap to the Screen" by Roderick Mann, *The Los Angeles Times*, July 31, 1977.

422. *Ibid.*

423. "One-on-One Interview with Producer Ilya Salkind" by Barry M. Freiman, *SupermanHomepage.com*, June 30, 2006, http://www.supermanhomepage.com/movies/movies.php?topic=interview-salkind.

424. "Superman Makes the Leap to the Screen" by Roderick Mann, *The Los Angeles Times*, July 31, 1977.

425. Petrou, David Michael, *The Making of Superman: The Movie*, (c) 1978 David Michael Petrou, published by Warner Books, NY, p. 35.

426. "'Superman' Reeve a Born Flier," by Roderick Mann, *The Los Angeles Times*, Nov. 19, 1978.

427. "Interview" by Albin Krebs, *The New York Times*, March 6, 1977.

428. Reeve, Christopher, *Still Me*, (c) 1998 Cambria Productions Inc., published by Random House, NY, p. 197.

429. "On Krypton, Superman Might Have Been a Plumber" by Dan Carlinsky, *The New York Times*, Dec. 10, 1978.

430. "A Hero's Welcome: Christopher Reeve Simply Was Superman" by Katharine Whittemore, *American Movie Classics Magazine*, April 1998, p. 5.

431. "Interview" by Albin Krebs, *The New York Times*, March 6, 1977.

432. Reeve, Christopher, *Still Me*, (c) 1998 Cambria Productions Inc., published by Random House, NY, p. 173.

433. *Ibid.*, 185.

434. *Ibid.*, 186.

435. *Ibid.*, 188.

436. *Ibid.*, 189.

437. "Career is Airborne But He's Got Feet on the Ground" by Wayne Warga, *The Los Angeles Times*, July 15, 1979.

438. Petrou, David Michael, *The Making of Superman: The Movie*, (c) 1978 David Michael Petrou, published by Warner Books, NY, p. 44.

439. *Ibid.*, 69.

440. "It's A Bird! It's A Plane! It's A Movie!" by Susan Heller Anderson, *The New York Times*, June 26, 1977.

441. Petrou, David Michael, *The Making of Superman: The Movie*, (c) 1978 David Michael Petrou, published by Warner Books, NY, p. 48.

442. "A Nice Canadian Girl Grounds Superman" by Colin Dangaard, *Winnipeg Free Press*, Oct. 21, 1978.

443. Petrou, David Michael, *The Making of Superman: The Movie*, (c) 1978 David Michael Petrou, published by Warner Books, NY, p. 45.

444. "Superman Makes the Leap to the Screen" by Roderick Mann, *The Los Angeles Times*, July 31, 1977.

445. Reeve, Christopher, *Still Me*, (c) 1998 Cambria Productions Inc., published by Random House, NY, p. 198.

446. "Superman Makes the Leap to the Screen" by Roderick Mann, *The Los Angeles Times*, July 31, 1977.

447. "Ilya Salkind: Creative Producer" by Dharmesh, *SupermanCinema.com*, http://www.supermancinema.co.uk/special_features/interviews/ilya_salkind/ilya-stm.asp.

448. Petrou, David Michael, *The Making of Superman: The Movie*, (c) 1978 David Michael Petrou, published by Warner Books, NY, p. 101–102.

449. "Superman Makes the Leap to the Screen" by Roderick Mann, *The Los Angeles Times*, July 31, 1977.

450. "'Superman II' Wraps Shooting In London On High Note" by Simon Perry, *Daily Variety*, March 19, 1980.

451. "Superman Makes the Leap to the Screen" by Roderick Mann, *The Los Angeles Times*, July 31, 1977.

452. Reeve, Christopher, *Still Me*, (c) 1998 Cambria Productions Inc., published by Random House, NY, p. 198.

453. Petrou, David Michael, *The Making of Superman: The Movie*, (c) 1978 David Michael Petrou, published by Warner Books, NY, p. 101–102.

454. *Ibid.*, 122.

455. *Ibid.*, 126.

456. "Young Fan Has Role in 'Superman,'" *Oakland Tribune*, Aug. 8, 1977.

457. Petrou, David Michael, *The Making of Superman: The Movie*, (c) 1978 David Michael Petrou, published by Warner Books, NY, p. 133–135.

458. *Ibid.*, 139.

459. *Ibid.*, 148.

460. *Ibid.*, 152.

461. *Ibid.*, 157.

462. *Ibid.*, 162–163.

463. *Ibid.*, 166.

464. *Ibid.*, 175–178.

465. *Ibid.*, 182–183.

466. *Ibid.*, 183–184.

467. *Ibid.*, 184–185.

468. *Ibid.*, 188.

469. "'Superman' Reeve a Born Flier," by Roderick Mann, *The Los Angeles Times*, Nov. 19, 1978.

470. Petrou, David Michael, *The Making of Superman: The Movie*, (c) 1978 David Michael Petrou, published by Warner Books, NY, p. 203.

471. *Ibid.*, 204.

472. "Salkinds' Lucrative 'Superman' Films Also Costly And Litigious" by Todd McCarthy, *Variety*, July 8, 1987.

473. "'Superman': Leaping Tall Budgets" by Roderick Mann, *The Los Angeles Times*, April 6, 1978.

474. "The Life and Exceedingly Hard Times of Superman" by Aljean Harmetz, *The New York Times*, June 14, 1981.

475. http://www.supermancinema.co.uk/special_features/interviews/ilya_salkind/ilya-stm.asp.

476. "The Marketing of Superman and His Paraphernalia" by Aljean Harmetz, *The New York Times*, June 21, 1981.

477. "Newsmakers: Too Bad, Lois–Clark's Seeing Eunice," *The Los Angeles Times*, Nov. 21, 1978.

478. http://www.supermancinema.co.uk/special_features/interviews/ilya_salkind/ilya-stm.asp.

479. "Yipes! 'Superman' Jackpot Goes Tilt! Or, Lawsuits, Litigation and the American Way," by Gregg Kilday, *The Los Angeles Herald Examiner*, January 28, 1979.

480. "Salkinds' Lucrative 'Superman' Films Also Costly And Litigious" by Todd McCarthy, *Variety*, July 8, 1987.

481. "Yipes! 'Superman' Jackpot Goes Tilt! Or, Lawsuits, Litigation and the American Way," by Gregg Kilday, *The Los Angeles Herald Examiner*, January 28, 1979.

482. "The Salkind Heroes Wear Red and Fly High" by Sandra Salmans, *The New York Times*, July 17, 1983.

483. "The Life and Exceedingly Hard Times of Superman" by Aljean Harmetz, *The New York Times*, June 14, 1981.

484. "Future Events: Superstuff" by Lillian Bellison, *The New York Times*, Dec. 3, 1978.

485. "'Superman' Road Show For the Special Olympics Rolls Into New York," by Judy Klemesrud, *The New York Times*, Dec. 12, 1978.

486. "'Superman' L.A. Opening Will Benefit the Special Olympics," *The Los Angeles Times*, July 22, 1978.

487. "Screen: It's a Bird, It's a Plane, It's a Movie!" by Vincent Canby, *The New York Times*, Dec. 15, 1978.

488. "Critic At Large: Man of Steel, Feat of Clay" by Charles Champlin, *The Los Angeles Times*, Dec. 15, 1978.

489. "Supeman" by James Harwood, *Variety*, Dec. 13, 1978.

490. http://www.imdb.com/title/tt0078346/business.

491. "Salkinds' Lucrative 'Superman' Films Also Costly And Litigious," by Todd McCarthy, *Weekly Variety*, July 8, 1987.

492. "Superman Gears Up For Success," by Dick Kleiner, *The Frederick (MD) News-Post*, Dec. 15, 1978.

493. *Ibid.*

494. Reeve, Christopher, *Still Me*, (c) 1998 Cambria Productions Inc., published by Random House, NY, p. 201.

495. "Up, Up, and Awaaay!!!" by Otto Friedrich, *TIME* magazine, March 14, 1988.

496. Reeve, Christopher, *Still Me*, (c) 1998 Cambria Productions Inc., published by Random House, NY, p. 201.

497. "They're Standing In Line for Christopher Reeve" by Roderick Mann, *The Los Angeles Times*, April 13, 1980.

498. "Reeve Shaking Off His Superman Image" by Aljean Harmetz, *The New York Times*, Aug. 20, 1979.

499. "Somewhere in Time Review" by Betsy Mahon, *The Christopher Reeve Homepage*, http://www.chrisreevehomepage.com/m-sit.html.

500. "Reeve Shaking Off His Superman Image" by Aljean Harmetz, *The New York Times*, Aug. 20, 1979.

501. "'Superman' Sequel: Flying in the Soup" by Roderick Mann, *The Los Angeles Times*, March 20, 1979.

502. "Late Flashes Re 'Superman II' Pic," *Daily Variety*, March 21, 1979.

503. "One-on-One Interview with Producer Ilya Salkind" by Barry M. Freiman, *SupermanHomepage.com*, June 30, 2006, http://www.supermanhomepage.com/movies/movies.php?topic=interview-salkind.

504. "'Superman 2' May Fall From Sky If Work Sked Not Met" by Dale Pollock, *Daily Variety*, January, 1979.

505. "Richard Lester Once Again Best Bet For 'Superman 2' Director," *Daily Variety*, July 19, 1979.

506. Interview with George MacDonald Fraser conducted by John Cork, August 22, 2006.

507. "Reeve Peace With Salkinds Lacking Confirming Word," *Daily Variety*, April 4, 1979.

508. "'Superman' Sequel: Flying in the Soup" by Roderick Mann, *The Los Angeles Times*, March 20, 1979.

509. "Reeve Shaking Off His Superman Image" by Aljean Harmetz, *The New York Times*, Aug. 20, 1979.

510. "'Superman' Sequel: Flying in the Soup" by Roderick Mann, *The Los Angeles Times*, March 20, 1979.

511. "Richard Lester Once Again Best Bet For 'Superman 2' Director," *Daily Variety*, July 19, 1979.

512. "Superman, Take Three" by Karen Stabiner, *Moviegoer*, June, 1983, p. 8.

513. Reeve, Christopher, *Still Me*, (c) 1998 Cambria Productions Inc., published by Random House, NY, p. 202.

514. "'Superman 2' On Launching Pad" by Roderick Mann, *The Los Angeles, Times*, Oct. 9, 1979.

515. *Ibid.*

516. *Ibid.*

517. "They're Standing In Line for Christopher Reeve" by Roderick Mann, *The Los Angeles Times*, April 13, 1980.

518. "One-on-One Interview with Producer Ilya Salkind" by Barry M. Freiman, *SupermanHomepage.com*, June 30, 2006, http://www.supermanhomepage.com/movies/movies.php?topic=interview-salkind.

519. "'Superman's' Battle of the Red Ink" by Roderick Mann, *The Los Angeles Times*, May 27, 1980.

520. "'Superman 2' On Launching Pad" by Roderick Mann, *The Los Angeles, Times*, Oct. 9, 1979.

521. "They're Standing In Line for Christopher

Reeve" by Roderick Mann, *The Los Angeles Times*, April 13, 1980.

522. Reeve, Christopher, *Still Me*, (c) 1998 Cambria Productions Inc., published by Random House, NY, p. 207.

523. "'Superman II' Double the Pleasure of Original" by Steve Fogarty, *Elyria, Ohio Chronicle-Telegram*, June 26, 1981.

524. "They're Standing In Line for Christopher Reeve" by Roderick Mann, *The Los Angeles Times*, April 13, 1980.

525. "'Superman's' Battle of the Red Ink" by Roderick Mann, *The Los Angeles Times*, May 27, 1980.

526. "'Superman II' Wraps Shooting In London On High Note" by Simon Perry, *Daily Variety*, March 19, 1980.

527. "One-on-One Interview with Producer Ilya Salkind" by Barry M. Freiman, *SupermanHomepage.com*, June 30, 2006, http://www.supermanhomepage.com/movies/movies.php?topic=interview-salkind.

528. "When Does A Creative Idea Become Intellectual Property" by Tamar Lewin, *The New York Times*, March 27, 1983.

529. "They're Standing In Line for Christopher Reeve" by Roderick Mann, *The Los Angeles Times*, April 13, 1980.

530. "Reeve Doesn't Worry About Being 'Superman' Forever" by Joan E. Vadeboncoeur, *Syracuse Herald-Journal*, June 1, 1981.

531. "The Marketing of Superman and His Paraphernalia" by Aljean Harmetz, *The New York Times*, June 21, 1981.

532. "The Life and Exceedingly Hard Times of Superman" by Aljean Harmetz, *The New York Times*, June 14, 1981.

533. "'Superman II': A Human Touch to the Invincible" by Sheila Benson, *The Los Angeles Times*, June 18, 1981.

534. "Screen: 'Superman II' Is Full of Tricks," by Janet Maslin, *The New York Times*, June 19, 1981.

535. "Canadian Kidder Works Both Sides of the Border" by Roderick Mann, *The Los Angeles Times*, Nov. 18, 1982.

536. "'Superman II' Double the Pleasure of Original" by Steve Fogarty, *Elyria, Ohio Chronicle-Telegram*, June 26, 1981.

537. "Salkinds' Lucrative 'Superman' Films Also Costly And Litigious," by Todd McCarthy, *Weekly Variety*, July 8, 1987.

538. "The Marketing of Superman and His Paraphernalia" by Aljean Harmetz, *The New York Times*, June 21, 1981.

539. "'Protect Children Act' Aims to Ban Cigarette Deals in Films" by Myron Levin, *The Los Angeles Times*, March 8, 1989.

540. "Salkinds Settle Brando, Puzo 'Superman' Suits" by Al Delugach, *The Los Angeles Times*, April 6, 1982.

541. "The Salkind Heroes Wear Red and Fly High" by Sandra Salmans, *The New York Times*, July 17, 1983.

542. "One-on-One Interview with Producer Ilya Salkind" by Barry M. Freiman, *SupermanHomepage.com*, June 30, 2006, http://www.supermanhomepage.com/movies/movies.php?topic=interview-salkind.

543. "Dialogue on Film: David and Leslie Newman," by Don Shewey, *American Film*, July/August 1983, p. 24.

544. "Superman, Take Three" by Karen Stabiner, *Moviegoer*, June, 1983, p. 8.

545. *Superman III* Presskit, (c) 1983 Warner Bros.

546. "Dialogue on Film: David and Leslie Newman," by Don Shewey, *American Film*, July/August 1983, p. 24.

547. *Superman III* Presskit, (c) 1983 Warner Bros.

548. "Success Holds No Laughter for Richard Pryor" by Stephen Farber, *The Los Angeles Times*, June 12, 1983.

549. "The Panning of 'Monsignor'—Reeve, Perry and Yablans Defend Film," by Dick Kleiner, *The Post, Frederick (MD)*, December 14, 1982.

550. "The Salkind Heroes Wear Red and Fly High" by Sandra Salmans, *The New York Times*, July 17, 1983.

551. "Canadian Kidder Works Both Sides of the Border" by Roderick Mann, *The Los Angeles Times*, Nov. 18, 1982.

552. *Superman III* Presskit, (c) 1983 Warner Bros.

553. *Ibid.*

554. "Dialogue on Film: David and Leslie Newman," by Don Shewey, *American Film*, July/August 1983, p. 24.

555. *Superman III* Presskit, (c) 1983 Warner Bros.

556. *Ibid.*,

557. *Ibid.*

558. "Superman 'Has Done Only Good,'" *The Lethbridge (Alberta) Herald*, June 17, 1983.

559. "Why Reeve Is Hanging Up His Cape," by Deborah Caulfield, *The Los Angeles Times*, June 20, 1983.

560. "Superman, Take Three" by Karen Stabiner, *Moviegoer*, June, 1983, p. 9.

561. *Ibid.*, 10.

562. "Success Holds No Laughter for Richard Pryor" by Stephen Farber, *The Los Angeles Times*, June 12, 1983.

563. "Superman, Take Three" by Karen Stabiner, *Moviegoer*, June, 1983, p. 10–11.

564. "The Longest Hottest Summer" by Dale Pollock, *The Los Angeles Times*, May 8, 1983.

565. "Politics and Fantasy: A Curious Combination" by Deborah Caulfield, *The Los Angeles Times*, June 15, 1983.

566. *Superman III* Presskit, (c) 1983 Warner Bros.

567. "Film: 'Superman III': Reeve Joined by Pryor" by Janet Maslin, *The New York Times*, June 17, 1983.

568. "Feet of Clay for Earthier Man of Steel" by Sheila Benson, *The Los Angeles Times*, June 17, 1983.

569. "Hustle—Albert Stroller (Robert Vaughn)," *Hustle* press release, January 1, 2004, from http://www.bbc.co.uk/pressoffice/pressreleases/stories/2004/01_january/20/hustle_robert_vaughn.shtml.

570. "'Man of Steel' Role Gets Rusty: Christopher Reeve Looks Forward to Life After 'Superman'" by Richard Freedman, *Syracuse Herald-Journal*, July 1, 1983.

571. Reeve, Christopher, *Still Me*, (c) 1998 Cambria Productions Inc., published by Random House, NY, p. 203.

572. "Salkinds' Lucrative 'Superman' Films Also Costly And Litigious," by Todd McCarthy, *Weekly Variety*, July 8, 1987.

573. "Superman 'Has Done Only Good,'" *The Lethbridge (Alberta) Herald*, June 17, 1983.

574. "Why Reeve Is Hanging Up His Cape," by Deborah Caulfield, *The Los Angeles Times*, June 20, 1983.

575. "'Man of Steel' Role Gets Rusty: Christopher Reeve Looks Forward to Life After 'Superman'" by Richard Freedman, *Syracuse Herald-Journal*, July 1, 1983.

576. Reeve, Christopher, *Still Me*, (c) 1998 Cambria Productions Inc., published by Random House, NY, p. 213.

577. "Ilya Salkind Interview: Supergirl" conducted April 13, 2000 by Scott Michael Bosco,(c) 2000 Scott Michael Bosco, http://www.geocities.com/Hollywood/Palace/3454/ilyasupergirl.html.

578. "One-on-One Interview with Producer Ilya Salkind" by Barry M. Freiman, *SupermanHomepage.com*, June 30, 2006, http://www.supermanhomepage.com/movies/movies.php?topic=interview-salkind.

579. "Ilya Salkind Interview: Supergirl" conducted April 13, 2000 by Scott Michael Bosco,(c) 2000 Scott Michael Bosco, http://www.geocities.com/Hollywood/Palace/3454/ilyasupergirl.html.

580. "Jeannot Szwarc Interview: Supergirl" conducted November 27, 1999 by Scott Michael Bosco,(c) 1999 Scott Michael Bosco, http://www.geocities.com/hollywood/palace/3454/jeannotsupergirl.html.

581. "Ilya Salkind Interview: Supergirl" conducted April 13, 2000 by Scott Michael Bosco,(c) 2000 Scott Michael Bosco, http://www.geocities.com/Hollywood/Palace/3454/ilyasupergirl.html.

582. *Ibid.*

583. "Jeannot Szwarc Interview: Supergirl" conducted November 27, 1999 by Scott Michael Bosco,(c) 1999 Scott Michael Bosco, http://www.geocities.com/hollywood/palace/3454/jeannotsupergirl.html.

584. "The Salkind Heroes Wear Red and Fly High" by Sandra Salmans, *The New York Times*, July 17, 1983.

585. "One-on-One Interview with Producer Ilya Salkind" by Barry M. Freiman, *SupermanHomepage.com*, June 30, 2006, http://www.supermanhomepage.com/movies/movies.php?topic=interview-salkind.

586. "'She-roes' Are Made, Not Born" by Roderick Mann, *The Los Angeles Times*, June 19, 1983.

587. "One-on-One Interview with Producer Ilya Salkind" by Barry M. Freiman, *SupermanHomepage.com*, June 30, 2006, http://www.supermanhomepage.com/movies/movies.php?topic=interview-salkind.

588. "Jeannot Szwarc Interview: Supergirl" conducted November 27, 1999 by Scott Michael Bosco,(c) 1999 Scott Michael Bosco, http://www.geocities.com/hollywood/palace/3454/jeannotsupergirl.html.

589. *Ibid.*

590. "One-on-One Interview with Producer Ilya Salkind" by Barry M. Freiman, *SupermanHomepage.com*, June 30, 2006, http://www.supermanhomepage.com/movies/movies.php?topic=interview-salkind.

591. "Jeannot Szwarc Interview: Supergirl" conducted November 27, 1999 by Scott Michael Bosco,(c) 1999 Scott Michael Bosco, http://www.geocities.com/hollywood/palace/3454/jeannotsupergirl.html.

592. *Ibid.*

593. "The Screen: Helen Slater as 'Supergirl'" by Janet Maslin, *The New York Times*, Nov. 22, 1984.

594. "Supergirl" by Rogert Ebert, *The Chicago Sun-Times*, Jan. 1, 1984.

595. "Salkinds' Lucrative 'Superman' Films Also Costly And Litigious," by Todd McCarthy, *Weekly Variety*, July 8, 1987.

596. "... And the Adventures of Superboy" by David McDonnell and Daniel Dickholtz, *Comics Scene # 5*, September 1988.

597. "Cannon Films: The Life, Death and Resurrection" by Patrick Runkle, *Cannonfilms.com*, http://www.cannonfilms.com/cannon2.htm.

598. "Cannon Buys The Rights to Future 'Superman' Films" by Ray Loynd, *Daily Variety*, June 19, 1985.

599. "... And the Adventures of Superboy" by David McDonnell and Daniel Dickholtz, *Comics Scene # 5*, September 1988.

600. "Cannon Acquires Rights to Produce 'Superman 4,'" *Cannon Publicity Dept. Press Release*, June 21, 1985.

601. "Cannon Cuts WB Deal, Gets More Financing" by James Greenberg, *Daily Variety*, July 29, 1985.

602. "At the Movies: Superman or Not, Choices are the Goal," by Lawrence Van Gelder, *The New York Times*, July 4, 1986.

603. *Superman IV* presskit.

604. "Clark Kent Tries On A New Role," *Northbrook (IL) Daily Herald*, UPI, March 22, 1987.

605. "Superman IV: The Quest for Peace: A History of the Production," by Ahem, *Superman Cinema* website, http://www.supermancinema.co.uk/superman4/s4_production/history/sr_history_page1.htm.

606. *Hollywood Reporter*, March 12, 1986.

607. Reeve, Christopher, *Still Me*, (c) 1998 Cambria Productions Inc., published by Random House, NY, p. 224–225.

608. "Clark Kent Tries On A New Role," *Northbrook (IL) Daily Herald*, UPI, March 22, 1987.

609. "Reeve to Fly Again As Filming of 'Superman IV' Gets Underway" by Matt Wolf, *The Gettysburg Times*, Jan. 9, 1987.

610. "Superman IV: Reeve Assists Screenplay," *Screen International*, March 1, 1986.

611. Reeve, Christopher, *Still Me*, (c) 1998 Cambria Productions Inc., published by Random House, NY, p. 227–228.

612. *Ibid.*, 224–225.

613. "Clark Kent Tries On A New Role," *Northbrook (IL) Daily Herald*, UPI, March 22, 1987.

614. "At the Movies: Superman or Not, Choices are the Goal," by Lawrence Van Gelder, *The New York Times*, July 4, 1986.

615. "Reeve to Fly Again As Filming of 'Superman IV' Gets Underway" by Matt Wolf, *The Gettysburg Times*, Jan. 9, 1987.

616. "The Sound, The Furie & 'Superman IV'" by Edward Gross, *Starlog # 123*, October 1987, p. 48.

617. "Superman IV: The Quest for Peace: A History of the Production," by Ahem, *Superman Cinema* website, http://www.supermancinema.co.uk/superman4/s4_production/history/sr_history_page1.htm.

618. "The Sound, The Furie & 'Superman IV'" by Edward Gross, *Starlog # 123*, October 1987, p. 48.

619. *Ibid.*

620. "Superman IV: The Quest for Peace: A History of the Production," by Ahem, *Superman Cinema* website, http://www.supermancinema.co.uk/superman4/s4_production/history/sr_history_page1.htm.

621. "At the Movies: Superman or Not, Choices are the Goal," by Lawrence Van Gelder, *The New York Times*, July 4, 1986.

622. "The Sound, The Furie & 'Superman IV'" by Edward Gross, *Starlog # 123*, October 1987, p. 49

623. *Ibid.*, 50.

624. *Ibid.*

625. "Superman IV: The Quest for Peace: A History of the Production," by Ahem, *Superman Cinema* website, http://www.supermancinema.co.uk/superman4/s4_production/history/sr_history_page1.htm.

626. *Ibid.*

627. Reeve, Christopher, *Still Me*, (c) 1998 Cambria Productions Inc., published by Random House, NY, p. 225.

628. *Ibid.*, 203.

629. "The Region," *The Los Angeles Times*, March 11, 1987.

630. "Man of Steal?" by Pat H. Broeske, *The Los Angeles Times*, April 26, 1987.

631. "Writers Vs. Reeve: 'Superman' Dispute Going To Trial" by Joseph McBride, *Daily Variety*, March 10, 1989.

632. "Judge Throws Out 'Superman' Suit" by Michael Martinez, *The Hollywood Reporter*, Oct. 24, 1990.

633. "Superman Summer," *The Hollywood Reporter*, Jan. 28, 1987.

634. "Superman IV: The Quest for Peace: A History of the Production," by Ahem, *Superman Cinema* website, http://www.supermancinema.co.uk/superman4/s4_production/history/sr_history_page1.htm.

635. "Movie: 'Superman IV: Quest for Peace'" by Janet Maslin, *The New York Times*, July 25, 1987.

636. "Superman IV: The Quest for Peace," *Variety Movie Guide*, (c) 1992 Variety Inc., published by Prentice Hall General Reference, NY, p. 587.

637. "Reeve to Fly Again As Filming of 'Superman IV' Gets Underway" by Matt Wolf, *The Gettysburg Times*, Jan. 9, 1987.

638. Reeve, Christopher, *Still Me*, (c) 1998 Cambria Productions Inc., published by Random House, NY, p. 228.

639. "Cannon Films: The Life, Death and Resurrection" by Patrick Runkle, *Cannonfilms.com*, http://www.cannonfilms.com/cannon2.htm.

640. Reeve, Christopher, *Still Me*, (c) 1998 Cambria Productions Inc., published by Random House, NY, p. 225.

641. "Biography: Christopher Reeve," *Chris Reeve Home Page*, http://www.chrisreevehomepage.com/biography.html.

642. Reeve, Christopher, *Still Me*, (c) 1998 Cambria Productions Inc., published by Random House, NY, p. 77.

643. "In Confidence," *Screen International*, April 7, 1990.

644. "One-on-One Interview with Producer Ilya Salkind" by Barry M. Freiman, *SupermanHomepage.com*, June 30, 2006, http://www.supermanhomepage.com/movies/movies.php?topic=interview-salkind.

645. "Hollywood Vine," *The Hollywood Reporter*, Nov. 27, 1991.

646. "Salkind's 'Superman' Shows Pre-Sales of Steel" by James Ulmer, *The Hollywood Reporter*, Oct. 27, 1992.

647. "Christopher Reeve's Most Famous Role? Guess Again—The Man of Steel is Better Known for 'Somewhere in Time'" by Dann Gire, *Northbrook (IL) Daily Herald*, Dec. 27, 1994.

648. "One-on-One Interview with Producer Ilya Salkind" by Barry M. Freiman, *SupermanHomepage.com*, June 30, 2006, http://www.supermanhomepage.com/movies/movies.php?topic=interview-salkind.

649. Reeve, Christopher, *Still Me*, (c) 1998 Cambria Productions Inc., published by Random House, NY, p. 94.

650. *Ibid.*, 232.

651. *Ibid.*, p. 7.

652. *Ibid.*, 14.

653. *Ibid.*, 8–15.

654. *Ibid.*, 14–19.

655. *Ibid.*, 21–22.

656. *Ibid.*, 32.

657. "Biography: Christopher Reeve," *Christopher Reeve Home Page*, http://www.chrisreevehomepage.com/biography.html.

658. *Ibid.*

659. Reeve, Christopher, *Still Me*, (c) 1998 Cambria Productions Inc., published by Random House, NY, p. 78.

660. "Biography: Christopher Reeve," *Christopher Reeve Home Page*, http://www.chrisreevehomepage.com/biography.html.

661. *Ibid.*

662. *Ibid.*

663. Reeve, Christopher, *Still Me*, (c) 1998 Cambria Productions Inc., published by Random House, NY, p. 273.

Chapter 8

664. "Superman Through the Ages: The End of History" by Peter Sanderson, *Fortress-of-Solitude.net*, excerpted from *Amazing Heroes* # 96, June, 1986, http://theages.superman.ws/History/end.php.

665. "TV Review; Superman At 50, A Special" by John O'Connor, *The New York Times*, Feb. 29, 1988.

666. "Beau Weaver," *Wikipedia*, http://en.wikipedia.org/wiki/Beau_Weaver.

667. "One-on-One Interview with Producer Ilya Salkind" by Barry M. Freiman, *SupermanHomepage.com*, June 30, 2006, http://www.supermanhomepage.com/movies/movies.php?topic=interview-salkind.

668. *Ibid.*

669. "... And the Adventures of Superboy" by David McDonnell and Daniel Dickholtz, *Comics Scene* # 5, September 1988.

670. "One-on-One Interview with Producer Ilya Salkind" by Barry M. Freiman, *SupermanHomepage.com*, June 30, 2006, http://www.supermanhomepage.com/movies/movies.php?topic=interview-salkind.

671. "... And the Adventures of Superboy" by David McDonnell and Daniel Dickholtz, *Comics Scene* # 5, September 1988.

672. "Interview With Stacy Haiduk" by Daniel Dickholtz, *Spectacular*, 1991, http://www.geocities.com/dmwc/.

673. *Ibid.*

674. "... And the Adventures of Superboy" by David McDonnell and Daniel Dickholtz, *Comics Scene* # 5, September 1988.

675. "Interview With Stacy Haiduk" by Daniel Dickholtz, *Spectacular*, 1991, http://www.geocities.com/dmwc/.

676. "One-on-One Interview with Producer Ilya Salkind" by Barry M. Freiman, *SupermanHomepage.com*, June 30, 2006, http://www.supermanhomepage.com/movies/movies.php?topic=interview-salkind.

677. "The Adventures of Superboy When He Was An Actor" by Edward Gross, *Comics Scene* # 6, February 1989.

678. "John Haymes Newton," *Superman Homepage*, http://www.supermanhomepage.com/tv/tv.php?topic=cast-crew/john-h-newton.

679. *Ibid.*

680. *Ibid.*

681. "... And the Adventures of Superboy" by David McDonnell and Daniel Dickholtz, *Comics Scene* # 5, September 1988.

682. *Ibid.*

683. "The Adventures of Superboy When He Was An Actor" by Edward Gross, *Comics Scene* # 6, February 1989.

684. *Ibid.*

685. *Ibid.*

686. "... And the Adventures of Superboy" by David McDonnell and Daniel Dickholtz, *Comics Scene* # 5, September 1988.

687. *Ibid.*

688. *Ibid.*

689. "John Haymes Newton," *Superman Homepage*, http://www.supermanhomepage.com/tv/tv.php?topic =cast-crew/john-h-newton.

690. "Behind the Scenes of Superboy," *Deluxe Format DC Books*, March 1990; http://www.geocities.com/dmwc/.

691. "One-on-One Interview with Producer Ilya Salkind" by Barry M. Freiman, *SupermanHomepage. com*, June 30, 2006, http://www.supermanhomepage. com/movies/movies.php?topic=interview-salkind.

692. "Interview With Stacy Haiduk" by Daniel Dickholtz, *Spectacular*, 1991, http://www.geocities.com/dmwc/.

693. "The Adventures of Superboy When He Was An Actor" by Edward Gross, *Comics Scene # 6*, February 1989.

694. "Behind the Camera: A Spotlight on Stacy Haiduk," http://www.geocities.com/dmwc/.

695. "The Adventures of Superboy When He Was An Actor" by Edward Gross, *Comics Scene # 6*, February 1989.

696. *Ibid.*

697. "One-on-One Interview with Producer Ilya Salkind" by Barry M. Freiman, *SupermanHomepage. com*, June 30, 2006, http://www.supermanhomepage. com/movies/movies.php?topic=interview-salkind.

698. "The Adventures of Superboy When He Was An Actor" by Edward Gross, *Comics Scene # 6*, February 1989.

699. *Ibid.*

700. *Ibid.*

701. "One-on-One Interview with Producer Ilya Salkind" by Barry M. Freiman, *SupermanHomepage. com*, June 30, 2006, http://www.supermanhomepage. com/movies/movies.php?topic=interview-salkind.

702. "John Haymes Newton," *Superman Homepage*, http://www.supermanhomepage.com/tv/tv.php?topic=-cast-crew/john-h-newton.

703. "One-on-One Interview with Producer Ilya Salkind" by Barry M. Freiman, *SupermanHomepage. com*, June 30, 2006, http://www.supermanhomepage. com/movies/movies.php?topic=interview-salkind.

704. "Interview with Gerard Christopher" by Brian McKernan, *Superboy Home Page*, http://www.superboyhomepage.com/home.htm.

705. "Gerard Christopher Bio," *Superman Homepage*, http://www.superboyhomepage.com/home.htm.

706. *Ibid.*

707. *Ibid.*

708. *Ibid.*

709. "Interview With Stacy Haiduk" by Daniel Dickholtz, *Spectacular*, 1991, http://www.geocities.com/dmwc/

710. *Ibid.*

711. "Interview with Gerard Christopher" by Brian McKernan, *Superboy Home Page*, http://www.superboyhomepage.com/home.htm.

712. *Ibid.*

713. "One-on-One Interview with Producer Ilya Salkind" by Barry M. Freiman, *SupermanHomepage. com*, June 30, 2006, http://www.supermanhomepage. com/movies/movies.php?topic=interview-salkind.

714. "Behind the Scenes of Superboy," *Deluxe Format DC Books*, March 1990; http://www.geocities.com/dmwc/.

715. "Interview with Gerard Christopher" by Brian McKernan, *Superboy Home Page*, http://www.superboyhomepage.com/home.htm.

716. "Behind the Camera: A Spotlight on Stacy Haiduk," http://www.geocities.com/dmwc/.

717. "Interview With Stacy Haiduk" by Daniel Dickholtz, *Spectacular*, 1991, http://www.geocities.com/dmwc/.

718. "Gerard Christopher Bio," *Superman Homepage*, http://www.superboyhomepage.com/home.htm.

719. "Interview with Gerard Christopher" by Brian McKernan, *Superboy Home Page*, http://www.superboyhomepage.com/home.htm.

720. *Ibid.*

721. "Gerard Christopher Bio," *Superman Homepage*, http://www.superboyhomepage.com/home.htm

722. "One-on-One Interview with Producer Ilya Salkind" by Barry M. Freiman, *SupermanHomepage. com*, June 30, 2006, http://www.supermanhomepage. com/movies/movies.php?topic=interview-salkind.

723. "Superboy: The Series" by Doug Chambers, *DMWC's Superboy: The Series* website, http://www.geocities.com/dmwc.

724. "Interview with Gerard Christopher" by Brian McKernan, *Superboy Home Page*, http://www.superboyhomepage.com/home.htm.

725. *Ibid.*

726. "One-on-One Interview with Producer Ilya Salkind" by Barry M. Freiman, *SupermanHomepage. com*, June 30, 2006, http://www.supermanhomepage. com/movies/movies.php?topic=interview-salkind.

727. *Ibid.*

728. "Ilya Salkind's Siegel & Shuster," http://www.ilyasalkindcompany.com.

729. "One-on-One Interview with Producer Ilya Salkind" by Barry M. Freiman, *SupermanHomepage. com*, June 30, 2006, http://www.supermanhomepage. com/movies/movies.php?topic=interview-salkind.

730. *Ibid.*

731. "Dish: Thest Trio Eye 'Nurse'; 'Superman' May Fly" by Michael Fleming, *Variety*, Sept. 29, 1998.

Chapter 9

732. Lois & Clark: A Day in the Life of the Daily Planet" by Edward Gross & Mark A. Altman, *Not Of This Earth*, March 1994, Vol. 1, No. 2, p. 31–32.

733. *Ibid.*, 32

734. "Personality Parade" by Walter Scott, *Parade*, Dec. 25, 1994 and "In Step With(r) ... Teri Hatcher" by James Brady, *Parade*, April 16, 2006 and "Teri Hatcher," *The Superman Supersite*, http://www.supermansupersite. com/hatcher.html.

735. "Lady of the Lane" by Dan Glaister, *The Guardian*, February 14, 2005.

736. "Looking Good: Teri Hatcher" US, October 1993, p. 51.

737. "Super Chat" by Rick Marin, *TV Guide*, Nov. 6, 1993, p. 28.

738. "Interview with Gerard Christopher" by Brian McKernan, *Superboy Home Page*, http://www.superboyhomepage.com/home.htm

739. *Ibid.*

740. Interview with Kevin Sorbo, April 23, 2006.

741. "Lois & Clark: A Day in the Life of the Daily Planet" by Edward Gross & Mark A. Altman, *Not Of This Earth*, March 1994, Vol. 1, No. 2, p. 32.

742. "Dean Cain" *People*, May 9, 1994.

743. "One To Watch: Teri Hatcher" *Variety*, Aug. 30, 1993.

744. "Lois & Clark: A Day in the Life of the Daily Planet" by Edward Gross & Mark A. Altman, *Not Of This Earth*, March 1994, Vol. 1, No. 2, p. 32.

745. "Super Chat" by Rick Marin, *TV Guide*, Nov. 6, 1993, p. 28.

746. "Lois & Clark: A Day in the Life of the Daily Planet" by Edward Gross & Mark A. Altman, *Not of This Earth*, March 1994, Vol. 1, No. 2, p. 34.

747. "Dean Cain" by Brett Tam, *Yolk*, Summer 1995, p. 19.

748. "Cain, Able" by Michelle Tauber, *People*, Oct. 13, 2003, p. 80.

749. "Dean Cain Uncaped" by Joe Rhodes, *TV Guide*, July 22, 1995.

750. "Cain, Able" by Michelle Tauber, *People*, Oct. 13, 2003, p. 80.

751. "Superman Superceded" by Mark Olsen, *The Los Angeles Times*, May 22, 2005.

752. "Lois & Clark: A Day in the Life of the Daily Planet" by Edward Gross & Mark A. Altman, *Not of This Earth*, March 1994, Vol. 1, No. 2, p. 35.

753. "Lane Smith," *What A Character.com*, http://www.what-a-character.com/cgi-bin/display.cgi?id=982796316.

754. "Lane Smith Interview" by M.J. Simpson, *MJSimpson.co.uk*, http://www.mjsimpson.co.uk/interviews/lanesmith.html.

755. Ibid.

756. "The Final Problem" by Sir Arthur Conan Doyle, *The Memoirs of Sherlock Holmes*, 1893.

757. "John Shea Bio" by Russ Dimino, *Kryptonsite.com*, http://www.kryptonsite.com/loisclark/johnshea.htm.

758. Ibid.

759. "Interview: John Shea" by Kathie Huddleston, *SciFi.com*, http://www.scifi.com/sfw/issue256/interview.html.

760. "Lois & Clark: A Day in the Life of the Daily Planet" by Edward Gross & Mark A. Altman, *Not of This Earth*, March 1994, Vol. 1, No. 2, p. 35.

761. "Eddie Jones Bio" by Russ Dimino, *Kryptonsite.com*, http://www.kryptonsite.com/loisclark/eddiejones.htm.

762. "K Callan: Superman's Mother" by Michelle Erica Green, *LittleReview.com*, http://www.littlereview.com/getcritical/interviews/callan.htm.

763. "Tracy Scoggins Bio" by Russ Dimino, *Kryptonsite.com*, http://www.kryptonsite.com/loisclark/tracyscoggins.htm.

764. "Super Chat" by Rick Marin, *TV Guide*, Nov. 6, 1993, p. 29.

765. "Dean Cain" by Brett Tam, *Yolk*, Summer 1995, p. 70.

766. "Reader's Poll '96," TV Guide, Aug. 17–23, 1996, p. 16.

767. "Man and Superman" by Mark Morrison, *US*, January 1995, p. 78.

768. "Dean Cain" *People*, May 9, 1994.

769. "Looking Good: Teri Hatcher" *US*, October 1993, p. 51.

770. "Personality Parade" by Walter Scott, *Parade*, July 31, 1994.

771. "This Superman Aims To Keep His Feet Firmly On the Ground" by Tom Shales, *The Los Angeles Times*, Oct. 3, 1993, p. 9.

772. "Pebble Mill interviews Teri Hatcher," *BBC*, Friday, February 16, 1996, http://www.stack.nl/~boris/Teri/Text/pebble.txt.

773. "Super Chat" by Rick Marin, *TV Guide*, Nov. 6, 1993, p. 29.

774. "Classic Pinups," *People*, May 6, 1996.

775. "Lois & Clark: A Day in the Life of the Daily Planet" by Edward Gross & Mark A. Altman, *Not Of This Earth*, March 1994, Vol. 1, No. 2, p. 31.

776. "ABC Opens Fire on Vid Violence" by Brian Lowry, *Variety*, June 11, 1993.

777. "Lois & Clark: A Day in the Life of the Daily Planet" by Edward Gross & Mark A. Altman, *Not Of This Earth*, March 1994, Vol. 1, No. 2, p. 29.

778. "Singer Leaps to Lofty 'Lois' Slot" by Brian Lowry, *Variety*, Nov. 2, 1993.

779. "Super Chat" by Rick Marin, *TV Guide*, Nov. 6, 1993, p. 29.

780. "Lois & Clark: A Day in the Life of the Daily Planet" by Edward Gross & Mark A. Altman, *Not Of This Earth*, March 1994, Vol. 1, No. 2, p. 34.

781. "Look! Up On the Screen! It's ... Lois Lane?" by Rip Rense, *The Los Angeles Times*, April 5, 1994.

782. "Lane Smith Interview" by M.J. Simpson, *MJSimpson.co.uk*, http://www.mjsimpson.co.uk/interviews/lanesmith.html.

783. "Dean Cain" by Brett Tam, *Yolk*, Summer 1995, p. 55, 70.

784. "John Shea Bio" by Russ Dimino, *Kryptonsite.com*, http://www.kryptonsite.com/loisclark/johnshea.htm.

785. "Interview: John Shea" by Kathie Huddleston, *SciFi.com*, http://www.scifi.com/sfw/issue256/interview.html.

786. "Justin Whalin Bio" by Russ Dimino, *Kryptonsite.com*, http://www.kryptonsite.com/loisclark/justinwhalin.htm.

787. "Lane Smith Interview" by M.J. Simpson, *MJSimpson.co.uk*, http://www.mjsimpson.co.uk/interviews/lanesmith.html.

788. "Justin Whalin Bio" by Russ Dimino, *Kryptonsite.com*, http://www.kryptonsite.com/loisclark/justinwhalin.htm.

789. "Dean Cain" by Brett Tam, *Yolk*, Summer 1995, p. 55.

790. "This Cain is Able" by Susan King, *Los Angeles Times*, July 30, 1994, p. 7.

791. "Dean Cain" by Brett Tam, *Yolk*, Summer 1995, p. 70.

792. "This Cain is Able" by Susan King, *Los Angeles Times*, July 30, 1994, p. 7.

793. "Lois in the Fast Land" by Tim Cogshell, *Entertainment Today*, May 17–23, 1996 p. 4.

794. "Brad Buckner" Interview by Craig Byrne, *Kryptonsite.com*, August 2003, http://www.kryptonsite.com/loisclark/buckner2003.htm.

795. TV Guide, May 10–16, 1997.

796. "K Callan: Superman's Mother" by Michelle Erica Green, *LittleReview.com*, http://www.littlereview.com/getcritical/interviews/callan.htm.

797. "Clark Can't," People, 10/09/2000.

798. "Meanwhile, Back at the Ranch ..." by Eric Messinger, *InStyle*, Oct. 2003, p. 419.

799. "Crash Landing," *People*, Sept. 7, 1998, p. 86.

800. "Cain, Able" by Michelle Tauber, *People*, Oct. 13, 2003, p. 80.

801. "Split," People, March 24, 2003.

802. "Desperately Happy To Be Back," by John Harlow, *The London Sunday Times*, Feb. 13, 2005.

803. "Hatcher Takes a Stand" by Marc Peyser, *Newsweek*, March 20, 2006.

Chapter 10

804. "Postscript," Vanity Fair, June 2006, p. 50.

805. "The Ever-Lovin' Blue-Eyed Timm!" by Brian Saner Lamken, *Comicology #1*, Spring 2000, http://www.twomorrows.com/comicology/articles/01timm.html

806. *Ibid.*

807. *Ibid.*

808. *Ibid.*

809. *Ibid.*

810. *Ibid.*

811. *Ibid.*

812. *Ibid.*

813. *Ibid.*

814. *Ibid.*

815. *Ibid.*

816. "An Interview with Paul Dini" by Jayme Lynn Blaschke, Revolution Science Fiction website, (c) Jayme Lynn Blaschke, August 14, 2004, http://www.revolutionsf.com/article.html?id=2352.

817. "Superman: Learning To Fly," *Superman: The Animated Series Vol. 1, Disc 2*, (c) 2004 Warner Bros. Entertainment Inc. .

818. "The Ever-Lovin' Blue-Eyed Timm!" by Brian Saner Lamken, *Comicology #1*, Spring 2000, http://www.twomorrows.com/comicology/articles/01timm.html.

819. "Being Batman Can Be Grunt Work" by Brian Lowry, *The Los Angeles Times*, Dec. 8, 2002, pg. E.30.

820. *Ibid.*

821. "Superman: Learning To Fly," *Superman: The Animated Series Vol. 1, Disc 2*, (c) 2004 Warner Bros. Entertainment Inc.

822. "The Ever-Lovin' Blue-Eyed Timm!" by Brian Saner Lamken, *Comicology #1*, Spring 2000, http://www.twomorrows.com/comicology/articles/01timm.html.

823. "Superman: Learning To Fly," *Superman: The Animated Series Vol. 1, Disc 2*, (c) 2004 Warner Bros. Entertainment Inc.

824. "Tim Daly Biography," *Wikipedia*, http://en.wikipedia.org/wiki/Timothy_Daly

825. *Ibid.*

826. *Ibid.*

827. "Tim Daly: What's Next for *The Nine*'s Nick?" by Matt Webb Mitovich, *TVGuide.com*, Oct. 11, 2006.

828. "Lois Long: An Interview with Actress Dana Delany" by Barry Freiman, *The Superman Homepage*, June 14, 2005, http://www.supermanhomepage.com/tv/tv.php?topic=interviews/dana-delany.

829. *Ibid.*

830. *Ibid.*

831. *Ibid.*

832. *Ibid.*

833. *Ibid.*

834. *Ibid.*

835. "Being Batman Can Be Grunt Work" by Brian Lowry, *The Los Angeles Times*, Dec. 8, 2002, pg. E.30

836. *Ibid.*

837. "Lois Long: An Interview with Actress Dana Delany" by Barry Freiman, *The Superman Homepage*, June 14, 2005, http://www.supermanhomepage.com/tv/tv.php?topic=interviews/dana-delany.

838. "Being Batman Can Be Grunt Work" by Brian Lowry, *The Los Angeles Times*, Dec. 8, 2002, pg. E.30.

839. "A Little Piece of Trivia," *Superman: The Animated Series Vol. 1, Disc 1*, (c) 2004 Warner Bros. Entertainment Inc.

840. *Ibid.*

841. *Ibid.*

842. "Lois Long: An Interview with Actress Dana Delany" by Barry Freiman, *The Superman Homepage*, June 14, 2005, http://www.supermanhomepage.com/tv/tv.php?topic=interviews/dana-delany

843. "Justice League's Superman," The Comics Continuum, March 20, 2003, http://www.comicscontinuum.com/stories/0303/20/index.htm

844. *Ibid.*

845. *Ibid.*

846. "Lois Long: An Interview with Actress Dana Delany" by Barry Freiman, *The Superman Homepage*, June 14, 2005, http://www.supermanhomepage.com/tv/tv.php?topic=interviews/dana-delany

847. "Tim Daly Biography," *Wikipedia*, http://en.wikipedia.org/wiki/Timothy_Daly.

Chapter 11

848. "First look: 'Smallville'" by Michael Schneider, *Variety*, Sept. 13, 2001.

849. "For Whom Production Tolls" by Michael Freeman, *Electronic Media*, Aug. 12, 2002.

850. "Leaps tall ratings" by Rick Kissell, *Variety*, Jan. 25, 2006.

851. "KryptonSite Interview #1 With Smallville Executive Producer Alfred Gough" by Craig Byrne, *KryptonSite.com*, April 6, 2001.

852. *Ibid.*

853. *Ibid.*

854. "Leaps tall ratings" by Rick Kissell, *Variety*, Jan. 25, 2006.

855. "KryptonSite Interview #1 With Smallville Executive Producer Alfred Gough" by Craig Byrne, *KryptonSite.com*, April 6, 2001.

856. "Leaps tall ratings" by Rick Kissell, *Variety*, Jan. 25, 2006.

857. "KryptonSite Interview #1 With Smallville Executive Producer Alfred Gough" by Craig Byrne, *KryptonSite.com*, April 6, 2001.

858. "Undressed for Success?" by Geoff Boucher, *The Los Angeles Times*, Aug. 28, 2001.

859. "In Touch With Their Inner Teen" by Kathy Tracy, *Variety*, Jan. 25, 2006.

860. *Ibid.*

861. "Teen Clark Kent Slipping Into Phone Booth at WB" by Josef Adalian and Michael Schneider, *Variety*, Sept. 19, 2000.

862. "Kristin Kreuk" by Jill Feiwell, *Variety*, Feb. 5, 2001.

863. "KryptonSite Interview #1 With Smallville Executive Producer Alfred Gough" by Craig Byrne, *KryptonSite.com*, April 6, 2001.

864. "The Clark & Lana Files: Gene Geter Talks To Kristin Kreuk" by Gene Geter, *KryptonSite.com*, May 13, 2003.

865. "Kristin Kreuk Bio" by Craig Byrne, *Kryptonsite.com*.

866. "The Clark & Lana Files: Gene Geter Talks To Kristin Kreuk" by Gene Geter, *KryptonSite.com*, May 13, 2003.

867. "Smallville Interview" by Haggay Kraus, *MichaelRosenbaum.com*, April 2002.

868. "KryptonSite Interview #1 With Smallville Exec-

utive Producer Alfred Gough" by Craig Byrne, *Krypton-Site.com*, April 6, 2001.

869. "Super-Natural: A Conversation With Tom Welling" by Robert Falconer, Hollywood North Report, May 30, 2005, http://www.hollwoodnorthreport.com/article.php?Article=1323.

870. "Tom Welling Bio" by Craig Byrne, *Krypton Site.com*.

871. "'Smallville' Hero Started Out as a Model" by Taylor Michaels, *Zap2It, Star-Herald TV Week*, March 20, 2004.

872. "Tom Welling Bio" by Craig Byrne, *Krypton Site.com*.

873. "Smallville Interview" by Haggay Kraus, *MichaelRosenbaum.com*, April 2002.

874. "He's Not Super, He's Special" by John Levesque, *Seattle-Post Intelligencer*, July 19, 2001.

875. "Smallville Interview" by Haggay Kraus, *MichaelRosenbaum.com*, April 2002.

876. "A Special Guest on 'Smallville'" by Frazier Moore, *Associated Press, The Elyria, Ohio Chronicle-Telegram*, February 25, 2003.

877. "Indiana Man Helps Re-invent Superman Story" by Marc D. Allan, *The Indianapolis Star*, July 17, 2001.

878. *Ibid.*

879. "KryptonSite Interview #1 With Smallville Executive Producer Alfred Gough" by Craig Byrne, *KryptonSite.com*, April 6, 2001.

880. "Deadly Disciples" by Tara DiLullo, *Smallville Magazine*, July/August 2006, p. 63.

881. "Indiana Man Helps Re-invent Superman Story" by Marc D. Allan, *The Indianapolis Star*, July 17, 2001.

882. "Smallville Interview" by Haggay Kraus, *MichaelRosenbaum.com*, April 2002.

883. *Ibid.*

884. "Michael Rosenbaum Bio" by Craig Byrne, *Kryptonsite.com*.

885. "Smallville Interview" by Haggay Kraus, *MichaelRosenbaum.com*, April 2002.

886. "Without Tights or Flights, Smallville's Second Season Continues to Soar" by Patrick Lee, *Science Fiction Weekly*, March 2003.

887. "Indiana Man Helps Re-invent Superman Story" by Marc D. Allan, *The Indianapolis Star*, July 17, 2001.

888. "Without Tights or Flights, Smallville's Second Season Continues to Soar" by Patrick Lee, *Science Fiction Weekly*, March 2003.

889. "John Glover Bio" by Craig Byrne, *KryptonSite.com*.

890. "Other Worlds" by Kate O'Hare, *Zap2it, The Dominion Post*, Feb. 16–22, 2003.

891. "Without Tights or Flights, Smallville's Second Season Continues to Soar" by Patrick Lee, *Science Fiction Weekly*, March 200.

892. "Other Worlds" by Kate O'Hare, *Zap2it, The Dominion Post*, Feb. 16–22, 2003

893. *Ibid.*

894. *Ibid.*,

895. "Raising a Hero" by Janice Rhoshalle Littlejohn, *The Los Angeles Times*, Oct. 21, 2001.

896. "KryptonSite Interview #1 With Smallville Executive Producer Alfred Gough" by Craig Byrne, *KryptonSite.com*, April 6, 2001.

897. "He's Not Super, He's Special" by John Levesque, *Seattle-Post Intelligencer*, July 19, 2001.

898. "John Schneider of *Smallville* Interview" by Daniel Robert Epstein, *Sci-fi/Fantasy*, Fall 2004.

899. "John Schneider Bio" by Craig Byrne, *Krypton Site.com*.

900. *Ibid.*

901. "John Schneider of *Smallville* Interview" by Daniel Robert Epstein, *Sci-fi/Fantasy*, Fall 2004.

902. "Jeph Loeb Talks 'Insurgence'" by Craig Byrne, *KryptonSite.com*, December 2002.

903. "KryptonSite Interview #1 With Smallville Executive Producer Alfred Gough" by Craig Byrne, *Krypton-Site.com*, April 6, 2001.

904. "Sam Jones III Bio" by Craig Byrne, *Krypton Site.com*.

905. "Allison Mack Bio" by Craig Byrne, *Krypton Site.com*.

906. "KryptonSite Interview #1 With Smallville Executive Producer Alfred Gough" by Craig Byrne, *Krypton-Site.com*, April 6, 2001.

907. "Indiana Man Helps Re-invent Superman Story" by Marc D. Allan, *The Indianapolis Star*, July 17, 2001.

908. "Teen Clark Kent Slipping Into Phone Booth at WB" by Josef Adalian and Michael Schneider, *Variety*, Sept. 19, 2000.

909. "Exclusive Preview: Smallville" by Edward Gross, *Retrovision*, http:www.retrovisionmag.com/smallville.htm

910. *Ibid.*

911. *Ibid.*

912. "Smallville Interview" by Haggay Kraus, *MichaelRosenbaum.com*, April 2002.

913. "Smallville (TV Series)," *Wikipedia*, http://en.wikipedia.org/wiki/Smallville_(TV_series).

914. "Indiana Man Helps Re-invent Superman Story" by Marc D. Allan, *The Indianapolis Star*, July 17, 2001.

915. "Smallville: The definitive WB" by Addie Morfoot, *Variety*, Jan. 20, 2005.

916. *Ibid.*

917. "Rosenbaum Enjoys Playing 'Lex,' The Bad Boy on 'Smallville' Series" by Terry Morrow, Scripps Howard News Service, April 25, 2004.

918. "Super writers, WBTV staying in 'Smallville'" by Josef Adalian, *Variety*, March 25, 2003.

919. "Curiosidades sobre Smallville" by Mariano Bayona Estradera, *smallville.cinecin.com/otramartha.htm*, 2004.

920. "Annette O'Toole Bio" by Craig Byrne, *Krypton Site.com*.

921. "Jeph Loeb Talks 'Insurgence'" by Craig Byrne, *KryptonSite.com*, December 2002.

922. "'Smallville' bow super for the WB" by Rick Kissell, *Variety*, Oct. 17, 2001.

923. "'Smallville' gets super order" by Josef Adalian, *Variety*, Oct. 24, 2001.

924. "In Step With Kristin Kreuk" by James Brady, *Parade*, June 9, 2002.

925. "Christopher Reeve Joins 'Smallville' in a Guest Role" by Frazier Moore, *TV Times*, Feb. 22, 2003.

926. "KryptonSite Interview #1 With Smallville Executive Producer Alfred Gough" by Craig Byrne, *Krypton-Site.com*, April 6, 2001.

927. "Other Worlds" by Kate O'Hare, *Zap2it, The Dominion Post*, Feb. 16–22, 2003.

928. *Ibid.*

929. "*Smallville*'s Dr. Bryce: Emmanuelle Vaugier" by Ted Weiland, *KryptonSite.com*, December 2002.

930. "A Special Guest on 'Smallville'" by Frazier Moore, *Associated Press, The Elyria, Ohio Chronicle-Telegram*, February 25, 2003.

931. "Without Tights or Flights, Smallville's Second Season Continues to Soar" by Patrick Lee, *Science Fiction Weekly*, March 2003.

932. "A Special Guest on 'Smallville'" by Frazier Moore, *Associated Press, The Elyria, Ohio Chronicle-Telegram*, February 25, 2003.

933. "AOL synergies for 'Smallville' CD" by Phil Gallo, *Variety*, Jan. 20, 2003.
934. "Superman Reeve will guest on 'Smallville'" by Michael Schneider, *Variety*, Jan. 6, 2003.
935. "Without Tights or Flights, Smallville's Second Season Continues to Soar" by Patrick Lee, *Science Fiction Weekly*, March 2003.
936. "Jeph Loeb Talks About 'Legacy'" by Craig Byrne, *KryptonSite.com*, December 2002.
937. "Save Me (Remy Zero song), *Wikipedia*, http://en.wikipedia.org/wiki/Save_Me_(Remy_Zero_song).
938. "AOL synergies for 'Smallville' CD" by Phil Gallo, *Variety*, Jan. 20, 2003.
939. "Jeph Loeb Talks About 'Legacy'" by Craig Byrne, *KryptonSite.com*, December 2002.
940. "Super writers, WBTV staying in 'Smallville'" by Josef Adalian, *Variety*, March 25, 2003.
941. *Ibid.*
942. "Mark Verheiden Talks About 'Perry'" by Craig Byrne, *KryptonSite.com*
943. *Ibid.*
944. *Ibid.*
945. *Ibid.*
946. "KryptonSite Interview With *Smallville* Executive Producer Alfred Gough" by Craig Byrne, *KryptonSite.com*, Sept. 10, 2004
947. *Ibid.*
948. "Erica Durance Bio" by Craig Byrne, *KrytonSite.com*.
949. *Ibid.*
950. "KryptonSite Interview With *Smallville* Executive Producer Alfred Gough" by Craig Byrne, *KryptonSite.com*, Sept. 10, 2004
951. *Ibid.*
952. "Smallville: The definitive WB" by Addie Morfoot, *Variety*, Jan. 20, 2005.
953. "Alfred Gough Interview" by Bill Radford, *The Gazette*, Sept. 21, 2006.
954. "Leaps tall ratings" by Rick Kissell, *Variety*, Jan. 25, 2006.
955. *Ibid.*
956. *Ibid.*
957. "Frog gets into swim of things: WB's 'Smallville' living large" by Rick Kissell, *Variety*, Oct. 23, 2005.
958. "WB Dives Into 'Aquaman': Frog Turns DC Comics Hero Into Primetime Star" by Josef Adalian, *Variety*, Nov. 13, 2005.
959. *Ibid.*
960. "The Year in Review" by Craig Byrne, *Smallville Magazine*, July/August 2006, p. 11.
961. "John Schneider Bio" by Craig Byrne, *KryptonSite.com*.
962. "The Year in Review" by Craig Byrne, *Smallville Magazine*, July/August 2006, p. 11.
963. "Will the Senator From Smallville Please Rise" by Jay Bobbin, *Zap2it.com*, April 13, 2006 .
964. "Lex Luthor Played By Michael Rosenbaum" by Bryan Cairns, *Smallville Magazine*, July/August 2006, p. 39.
965. "Five Talking" by Ian Spelling, *Smallville Magazine*, July/August 2006, p. 87.
966. "Alfred Gough Interview" by Bill Radford, *The Gazette*, Sept. 21, 2006.
967. "Breaking News," *The Futon Critic*, www.thefutoncritic.com/news.aspx?id=20061003cw01, Oct. 4, 2006.
968. "Leaps tall ratings" by Rick Kissell, *Variety*, Jan. 25, 2006.
969. "Michael Rosenbaum Bio" by Craig Byrne, *Kryptonsite.com*.
970. "Rosenbaum Enjoys Playing 'Lex,' The Bad Boy on 'Smallville' Series" by Terry Morrow, *Scripps Howard News Service*, April 25, 2004.
971. "The Clark & Lana Files: Gene Geter Talks To Kristin Kreuk" by Gene Geter, *KryptonSite.com*, May 13, 2003.
972. "Without Tights or Flights, Smallville's Second Season Continues to Soar" by Patrick Lee, *Science Fiction Weekly*, March 2003.
973. "Alfred Gough Interview" by Bill Radford, *The Gazette*, Sept. 21, 2006.
974. "Five Talking" by Ian Spelling, *Smallville Magazine*, July/August 2006, p. 90.

Chapter 12

975. "Brave new world for summer tie-ins" by Gail Schiller, *Reuters*, May 30, 2006.
976. *Superman: The Complete History* by Les Daniels, (c) 1998 by DC Comics, published by Chronicle Books, San Francisco, CA, p. 47.
977. Interview with Peter Lupus, May 16, 2006.
978. Interview with Denny Miller, 2004.
979. "Truth, Justice and the American (Express) Way" by Jackson King, *JimHillMedia.com*, May 20, 2004, http://jimhillmedia.com/blogs/jackson_king/archive/2004/05/20/1124.aspx.
980. "American Express Campaign Includes Television Commercials for Online Advertisements" by Ed Martin, *Mediavillage.com*, April 13, 2004.
981. "Commercial Message" by Jim Nolt, *TAC, Jr.* #16, January 5, 1998, http://www.jimnolt.com/amex.htm.
982. Interview with Jack Larson, December 11, 2006.
983. *Ibid.*
984. *Ibid.*
985. "Commercial Message" by Jim Nolt, *TAC, Jr.* #16, January 5, 1998, http://www.jimnolt.com/amex.htm.
986. *Ibid.*
987. *Jerry Seinfeld: The Entire Domain* by Kathleen Tracy, Birch Lane Press, 1998.
988. "Truth, Justice and the American (Express) Way" by Jackson King, *JimHillMedia.com*, May 20, 2004, http://jimhillmedia.com/blogs/jackson_king/archive/2004/05/20/1124.aspx.
989. Seinfeld and Superman Take On the Web: The Internet Becomes Home For Two of the Entertainment Industry's Strongest Stars" by Ken McGorry, *Post*, April, 2004.
990. *Ibid.*
991. "The Problem With Superman" by Lev Grossman, *TIME Magazine*, May 17, 2004.
992. Noel Neill interview March 16, 2005.
993. "Seinfeld-Superman Video Gets Results" by Janis Mara, *ClickZ News*, April 13, 2004, http://www.clickz.com/showPage.html?page=3339791.
994. "Seinfeld And Superman Return To The Web Today With Their Highly Anticipated Second Webisode," *AmericanExpress.com*, May 20, 2004, http://home3.americanexpress.com/corp/pc/2004/webisode2.asp.
995. *Ibid.*
996. Seinfeld and Superman Take On the Web: The Internet Becomes Home For Two of the Entertainment Industry's Strongest Stars" by Ken McGorry, *Post*, April, 2004.
997. "Seinfeld-Superman Video Gets Results" by Janis Mara, *ClickZ News*, April 13, 2004, http://www.clickz.com/showPage.html?page=3339791.

998. "Seinfeld And Superman Return To The Web Today With Their Highly Anticipated Second Webisode," *AmericanExpress.com*, May 20, 2004, http://home3.americanexpress.com/corp/pc/2004/webisode2.asp.

999. "The Adventures of Seinfeld and Superman Land on TBS," *TimeWarner.com*, June 9, 2004, http://www.timewarner.com/corp/newsroom/pr/0,20812,6704 51,00.html.

1000. "The Problem With Superman" by Lev Grossman, *TIME Magazine*, May 17, 2004.

1001. "It's a Bird! It's a Plane! It's a ... Webisode?" by Seth Stevenson, *Slate.com*, April 19, 2004, http://www.slate.com/id/2099152/.

1002. ADDY Award Show & Winners, *aaf.org*, http://www.aaf.org/awards/addys_silver_2005.html.

Chapter 13

1003. "The Disappearing Comic Book" by Glenn Gaslin, *The Los Angeles Times*, July 17, 2001.

1004. *Ibid.*

1005. "Superman Lives!–The Development Hell of an Unmade Film" by Edward Gross, *Cinemania*, http://www.mania.com/20991.html, May 5, 2000.

1006. "The Death of Superman," *Wikipedia*, http://en.wikipedia.org/wiki/Death_of_Superman#Audience_and_media_response.

1007. "B is for Big Book Sales" by Calvin Reid, *Publishers Weekly*, http://www.publishersweekly.com/article/CA6321550.html, April 4, 2006.

1008. "Superman Lives!–The Development Hell of an Unmade Film" by Edward Gross, *Cinemania*, http://www.mania.com/20991.html, May 5, 2000.

1009. "A Man-Child in Lotusland" by Rebecca Mead, *The New Yorker*, May 20, 2002.

1010. "Just for Variety" by Army Archerd, *Variety*, Sept. 18, 1996.

1011. "Steel" by Leonard Klady, *Variety*, Aug. 18, 1997.

1012. "Untitled" by Anita M. Busch, *Variety*, April 4, 1997.

1013. "Superman Lives!—The Development Hell of an Unmade Film" by Edward Gross, *Cinemania*, http://www.mania.com/20991.html, May 5, 2000.

1014. *Ibid.*

1015. "Superman Lives, Part 2: Writer Kevin Smith" by Edward Gross, *Cinemania*, http://www.mania.com/20991.html, May 12, 2000

1016. *Ibid.*

1017. *Ibid.*

1018. "WB Courting BK: Studio Hopes To Lock In 'Superman' Partner" by Anita M. Busch, *Variety*, Jan. 14, 1997.

1019. "Inside Moves: Cage, Man of Steel?" by Ted Johnson & Anita M. Busch, *Variety*, Feb. 21, 1997.

1020. "Nicolas Cage," *Wikipedia*, http://en.wikipedia.org/wiki/Nicolas_Cage.

1021. *Ibid.*

1022. "Superman Lives, Part 2: Writer Kevin Smith" by Edward Gross, *Cinemania*, http://www.mania.com/20991.html, May 12, 2000.

1023. "Untitled" by Anita M. Busch, *Variety*, April 4, 1997.

1024. "Superman Lives, Part 2: Writer Kevin Smith" by Edward Gross, *Cinemania*, http://www.mania.com/20991.html, May 12, 2000.

1025. *Ibid.*

1026. "WB, Burton Flirtin'" by Anita M. Busch, *Variety*, April 9, 1997.

1027. "Cage Wrestling Match" by Anita M. Busch, *Variety*, May 20, 1997.

1028. "'Superman' Un-Caged as 'Snake Eyes' Rolls" by Anita M. Busch, *Variety*, May 28, 1997.

1029. "'Superman' Restarted" by Anita M. Busch, *Variety*, July 11, 1997.

1030. "'Superman' Reskeds Start Date–Again" by Chris Petrikin & Paul Karon, *Variety*, October 8, 1997.

1031. "Dish: Spacey May Use Kryptonite; Scary TV" by Michael Fleming, *Variety*, March 3, 1998.

1032. "Kryptonite for WB's 'Superman'" by Paul Karon & Chris Petrikin, *Variety*, April 17, 1998.

1033. "WB to Roll Back Output, Cut Down on Event Pix" by Dan Cox, *Variety*, May 4, 1998.

1034. "Kryptonite for WB's 'Superman'" by Paul Karon & Chris Petrikin, *Variety*, April 17, 1998.

1035. "WB to Roll Back Output, Cut Down on Event Pix" by Dan Cox, *Variety*, May 4, 1998.

1036. "It's a Bird! It's a Plane! It's 'Superman' on Hold Again" by Amy Wallace, *The Los Angeles Times*, April 17, 1998.

1037. "Kryptonite for WB's 'Superman'" by Paul Karon & Chris Petrikin, *Variety*, April 17, 1998.

1038. "It's a Bird! It's a Plane! It's 'Superman' on Hold Again" by Amy Wallace, *The Los Angeles Times*, April 17, 1998.

1039. "WB 'Superman' Won't Be Flying By Summer '99" by Josh Chetwynd, *The Hollywood Reporter*, April 17, 1998.

1040. "Dish: Thesp Trio Eyes 'Nurse'; 'Superman' May Fly" by Michael Fleming, *Variety*, Sept. 29, 1998.

1041. "A Head of Its Time," by Christopher Nashawaty, *Entertainment Weekly*, November, 1999, p. 39+, reprinted in *Tim Burton Interviews*, edited by Kristian Fraga, (c) 2005 University Press of Mississippi, p. 130.

1042. "Dish: Thesp Trio Eyes 'Nurse'; 'Superman' May Fly" by Michael Fleming, *Variety*, Sept. 29, 1998.

1043. "WB Puts 'Superman' Into the Wisher Well" by Michael Fleming, *Variety*, June 30, 1999.

1044. "Attanasio 'Good' For Warners" by Michael Fleming, *Variety*, April 18, 2001.

1045. "WB Powers Up Super Team" by Dana Harris & Michael Fleming, *Variety*, Aug. 7, 2001.

1046. "WB Finds Helmer for 'Batman Vs. Superman'" by Dana Harris, *Variety*, July 8, 2002.

1047. "Petersen Teams With Warners on Superhero Epic" by Zorianna Kit, *The Hollywood Reporter*, July 9, 2002.

1048. "WB Finds Helmer for 'Batman Vs. Superman'" by Dana Harris, *Variety*, July 8, 2002.

1049. "WB's Man of Steel Flexing His Muscles" by Dana Harris & Claude Brodesser, *Variety*, Feb. 13, 2002.

1050. *Ibid.*

1051. "Superheroes Alter Script in Screen Clash of Titans" by Katty Kay, *The Times of London*, July 11, 2002.

1052. "Inside Move: Warners Superheroes Suit Up For Toy Wars" by David Bloom, *Variety*, July 14, 2002.

1053. "Petersen Marches Into 'Troy'" by Dana Harris, *Variety*, August 12, 2002.

1054. "Petersen On Trek to Attack 'Troy'" by Gregg Kilday, *The Hollywood Reporter*, Aug. 13, 2002.

1055. "Ratner Steels For Gig Helming 'Superman'" by Cathy Dunkley, *Variety*, Sept. 25, 2002.

1056. "Ratner Wearing Director's Cape for 'Superman'" by Zorianna Kitt, *The Hollywood Reporter*, Sept. 26, 2002.

1057. "Canceled Superman Films," *Wikipedia*, http://en.wikipedia.org/wiki/Superman_Lives.

1058. "Scribe Abrams Defuses Kryptonite Web Review" by Gregg Kilday, *The Hollywood Reporter*, Oct. 4, 2002.

1059. "New Team Tackles Tricky Tentpoles" by Cathy Dunkley, *Variety*, Oct. 6, 2002.

1060. "The Next Superman Could Be a Nobody" by Sam Lister, The Times of London, Dec. 23, 2002.

1061. "Ratner Cites Lack of Lead Actor for 'Superman' Exit" by Zorianna Kit, *The Hollywood Reporter*, March 20, 2003.

1062. "Dish: Ratner's Still WB's Choice for Man of Steel" by Michael Fleming, *Variety*, Jan. 30, 2003.

1063. "Inside Move: 'Superman' May Fly With Fresh Face" by Dana Harris & Claude Brodesser, *Variety*, Feb. 9, 2003.

1064. "Walker Won't Don Cape for WB" by Michael Fleming & Cathy Dunkley, *Variety*, March 13, 2003.

1065. "Inside Move: Dark 'Superman' Curse?" by Claude Brodesser, *Variety*, March 16, 2003.

1066. "Ratner Rushes Out of 'Superman'" by Dana Harris & Cathy Dunkley, *Variety*, March 19, 2003.

1067. "Ratner Cites Lack of Lead Actor for 'Superman' Exit" by Zorianna Kit, *The Hollywood Reporter*, March 20, 2003.

1068. "Ratner Rushes Out of 'Superman'" by Dana Harris & Cathy Dunkley, *Variety*, March 19, 2003.

1069. "Inside Move: New Dynamic for WB Duo" by Cathy Dunkley & Jonathan Bing, *Variety*, Sept. 7, 2003.

1070. "'Superman' Back in Orbit" by Michael Fleming & Cathy Dunkley, *Variety*, June 16, 2004.

1071. "High Noon: Super Pooper?" by Stella Papamichael, BBC, Nov. 10, 2003.

1072. "'Superman' Seeking New Helmer of Steel" by Jonathan Bing, *Variety*, July 11, 2004.

1073. "Back To The Launch Pad for 'Superman'" by John Horn, *The Los Angeles Times*, July 21, 2004.

1074. "Producing a 'Superman' Sequel Is Like Leaping Tall Buildings" by Laura M. Holson, *The New York Times*, July 22, 2004.

1075. "Producing a 'Superman' Sequel Is Like Leaping Tall Buildings" by Laura M. Holson, *The New York Times*, July 22, 2004.

1076. "Back To The Launch Pad for 'Superman'" by John Horn, *The Los Angeles Times*, July 21, 2004.

1077. "Producing a 'Superman' Sequel Is Like Leaping Tall Buildings" by Laura M. Holson, *The New York Times*, July 22, 2004.

1078. "Back To The Launch Pad for 'Superman'" by John Horn, *The Los Angeles Times*, July 21, 2004.

1079. "Producing a 'Superman' Sequel Is Like Leaping Tall Buildings" by Laura M. Holson, *The New York Times*, July 22, 2004.

1080. *Ibid.*

1081. "Super's On With 'X' Man" by Cathy Dunkley & Michael Fleming, *Variety*, July 18, 2005.

1082. "Bryan Singer: Superman Returns" by Daniel Restuccio, *Post Magazine*, June 2006, p. 16.

1083. "Warner Bros. Believe Bryan Singer is Superman," no author credited, *Empire* magazine, February 2006, p. 75.

1084. "Man of Steel: Bryan Singer Overcame a Path Paved With Kryptonite to Bring Back Superman" by Scott Foundas, *L.A. Weekly*, June 16–22, 2006, p. 43.

1085. *Ibid.*

1086. *Ibid.*

1087. "Comic book crusader: Bryan Singer," *BBC.com*, July 13, 2006.

1088. "Super Troupers" by Tim Swanson, *Premiere* magazine, February 2006, p. 59.

1089. "Greatest American Hero?" by Jeff Jensen, *Entertainment Weekly*, June 18, 2006.

1090. "Man of Steel: Bryan Singer Overcame a Path Paved With Kryptonite to Bring Back Superman" by Scott Foundas, *L.A. Weekly*, June 16–22, 2006, p. 43.

1091. "Returning the Man of Steel to the Silver Screen" by Michael Dougherty and Dan Harris, *scr(i)pt Magazine*, May/June 2006, p. 42–47.

1092. *Ibid.*

1093. "Greatest American Hero?" by Jeff Jensen, *Entertainment Weekly*, June 18, 2006.

1094. "Returning the Man of Steel to the Silver Screen" by Michael Dougherty and Dan Harris, *scr(i)pt Magazine*, May/June 2006, p. 42–47.

1095. *Ibid.*

1096. *Ibid.*

1097. "Greatest American Hero?" by Jeff Jensen, *Entertainment Weekly*, June 18, 2006.

1098. "Warner Bros. Believe Bryan Singer is Superman," no author credited, *Empire* magazine, February 2006, p. 75.

1099. "Greatest American Hero?" by Jeff Jensen, *Entertainment Weekly*, June 18, 2006.

1100. *Ibid.*

1101. *Ibid.*

1102. *Ibid.*

1103. *Ibid.*

1104. *Ibid.*

1105. "Caviezel Poised To Sign Superman Deal," *WENN*, Sept. 2, 2004.

1106. "Caviezel Wants Superman Role" *WENN*, Oct. 15, 2004.

1107. "Greatest American Hero?" by Jeff Jensen, *Entertainment Weekly*, June 18, 2006.

1108. "Interview with Bryan Singer," Harry Knowles, *Ain't It Cool News*, June 10th, 2006, http://www.aintitcool.com/display.cgi?id=23557.

1109. "Singer's Superman Ready To Don Cape" by Cathy Dunkley, *Variety*, October 20, 2004, p. 5.

1110. "Super Troupers" by Tim Swanson, *Premiere* magazine, February 2006, p. 59.

1111. "Interview: Brandon Routh 'Superman Returns'" by Paul Fischer, *DarkHorizons.com*, June 16, 2006.

1112. *Ibid.*

1113. *Ibid.*

1114. *Ibid.*

1115. "Laurie offering Super support with Marsden," *The Hollywood Reporter*, Jan. 13, 2005.

1116. "Huntington files story as Jimmy Olsen," *The Hollywood Reporter*, Jan. 31, 2005.

1117. "Interview with Bryan Singer," Harry Knowles, *Ain't It Cool News*, June 10th, 2006, http://www.aintitcool.com/display.cgi?id=23557.

1118. "Super Troupers" by Tim Swanson, *Premiere* magazine, February 2006, p. 59.

1119. "Greatest American Hero?" by Jeff Jensen, *Entertainment Weekly*, June 18, 2006.

1120. "On Screen: Eva Marie Saint on Life Between Brando's Babe and Superman's Mom" by Elliot V. Kotek, *Moving Pictures Magazine*, Volume 3, Issue 11, June/July 2006, p. 20.

1121. "Super Troupers" by Tim Swanson, *Premiere* magazine, February 2006, p. 59.

1122. "Superman is 'Greatest Superhero,'" *BBC.com*, Dec. 12, 2004.

1123. "The Genesis of Superman Returns" by Daniel Restuccio, *Post Magazine*, June 2006, p. 15.

1124. "Director's Chair: Bryan Singer: Superman Returns" by Daniel Restucio, *Post Magazine*, June 2006, p. 16.

1125. "The Genesis of Superman Returns" by Daniel Restuccio, *Post Magazine*, June 2006, p. 15.

1126. "Interview with Bryan Singer," Harry Knowles, *Ain't It Cool News*, June 10th, 2006, http://www.aintitcool.com/display.cgi?id=23557.

1127. "Director's Chair: Bryan Singer: Superman Returns" by Daniel Restucio, *Post Magazine*, June 2006, p. 16.

1128. "Interview with Bryan Singer," Harry Knowles, *Ain't It Cool News*, June 10th, 2006, http://www.aintitcool.com/display.cgi?id=23557.

1129. "New Superman actor tries on suit," *BBC.com*, April 22, 2005.

1130. "Interview with Bryan Singer," Harry Knowles, *Ain't It Cool News*, June 10th, 2006, http://www.aintitcool.com/display.cgi?id=23557.

1131. *Ibid.*

1132. "Greatest American Hero?" by Jeff Jensen, *Entertainment Weekly*, June 18, 2006.

1133. "Interview: Brandon Routh 'Superman Returns'" by Paul Fischer, *DarkHorizons.com*, June 16, 2006.

1134. *Ibid.*

1135. "Greatest American Hero?" by Jeff Jensen, *Entertainment Weekly*, June 18, 2006.

1136. *Ibid.*

1137. "Warner Bros. Believe Bryan Singer is Superman," no author credited, *Empire* magazine, February 2006, p. 75.

1138. *Ibid.*

1139. "Comic-Con falls in love with new Man of Steel," *The Hollywood Reporter*, July 18, 2005.

1140. "Warner Bros. Believe Bryan Singer is Superman," no author credited, *Empire* magazine, February 2006, p. 75.

1141. "Interview with Bryan Singer," Harry Knowles, *Ain't It Cool News*, June 10th, 2006, http://www.aintitcool.com/display.cgi?id=23557.

1142. "Warner Bros. Believe Bryan Singer is Superman," no author credited, *Empire* magazine, February 2006, p. 75.

1143. "Greatest American Hero?" by Jeff Jensen, *Entertainment Weekly*, June 18, 2006.

1144. "Warner Bros. Believe Bryan Singer is Superman," no author credited, *Empire* magazine, February 2006, p. 75.

1145. "Is the New Superman Meant to Be Jesus?" by Finlo Rohrer, *BBC News Magazine*, July 28, 2006.

1146. "'Superman Returns' to His Bodhisattva Career" by Shen Shi'an, *The Buddhist Channel*, July 17, 2006, http://www.buddhistchannel.tv/index.php?id=12,2919,0,0,1,0.

1147. "London Life: 'Superman Returns,'" *BBC.co.uk*, http://downloads.bbc.co.uk/worldservice/learning english/londonlife/scripts/londonlife_060719_superman.pdf.

1148. "Superman Returns" by Todd McCarthy, *Variety*, June 18, 2006.

1149. "Film review: Superman Returns" by Neil Smith, *BBC News*, July 13, 2006.

1150. "Movie Review: Earthbound Superhero; It's Fine in the Air, but the Cumbersome 'Superman Returns' Stumbles Over Its Story Line" by Kenneth Turan, *The Los Angeles Times*, June 27, 2006, pg. E.1.

1151. "The Current Cinema: Kryptology—'Superman Returns'" by Anthony Lane, *The New Yorker*, July 3, 2006, p. 87.

1152. "'Superman Returns' to Save Mankind From Its Sins" by Manohla Dargis, *The New York Times*, June 27, 2006.

1153. "Hero's Return Wows Original Director" by James Christie, *BBC.com*, July 13, 2006.

1154. "'Superman Returns' Flies High With $21 Mil Debut" by Brian Fuson, *BBC.com*, June 30, 2006.

1155. "'Superman' flies over box office," *Associated Press*, July 3, 2006.

Bibliography

This bibliography is subdivided into six parts: Books, Interviews, Magazine Articles, Newspaper Articles, Web Sites, Other Sources.

Books

Alyn, Kirk. *A Job for Superman.* Self-published, 1971.

Benton, Mike. *The Illustrated History—Superhero Comics of the Golden Age.* Dallas, TX: Taylor, 1992.

Bifulco, Michael. *Superman on Television Tenth Anniversary Edition.* Grand Rapids, MI: Michael Bifulco, 1998.

Conan Doyle, Arthur. *The Original Illustrated Strand Sherlock Holmes: The Complete Facsimile Edition,* New York: Mallard, 1990.

Daniels, Les. *Superman: The Complete History.* San Francisco, CA: Chronicle, 1998.

Dooley, Dennis, and Gary Engle, eds. *Superman at Fifty! The Persistence of a Legend!* Cleveland, OH: Octavia, 1987.

Fraga, Kristian, ed., *Tim Burton Interviews.* Jackson, MS: University Press of Mississippi, 2005.

Grossman, Gary. *Superman: Serial to Cereal.* New York: Popular Library, 1977.

Grossman, Gary H. *Saturday Morning TV.* New York: Dell, 1981.

Guernsey Jr., Otis L., ed., *The Best Plays of 1965-1966.* New York: Dodd, Mead, 1966.

Harter, Chuck. *Cult Movies Presents Superboy & Superpup: The Lost Videos.* Hollywood, CA: Cult Movies, 1993.

Holiday, Bob, and Chuck Harter. *Superman on Broadway.* Hollywood Hills, CA: Chuck Harter, 2003.

Jones, Gerard. *Men of Tomorrow: Geeks, Gangsters and the Birth of the Comic Book.* New York: Basic, 2004.

Kashner, Sam, and Nancy Schoenberger. *Hollywood Kryptonite: The Bulldog, The Lady and the Death of Superman.* New York: St. Martin's, 1996.

Petrou, David Michael. *The Making of Superman: The Movie.* New York: Warner, 1978.

Reeve, Christopher. *Still Me.* New York: Cambria Productions/Random House, 1998.

Tracy, Kathleen. *Jerry Seinfeld: The Entire Domain.* Birch Lane, 1998.

Variety. *Variety Movie Guide.* New York: Prentice Hall, 1992.

Ward, Larry Thomas. *Truth, Justice & The American Way: The Life and Times of Noel Neill, the Original Lois Lane.* Canon City, CO: Nicholas Lawrence, 2003.

Wolper, David L., with David Fisher. *Producer.* New York: Lisa Drew/Scribner, 2003.

Interviews

Collyer, Cynthia. April 25, 2006.

Croskery, Caroline. July 27, 2006.

Croskery, Sydney. July 27, 2006.

Fraser, George MacDonald (interview conducted by John Cork). August 22, 2006.

Hambrick, Jim. February 24, 2006.

Kasem, Casey. July 18, 2006.

Kirk, Steven. July 21, 2006.

Larson, Jack. December 11, 2006.

Lupus, Peter. May 16, 2006.

Miller, Denny. 2004.

Neill, Noel. March 16, 2005.

Magazine Articles

Brady, James. "In Step With ... Kristin Kreuk." *Parade,* June 9, 2002.

Brady, James. "In Step With ... Teri Hatcher." *Parade,* April 16, 2006.

Brown, B.B. "What A Super Guy! (And The Original, Too)." Source and date unknown, Academy of Motion Picture Arts & Sciences.

Byrne, Craig. "The Year in Review." *Smallville Magazine,* July/August 2006.

Cairns, Bryan. "Lex Luthor Played By Michael Rosenbaum." *Smallville Magazine,* July/August 2006.

"Clark Can't." *People,* 10/09/2000

"Classic Pinups." *People,* May 6, 1996.

Cogshell, Tim. "Lois in the Fast Land." *Entertainment Today*, May 17–23, 1996.

"Crash Landing." *People*, September 7, 1998.

"Dean Cain." *People*, May 9, 1994.

DiLullo, Tara. "Deadly Disciples." *Smallville Magazine*, July/August 2006.

Dougherty, Michael, and Dan Harris. "Returning the Man of Steel to the Silver Screen." *scr(i)pt Magazine*, May/June 2006.

Elliott, Jeff. "Kirk Alyn: Superman Remembers." *Starlog*, March, 1979.

Epstein, Daniel Robert. "John Schneider of *Smallville* Interview." *Sci-fi/Fantasy*, Fall 2004.

Freeman, Michael. "For Whom Production Tolls." *Electronic Media*, August 12, 2002.

Friedrich, Otto. "Up, Up, and Awaaay!!!" *Time*, March 14, 1988.

Gross, Edward. "The Adventures of Superboy When He Was An Actor." *Comics Scene #6*, February 1989.

Gross, Edward and Mark A. Altman. "Lois & Clark: A Day in the Life of the Daily Planet." *Not Of This Earth*, March 1994.

Gross, Edward. "The Sound, The Furie & 'Superman IV.'" *Starlog # 123*, October 1987.

Grossman, Lev. "The Problem With Superman." *Time*, May 17, 2004.

Jensen, Jeff. "Greatest American Hero?" *Entertainment Weekly*, June 18, 2006.

Kotek, Elliot V. "On Screen: Eva Marie Saint on Life Between Brando's Babe and Superman's Mom." *Moving Pictures Magazine*, Volume 3, Issue 11, June/July 2006.

Lane, Anthony. "The Current Cinema: Kryptology—'Superman Returns.'" *The New Yorker*, July 3, 2006.

Lee, Patrick. "Without Tights or Flights, Smallville's Second Season Continues to Soar." *Science Fiction Weekly*, March 2003.

"Looking Good: Teri Hatcher." *US*, October 1993.

McDonnell, David, and Daniel Dickholtz. " ... And the Adventures of Superboy." *Comics Scene #5*, September 1988.

McGorry, Ken. "Seinfeld and Superman Take On the Web: The Internet Becomes Home For Two of the Entertainment Industry's Strongest Stars." *Post*, April 2004.

Marin, Rick. "Super Chat." *TV Guide*, November 6, 1993.

Mead, Rebecca. "A Man-Child in Lotusland." *The New Yorker*, May 20, 2002.

Mesinger, Eric. "Meanwhile, Back at the Ranch ..." *InStyle*, October 2003.

Michaels, Taylor. "'Smallville' Hero Started Out as a Model." *Star-Herald TV Week*, March 20, 2004.

Moore, Frazier. "Christopher Reeve Joins 'Smallville' in a Guest Role." *TV Times*, February 22, 2003.

Morrison, Mark. "Man and Superman." *US*, January 1995.

Nashawaty, Christopher. "A Head of Its Time." *Entertainment Weekly*, November 1999.

O'Hare, Kate. "Other Worlds." *The Dominion Post*, February 16–22, 2003.

Peyser, Marc. "Hatcher Takes a Stand." *Newsweek*, March 20, 2006.

"Postscript." *Vanity Fair*, June 2006.

"Reader's Poll '96." *TV Guide*, August 17–23, 1996.

Restuccio, Daniel. "Director's Chair: Bryan Singer: Superman Returns." *Post*, June 2006.

Restuccio, Daniel. "The Genesis of Superman Returns." *Post*, June 2006.

Rhodes, Joe. "Dean Cain Uncaped." *TV Guide*, July 22, 1995.

Scott, Walter. "Personality Parade." *Parade*, December 25, 1994

Shewey, Don. "Dialogue on Film: David and Leslie Newman." *American Film*, July/August 1983.

Siegel, Jerry, "Lois Lane = Torchy Blane." *Time*, May 30, 1988.

Spelling, Ian. "Five Talking." *Smallville Magazine*, July/August 2006.

"Split." *People*, March 24, 2003.

Stabiner, Karen. "Superman, Take Three." *Moviegoer*, June, 1983.

Swanson, Tim. "Super Troupers." *Premiere*, February 2006.

Tam, Brett. "Dean Cain." *Yolk*, Summer 1995.

Tauber, Michelle. "Cain, Able." *People*, October 13, 2003.

Untitled. *TV Guide*, May 10–16, 1997.

"Warner Bros. Believe Bryan Singer is Superman." *Empire*, February 2006.

Whittemore, Katharine. "A Hero's Welcome: Christopher Reeve Simply Was Superman." *American Movie Classics Magazine*, April 1998.

Wilson, Patricia Ellsworth. "Present at the Creation of Superman and the Mole Men." *The Adventures Continue #14*, Jim Nolt, 1997.

Newspaper Articles

Adalian, Josef. "'Smallville' Gets Super Order." *Variety*, October 24, 2001.

_____. "Super writers, WBTV staying in 'Smallville.'" *Variety*, March 25, 2003.

_____. "WB Dives Into 'Aquaman': Frog Turns DC Comics Hero Into Primetime Star." *Variety*, November 13, 2005.

_____, and Michael Schneider. "Teen Clark Kent Slipping into Phone Booth at WB." *Variety*, September 19, 2000

Adams, Val. "CBS May Sign Duff, A Producer." *New York Times*, August 7, 1956.

Allan, Marc D. "Indiana Man Helps Re-invent Superman Story." *Indianapolis Star*, July 17, 2001.

Ames, Walter. "Superman George Reeves and Producers Disagree on New Television Deal." *Los Angeles Times*, September 27, 1954.

_____. "TV Tidbits." *Los Angeles Times*, June 27, 1951.

_____. Untitled. *Los Angeles Times*, March 29, 1953.

_____. Untitled. *Los Angeles Times*, July 6, 1953.

_____. Untitled. *Los Angeles Times*, July 31, 1956.

_____. "Video Actress Can't Convince Daughter." *Los Angeles Times*, March 29, 1953.

Anderson, Susan Heller. "It's a Bird! It's a Plane! It's a Movie!" *New York Times*, June 26, 1977.

Archerd, Army. "Just for Variety." *Variety*, September 18, 1996.

Associated Press. "Kirk Alyn Obituary." March 16, 1999.

Associated Press. "'Superman' Flies over Box Office." July 3, 2006.

Baker, Kathryn. "CBS Has Super Celebration for Man of Steel." Associated Press, February 28, 1988.

Bellison, Lillian. "Future Events: Superstuff." *New York Times*, December 3, 1978.

Benson, Sheila. "Feet of Clay for Earthier Man of Steel." *Los Angeles Times*, June 17, 1983.

_____. "'Superman II': A Human Touch to the Invincible." *Los Angeles Times*, June 18, 1981.

Bing, Jonathan. "'Superman' Seeking New Helmer of Steel." *Variety*, July 11, 2004.

Bloom, David. "Inside Move: Warners Superheroes Suit Up for Toy Wars." *Variety*, July 14, 2002.

Bolton, Whitney. "Stage Review: 'Superman' Is Camp And Mostly 'WHAM!'" *New York Morning Telegram*, March 31, 1966.

Boucher, Geoff. "Undressed for Success?" *Los Angeles Times*, August 28, 2001.

Brodesser, Claude. "Inside Move: Dark 'Superman' Curse?" *Variety*, March 16, 2003.

Broeske, Pat H. "Man of Steal?" *Los Angeles Times*, April 26, 1987.

Bruder, Leonard. "The Ubiquitous Mr. Collyer." *New York Times*, November 25, 1945.

Busch, Anita M. "Cage Wrestling Match." *Variety*, May 20, 1997.

_____. "'Superman' Restarted." *Variety*, July 11, 1997.

_____. "'Superman' Un-Caged as 'Snake Eyes' Rolls." *Variety*, May 28, 1997.

_____. Untitled. *Variety*, April 4, 1997.

_____. "WB, Burton Flirtin.'" *Variety*, April 9, 1997.

_____. "WB Courting BK: Studio Hopes To Lock In 'Superman' Partner." *Variety*, January 14, 1997.

Carlinsky, Dan. "On Krypton, Superman Might Have Been a Plumber." *New York Times*, December 10, 1978.

Caulfield, Deborah. "Politics and Fantasy: A Curious Combination." *Los Angeles Times*, June 15, 1983.

Caulfield, Deborah. "Why Reeve is Hanging Up His Cape." *Los Angeles Times*, June 20, 1983.

Champlin, Charles. "Critic at Large: Man of Steel, Feat of Clay." *Los Angeles Times*, December 15, 1978.

Chetwynd, Josh. "WB 'Superman' Won't Be Flying by Summer '99." *Hollywood Reporter*, April 17, 1998.

Colker, David. "A 'Superman' of the Literary Set." *Los Angeles Herald Examiner*, February 16, 1986.

Cox, Dan. "WB to Roll Back Output, Cut Down on Event Pix." *Variety*, May 4, 1998.

Daily Variety. "Late Flashes Re 'Superman II' Pic," March 21, 1979.

_____. "Richard Lester Once Again Best Bet For 'Superman 2' Director," July 19, 1979.

_____. "Reeve Peace with Salkinds Lacking Confirming Word," April 4, 1979.

Dalton, Joseph. "Anniversary for the Man of Steel: Death of First Superman Still a Supermystery." *Los Angeles Herald Examiner*, February 28, 1988.

Dangaard, Colin. "A Nice Canadian Girl Grounds Superman." *Winnipeg Free Press*, October 21, 1978.

Dargis, Manohla. "'Superman Returns' to Save Mankind From Its Sins." *New York Times*, June 27, 2006.

Delugach, Al. "Salkinds Settle Brando, Puzo 'Superman' Suits." *Los Angeles Times*, April 6, 1982.

Dunkley, Cathy. "New Team Tackles Tricky Tentpoles." *Variety*, October 6, 2002.

_____. "Ratner Steels for Gig Helming 'Superman.'" *Variety*, September 25, 2002.

_____. "Singer's Superman Ready to Don Cape." *Variety*, October 20, 2004.

_____, and Jonathan Bing. "Inside Move: New Dynamic for WB Duo." *Variety*, September 7, 2003.

_____, and Michael Fleming. "Super's on with 'X' Man." *Variety*, July 18, 2005.

Ebert, Roger. "Supergirl." *Chicago Sun-Times*, January 1, 1984.

Farber, Stephen. "Success Holds No Laughter for Richard Pryor." *Los Angeles Times*, June 12, 1983.

Feiwell, Jill. "Kristin Kreuk." *Variety*, February 5, 2001

Fleming, Michael. "Attanasio 'Good' For Warners." *Variety*, April 18, 2001.

_____. "Dish: Ratner's Still WB's Choice for Man of Steel." *Variety*, January 30, 2003.

_____. "Dish: Spacey May Use Kryptonite; Scary TV." *Variety*, March 3, 1998.

_____. "Dish: Thesp Trio Eyes 'Nurse'; 'Superman' May Fly." *Variety*, September 29, 1998.

_____. "WB Puts 'Superman' Into the Wisher Well." *Variety*, June 30, 1999.

_____ and Cathy Dunkley. "'Superman' Back in Orbit." *Variety*, June 16, 2004.

_____ and _____. "Walker Won't Don Cape for WB." *Variety*, March 13, 2003.

Fogarty, Steve. "'Superman II' Double the Pleasure of Original." *Elyria, Ohio Chronicle-Telegram*, June 26, 1981.

Foundas, Scott. "Man of Steel: Bryan Singer Overcame a Path Paved with Kryptonite to Bring Back Superman." *L.A. Weekly*, June 16–22, 2006.

Freedman, Richard. "'Man of Steel' Role Gets Rusty: Christopher Reeve Looks Forward to Life After 'Superman.'" *Syracuse Herald-Journal*, July 1, 1983.

Gallo, Phil. "AOL synergies for 'Smallville' CD." *Variety*, January 20, 2003.

Gaslin, Glenn. "The Disappearing Comic Book." *Los Angeles Times*, July 17, 2001.

Gire, Dann. "Christopher Reeve's Most Famous Role? Guess Again—The Man of Steel is Better Known for 'Somewhere in Time.'" *Northbrook (IL) Daily Herald*, December 27, 1994.

Glaister, Dan. "Lady of the Lane." *Guardian*, February 14, 2005.

Gould, Jack. "On the New Superman." *New York Times*, April 28, 1946.

_____. "TV: Paar as Symptom." *New York Times*, September 11, 1961.

Grant, Lee. "Superstar Lineup for Superman." *Los Angeles Times*, January 15, 1977.

Greenberg, James. "Cannon Cuts WB Deal, Gets More Financing." *Daily Variety*, July 29, 1985.

Harlow, John. "Desperately Happy To Be Back." *London Sunday Times*, February 13, 2005.

Harmetz, Aljean. "Reeve Shaking Off His Superman Image." *New York Times*, August 20, 1979.

_____. "The Life and Exceedingly Hard Times of Superman." *New York Times*, June 14, 1981.

_____. "The Marketing of Superman and His Paraphernalia." *New York Times*, June 21, 1981.

Harris, Dana. "Petersen Marches into 'Troy.'" *Variety*, August 12, 2002.

_____. "WB Finds Helmer for 'Batman Vs. Superman.'" *Variety*, July 8, 2002.

_____ and Cathy Dunkley. "Ratner Rushes Out of 'Superman.'" *Variety*, March 19, 2003.

_____ and Claude Brodesser. "Inside Move: 'Superman' May Fly With Fresh Face." *Variety*, February 9, 2003.

_____ and _____. "WB's Man of Steel Flexing His Muscles." *Variety*, February 13, 2002.

_____ and Michael Fleming. "WB Powers up Super Team." *Variety*, August 7, 2001.

Harvey, Steve. "Ex-Superman Has Place of His Own to Hang Up Suit." *Los Angeles Times*, March 28, 1974.

Harwood, James. "Superman." *Variety*, December 13, 1978.

Henry, Bill. "By The Way ... with Bill Henry." *Los Angeles Times*, October 2, 1952.

Holden, Stephen. "Theater: Superman as Dimwit in 1966 Parable." *New York Times*, June 20, 1992.

Hollywood Reporter. "Comic-Con Falls in Love with New Man of Steel," July 17, 2005.

_____. "Hollywood Vine," November 27, 1991.

_____. "Huntington Files Story as Jimmy Olsen," January 31, 2005.

_____. "Laurie Offering Super Support with Marsden," January 13, 2005.

_____. "Superman Summer," January 28, 1987.

_____. Untitled, March 12, 1986.

Holson, Laura M. "Producing a 'Superman' Sequel is Like Leaping Tall Buildings." *New York Times*, July 22, 2004.

Hopper, Hedda. "Looking at Hollywood." *Los Angeles Times*, March 8, 1943.

Horn, John. "Back to the Launch Pad for 'Superman.'" *Los Angeles Times*, July 21, 2004.

Hunter, Frank. " 'Man of Steel' Looks the Part: 10,026 Enjoy 'Superman' Exploits, Songs at Muny." *St. Louis Globe Democrat*, July 5, 1967.

"In Confidence." *Screen International*, April 7, 1990.

Johnson, Ted, and Anita M. Busch. "Inside Moves: Cage, Man of Steel?" *Variety*, February 21, 1997.

Karon, Paul, and Chris Petrikin. "Kryptonite for WB's 'Superman.'" *Variety*, April 17, 1998.

Kauffmann, Stanley. "Theater: 'It's A Bird ... It's a Plane ... It's Superman,' It's a Musical and It's Here." *New York Times*, March 30, 1966.

Kay, Katty. "Superheroes Alter Script in Screen Clash of Titans." *Times of London*, July 11, 2002.

Kilday, Gregg. "Petersen on Trek to Attack 'Troy.'" *Hollywood Reporter*, August 13, 2002.

_____. "Scribe Abrams Defuses Kryptonite Web Review." *Hollywood Reporter*, October 4, 2002.

_____. "Yipes! 'Superman' Jackpot Goes Tilt! Or, Lawsuits, Litigation and the American Way." *Los Angeles Herald Examiner*, January 28, 1979.

King, Susan. "This Cain is Able." *Los Angeles Times*, July 30, 1994.

Kissell, Rick. "Frog Gets Into Swim of Things: WB's 'Smallville' Living Large." *Variety*, October 23, 2005.

_____. "Leaps Tall Ratings." *Variety*, January 25, 2006.

_____. "'Smallville' Bow Super for the WB." *Variety*, October 17, 2001.

Kit, Zorianna. "Petersen Teams with Warners on Superhero Epic." *Hollywood Reporter*, July 9, 2002.

_____. "Ratner Cites Lack of Lead Actor for 'Superman' Exit." *Hollywood Reporter*, March 20, 2003.

_____. "Ratner Wearing Director's Cape for 'Superman.'" *Hollywood Reporter*, September 26, 2002.

Klady, Leonard. "Steel." *Variety*, August 18, 1997.

Kleiner, Dick. "The Panning of 'Monsignor'—Reeve, Perry and Yablans Defend Film." *The (Frederick, MD) Post*, December 14, 1982.

_____. "Superman Gears Up For Success." *The Frederick (MD) News-Post*, December 15, 1978.

Klemesrud, Judy. "'Superman' Road Show For the Special Olympics Rolls Into New York." *New York Times*, December 12, 1978.

Krebs, Albin. "Interview." *New York Times*, March 6, 1977.

Lethbridge (Alberta) Herald. "Superman 'Has Done Only Good,'" June 17, 1983.

Levesque, John. "He's Not Super, He's Special." *Seattle-Post Intelligencer*, July 19, 2001.

Levin, Myron. "'Protect Children Act' Aims to Ban Cigarette Deals in Films." *Los Angeles Times*, March 8, 1989.

Lewin, Tamar. "When Does a Creative Idea Become Intellectual Property?" *New York Times*, March 27, 1983.

Lister, Sam. "The Next Superman Could Be a Nobody." *Times of London*, December 23, 2002.

Little, Stuart W. "Rehearsals Begin—4 New Shows Due." *New York Times*, January 11, 1966.

Littlejohn, Janice Rhoshalle. "Raising a Hero." *Los Angeles Times*, October 21, 2001.

Los Angeles Times. "Children in Stores Visited by Superman." April 6, 1955.

_____. "First Runs Book Serial," July 7, 1948.

_____. "New Superman Series Slated," December 30, 1965.

_____. "Newsmakers: Too Bad, Lois—Clark's Seeing Eunice," November 21, 1978.

_____. "Notes on Our Cuffs-Top Secret," May 10, 1959.

_____. "Original Superman Returns for 50th," July 28, 1987.

_____. "The Region," March 11, 1987.

_____. "Singer Virginia O'Brien Tells Blow, Gets Decree," June 25, 1955.

_____. "Studio Briefs," February 1, 1950.

_____. "'Superman' L.A. Opening Will Benefit the Special Olympic, July 22, 1978.

_____. Untitled, February 9, 1953.

_____. "Virginia O'Brien to Become Mother," December 15, 1944.

_____. "The Week in Review," April 12, 1959.

Lowry, Brian. "ABC Opens Fire on Vid Violence." *Variety*, June 11, 1993.

_____. "Being Batman Can Be Grunt Work." *Los Angeles Times*, December 8, 2002.

_____. "Singer Leaps to Lofty 'Lois' Slot." *Variety*, November 2, 1993.

Lowry, Joseph F. "So I Said to Superman ..." *The Philadelphia Sunday Bulletin Magazine*, February 6, 1966.

Loynd, Ray. "Cannon Buys the Rights to Future 'Superman' Films." *Daily Variety*, June 19, 1985.

McBride, Joseph. "Writers vs. Reeve: 'Superman' Dispute Going to Trial." *Daily Variety*, March 10, 1989.

McCarthy, Todd. "Salkinds' Lucrative 'Superman' Films Also Costly and Litigious." *Variety*, July 8, 1987.

_____. "Superman Returns." *Variety*, June 18, 2006.

MacKenzie, Catherine . "'Superman,' 'Dick Tracy' et al. Here to Stay, Educators Find in an Evaluation of Comics." *New York Times*, December 15, 1944.

Manitowec (WI) Herald-Times. "Superman is in Demand Again," July 5, 1972.

Mann, Roderick. "Canadian Kidder Works Both Sides of the Border." *Los Angeles Times*, November 18, 1982.

_____. "'She-roes' Are Made, Not Born." *Los Angeles Times*, June 19, 1983.

_____. "'Superman': Leaping Tall Budgets." *Los Angeles Times*, April 6, 1978.

_____. "Superman Makes the Leap to the Screen." *Los Angeles Times*, July 31, 1977.

_____. "'Superman' Reeve a Born Flier." *Los Angeles Times*, November 19, 1978.

_____. "'Superman' Sequel: Flying in the Soup." *Los Angeles Times*, March 20, 1979.

_____. "'Superman 2' On Launching Pad." *Los Angeles, Times*, October 9, 1979.

_____. "'Superman's' Battle of the Red Ink." *Los Angeles Times*, May 27, 1980.

_____. "They're Standing in Line for Christopher Reeve." *Los Angeles Times*, April 13, 1980.

Martinez, Michael. "Judge Throws Out 'Superman' Suit." *Hollywood Reporter*, October 24, 1990.

Maslin, Janet. "Film: 'Superman III': Reeve Joined by Pryor." *New York Times*, June 17, 1983.

_____. "The Screen: Helen Slater as 'Supergirl.'" *New York Times*, November 22, 1984.

_____. "Screen: 'Superman II' Is Full of Tricks." *New York Times*, June 19, 1981.

_____. "Movie: 'Superman IV: Quest for Peace.'" *New York Times*, July 25, 1987.

Mitchell, John L. "Created Famed Character 47 Years Ago: Superman's Originators Warm Up After Long Freeze-Out." *Los Angeles Times*, June 18, 1981.

Mitchell, Lisa. "Superman is Alive and Well and Living in North Hollywood." *Los Angeles Times*, August 12, 1977.

Moore, Frazier. "A Special Guest on 'Smallville.'" *The Elyria (Ohio) Chronicle-Telegram*, February 25, 2003.

Morfoot, Addie. "Smallville: The Definitive WB." *Variety*, January 20, 2005.

Morrow, Terrry. "Rosenbaum Enjoys Playing 'Lex,' The Bad Boy on 'Smallville' Series." Scripps Howard News Service, April 25, 2004.

Morse, Tom. "Hal Prince Raps Philly as Tryout City; Local Critics 'Post-College Twerps.'" *Weekly Variety*, April 6, 1966.

Nadel, Norman. "'Superman,' Airy, Merry." *New York World Telegram and Sun*, March 30, 1966.

New York Herald Tribune. "'Superman' Plans Pricing Changes," January 11, 1966.

New York Daily News. "Superman! And Eligible!" June 2, 1966.

New York Times. "Bud Collyer Dies; Host of TV Shows." September 9, 1969.

_____. "Child Born to Virginia O'Brien." June 22, 1945.

_____. "Simple," January 29, 1950.

_____. Untitled, September 13, 1942.

Oakland Tribune. "Young Fan Has Role in 'Superman,'" August 8, 1977.

O'Connor, John. "TV Review; Superman at 50, a Special." *New York Times*, February 29, 1988.

Olsen, Mark. "Superman Superseded." *Los Angeles Times*, May 22, 2005.

Papamichael, Stella. "High Noon: Super Pooper?" *BBC*, November 10, 2003.

Peper, William. "That Bird is 'Superman.'" *New York World Telegram*, March 24, 1966.

Perry, Simon. "'Superman II' Wraps Shooting in London on High Note." *Variety*, March 19, 1980.

Petrikin, Chris, and Paul Karon. "'Superman' Reskeds Start Date—Again." *Variety*, October 8, 1997.

Pollack, Dale. "The Longest Hottest Summer." *Los Angeles Times*, May 8, 1983.

_____. "'Superman 2' May Fall From Sky if Work Sked Not Met." *Daily Variety*, January, 1979.

Radford, Bill. "Alfred Gough Interview." *Gazette*, September 21, 2006.

Rense, Rip. "A Crush More Powerful Than a Locomotive." *Los Angeles Times*, August 12, 1994.

_____. "Look! Up on the Screen! It's ... Lois Lane?" *Los Angeles Times*, April 5, 1994.

Roberts, Clark. "Kay Thompson and Williams Brothers Have Plans for Television Musical Comedy." *Los Angeles Times*, July 27, 1951.

Rohrer, Finlo. "Is the New Superman Meant to be Jesus?" *BBC News Magazine*, July 28, 2006.

Rosenberg, Howard. "A Visit with Lois & Jimmy." *Los Angeles Times*, February 16, 1979.

Salmans, Sandra. "The Salkind Heroes Wear Red and

Fly High." *New York Times*, July 17, 1983.

Schallert, Edwin. "Noel Neill Set For Superman Serial." *Los Angeles Times*, January 10, 1948.

Schiller, Gail. "Brave new world for summer tie-ins." Reuters, May 30, 2006.

Schneider, Michael. "First look: 'Smallville.'" *Variety*, September 13, 2001.

_____. "Superman Reeve will guest on 'Smallville.'" *Variety*, January 6, 2003.

Screen International. "Superman IV: Reeve Assists Screenplay," March 1, 1986.

Seder, Jennifer. "Arnold." *Los Angeles Times*, June 22, 1979.

Shales, Tom. "This Superman Aims to Keep His Feet Firmly on the Ground." *Los Angeles Times*, October 3, 1993.

Siegel, Joel. "Radio, It Was Magic!" *Los Angeles Times*, September 28, 1969.

Smith, Cecil. "Broadway 'Superman': It's a Bird." *Los Angeles Times*, April 1, 1966.

Smith, Neil. "Film review: Superman Returns." *BBC News*, July 13, 2006.

Standish, Myles. "'Superman' Opens Week's Run in Park." *St. Louis Post Dispatch*, July 5, 1967.

Stephens, William. "Film Superman Flies on Wings of Nostalgia." *Los Angeles Times*, September 4, 1972.

Syracuse Herald-American. "People, Etc.," March 27, 1977.

Tepper, Ron. "It's a Bird! A Plane! It's Reeves!—A Job for Superman? He Lets George Do It." *Los Angeles Times*, May 10, 1959.

Thomas Jr., Robert McG. "Jerry Siegel, Superman's Creator, Dies at 81." *New York Times*, January 31, 1996.

Tommasini, Anthony. "Golly, Jimmy Olsen Writes Librettos!" *New York Times*, May 15, 1998.

Tracy, Kathy. "In Touch With Their Inner Teen." *Variety*, January 25, 2006.

Turan, Kenneth. "Movie Review: Earthbound Superhero; It's Fine in the Air, but the Cumbersome 'Superman Returns' Stumbles Over Its Story Line." *Los Angeles Times*, June 27, 2006.

Ulmer, James. "Salkind's 'Superman' Shows Pre-Sales of Steel." *Hollywood Reporter*, October 27, 1992.

United Press International. "Clark Kent Tries on A New Role." *Northbrook (IL) Daily Herald*, March 22, 1987.

Valley News. "'Super Schumck' Irks Superman," April 22, 1977.

Vadeboncoeur, Joan E. "Reeve Doesn't Worry About Being 'Superman' Forever." *Syracuse Herald-Journal*, June 1, 1981.

Van Gelder, Lawrence. "At the Movies: Superman or Not, Choices are the Goal." *New York Times*, July 4, 1986

Variety. "One to Watch: Teri Hatcher," August 30, 1993.

_____. Untitled, October 13, 1957.

Vidal, David. "Mild-Mannered Cartoonists Go to Aid of Superman's Creators." *New York Times*, December 10, 1975.

Wallace, Amy. "It's a Bird! It's a Plane! It's 'Super-

man' on Hold Again." *Los Angeles Times*, April 17, 1998.

Warga, Wayne. "Career is Airborne but He's Got Feet on the Ground." *Los Angeles Times*, July 15, 1979

Watt, Douglas. "Nominees Chosen for Tony Awards." *Los Angeles Times*, June 1, 1966.

Webster, Kerry. "OK, Trivia Buffs, Name The Original Superman." *Los Angeles Herald-Examiner*, February 24, 1984.

WENN. "Caviezel Poised to Sign Superman Deal." September 2, 2004.

_____. "Caviezel Wants Superman Role." October 15, 2004.

Wiener, Rex. "A. Salkind Dead at 76." *Variety*, March 18, 1997

Wolf, Matt. "Reeve to Fly Again as Filming of 'Superman IV' Gets Underway." *Gettysburg Times*, January 9, 1987.

Zolotow, Sam. "Superman Toils for Musical Role." *New York Times*, November 17, 1965.

Websites

"ADDY Award Show & Winners." *aaf.org*, www.aaf.org/awards/addys_silver_2005.html.

"The Adventures of Seinfeld and Superman Land on TBS." *TimeWarner.com*, www.timewarner.com/corp/newsroom/pr/0,20812,670451,00.html, June 9, 2004.

Ahem. "Superman IV: The Quest for Peace: A History of the Production." *SupermanCinema*, www.supermancinema.co.uk/superman4/s4_production/history/sr_history_page1.htm.

"Beau Weaver." *Wikipedia*, http://en.wikipedia.org/wiki/Beau_Weaver.

"Behind the Camera: A Spotlight on Stacy Haiduk." *DMWC's Superboy-The Series Website*, www.geocities.com/dmwc/.

"Behind the Scenes of Superboy," *DMWC's Superboy-The Series Website*, www.geocities.com/dmwc/. Reprinted from *Deluxe Format DC Books*, March 1990.

"Biography: Christopher Reeve." *Chris Reeve Home Page*, www.chrisreevehomepage.com/biography.html.

Blaschke, Jayme Lynn. "An Interview with Paul Dini." *Revolution Science Fiction*, August 14, 2004, www.revolutionsf.com/article.html?id=2352.

Bobbin, Jay. "Will the Senator from Smallville Please Rise." *Zap2it.com*, April 13, 2006.

_____. "Ilya Salkind Interview: Supergirl." April 13, 2000. www.geocities.com/Hollywood/Palace/3454/ilyasupergirl.html.

_____. "Jeannot Szwarc Interview: Supergirl." November 27, 1999. www.geocities.com/hollywood/palace/3454/jeannotsupergirl.html.

"Box Office / Business for Superman (1978)." *Internet Movie Database*, www.imdb.com/title/tt0078346/business.

"The Brady Kids (1972–1974)." *Brady World*, www.bradyworld.com/episodes/kids.htm

"Breaking News." *The Futon Critic*, www.thefuton

critic.com/news.aspx?id=20061003cw01, October 4, 2006.

"Broadcasting Timeline." *FactMonster.com*, www.factmonster.com/ipka/AO151956.html.

Byrne, Craig. "Allison Mack Bio." *KryptonSite.com*.

_____. "Annette O'Toole Bio." *KryptonSite.com*.

_____. "Brad Buckner Interview." *Kryptonsite.com*, August 2003, www.kryptonsite.com/loisclark/buckner2003.htm.

_____. "Erica Durance Bio." *KrytonSite.com*.

_____. "Jeph Loeb Talks About 'Legacy.'" *KryptonSite.com*, December 2002.

_____. "Jeph Loeb Talks 'Insurgence.'" *KryptonSite.com*, December 2002.

_____. "John Glover Bio." *KryptonSite.com*.

_____. "John Schneider Bio." *KryptonSite.com*.

_____. "Kristin Kreuk Bio." *Kryptonsite.com*.

_____. "KryptonSite Interview #1 With Smallville Executive Producer Alfred Gough." *KryptonSite.com*, April 6, 2001.

_____. "KryptonSite Interview With *Smallville* Executive Producer Alfred Gough." *KryptonSite.com*, September 10, 2004.

_____. "Mark Verheiden Talks About 'Perry.'" *KryptonSite.com*.

_____. "Sam Jones III Bio." *KryptonSite.com*.

_____. "Tom Welling Bio." *KryptonSite.com*.

"Canceled Superman Films." *Wikipedia*, http://en.wikipedia.org/wiki/Superman_Lives.

Chambers, Doug. "Superboy: The Series." *DMWC's Superboy-The Series Website*, www.geocities.com/dmwc.

Christie, James. "Hero's Return Wows Original Director." *BBC.com*, July 13, 2006.

"Comic book crusader: Bryan Singer." *BBC.com*, July 13, 2006.

"Danny Dark." *SupermanHomepage*, www.supermanhomepage.com/tv/tv.php?topic=cast-crew/danny-dark.

"The Death of Superman." *Wikipedia*, http://en.wikipedia.org/wiki/Death_of_Superman#Audience_and_media_response.

Dharmesh. "Ilya Salkind: Creative Producer." *Superman Cinema.com*, www.supermancinema.co.uk/special_features/interviews/ilya_salkind/ilya-stm.asp.

Dickholtz, Daniel. "Interview sith Stacy Haiduk." *DMWC'S Superboy-The Series Website*, reprinted from *Spectacular*, 1991, www.geocities.com/dmwc/.

Dimino, Russ. "Eddie Jones Bio." *Kryptonsite.com*, www.kryptonsite.com/loisclark/eddiejones.htm.

_____. "John Shea Bio." *Kryptonsite.com*, www.kryptonsite.com/loisclark/johnshea.htm.

_____. "Justin Whalin Bio." *Kryptonsite.com*, www.kryptonsite.com/loisclark/justinwhalin.htm.

_____. "Tracy Scoggins Bio." *Kryptonsite.com*, www.kryptonsite.com/loisclark/tracyscoggins.htm.

Estradera, Mariano Bayona. "Curiosidades sobre Smallville." *smallville.cinecin.com/otramartha.htm*, 2004.

Falconer, Robert. "Super-Natural: A Conversation with Tom Welling." *Hollywood North Report*, May 30, 2005, www.hollwoodnorthreport.com/article.php?Article=1323.

Filichia, Peter. "It's Got Possibilities." *Theater Mania*, October 2, 2006, www.theatermania.com/peterfilichia/permalinks/2006/10/02/Its-Got-Possibilities/.

"Filmation." *Guide to Animated Star Trek*, www.danhausertrek.com/AnimatedSeries/Filmation.html#Show66.

Fischer, Paul. "Interview: Brandon Routh 'Superman Returns.'" *DarkHorizons.com*, June 16, 2006.

Freiman, Barry. "Lois Long: An Interview with Actress Dana Delany." *The Superman Homepage*, June 14, 2005, www.supermanhomepage.com/tv/tv.php?topic=interviews/dana-delany.

Freiman, Barry M. "One-on-One Interview with Producer Ilya Salkind, June 30, 2006." *SupermanHomepage.com*, www.supermanhomepage.com/movies/movies.php?topic=interview-salkind.

Fuson, Brian. "'Superman Returns' Flies High With $21 Mil Debut." *BBC.com*, June 30, 2006.

Garrett, Randy. "Metropolis and Mayberry." *The Adventures Continue*, www.jimnolt.com/fortyacres1.htm, Spring 2001.

"Gerard Christopher Bio." *SupermanHomepage*, www.superboyhomepage.com/home.htm.

Geter, Gene. "The Clark & Lana Files: Gene Geter Talks To Kristin Kreuk." *KryptonSite.com*, May 13, 2003.

Green, Michelle Erica. "K Callan: Superman's Mother." *LittleReview.com*, www.littlereview.com/getcritical/interviews/callan.htm.

Gross, Edward. "Exclusive Preview: Smallville." *Retrovision*, www.retrovisionmag.com/smallville.htm.

_____. "Superman Lives!—The Development Hell of an Unmade Film." *Cinemania*, www.mania.com/20991.html, May 5, 2000.

_____. "SUPERMAN LIVES, Part 2: Writer Kevin Smith." *Cinemania*, www.mania.com/20991.html, May 12, 2000. http://voices.fuzzy.com/actor.idc?actor_id=1875.

Huddleston, Kathie. "Interview: John Shea." *Sci Fi.com*, www.scifi.com/sfw/issue256/interview.html.

"Hustle—Albert Stroller (Robert Vaughn)." *Hustle* press release, www.bbc.co.uk/pressoffice/pressreleases/stories/2004/01_january/20/hustle_robert_vaughn.shtml, January 1, 2004.

"Ilya Salkind's Siegel & Shuster." www.ilyasalkindcompany.com.

"John Haymes Newton." *SupermanHomepage*, www.supermanhomepage.com/tv/tv.php?topic=cast-crew/john-h-newton.

"Justice League's Superman." *The Comics Continuum*, www.comicscontinuum.com/stories/0303/20/index.htm, March 20, 2003.

"Keith Sutherland." *The Internet Movie Database*, www.imdb.com/name/nm0840127/.

King, Jackson. "Truth, Justice and the American (Express) Way." *JimHillMedia.com*, , May 20, 2004, http://jimhillmedia.com/blogs/jackson_king/archive/2004/05/20/1124.aspx.

Knowles, Harry. "Interview with Bryan Singer." *Ain't*

It Cool News, June 10th, 2006, www.aintitcool. com/display.cgi?id=23557.

Kraus, Haggay. "Smallville Interview." *Michael Rosenbaum.com*, April 2002.

Lamken, Brian Saner. "The Ever-Lovin' Blue-Eyed Timm!" *Comicology #1*, Spring 2000, www.two morrows.com/comicology/articles/01timm.html.

"Lane Smith." *What A Character.com*, www.what-a-character.com/cgi-bin/display.cgi?id=982796316.

"London Life: 'Superman Returns.'" *BBC.co.uk*, http://downloads.bbc.co.uk/worldservice/learnin-genglish/londonlife/scripts/londonlife_060719_s uperman.pdf.

McKernan, Brian. "Interview with Gerard Christopher." *Superboy Home Page*, www.superboyhomepage. com/home.htm.

Mahon, Betsy. "Somewhere in Time Review." *The Christopher Reeve Homepage*, www.chrisreevehome-page.com/m-sit.html.

Mandelbaum, Ken. "Obscure Videos: Two By Strouse." *Broadway.com*, www.broadway.com/gen/Buzz_Story. aspx?ci-518409.

Mandell, Paul. *Adventures of Superman Notes*, http:// members.tripod.com/~davidschultz/superman music.htm.

Mara, Janis. "Seinfeld-Superman Video Gets Results." *ClickZ News*, April 13, 2004, www.clickz.com/show-Page.html?page=3339791.

Markstein, Don. "Betty Boop." *Don Markstein's Toono-pedia*, www.toonopedia.com/boop.htm.

Markstein, Don. "Mighty Mouse." *Don Markstein's Toonopedia*, www.toonopedia.com/mightym.htm.

Martin, Ed. "American Express Campaign Includes Television Commercials for Online Advertisements." *Mediavillage.com*, April 13, 2004.

"Max Fleischer." *Wikipedia*, http://en.wikipedia. org/wiki/Max_Fleischer.

Mitovich, Matt Webb. "Tim Daly: What's Next for *The Nine*'s Nick?" *TVGuide.com*, October 11, 2006.

"The New Adventures of Superman Cast & Crew List." *The Big Cartoon Database*, www.bcdb.com/ cartoon_characters/25361-New_Adventures_of_ Superman.html.

"New Superman actor tries on suit." *BBC.com*, April 22, 2005.

"Nicolas Cage." *Wikipedia*, http://en.wikipedia.org/ wiki/Nicolas_Cage.

Nolt, Jim. "Commercial Message." *TAC, Jr. #16*, January 5, 1998, www.jimnolt.com/amex.htm.

"Pebble Mill interviews Teri Hatcher," *BBC*, www.stack.nl/~boris/Teri/Text/pebble.txt, February 16, 1996.

Reid, Calvin. "B is for Big Book Sales." *Publishers Weekly*, www.publishersweekly.com/article/CA6321550 .html, April 4, 2006.

"Romeo Muller." *The Internet Movie Database*, www. imdb.com/name/nm0612239/bio.

Runkle, Patrick. "Cannon Films: The Life, Death and Resurrection." *Cannonfilms.com*, www.cannonfilms. com/cannon2.htm.

Sanderson, Peter. "Superman Through the Ages: The End of History." *Fortress-of-Solitude.net*, excerpted from *Amazing Heroes # 96*, June 1986, http://theages. superman.ws/History/end.php.

"Save Me (Remy Zero song)." *Wikipedia*, http://en. wikipedia.org/wiki/Save_Me_(Remy_Zero_song).

"Seinfeld and Superman Return to the Web Today with Their Highly Anticipated Second Webisode." *AmericanExpress.com*, http://home3.american express.com/corp/pc/2004/webisode2.asp, May 20, 2004.

Shi'an, Shen. "'Superman Returns' to His Bod-hisattva Career." *The Buddhist Channel*, July 17, 2006, www.buddhistchannel.tv/index.php?id= 12,2919,0,0,1,0.

Simpson, M.J. "Lane Smith Interview." *MJSimpson. co.uk*,www.mjsimpson.co.uk/interviews/lane smith.html

"Smallville (TV Series)." *Wikipedia*, http://en.wikipedia. org/wiki/Smallville_(TV_series).

Stevenson, Seth. "It's a Bird! It's a Plane! It's a ... We-bisode?" *Slate.com*, April 19, 2004, www.slate.com/ id/2099152/.

"Super Friends." *The Big Cartoon Database*, www. bcdb.com/cartoons/Hanna- Barbera_Studios/S/ Super_Friends/index.html.

"Super Friends." *Wikipedia*. http://en.wikipedia.org/ wiki/Superfriends.

"Teri Hatcher," *The Superman Supersite*, www.super-mansupersite.com/hatcher.html.

"Tim Daly Biography," *Wikipedia*, http://en.wikipedia. org/wiki/Timothy_Daly.

"TV Ratings 1951-1952." *Classic TV Hits*, www.clas-sictvhits.com/tvratings/1951.htm.

"TV Ratings 1956-1957." *Classic TV Hits*, www.clas-sictvhits.com/tvratings/1956.htm.

Weiland, Ted. "*Smallville*'s Dr. Bryce: Emmanuelle Vaugier." *KryptonSite.com*, December 2002.

Other Sources

"Cannon Acquires Rights to Produce 'Superman 4.'" Cannon Publicity Dept. Press Release, June 21, 1985.

Data for Bulletin of Screen Achievement Records. Academy of Motion Pictures Arts & Sciences.

Deutsch, Didier C. *It's A Bird, It's A Plane, It's Superman* CD liner notes. Sony Music Entertainment, 1992.

"A Little Piece of Trivia," *Superman: The Animated Series Vol. 1, Disc 1*, Warner Bros. Entertainment, 2004.

"Superman: Learning To Fly," *Superman: The Animated Series Vol. 1, Disc 2*, Warner Bros. Entertainment, 2004.

Superman II Premiere Program Book. Warner Bros., 1981.

Superman III Presskit. Warner Bros., 1983.

Superman IV Presskit. Warner Bros., 1987.

The Tonight Show with Johnny Carson. NBC-TV, April 22, 1969.

Whatever Became of ... Radio program. Richard Lamparski. 1966.

Index

Numbers in **bold italic** refer to photographs